Richard Perceval, Herbert David Croly

Bibliotheca hispanica

Containing a grammar, with a dictionarie in Spanish, English, and Latin

Richard Perceval, Herbert David Croly

Bibliotheca hispanica

Containing a grammar, with a dictionarie in Spanish, English, and Latin

ISBN/EAN: 9783744657297

Printed in Europe, USA, Canada, Australia, Japan

Cover: Foto ©Thomas Meinert / pixelio.de

More available books at **www.hansebooks.com**

BIBLIOTHECA HISPANICA.

Containing a Grammar, with a Dictionarie in SPANISH, English, and Latine gathered out of diuers good Authors: very profitable for the studious of the Spanish toong.

By Richard Percyuall Gent.

The Dictionarie being inlarged with the Latine, by the aduise and conference of Maister Thomas DOYLEY Doctor in Physicke.

Imprinted at London, by Iohn Iackson, for Richard Watkins.

1591

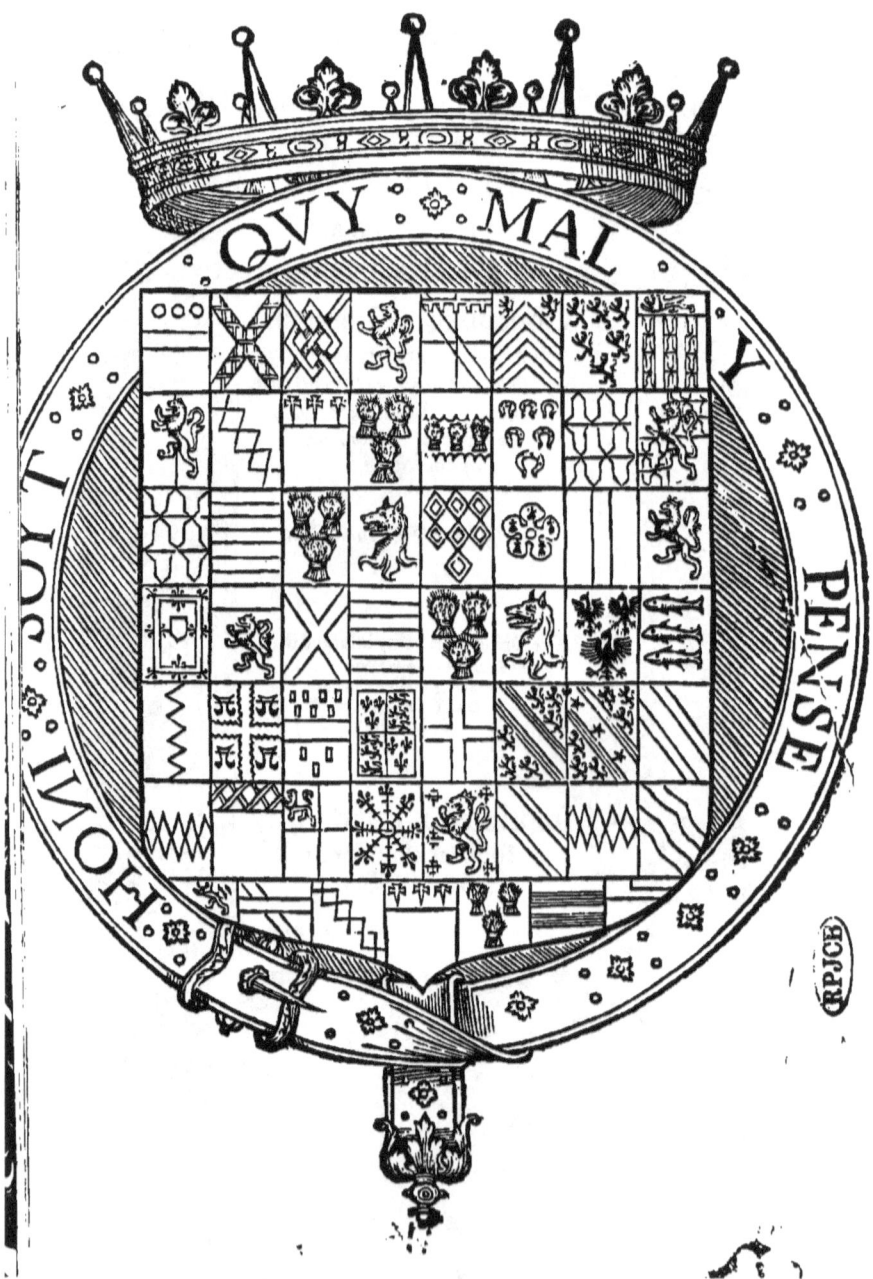

TO THE RIGHT HONO-
RABLE ROBERT EARLE OF ESSEX
AND EWE, VISCOVNT HEREFORD,
and Bourghchier, Lord Ferrers of Chart-
ley, *Bourghchier and Louaine*, *Master of the*
Queenes Maiesties Horse, and Knight of the
most noble order of the Garter, RICHARD
PERCYVALL, wisheth all increase
of Honor and Heroicall
vertues.

IGHT HONORABLE, after I had brought to light this sillie newe borne infant, as the first fruits of my poore trauails; beholding both hir weakenes, and the meanenes of mine own abilitie; I perceiued it would be verie needful for me, to procure it a vaile of greater brightnesse, which might increase the reputation of hir perfections if she had any; and shadowe hir wants and deformities. For hauing put foorth so far into the large sea of common opinion; I sawe that by reason of the shelues and rocks of iniurious conceits; which are ready to be found on euerie hand; we were like to passe no small aduenture: So extreame is the delight, which manie take to deface the well meaning attempts of others; as euen the smallest faults, which with great reason we might wish to be buried in obliuion; euerie one, yea of those that deserue best; maugre his head, heareth in the open streetes. And therefore Right Honorable, bethinking my selfe of all meanes, by which I might escape a danger so apparant; I resolued on this, that bearing in the foreship of my small vessell, the luckie streamer of your Honorable and happie name; there would not be a beagle of the cruell *Scylla*, that should dare to baye at vs; nor any other monster, were he neuer so fierce, that would aduenture to behold vs with a malitious eie. Yea further, that your Honors fauorable

A 2 coun-

The Epistle Dedicatorie.

countenance, would appeafe vs the moſt ſtormie tempeſts, with no leſſe authoritie,

Quàm fratres Helena, lucida ſydera.

True it is, that the great ods betweene my meane eſtate, and the high degree of honor, wherein, both the nobilitie of your birth, and the valour of your perſon haue worthelie placed you: brought me in great doubt to proceede any farther in this ſo bold an attempt. But vnderſtanding that your Honor beſtoweth much time with happie ſucceſſe, as well in the knowledge of the toongs; as of other commendable learnings beſeeming your place and perſon; and remembring that hauing emploied your ſelfe ſo honorablie againſt the Spanyard in Flanders, Spayne & Portugal; you had gained an immortall memorie with all poſteritie, & might perhaps encounter with them againe vpon like occaſion; I began to hope that your Honor would vouchſafe the entertainment of this your handmaid; that humblie offereth hir ſelfe, to attend on your Honorable ſtudies as a diligent ſeruant: and in the other occaſion, (if it be offered) to performe the part of a faithful Trucheman and interpretor. I beſeech your H. to receiue and protect hir as your owne; giuing vnto hir, by the brightnes of your Honorable fauor, that light which of hir ſelfe ſhe hath not; and to me the encouragement, to offer heereafter to your Honors viewe, ſome other fruits of my labour, perhaps of a pleaſanter taſte; which may manifeſtly witnes the feruent zeale enflaming me with a deſire vnquenchable, to ſerue your Honor in whatſoeuer my ſmall knowledge ſhall enable me.

Your Honors moſt humbly deuoted,

R. PERCYVALL.

TO THE READER.

Riendly Reader; the trauaile which I haue taken for thy behoofe, I may boldly say, doth require a fauourable acceptance at thy handes; for many in matters of as small moment as this, haue threatned on thee as great kindnesse, and receaued for their paines frendly entreatie. I open vnto thee a Librarie; wherein thou mayst finde layed readie to thy view and vse, the toonge with which by reason of the troublesome times, thou arte like to haue most acquaintance: hauing trauailed (though at home) with a more curious indeuour to search out the proprietie thereof; then many that haue spent some yeares in the Countrie where the toonge is naturall; yea then some Spaniardes, that haue dealt in the same argument. For no doubt, those things that to me being a straunger to the toonge, appeared vpon good reason to bee worth the obseruation: were so ordinarie with them, as they seemed needlesse to be drawen into rule. I am not so malicious as to detract from the labours of any that haue gone before me; but confesse, that I haue both seene and vsed them where I thought it conuenient: referring it to the indifferent iudgment of the discreete Reader, whether I haue reason to dissent from them, in such points as wee varie. The Methode I obserue, is so playne and easie, if thou marke my first Analytical *table; as thou shalt neede no long discourse to explane it; and though I assure thee I haue not concealed any thing which I knew to be needfull for thy furtheraunce herein; yet were the rule neuer so playne and perfect; the linely voice of the teacher, is the best light to the learner: Howbeit the more absolute and compleat the rule is; with the lesse time and trouble shalt thou attayne thy desired acquaintaunce with the language. I haue studied to be briefe, I hope without obscuritie, for sparing thy time the chiefest treasure. The Dictionarie hath coste me greatest paynes; for after that I had collected it into Spanish and English out of* Christoval de las Casas, *and* Nebrissensis; *casting in some small pittaunce of mine owne, amounting well neere two* 2000 *wordes; which neither of them had; I ranne it ouer twise with* Don Pedro de Valdes, and Don Vasco de Sylua, *to whome I had accesse, by the fauour of my worshipfull friend Maister* Richard Drake, *(a Gentleman as vertuouslie minded as any, to further any good attempt) and hauing by their helpe made it readie for the presse with the English interpretation onely: In very good time, I chaunced to be acquainted with the learned Gentleman, Master* Thomas Doyley *doctor in Phisicke; who had begunne a Dictionary in Spanish, English, and Latine; and seeing mee to bee more foreward to the presse then himselfe; very friendly gaue his consent to the publishing of mine; wishing me to adde the Latine to it as hee had begunne in his; which I performed, being not a little furthered therein by his aduise and conference. Make thy profite of it good Reader, and yeelde mee thy good worde for my paines: if any thing want the grace and perfection it ought to haue, upon friendly warning I will doe my best to polish it to thy contentment, which I am sure will be limited within the boundes of reason. The malicious who with their venemous toonges, seeke to deface the labours of others, themselues being vermine altogether vnprofitable, I would be loth to grace so much, as to vouchsafe them a word in their disgrace; but leaue them to the iust punishment of their repining consciences.*

R. P.

Thomas Doyleyus medicinæ doctor.

Quas nouus orbis opes, quas profert India fructus,
Quas mare, quas tellus gemmas, aurique fodinas;
Has habet Hispanus, Iasonis vellere diues:
    Cum populo aurato collubet ergò loqui.
Expetit Hispanus Belgas euincere, regem
Gallorum per vim regno depellere, regnum
Diripere Anglorum, quid non? cupit esse Monarcha:
    Cum rege'hoc tanto, collubet ergò loqui.
Cum quibus aut bellum cupimus, commercia, pacem;
Horum sermo placet: facilémque breuémque loquendi
Dat liber iste modum, dat Percyuallius author
    Cum populo Hispano quàm citò posse loqui.

Aduena quidam amicus.

Hactenus Hispanis, Hispanica lingua refulsit,
    Sed reliquis, sicut nocte Diana micans.
Latius at splendet nunc multis gentibus, almâ
    Sol velut excurrens, per sua signa, die.
Præstitit hoc Anglus, constanti pollice, scriptor,
    Vt Tartessiacæ detegerentur opes.
Non vnum Typhin Græcum, sed mille Britannos
    Spe lucri accendet, nominis atque magis,
Colchica qui leuibus volitent noua regna carinis,
    Aureaque apportent vellera mille domum.

To the practitioners in the Spanish,
Iames Lea.

Though Spanish speech lay long aside within our Brittish Ile,
(Our Courtiers liking nought saue French, or *Tuscane* stately stile)
Yet now at length,(I know not how) steps *Castile* language in,
And craues for credit with the first, though latest she begin:
Who lists not yeeld to neither both, of those rehearst before,
But iumpe as stately and as sweete, or rather stately more:
As full of prety prouerbs, and most dainty priuie quips,
Of graue aduices, bitter taunts, and passing gawling nips.
Though learned pens in Italy and France do florish more,
And in our happy Britaine, where are learned men such store:
Yet Spanish speech lists giue no ground: which here by painfull hand
Of Perciuall, is open laid, for all to vnderstand,
And soon to speake and write the same, by practise in his booke:
In practise, yeeld him praise and thanks, for thee such paines that tooke.
Then thanks, nought else he doth reqaire, though more he do deserue;
He sets before thee store of cates, spare not, but like and carue.

Ad Lectorem.

Quæ mihi continui, lector, peperêre labores,
  Insomnes lunæ, sudor & assiduus;
Exiguo prostant pretio tibi, nec tibi fructus
  Exiguus, ni me spes mea fallat, erit.
Quod Casas Italis, quod Nebrissensis Iberis,
  Pluraque, nostra tibi Bibliotheca dabit.
Si methodum spectes, summa hic compendia, verùm
  Vt constent numeris singula plena suis.
Fallimur interdum? & quis non? sed nostra meretur
  Cui bonus ignoscas paucula, lassa manus.

R. Perciual.

THE ANALYTICALL TABLE
for the Grammar.

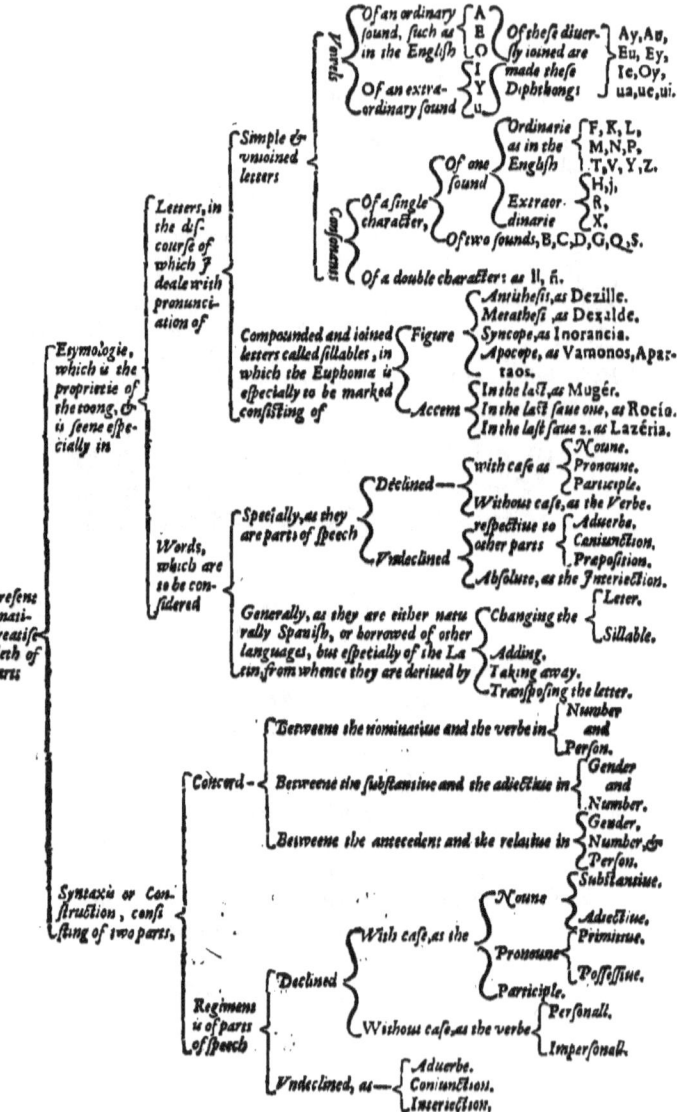

THE SPANISH GRAMMAR.
Of Letters.

VCH as teach Arithmetike and Geometrie, begin with points and vnities, things in shew of small moment, yet such as being neglected, would hinder the teacher, and entangle the learner in manie labyrinthes: in like maner, and for like reason, since I haue taken in hand to deale with this Grammaticall treatise; if I meane not to builde without a sure foundation: I must set before the eies, or rather make euident to the eares of the learner, the naturall force and efficacie of each letter. First, I finde that in placing and ordering them, there may be some question, since it is plaine that diuers languages obserue diuers courses: none that I knowe following that, which the naturall efficacie of the letter seemeth to require. And although in marshalling them I might well take for a patterne, the Hebrew as most ancient; some of the Spanish approching so neere it, as shall after appeere: yet bicause that course might seeme far fet, I will keepe me to the vsuall forme of our English: following notwithstanding in my particular diuision that method, which I gesse the nature of the toong afordeth. Neither let any man thinke this treatise of letters to be of small moment, the ods betweene the Spanish and our English being such, as doth necessarily require it. To begin therefore; The letters are in number xxiiij. besides two, which being written double, haue in this language a peculiar pronunciation.

A b c ç d e f g h i k l m n o p q r ſ t v x y z.
The letters written with a double character are, ll ñ.
They may well be diuided into vowels and consonants: the vowels yeeld a perfect sound of themselues: the consonants do not; without the helpe of the vowels. These vowels following differ not in pronunciation from the English.

A is pronounced with an open mouth plainly, as in Band, ſtand, ſo in Spanish Laſtimada, Paſmada.

E as in English, Tender, tempeſt, ſo in Spanish, Pebre, Peſebre. And the ſtudious muſt take heede of drowning it, as the French do their e feminine, or ſtraining it too ſmall like the double ee of the English, in Wee, ſee.

O with a plaine and open mouth as in other languages.

Theſe vary frō the ſound which we cōmonly giue them in English.
I and y with a ſlender tune as both French and Italians do in their proper toongs, and obſerue alſo in the Latin, as the double ee in English in wee, ſee; ſo in Spanish Viſita, oydos, and take heede you

B pronounce

Of Letters.

pronounce them not too broad, as we Englishmen do in the Latin, where the sillable is long, as in *Audire, Sentire*.

u with a full sound, as the Italian in *Aiuto, Alcuno, Costumi*, or as in some English words, as Surfet, pursie: so in Spanish Humo, çumo. And note that if h go before it, and a bowell follow it, it soundeth as w, Hueco, huevo. If g or q go before it, and e or i follow, the u is lost, and it soundeth as in English Guest, guift, as Guerra, gerra, Guiar, giar, Quemar, kemar, Quitar, kitar: except with g in these words Aguelo, çaraguelles, Cigueña, Aguero, Vergunça, Siguença, Guero, Garguero, Halagueño, Pedigueño, Regueldo, Deguello, and such verbes whose Infinitiues end in guar, as Menguar, Mengue, Fraguar, Frague: and except with q where the word is Latin, as Eloquente, Frequente, &c.

The consonants are either of a single, or of a double character. These consonants folowing of a single character, differ nothing from the sound which we allow them in English, F k l m n p t v y. But in these is difference.

H is seldome written in the beginning of a word, and where he is written many times he is not pronounced: but for this, bse of reading and speaking is the best teacher: where he commeth before ue he maketh it sound like a w, as Hueco, huevo: with c before him he is pronounced as in the English change, choise, so Charco, chupar: except in words deriued from the Græke, as Monarchia, jerarchia, where he soundeth much like k: with t the h is lost, as for *Theologo* they pronounce Teologo, &c. with p they both sound togither like F, as Philosopho.

j somwhat like the French in *Desja, joieux, juer*, but best like the Hebrew v with his point on the right horne, or sh in English, as Ojo, osho, Hijo, hisho, howbeit the *Andaluz* doth pronounce it rather like zh, as Ozho, bizho.

R is somwhat hard to be sounded by our countrimen if it be single in the mids of a word, as Parece, perece: where he must be pronounced very weakly, the toong lightly touching the roofe of the mouth: but if he be in the beginning of a word, or double in the midst, you cannot pronounce him too strong though you would, as Rey, Roble, Parra, Perro.

X like the j, the affinitie being so great as the one is often written for the other, Xara, shara, Lexia, leshia, Quexar, keshar.

These consonants being of a single character, haue notwithstanding two seuerall sounds, either as their places, the letters following, or the nature of the word doth require.

B is a lip letter, and pronounced as in the English, Barbour, basen: either where it is the first letter in the word, as Bevo, Biuda, Boca, or in the middle of a word, if it be deriued from the Latin, as Liberalidad, &c. otherwise it is manifest to any that obserueth it in the speech of any right Spaniard: that very often and commonly it is sounded like the Hebrew ב when it is in the middest of a word without daggesh, or as wee sound v the consonant: as Bobo, bovo, Cabo,

Of Letters.

Cabo, cavo, Cobrar, covrar, being a thing so vsuall and ordinarie, as that very often the one is printed for the other.

C before a o u like k, as Cabo, Cobrar, saue that if the nature of the word require any other pronunciation, it is noted with a little taile, as ç, and is called Cerilla, sounding almost as the Italian z in *Senza, Anzi,* or their t before ia or io, as in *Prudentia, Congregatione,* or like the Hebrew צ as our ts in English, but not altogither so strong vpon the r, Coraça, Coratsa, çarça, Tsartsa, keeping the same sound of Cerilla, though not the same forme: before e and i as Cerca, Tserca, Cierto, Tsierto.

D in the beginning of a word (except in Dios) is pronounced as in English Dosen, Dauid, so in Spanish Dar, Dezir, or if the word be deriued from the Latin, as Blando, Prudente. In other places it is very commonly sounded like the Hebrew ד in the midst of a word without daggesh, or as many pronounce ∂ in the Græke, or rather like, th, in these English words, Them, Then, These, as in Ciudad, Caredad, Cordero.

G before a o u as in English Garter, gurner, gorge, so Garça, Golpe, gusano: before e, as in Gwin, Gweneuer, so Agua, guardar: before ue and ui the u is lost, and it soundeth as in Guell, beguile, so Guerra, Guiar: except such words as are before set downe in the treatise of the bowell u. Before e and i the g is pronounced somewhat like our English, as in Ginger, but rather like the French in *Age, Sagesse :* to be briefe, altogither like the Spanish j, as Gente, Elegir.

Q before ua, as Quarry, quagmire, so Quatro, Quando: before ue and ui the u is lost, and the q soundeth like k, as in the French *Querelle, Antiquite,* so in Spanish Quemar, kemar, Quitar, kitar, except as before in the rule of u.

S if he be single in the midst of a word, or if he be in the end of a word, is pronounced with a milde sound betweene s and z, as the French do in *Chose, Maison,* or we in English in Pleasure, desire, so in Spanish Cosa, uso, Dios, Palabras. But in the beginning of a word, or if he be double in the middle, or come before a consonant, he keepeth the sound which we giue him in English, in Saue, Passed, Dust, Señor Huesso, Hasta.

These two following are of a double character, and haue their peculiar pronunciation.

Ll almost like the French in *Baille, Taylle, Famille, Oreille,* or as the Italian *gl Pigliar, Figliol,* sounding the latter l like the y consonant l going before it, yet so as you make all but one sillable, as Llamar, lyamar, Lleno, lyeno, Llorar, lyorar.

ñ somwhat like the French in *gn* in *Mignon,* or the Italian in *Ogni, Bagno,* or the Hebrew י in יוד: like y the consonant hauing n before it, as Año, Ynyo, Paño, Panyo.

OF DIPHTHONGS.

A diphthong is a ioint and mixt sound of two bowels comming togither, as in the Græke αι, οι, ευ, &c. in the Latin *au* in *Audio,* &c. both the bowels being so pronounced, as you heare the sound of both, yet so as

Of Sillables, and in them of Euphonia.

You seuer them not, neither make any moze than one sillable of them, as Ey in Ley, Reyna, Ay in Ayre, Au in Causa, Eu in Deudo, ie in Tiene, Viene, Oy in Oygo, ua in Suave, Cuajo, ue in Suegro, Sueño, ui in Cuitado, Cuidado.

Of Sillables, and in them
of Euphonia.

Nowe that we knowe the proper and peculiar force of ech letter; it followeth that we learne how the Spaniards frame their pronunciatiō of syllables, in respect of pleasantnes or easines of sound or vtterance, called Euphonia: which consisteth of two parts, Figure and Accent. The figures that they vse are commonly these fower.

Antithesis, or Antistœchon: where if I followe immediately after r being the last of the infinitiue moode, they change r into l, to make the sound the pleasanter, as for Dexarle, dexalle, Dezirle, dezille.

Metathisis, when after the second person plurall of the Imparatiue moode, I following: d and l chaunge places, as for Dexadle, they say and write dexalde, for Ponedle, ponelde.

Syncope, where two consonants comming togither in the midst of a word, would make the pronunciation somewhat hard, they cut off the former, if it be b c p: or g before n, as for Subtil, they say sutil, for Acto ato, for Captivo, cativo, for Ignorancia ignominia, inorancia inominia.

Apocope, where after the first person plurall of a Uerbe ending in os, nos, the Pronoune following; they cut off the s of the Uerbe as for Vamos nos, they say Vamonos, &c. So from the second person plural of the same moode, they take the d, as Apartados, for Apartados, Dezime for dezidme, otherwise, these rules excepted, you haue no letter clipped or drowned, as they are in the French, but are all wholie and fullie pronounced.

Of Accent.

Accent, being the second pillar of *Euphonia*, is the sounding of a syllable sharpe or soft, or the pronouncing it long or short, and disgraceth the speaker if it be not obserued: varying so much from the opinion of the learner, as it necessarily requireth a rule.

In the laste.   The accent is in the last sillabic in euery worde that endeth in r, as Amár, paladár, mugér, &c. yea although in the last sillable saue one, there be two consonants togither, which the Latines call Position, as Alcançar, Esparzir, out of this rule some fewe are excepted, as Açúcar, Acíbar, Alcáçar. Guerie Noune ending in d l i n s z, hath the accent in the last, Bondád, Alguazíl, Coraçón, Albañi, Pavés, Almiréz, except some ending in l, p and n, deriued from the Latin, which keepe the accent which they haue in the primitiue, as Fácil, árbol, órden, vírgen. Nownes in ion follow the generall rule, as veneración, afición.

In Uerbs it shall be sufficient to aduise the reader to marke the examples hereafter set downe, in which I haue diligently set the accent in his due place, bicause the rule would be to intricate: noting with al these

Of Accents.

These two points: First, that where the first and third person singular of the Preterperfectences of the Indicatiue mood of al regular Verbs, haue the accent in the last sillable, as Lastimé, lastimó, Pedí, pidió, &c. the Verbs irregular do commonly differ from this rule, as andúve dixe, and some Verbs regular in the third person of the Preterperfectense of the second & third coniugation: Secondly, that where al in general, in the third person plurall of the Indicatiue and present tense haue the accent in the last saue one, some irregular differ, as Están.

Aduerbes ending in a or i as Acá, aquí, Aí acullá, the Prepositions Hasta, házia, fuéra, differ from this rule.

All deriuatiues in Ado, eta, ido, udo, ico, ito, illo, üelo, haue the accent in the last saue one, as Barbádo, arquéta, abatído, cabeçúdo, chiquíto, pañizuélo, hombrezillo: and also many Nounes ending in ea, ia, eo, io, as Melibéa, abogacía, desséo, rocío, except where the word is Latine, as, Miséria, domínio, but this rule hath so many exceptions, as for the more certeinty I refer the Reader to the Dictionary, where commonly I prouide for this ambiguitie. *In the last saue one.*

Nownes deriued from the Latine, keepe the accent of the Latin, as Précio, Domínio, Lágrimas, &c. except where they be checkt by the former rules, as Caridád, afición, &c. *In the last saue two.*

And although these rules of the accent in some points may receaue exception (as what rule is so general but may?) yet they are ordinarily so true, as the studious shal receaue great light by them, and auoid manie absurdities in pronunciation, which otherwise he woulde commit: what falleth not within the compasse of this rule, shall be holpen by the Dictionarie, where in words doubtful, I commonly set the accent ouer the sillable.

Of parts of speech.

Hauing thus finished our briefe discourse of letters and sillables, order requireth that we deale with words, which considered as they are parts of speech, may be reduced to these eight generall heads, as in the Latine.

Noune,
Pronoune,
Verbe,
Participle,
} declined,

Aduerbe
Coniunction,
Preposition,
Interiection,
} vndeclined.

Of a Noune.

A Noune is the name of a thing that may be seene, felt, heard, or vnderstoode, as of a man, the name is Hombre, of vertue Virtud, &c. Of Nounes some be called substantiues, which in speech stande by themselues, and require not another worde to declare their signification, as el Hombre, a man, la Muger, a woman: some be called adiectiues, which cannot be vnderstoode of themselues throughly, vnlesse some other

Of Numbers.

other word be ioyned with them, as Negro,blacke,Blanco,white. Of the Subſtantiues likewiſe, ſome be proper, as Vaſco Alonſo. Some common,called alſo appellatiues, as Arbol,cabo,a tree,an end,Cuerpo,a bodie,Cabeça,a head,&c. In Nouns theſe ſixe things are eſpecially to be conſidered,kinde,number,caſe,gender, declenſon and compariſon.

There are two kinds of Nounes, Primitiues,and Deriuatiues: the Primitiue is deriued of no other, as Hombre a man : the Deriuatiue is drawen from the Primitiue, as Hombrezillo.

Primitiues.   Of Primitiues the numerals are eſpecially worth the noting, they are either Cardinall,that is,principall, vpon which the reſt depend, as Vno,dos, tres,quatro,cinco,ſeys,ſiete,ocho, nueue,diez,unze, doze,treze, catorze,quinze,diez y ſeys, diez y ſiete, diez y ocho, diez y nueue, veynte, veynte uno, veynte dos, &c. treynta,quarenta,cinquenta,ſeſſenta,ſetenta, ochenta, nouenta, ciento y cien, Docientos, trezientos,quatrocientos, quinientos,&c. Mil.

The ordinals are, which declare the order of place or time, as Primero, ſegundo, tercero, quarto, quinto, ſexto, ſeteno, octauo, noueno, diezmo, vnzeno, &c.

The Aduerbialls, vna vez, once, dos vez, twiſe, &c.

Deriuatiues.   Of Deriuatiues, theſe kinds are eſpecially to be marked, ſuch as ſig= nifie plentie, ende commonly in oſo, as virtuoſo, honrroſo, dichoſo.

Such as ſignifie exceſſe, in udo, as Cabeçudo, membrudo, &c. and ſub= ſtantiues in azo, as Hombrazo, perrazo.

Diminitiues ende commonly in ito, illo, illa, eta, uelo, ico, as Chiqui= to, delgadillo, hombrezillo, delgadito, pañizuelo, arqueta, vaqueta.

Of Adiectiues in o or e are formed Subſtantines, ſignifieng forme or qualitie in ad, eza, ura, of Bueno, bondad, of torpe, torpeza, of hecho, hechura.

OF NVMBERS.

There are two numbers, the ſingular ſpeaking of one, the plurall of moe, as Hombre, a man : Hombres, men. And this rule may be generally obſerued to forme the plurall number of the nowne: that if the ſingular ende in a bowell, the plurall is made by putting s to it, as Padre, padres, except ſome fewe, to which es muſt be added, as Ley, leyes, Rey, reyes, Fe, fees. But if the ſingular ende in a conſonant, the plurall is alwaies for= med by putting to es, as Amiſtad, amiſtades.

OF CASES.

The Spaniſh Nouns haue no diuerſitie in the termination of anie caſe, but the caſe is knowen by the article and prepoſition, the nomina= tiue hath no prepoſition, the genetiue hath de, the datiue para, the ac= cuſatiue a, the ablatiue de.

OF GENDERS.

Genders are three, the Maſculine, the Feminine, and the Neuter, and to knowe the genders of Subſtantiues, theſe rules following muſt be marked.

Sometime the Noune that in the Latine is of the Maſculine and Feminine, keepeth the ſame in the Spaniſh, but it varieth ſo often, as no certaine rule can be giuen in this point : the Neuter gender ſerueth onely

Of a Noune.

onely for Adiectiues vsed Substantiuely, as Lo justo, Lo bueno.

All nouns that ende in o,l,r, are commonly of the masculine gender, as Desseo, Alguazil, Paladar: but such as end in ion, a, or d, are commonly the feminine, as Aficion, Cama, Amistad, except la mar, and some few others.

Names of trees are commonly of the masculine: and of the fruites the feminine, as el mançano, la mançana, except some fewe, as el higo, la higuera, la palma, el datil, la parra, el razimo. 3

Herbals in or, are of the masculine gender, and haue their feminine by putting to a, as comprador, compradora: nownes in o, make the feminine by changing o into a. Amo, ama, bueno, buena. 4

OF DECLENSONS.

There is no diuersitie of Declensons, all Nownes following one & the same course, vz. to be declined with the Preposition and the article, the article is thus declined.

Sing. { Nom. el, la, lo.
Genit. del, dela, delo.
Dat. para el, para la, para lo.
Acc. a l, or a la, a lo.
Ab. del, de la, de lo. } Plur. { Nom. los, las.
Gen. de los, de las.
Dat. para los, para las.
Acc. a los, a las.
Abl. de los, de las.

And note that in speech: the article is to Nownes appellatiues a companion inseparable: but is not vsed with Nownes proper; as we say el hombre, la muger: but not el Iuan, la Catelina: neyther is the article vsed with the word Dios, vnlesse there be ioyned to it some epithyte, as el Dios todo poderoso &c. Nownes substantiues of the masculine gender are thus declined.

Sing. { Nom. el hombre.
Gen. del hombre.
Dat. para el hombre.
Acc. a el or al hombre.
Abl. del hombre. } Plur. { Nom. los hombres.
Gen. de los hombres.
Dat. para los hombres.
Acc. a los hombres.
Abl. de los hombres.

Of the Feminine gender thus.

Sing. { Nom. la muger.
Gen. de la muger.
Dat. para la muger.
Acc. a la muger.
Abl. de la muger. } Plur. { Nom. las mugeres.
Gen. de las mugeres.
Dat. para las mugeres.
Acc. a las mugeres.
Abl. de las mugeres.

OF NOVNES ADIECTIVES.

Adiectiues are of two sorts, some of all genders vnder one termination, as Eloquente, frequente: some of three diuers ending, as Bueno, buena, bueno, the Masculine being declined like the Substantiue of the Masculine gender, the Feminine as the Substantiue of the Feminine gender, and the newter with the article of the newter gender, in the singular number onely: & with the other two genders, in the plural also.

OF COMPARISON.

There be three degrees of Comparison of nownes adiectiues: the positiue of absolute signification, as justo, iust, Hermoso, fayre.

The comparatiue exceedeth the positiue, and in English is knowen by

A Pronoune.

by the termination er as iuster, fayrer, or by the worde more, as more iust, more fayre, which in Spanish is alway mas, as mas justo.

The Superlatiue in signification excœdeth his positiue in the highest degrœ, and in English hath the termination, est, as iustest, or the word most, as most iust; in Spanish it chaungeth o of the positiue into issimo, as justissimo, or else hath the word muy, & sometimes mas ioyned with it, as muy justo, muy hermoso. Fulano es el mas esforçado, de todos los soldados, de su tercio. Such a one is the most valient of all the souldiors of his bande. Out of this rule are excepted, Bueno, malo, mucho, poco, grande, chico, which are thus compared.

    Bueno, mejor, o mas bueno; muy bueno.
    Malo, peor, muy malo.
    Mucho, mas, muy mucho, o muchissimo.
    Poco, menos, muy poco.
    Grande, mayor, muy grande o grandissimo.
    Chico, menor, o mas chico; muy chico.

A Pronoune.

A Pronoune is a parte of speach very like the Noune, and is vsed in shewing & rehearsing. Of pronounes some are primitiues, as yo, tu, si, este, aquel, el, el qual, que, quien, mismo.

Some are deriuatiues called also possessiues: because they signifie possession, appertaining or belonging vnto some other thing, as Mio or mi, tuyo or tu, suyo or su, nuestro and vuestro.

Of Primitiues, some are called demonstratiues, because they shew a thing not spoken of before: as yo, tu, si, aquel, este, el.

Some are Relatiues, as rehearsing something, or hauing reference to something spoken of before, as el, este, que, quien, el qual.

In a Pronoune are especially to be noted these two thinges: declenson and person, there be thrœ declensons of pronounes, of the first are yo, tu, si, thus.

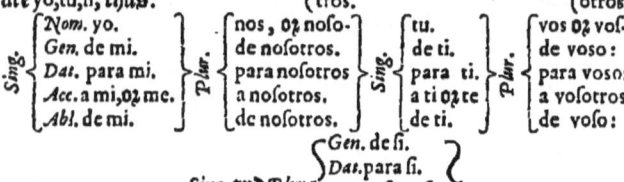

Of the second declenson are el, aquel, este, mio, tuyo, suyo, nuestro, vnestro, mismo, & note that el where he serueth as an article is declined, as is shewed in the Noune: where he is a pronoune, thus.

Sing.
  Nom. el, ella, ello.
  Gen. d'el, d'ella, d'ello.
  Dat. para el, para ella, para ello.
  Acc. a el, a ella, a ello.
  Abl. del, della, dello.

Plur.
  Nom. ellos, ellas.
  Gen. dellos, dellas.
  Dat. para ellos, para ellas.
  Acc. a ellos, a ellas.
  Abl. dellos, dellas. So aquel, aquella,

A Verbe.

aquella, aquello, este, esse, esta, essa, esto, esso, mismo, misma, mismo: and note that mismo, is commonly ioyned to some other Pronoune: as *ipse* in Latine, yo mismo, I my selfe, tu mismo, thou thy selfe, &c.

Of the third declenson are que, quien, el qual, noting that que is all one in both nūbers, el qual, maketh los quales in the plurall thus.

Sing. { *Nom.* el qual.
{ *Gen.* del qual.
{ *Dat.* para el qual, &c.

Plur. { *Nom.* los quales.
{ *Gen.* de los quales.
{ *Dat.* para los quales, &c.

OF PERSONS.

There be three persons, the first speaketh of himselfe, as yo, I, nos or nosotros, wee.

The second person is spoken to, as Tu, thou: vos or vosotros, yee.

The third person is spoken of, as aquel hee, aquellos they: and note that of this person are all Nounes, Pronounes & Participles, sauing the Pronounces last aforesaid.

A Verbe.

A Verbe is a part of speach declined with moode and tence, signifying doing: as lastimo, I hurt: suffering, as soy lastimado, I am hurt, or beyng, as soy, I am. Of verbes there are two sorts: Personals, and Impersonals. A verbe personall is, that is declined with three persons, both in the singular and plurall: a Verbe impersonall, that though all moodes and tences is declined by the third person singuler onely.

Of Verbs personals there be three kinds, Actiue, Passiue & neuter.

A Verbe actiue endeth in o, and signifieth to do, as Lastimo, I hurt: Amo, I loue; and may be made passiue by ioyning soy to the participle: as soy lastimado.

A Verbe passiue signifieth suffering, & is either formed by the verbe soy, and the participle, as soy lastimado, I am hurt, or els the accusatiue case se, with the third person of the actiue & singuler or plurall number, hath a passiue signification, as todo esto se lee en el nueuo testamento de nuestro señor. All this is read in the new testament, &c. Muchos libros se leen, los quales no se entienden. Many bookes are read which are not vnderstood.

A Verbe neuter endeth in o, or y, as soy, duermo, voy, and cannot take soy to make him a passiue.

To a Verbe belong moode, tence, number, person, gerund, coniugatiō.

The moodes are the indicatiue, shewing a reason true or false, or asking a question, as yo lastimo, I hurt, or lastimo? doe I hurt?

The imperatiue bidding or commaunding, as tu lastima, hurt thou.

The Optatiue wishing or desiring, as oxala yo lastime, I pray God I hurt. The Potentiall ioyned with these signes, may, can, might, would, should, or ought: the subiunctiue hauing a coniunction with it, the infinitiue knowen by the signe to, as lastimar, to hurt.

The tences are fiue, the present tence, signifying the time that now is: the preterimperfectence, the time not perfectly past: the preterperfectence the time perfectly past: the preterpluperfectence the time more

then

Of a Verbe.

then perfectly past: the future tence the time to come.

The numbers are two as in a Noune: the persons three in both numbers.

There is only one Gerund ending in do: hauing the English of the participle of the present tence, vsed oft in steede thereof: as *lastimando: creyendo, durmiendo*: that which in Latine is the Gerund in di, is expressed in Spanish by the infinitiue moode, and the preposition de: as *Gran desseo tengo de verle*, I haue great desire to see him; the Gerund in dum, by the infinitiue mood and the preposition *para* or *a*, as *voy me, para ver le*, I go to see him.

OF CONIVGATIONS.

A Coniugation is the course of declining a verbe, by mood and tense: there be sixe coniugations; three of verbes regular, and three of verbes irregular.

The first coniugations of verbes regular and irregular ende in *ar*, as *Lastimar, Dessear*.

The second in *er*, as *Creer, Leer, ver*.

The third in *ir*, as *Dormir, Reyr, Freyr*.

Except Adereçar, Aderesco, and enderecir, enderesco.

The tenses are thus deriued. In the first coniugation by changing *ar* into *o* you shall haue the first person of the present tence of the Indicatiue moode: whose third person singular endeth in *a*, to which adde *va*, and you haue the preterimperfect tense of the same moode: as of *Lastimar, lastimo, lastima, lastimaua*: by turning the *a* into *e* long you haue the first preterperfect tense of the same moode, as *Lastimé*: by adding *re* long, the future of the same moode, as *Lastimaré*. the Imperatiue moode is all one with the said third person of the Indicatiue: of which also by turning *a* into *e* short, you haue the present tense of the Subiunctiue, as *Lastime*: by adding *ra, ria, sse*, you make the voices of the preterimperfect tense of the Subiunctiue, as *Lastimara, lastimaria, lastimasse*: by putting to it *re* short the first future of the Subiunctiue, as *Lastimare*: by adding *ndo* the gerund: by adding *do* onely, the participle of the preter tense: so as in manner all your tenses of all moodes in this coniugation are formed by the verbe He, and the participle. *Perf.sec*. He Lastimado. *Plusquamperf*. Avia Lastimado, &c. which, by example shall be shewed more at large.

In the second coniugation change *er* into *o*, you haue the first person of the present tense of the Indicatiue mood, as *Leer, leo, Creer, creo*, whose third person singular endeth in *e*, which if you change into *y*, and put a *to* it, you haue the preterimperfect tense of the same moode, as *Leya*, from which take *a*, and you haue the first preterperfect tense of the same mood, as *Crey*: to the Infinitiue mood adde *e* long, you haue the future tense of the Indicatiue, as *Creeré*. The Imperatiue and third

Of a Verbe.

third perſon of the Indicatiue are all one : by adding era, eſſe, to the preterperfect tenſe of the indicatiue are formed two voices of the preterimperfect tenſe of the Subiunctiue : by putting to it ere the firſt future of the ſame moode: by changing the laſt e of the third perſon ſingular of the preſent tenſe of the Indicatiue into a, you haue the preſent tenſe of the Subiunctiue: by changing e of the future of the Indicatiue into ia, you make the third voice of the preterimperfect tenſe of the Subiunctiue, as of Crey, creyera, creyeſſe, creyére : of Cree, ſi yo crea, of Creeré commeth Creeria.

In the third coniugation change ir into o you make the preſent tenſe of the Indicatiue moode, ſaue that e in the laſt ſillable ſaue one is often changed into i, and o into ue, as Pido, eſcrivo, duermo, and verbs ending in zir, haue g before o, as Induzir, induzgo, induzes, læſing it againe in the ſecond perſon : change r of the Infinitiue moode into a, you haue the preterimperfect tenſe of the Indicatiue, as Dormia : take away r the firſt preterperfect tenſe : adde re long, the future tenſe; as of Dormir commeth dormi and dormire : the Imperatiue moode and the third perſon of the preſent tenſe of the Indicatiue are all one : the preſent tenſe of the Subiunctiue is formed of the firſt perſon of the preſent tenſe of the Indicatiue, by changing o into a, as of Duermo, duerma : by adding ia to the Infinitiue moode is formed one voice of the preterimperfect tenſe of the Subiunctiue : by changing r into era, eſſe, the two other voices : into ere, the future of the Subiunctiue moode, as of Dormir; commeth dormiria, dormiera, dormieſſe, dormiére.

For the forming of the tenſes of verbes irregular, no certaine rule can be giuen, although their coniugation be knowen by the ſame termination as the other : wherefore in theſe, in ſtæde of rule, I will ſet downe ſuch varietie of examples in euery coniugation, as ſhall giue great light to the reader.

Before we come to ſet downe examples of the verbes, bicauſe none of them can be declined without the verbe He, which belongeth to the ſecond coniugation of the irregulars : for helpe of the Reader (though ſomwhat diſorderly) we will begin with him.

The Indicatiue moode, and preſent tenſe.

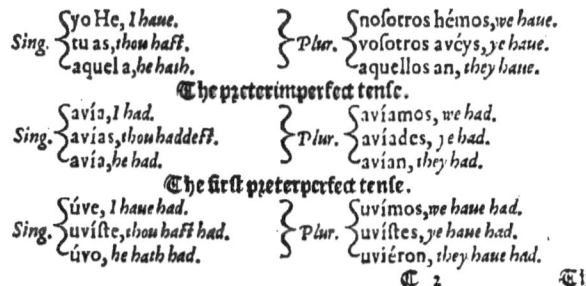

Sing. { yo He, *I haue.*
{ tu as, *thou haſt.*
{ aquel a, *he hath.*

Plur. { noſotros hémos, *we haue.*
{ voſotros avéys, *ye haue.*
{ aquellos an, *they haue.*

The preterimperfect tenſe.

Sing. { avía, *I had.*
{ avías, *thou haddeſt.*
{ avía, *he had.*

Plur. { avíamos, *we had.*
{ avíades, *ye had.*
{ avían, *they had.*

The firſt preterperfect tenſe.

Sing. { úve, *I haue had.*
{ uvíſte, *thou haſt had.*
{ úvo, *he hath had.*

Plur. { uvímos, *we haue had.*
{ uvíſtes, *ye haue had.*
{ uviéron, *they haue had.*

Of a Verbe.

The second preterperfect tense.

Sing. { yo he avído, *I haue had.*
as avido
a avido.

Plur. { hemos avido
aveys avido
an avido.

The preterpluperfect tense.

Sing. { avía avído, *I had had.*
avias avido
avia avido.

Plur. { avíamos avido
aviades avido
avian avido.

The future tense.

Sing. { avré, *I shall or will haue.*
avrás
avrá.

Plur. { avrémos
avreís
avrán.

The imperatiue moode.

Sing. { áyas tu, *haue thou.*
aquel áya, *let him haue.*

Plur. { nos ayámos, *let vs haue.*
vos avéd, *haue ye.*
aquellos áyan, *haue they.*

The imperatiue of this verbe is often borrowed of Tengo, as Ten, tenga, &c. Which verbe also in many tenses of other moodes is vsed in steede of He.

The optatiue and potentiall, are in all points like the subiunctiue, saue that to the optatiue you ioine Oxala, would God, or such like : to the potentiall his signes, to the subiunctiue Si. Wherefore both in this and in the examples of all other verbs; to auoid tedious repetition, I will set downe the subiunctiue onely.

The subiunctiue and present tense.

Sing. { Si ayá, *if I haue.*
áyas
áya

Plur. { ayámos
ayáys
áyan.

The preterimperfect tense.

Sing. { uviéra, uviésse, avría, *if I had.*
uviéras, uviésses, avrías
uviéra, uviésse, avría.

Plur. { uviéramos, uviéssemos, avríamos,
uviérades, uviéssedes, avríades
uvieran, uviéssen, avrían.

The preterperfect tense.

Sing. { Si yo áya avído, *if I haue*
ayas avido *(had.*
aya avido.

Plur. { ayamos avido
ayáys avido
ayan avido.

The preterpluperfect tense.

Sing. { uviésse avido, *if I had had.*
uviésses avido
uviésse avido.

Plur. { uviéssemos avido
uviéssedes avido
uviéssen avido.

The first future.

Sing. { uviére, *if I shall haue.*
uviéres
uviére

Plur. { uviéremos
uviéredes
uviéren.

Of a Verbe.

The second future.

Sing. {avré avido *I shall haue had.* / avrás avido / avrá avido.} Plur. {avrémos avido / avréys avido / avrán avido.}

The infinitiue and present tense.
Avér, *to haue.*

Preterperfect tense.
Aver avido. *To haue had.*

The future.
By some other verbe, as Espero de aver, *I hope to haue, &c.*

The gerund.
Aviendo, *hauing.*

The participle.
Avído, *had,* which I adde to the actiue though it haue a passiue signi=
fication, partly bicause it is formed of the actiue: partly bicause there
is no passiue in maner, but that which is formed by this participle.

And thus much of the verbe, He.

The first coniugation of the regular verbs endeth in ar, as Lasti-   1. Coniuga-
mar, Comprar, Tomar, and is thus formed.   tion.

The indicatiue moode and present tense.

Sing. {yo lastímo, *I hurt.* / tu lastímas, *thou hurtest.* / aquel lastíma, *he hurteth.*} Plur. {nosotros lastimámos / lastimáys / lastíman, *they hurt.*}

The preterimperfect tense.

Sing. {lastimáva, *I did hurt.* / lastimávas / lastimáva.} Plur. {lastimávamos / lastimávades / lastimávan.}

The first preterperfect tence.

Sing. {lastimé, *I hurt.* / lastimáste / lastimó.} Plur. {lastimámos / lastimástes / lastimáron.}

The second preterperfect tense.

Sing. {he lastimado, *I haue hurt.* / as lastimádo / a lastimado.} Plur. {hémos lastimado / avéys lastimado / an lastimado.}

The preterpluperfect tense.

Sing. {avía lastimádo, *I had hurt.* / avias lastimado / avia lastimado.} Plur. {avíamos lastimado / avíades lastimado / avían lastimado.}

The future.

Sing. {lastimaré, *I shal or wil hurt.* / lastimarás / lastimará.} Plur. {lastimarémos / lastimaréys / lastimarán,}

Note that in steed of this future tense of the indicatiue moode, both
in this and all other coniugations, there is often vsed the infinitiue
moode, and the termination of this future tense, as

Sing.

Of a Verbe.

Sing. {laſtimar lo he / laſtimar lo as / laſtimar lo a}   Plur. {laſtimar lo emos / laſtimar lo eys / laſtimar lo an}. So Creer lo he, dezir lo he, tener lo he, of which for auoiding tediousnes, it shall be sufficient this once to admonish the Reader.

The imperatiue moode.

Sing. {tu laſtima, *hurt thou* / aquel laſtime, *let him hurt*}   Plur. {laſtimámos, *let vs hurt* / laſtimád, *hurt ye* / laſtimen, *hurt they*}

The subiunctiue moode and preſent tenſe.

Sing. {Si yo laſtime, *if I hurt* / laſtimes / laſtime.}   Plur. {laſtimémos / laſtiméys / laſtimen.}

The preterimperfect tenſe.

Sing. {Si laſtimára, laſtimaría, laſtimáſſe, *if I did hurt* / laſtimáras, laſtimarías, laſtimáſſes / laſtimára, laſtimaría, laſtimáſſe.}

Plur. {laſtimáramos, laſtimaríamos, laſtimáſſemos / laſtimárades, laſtimaríades, laſtimáſſedes / laſtimáran, laſtimarían, laſtimáſſen.}

Note that the firſt of theſe voices is often found to haue an indicatiue ſignification: and ſometime the ſignification of the preterpluperfect tenſe of the potentiall moode, the ſecond voice both in this and all other verbs is often diuided in the potentiall moode, and is vſed with the infinitiue moode, Le, los, &c, comming betweene them, as Laſtimar le ia, Creyr le ia, Dezir le ia, Conocer le ia, and ſo forth through al perſons.

The preterperfect tenſe.

Sing. {Siyo, áya laſtimado *If I haue hurt* / áyas laſtimado / áya laſtimado.}   Plur. {ayámos laſtimado / ayáys laſtimado / áyan laſtimado.}

The preterpluperfectenſe.

Sing. {uuieſſe laſtimado *If I had hurt* / uuieſſes laſtim: / uuieſſe laſtim:}   Plur. {uuieſſemos laſtimado / uuieſſedes laſtimado / uuieſſen laſtimado.}

The firſt future.

Sing. {laſtimáre *If I ſhall hurt* / laſtimáres / laſtimáre.}   Plur. {laſtimáremos / laſtimáredes / laſtimáren.}

The ſecond future.

Sing. {avré laſtima: *If I ſhall haue hurt* / avrás laſtimado / avrá laſtimado.}   Plur. {avrémos laſtimado / avréys laſtimado / avrán laſtimado.}

The infinitiue preſent tenſe.

Laſtimar, *To hurt*.

The

Of a Verbe.

The preterperfect tense.
Aver lastimado, *To haue hurt.*
      The gerunde.
Lastimando, *Hurting.*
      The participle.
Lastimado, *Hurt.*

The second coniugation endeth in er, and is thus formed.   2. Coniugation.
      The indicatiue moode present tense.

Sing. { créo *I beleeue.*
       { crées
       { crée.

Plur. { creémos
      { creéys
      { créen.

The preterimperfect tense.

Sing. { creýa *I did beleeue.*
       { creýas
       { creýa.

Plur. { creyámos
      { creyádes
      { creýan.

The preterperfect tense.

Sing. { creýa *I beleeued.*
       { creýste
       { creyó.

Plur. { creýmos
      { creýstes
      { creyéron.

The second preterperfect tense.

Sing. { he creýdo *I haue beleeued.*
       { as creýdo
       { a &c. *as is before in the first coniugation.*

The preterpluperfect tense.
I had beleeued.
Sing. avía, creýdo, avías, avía, *as in the first.*

The future tense.

Sing. { creeré *I shall or will beleeue.*
       { creerás
       { creerá.

Plur. { creerémos
      { creeréys
      { creerán.

The imperatiue.

Sing. { crée *Beleeue thou.*
       {
       { créa

Plur. { creámos
      { creéd
      { créan.

The subiunctiue present tense.

Sing. { créa *If I beleeue.*
       { créas
       { créa.

Plur. { creámos
      { creáys
      { créan.

The preterimperfect tense.

Sing. { creyéra, creería, creyésse   *If I did beleeue.*
       { creyéras, creerías, creyésses
       { creyéra, creería, creyésse.

Plur. { creyéramos, creeríamos, creyéssemos
      { creyérades, creeríades, creyéssedes
      { creyéran, creerían, creyéssen.

The preterperfect tense and preterpluperfect tense.

The preterperfect, aya creydo, **the preterpluperfect** uviesse creydo, *as in the first coniugation.*

The

Of a Verbe.

The first future.
Sing. {creyére *If I shall beleeue.* / creyéres / creyére.}   Plur. {creyéremos / creyéredes / creyéren.}

The second future.
Sing. si yo avré creydo, avras creydo, *as in the first coniugation.*

The infinitiue present tense.
Creér *To beleeue.*

The preterimperfect tense.
Aver creydo, *To haue beleeued.*

The gerunde.
Creyendo, *Beleeuing.*

The participle.
Creydo, *Beleeued.*

The third coniugation endeth in yr or ir, as Dormir, pedir, oyr, **and is thus formed.**

The indicatiue moode present tense.
Sing. {pído, *I require.* / pídes / píde}   Plur. {pedímos / pedís / píden.}

The preterimperfect tense.
Sing. {pedía *I did require.* / pedías / pedía.}   Plur. {pedíamos / pedíades / pedían.}

The preterperfect tense.
Sing. {pedí *I required* / pedíste / pidió.}   Plur. {pedímos / pedístes / pidiéron.}

The second preterperfect and preterpluperfect tense.
The second preterperfect tense, he pedido, **the preterpluperfect tense,** avia pedido.

The future tense.
Sing. {pediré *I shall or will require.* / pedirás / pedirá.}   Plur. {pedirémos / pediréys / pedirán.}

The imperatiue.
Sing. {pide *Require thou.* / pída.}   Plur. {pidámos / pedíd / pídan.}

Subiunctiue present tense.
Sing. {pída *If I require.* / pídas / pída.}   Plur. {pidámos / pidáys / pídan.}

The preterimperfect tense.
Sing. {pidiéra, pediría, pidiésse, *If I did require.* / pidiéras, pedirías, pidiésses. / pidiéra, pediría, pidiésse.}

Plur.

Of a Verbe.

Plur. {pidiéramos, pediríamos, pidiéssemos
{pidiérades, pediríades, pidiéssedes
{pidiéran, pedirían, pidiéssen.

The preterperfect and preterpluperfect tense.
The preterperfect, aya pedido, **the preterpluperfect** uviesse pedido, &c.

The first future.

Sing. {pidiére *I shall or will require.*   Plur. {pidiéremos
{pidiéres   {pidiéredes
{pidiére.   {pidiéren.

The second future.
Si yo avre pedido, si tu avras pedido, &c.

The infinitie moode present tense.
Pedír, *To require.*

The preterperfect tense.
Aver pedido, *To haue required.*

The gerund.
Pidiendo, *Requiring.*

The participle.
Pedido, *Required.*

Of verbes irregular.
The first coniugation endeth in ar, as Estar, dar, **and are thus formed,** 1. Coniugacion.
The indicatiue present tense.

Sing. {estóy *I stand or I am.*   Plur. {estámos
{estás   {estáys
{está   {están.

The preterimperfect tense.
Estáva estavas, &c. *Like the regular.*

The first preterperfect tense.

Sing. {estúve *I haue stood.*   Plur. {estuvimos
{estuviste   {estuvistes
{estúvo.   {estuvieron.

The second preterperfect tense, and preterpluperfect tense.
The preterperfect, he estado, **the preterpluperfect** avia estado, &c.

The future.
Estaré, as, a, as the regulare.

The imparatiue.

Sing. {esta, sta *Stand then.*   Plur. {estémos
{este.   {estád
                                        {estén.

The subiunctiue present tense. Si

Sing. {esté *If I stand.*   Plur. {estémos
{estés   {esteys
{esté   {esten.

Of a Verbe.

Plur. {eſtuviéramos,eſtaríamos,eſtuviéſſemos,
      eſtuviérades,eſtaríades,eſtuvéſſedes,
      eſtuvieran,eſtarian,eſtuvieſſen.

The preterperfect and preterpluperfect tenſe.

The preterperfect aya eſtado, the preterpluperfect uviéſſe eſtado, &c.

The firſt future.

Sing. {eſtuviére *If I ſhall or will ſtand.*   Plur. {eſtuviéremos
       eſtuvieres   eſtuviéredes
       eſtuviére   eſtuviéren.

The ſecond future.

Avre eſtado, avras eſtado, avra eſtado, &c.

The infinitiue preſent tenſe.

Eſtar *to ſtande or to be.*

The preterperfect.

Aver eſtado, *To haue beene, or ſtood.*

The gerund.

Eſtando, *Standing or beeing.*

The participle.

Eſtado, *Stood or beene.*

So is Doy declined, following the regular in all tenſes, ſaue the firſt preterperfect of the indicatiue; and the tences thereof deriued, which are formed thus.

The firſt preterperfect of the indicatiue.

Sing. {dí *I haue giuen.*   Plur. {dimos
       diſte   diſtes
       dió.   diéron.

The preterimperfect of the ſubiunctiue. Si,

Sing. {diéra, daría, diéſſe, *If I did giue.*
       dieras, darias, dieſſes,
       diera, daria, dieſſe.

Plus. {diéramos, daríamos, diéſſemos,
       dierades, dariades, dieſſedes,
       dieran, darian, dieſſen.

The future of the ſubiunctiue.

Sing. {diére, *If I ſhall or will giue.*   Plur. {diéremos
       dieres   dieredes
       diere   dieren.

The infinitiue preſent.

Dar, *To giue.* Aver dado, *To haue giuen.* Dando, &c.

So is Ando, andas, to go, declined, making Audúve in the preterperfect of the indicatiue Auduviéra, andaría; auduviéſſe in the preterimperfect of the ſubiunctiue, and Auduviére in the future.

2. Coniugation.

The ſecond coniugation of irregulare verbes endeth in er, as hazér, Tenér, ponér, podér, and is thus formed.

Indicatiue preſent.

Sing. {hago *I do or make.*   Plur. {hazémos
       hazes   hazeys
       haze   hazen.

The

Of a Verbe.
The preterimperfect.
Sing. {hazía *I did, or made,*
hazías
hazía.

Plur. {hazíamos
hazíades
hazían.

The first preterperfect.
Sing. {hize *I did, or haue done,*
hezifte
hízo.

Plur. {hezímos
heziftes
hiziéron.

The second preterperfect, and preterpluperfect.
The preterperfect: he hecho, **the preterpluperfect**: auia hecho, auias hecho, as in other verbes.

The future.
Sing. {haré *I will doe,*
harás
hará.

Plur. {harémos
haréys
harán.

The imperatiue moode.
Sing. {haz *Doe thou,*
haga.

Plur. {hagámos
hazéd
hágan.

The subiunctiue present tense.
Sing. {híga *If I doe,*
hígas
haga.

Plur. {hagámos
hagáys
hágan.

The preterimperfect tense. (mos
Sing. {hiziéra, haría, hiziéffe *If I did,*
hizieras, harias, hizieffes
hiziera, haria, hizieffe.

Plur. {hiziéramos, haríamos, hiziéffe-
hizierades, hariades, hizieffedes
hizieran, harian, hizieffen.

The preterperfect tense, and preterpluperfect tense.
The preterperfect tense, aya hecho, **the preterpluperfect tense**, uviéffe hecho, uviéffes hecho, &c.

The first future.
Sing. {hiziére *If I shall doe,*
hiziéres
hiziére.

Plur. {hiziéremos
hiziéredes
hiziéren.

The seconde future.
Avre hecho, avras hecho, &c. as in other verbes.

The infinitiue present.
Hazer, *To doe, or to make.*

The preterfect.
Auer hecho, *To haue done.*

Gerunde.
Haziendo, *Doing.*

Participle.
Hecho, *Done, made.*

D 2   Tener,

Of a Verbe.

Tener, *To holde, or to haue.*

The indicatiue present.

Sing. { tengo *I hold or I haue.* / tienes / tiene. } Plur. { tenémos / tenéys / tienen. }

Imperfect.

Tenía, *I did hold.* tenias, as the regulare.

First perfect tense.

Sing. { túve *I helde.* / túviste / túvo. } Plur. { tuvímos / tuvistes / tuvieron. }

Second preterperfect: and preterpluperfect:
The preterfect. He tenido, the preterplupersect, avia tenido, auias tenido, &c.

The future.

Sing. { tendré o terné *I shall or will hold.* / tendras o ternas / tendra o terna. } Plur. { tendrémos o ternémos / tendréys o terneys / tendrán o ternán. }

The imperatiue.

Sing. { ten *Holde thou.* / tenga. } Plur. { tengamos / tenéd / tengan. }

The subiunctiue present.

Tenga *If I holde,* tengas, as in the regular.

The preterimperfect.

Sing. { tuviéra, ternía, tuviéste *If I did hold.* / tuvieras, ternias, tuvieses / tuviera, ternia, tuviesse. }

Plur. { tuviéramos, terniamos, tuviéssemos / tuvierades, terniades, tuviessedes / tuvieran, ternian, tuviessen. }

The preterperfect: and preterpluperfect.

The preterperfect. aya tenido, the preterplupersect, uviesse tenido.

The first future.

Sing. { tuviére *If I shall holde.* / tuvieres / tuviere. } Plur. { tuviéremos / tuvieredes / tuvieren. }

The second future.

Avre tenido, avras tenido, &c.

Infinitiue present.

Tenér *To haue, to holde.*

Preterperfect.

Aver tenido *To haue helde.*

Gerunde.

Teniendo, *Holding, hauing.*

Participle.

Tenído, *Had, helde.*

So is Pongo, pones, declined: forming Púse in the first preterperfect.

Porné

Of a Verbe.

Porné in the future. Pusiera pornia pusiesse in the preterinperfect of the subiunctiue, and Pusiére in the first future, Poner in the infinit. and Puesto the participle. So puedo, podia, pude, podre, the subiunct. Pueda, pudiera, podria, pudiesse: future pudiere: infinit. podér: participle Podido. Likewise se, *I know*: sabes, sabia, súpe, sabré. subiunct. sepa, supiera, sabria, supiésse. futur. supiere. infinit. sabér. participle, sabido. The verbe Soy, *I am*, varieth somwhat from the rest of the irregulars of this coningation, thus:

Indicatiue present.

Sing. { Soy, *I am*. / éres / es }   Plur. { somos / soys / son. }

The preterimperfect.

Sing. { éra, *I was*. / eras / era. }   Plur. { éramos / erades / eran. }

The first preterperfect.

Sing. { fúe, *I haue bene*. / fueste / fue. }   Plur. { fuymos / fuestes / fueron. }

Second preterperfect, and preterpluperfect.

he sido.   avia sido.

Future.

Sing. { seré, *I shall or will be*. / serás / será. }   Plur. { seremos / seréys / seran. }

Imperatiue.

Sing. { se, *Be thou*. / sea. }   Plur. { seamos / sed / sean. }

The subiunctiue present.

Sing. { sea, *If I be*. / seas / sea. }   Plur. { seamos / seáys / sean. }

Imperfect.

Sing. { fuéra, seria, fuésse, *If I were*. / fueras, serias, fuesses / fuera, seria, fuesse. }   Plur. { fuéramos, seriamos, fuéssemos / fuerades, seriades, fuessedes / fueran, serian, fuessen. }

Perfect and pluperfect.

Aya sido.   uviesse sido.

First future.

Sing. { fuére, *If I shall or will be*. / fueres / fuere. }   Plur. { fuéremos / fueredes / fueren. }

Second future.

Avré sido, avras sido, &c.

Infinitiue present.

Ser, *To bee*.

Perfect.

Of a Verbe.

Perfect.
Auer sido, *To haue beene.*

Gerunde.
Siendo, *Being.*

Participle.
Sido. *Beene.*

3.Coniug. **The third coniugation endeth in yr, or ir, as the regular, and is thus declined.**

Indicat. present.
Sing. { voy *I goe.* / vas / va. } Plur. { vámos / vays / van. }

Imperfect.
Sing. { íva *I did goe.* / ivas / iva. } Plur. { ívamos / ivades / ivan. }

First preterperfect.
Sing. { fuý *I went.* / fuiste / fue. } Plur. { fuímos / fuistes / fueron. }

Second perfect. and preterpluperfect.
He ydo, *I haue gone.* avia ydo. &c.

Future.
Sing. { yré *I shall or will goe.* / yrás / yrá. } Plur. { yrémos / yréys / yrán. }

Imperatiue.
Sing. { va, y, ve *Goe thou.* / váya. } Plur. { vamos / yd / vayan. }

Subiunctiue present.
Sing. { váya *If I goe.* / vayas / vaya. } Plur. { vámos / vays / vayan. }

Imperfect.
Sing. { fuéra, yría, fuésse *If I went.* / fueras, yrias, fuesses / fuera, yria, fuesse. } Plur. { fuéramos, yríamos, fuéssemos / fuerades, yriades, fuessedes / fueran, yrian, fuessen. }

The preterperfect. Aya, ydo: **the preterpluperfect.** uviesse ydo.

The first future.
Sing. { fuére *If I shall or will goe.* / fueres / fuere. } Plur. { fuéremos / fueredes / fueren. }

Infinitiue present.
yr, *To goe.*

Perfect.
Aver ydo, *To haue gone.*

Gerunde.

Of a Verbe.

Gerunde.
Yendo, not vsed, but instead therof andando, *Going*.
Participle.
Ydo, *Gone*.

Vengo, vienes, is declined like Tengo: saue that in the first preterperfect of the indicatiue, it maketh vine, veniste, vino: the future verne, or vendre: the imperfect tense of the subiunct. viniera, vernia, viniesse: the first future viniére: infinitiue: venir: participle venido: Digo is thus declined.

Indicat. present.

Sing. { digo *I say.*
       dizes
       dize.

Plur. { dezimos
       dezís
       dízen.

Imperfect.
Dezia *I did say*, dezias as the regular.

First perfect.

Sing. { díxe *I sayd.*
       dixíste
       díxo.

Plur. { diximos
       dixistes
       dixéron.

The second perfect tence, he dicho: the preterpluperfect, auia dicho, &c.

Future.

Sing. { diré *I shall or will saie.*
       diras
       dira.

Plur. { dirémos
       diréys
       dirán.

Imperatiue.

Sing. { di *Saie thou.*
       diga.

Plur. { digámos
       dezíd
       digan.

Subiunct. present.

Sing. { diga *If I say.*
       digas
       diga.

Plur. { digámos
       digáys
       digan.

Imperfect tense.

Sing. { dixéra, diría, dixésse, *if I did*
       dixéras, dirías, dixésses, *(say.)*
       dixéra, diría, dixésse.

Plur. { dixéramos, diríamos, dixéssemos
       dixérades, diríades, dixéssedes
       dixéran, dirían, dixéssen.

The preterperfect, Aya dicho: the preterpluperfect, uviésse dicho, &c.

The first future.

Sing. { dixére, *if I shall or will say.*
       dixéres
       dixére

Plur. { dixéremos
       dixéredes
       dixeren.

Infinitiue present, Dézir *to say.*
Perfect,   Aver dicho, *to haue said.*
Gerund,   Diziendo, *saying.*
Participle,   Dicho, *saied.*

The rest of the verbes irregulars may be formed after these examples: for the difference will not be so great, but that by some tense or other knowen, you may perceiue what example to follow.

A

Of a Participle.

A VERBE PASSIVE.

The verbe Passiue, as is aforesaid, is formed of the participle of the preter tense, ioined to the verbe Soy in euery tense, and person as occasion requireth: as

Indicatiue present.

Sing. {Soy lastimado, *I am hurt.*
eres lastimado
es lastimado.}

Plur' {somos lastimados
soys lastimados
son lastimados.}

So era lastimado, fue lastimado, avia sido lastimado, &c. and so forth of all verbes, that will admit a passiue signification, in all moodes and tenses.

Also se with the thirde person singular and plurall of the actiue, maketh the verbe to haue a passiue signification, as is before abused.

VERBES IMPERSONALS.

Impersonals are declined with the thirde person onely through all moodes and tences, as Es, *it is*, era, fue, avia sido será, &c.

Cumple, cumplia, cumplió, avia cumplido, &c. *It must, or it behooueth.*
Pertenece, pertenecia, perteneció.&c.

A Participle.

A Participle is a part of speech taking part both of a Noune, as declension, of the verbe as tense and signification: in Spanish there is one onely participle, and that of the pretertense, the English whereof endeth in *d, t,* or *n*: as *loued, taught, slain*: the Spanish in ado, or ydo: it is formed thus in the regular verbs. From the present tense of the infinitiue take r, in the first and thirde coniugation, and put do to that which remaineth, as of Lastimár, lastimado, pedír, pedido: in the second change er into ydo, creer creydo, in the irregulars there is no certaintie, for sometime they follow this rule, sometime they are deriued of the Latin participles, by changing or displacing letters, as of *Positus*, puesto, of *Dictus*, dicho, of *Factus*, fecho, they are all declined like adiectiues of three terminations, as Lastimado, lastimada, lastimado.

      Creydo, creyda creydo.
      Pedido, pedida, pedido.
      Dicho, dicha, dicho.

You shall sometime finde a participiall voice of the present tense, as Amante, Embargante, Poniente, but they are rather nounes adiectiues then participles, but as well of this tense, as of the others are expressed by the verbes, as
    El que lastima,
    El que dize.

Of the future.

    El que lastimará.
    El que dirá, and so forth of the rest.

An Aduerbe.

An Aduerbe is a part of speech, ioined to the verbe to declare his signification, or to expresse some circumstances.

Some be of Tyme. as, Oy, *to day*: Mañana, *to morrow*: Antier, *the other day*: Poco ha, *a little since*: Mucho à, *long since*: Ogaño, *this yeere*: Antaño, *the last yeere*: Entonces, *then*: Siempre, *alwaie*: Mientras, en el interim, entre tanto, *in the meane while*.

Of Place. as, Aqui, *heere*: Ay, alli, allá *there*: Acá, *hither*: Acullá, *that way*: De alli, de allá, *from thence*: De aqui, *from hence*: Arriba, *aboue*: Abaxo, *beneath*: Cerca, cabe, junto, *neere*: Fuera, *abroade*.

Of Number. Vna vez, *once*: Dos vezes, *twyse*: Cien vezes, *an hundred times*: Mil vezes, *a thousand times*: Pocas vezes, *seldome*, &c.

Of Affirming. Si, *yea*: Mas, *rather*: Antes, *rather*: Cierto, certamente, *truly*, I ambien, *aswell*.

Of Deniall. as, No *not*: Ni, tampoco, *neither*: Paraque no, *that not*.

Of Shewing. as, He aqui, *behold*.

Of Wishing. as, Oxala, *would God*: Ofi, *o if*.

Of Exhorting. as, Ea, *go to*: Ea pues, *go to then*.

Of Order. as, Primeramente, *first*: Despues, *after*: Allende de esto, *furthermore*: Al cabo, finalmente, *finallie*.

Of Asking. as, Porque, *why?* Paraque, *to what ende?* Quando, *when?* Que tanto ha, *how long since?* Que, *what?* Adonde, *whether?* Donde, *where?* De donde, *whence?* Porventura, *what?*

Of Doubting. as, Porventura, *peraduenture*: Quiça, *perhaps*.

Of Likenes. as, Alli, *so*: Como, *as*.

Of Chaunce. as, A caso, por dicho, *by chaunce, by hap*.

Of Qualitie. as, Doctamente, *learnedly*: Eloquentemente, *eloquentlie*: Bien, *well*: Mal, mal, mente, *ill*: and commonly most of the Aduerbes of Qualitie are formed of the Adiectiue of the Feminine gender, by adding mente, as, Sabiamente, seamente, &c.

Of Quantitie. as, Mucho, *much*: Poco, *little*: Muy verie: Mas, *more*: Por demas, *superfluouslie*: Demasiado y demasiadamente, *ouermuch*.

Of Gathering togither. as, Comigo, *with me*: Contigo, *with thee*: Consigo *with him*: junto, juntamente, *togither*.

Of Seuering. as, A parte, *a sunder*: De tras, *after*: A bocados, *by morsels*: A cada hombre, *man by man*.

Of Chosing. as, Mucho mas, *much rather*: Mas ayna, *rather*.

Of Comparison. as, Mas, *more*: Menos, *lesse*: Doctissimamente *most learnedly*.

A Coniunction.

A Coniunction is a part of speech, ioining moods and tenses togither, some are, Copulatiues.

as, Y and E. *and*: Tambien, *also*: Mas, *moreouer*.

Disiunctiues. as, O, *either*: ni, *neither*.

Exceptiues

Of a Coniunction.

Exceptiues. as, Cierto, *truely*: Alomenos, *at least*.
Ouersatiues. as, Aunque, como que, puestoque, *although*: Pero, *but*: Mas si, *but if*: Toda via, *notwithstanding*: No embargante, *yet notwithstanding*, &c.
Causals. as, Si, *if*: Dado que, *if so*: Como si, *as if*: Porque, *wherefore*: Puesque, *wherefore, or therefore*.
Illatiues. as, Assi, *so*: Que, *then*: Porque, *wherefore*: Pues, *therefore*: Por ello, *for this cause*.

A Preposition.

A Preposition is a part of speech, set before other parts, either in Composition, as, Contrahecho, entretener, injusto, or in Apposition, as, En la casa, *in the house*: De la yglesia, *of the church*.

These Prepositions following, are ioined to the Noune onely, with the article, or to the Pronoune, without the articles, seruing as it were to the nominatiue case. as,

Contra el Principe, *against the Prince*: A la yglesia, *to the church*: De la casa, *of the house, or from the house*: En, *in*: Cabe, *neere*: Por, *for, or by*: Entre, *betweene*: Con, *with*: Desde, *from, or since*: Sin, *without*: Hasta, or hazia, *to, or towards*: Sobre, *vpon, or aboue*.

These Prepositions following, are ioined to the Noune or Pronoune with de, as to the Genitiue or Ablatiue. as, Acerca o cerca de la yglesia, *neere the church*: Aquende, *of this side*: Allende, *of that side, or beyonde*: Fuera, *without*: Al deredor, or entorno, *about*: Detras, *behinde, after*: Debaxo, *vnder*: Encima, *on the top*.

This Preposition junto, is ioyned to the accusatiue case, as junto a la yglesia, *neere, &c*.

An Interiection.

An Interiection sheweth a sodaine passion of the minde, whereof some are of   Mirth or Reioising. as,
O bueno, *O well*.
Some of Laughter. as, Hi, hi, hi.
Some of Sorrowe. as, Ay, ay, *alas*: Oy, oy, *heigh*.
Some of Wondring. as, Iesus, Vala me dios, *Iesus, Lord helpe vs*.

Of Spanish words in generall.

IT would be a tedious peece of worke, to search out what should be the proper language of the Spanish nation; the countrie hauing bin mastered by so many dyuers kinds of people, as either of ambition to enlarge their dominions, or of necessitie to seeke habitation for such surplus, as their owne lymits could not conteyne: haue beene
inuited

Of Spanish words.

inuited to make inuasions. True it is that the Spanyard, as in all things he standeth highly vpon his reputation; so he glorieth not a little of his antiquitie, deriuing his pedegree from Tubal, the nephewe of Noe. But howe often the line of Tubal (especially as they drawe it) hath bæne bastarded, hath degenerated, hath bæne quite expelled, by the inuasions of the Phoenicians, the oppressions of the Græbes, the incursions of the Carthaginians, the conquest and planting of prouinces, colonies and garrisons of the Romaines; the generall Deluge of the Gothes Hunes and Vandals, which ouerran all Europe; and finally by the long and intolerable tyrannie of the Mores, whose yoake in 800. yæres he could scarsely shake off; his own histories giue sufficient testimonie. It is then verie manifest, that this mixture of nations must of necessitie make a mixt and compounded language: such as hauing affinitie with many, hath no perfection in any one. But as the Romane conquerors were most polityke, in planting where they swone; making their language most desired, as that of most necessarie vse; and as the tyrannie of the Mores, mixing themselues with such as would yæld to their gouernment, and driuing the rest to the mountaynes, endured longest: So hath the Spanish most resemblance, of the Romane and Morish toongs, retaining also some of the Gotishe: verie lyttle of the Græke, of the Hebrue some one or two letters, and a fewe, yea very fewe words. The Morish words sounde most vpon l r and x as Arrabal, Almofia, Almoxarife, of the Roman some are whole: as, Miseria, Frequente, Eloquente: but most so mangled broken & changed, as they are not easely knowne without great vse or speciall obseruation. Wherfore that the Latined Reader, may be the sooner acquainted with this toong, without troubling himself with to often recourse to his Dictionarie; let him marke this table following, which I set downe in Latine, as impertinent to be written in English), since the English Reader can take no profite by it.

C 2

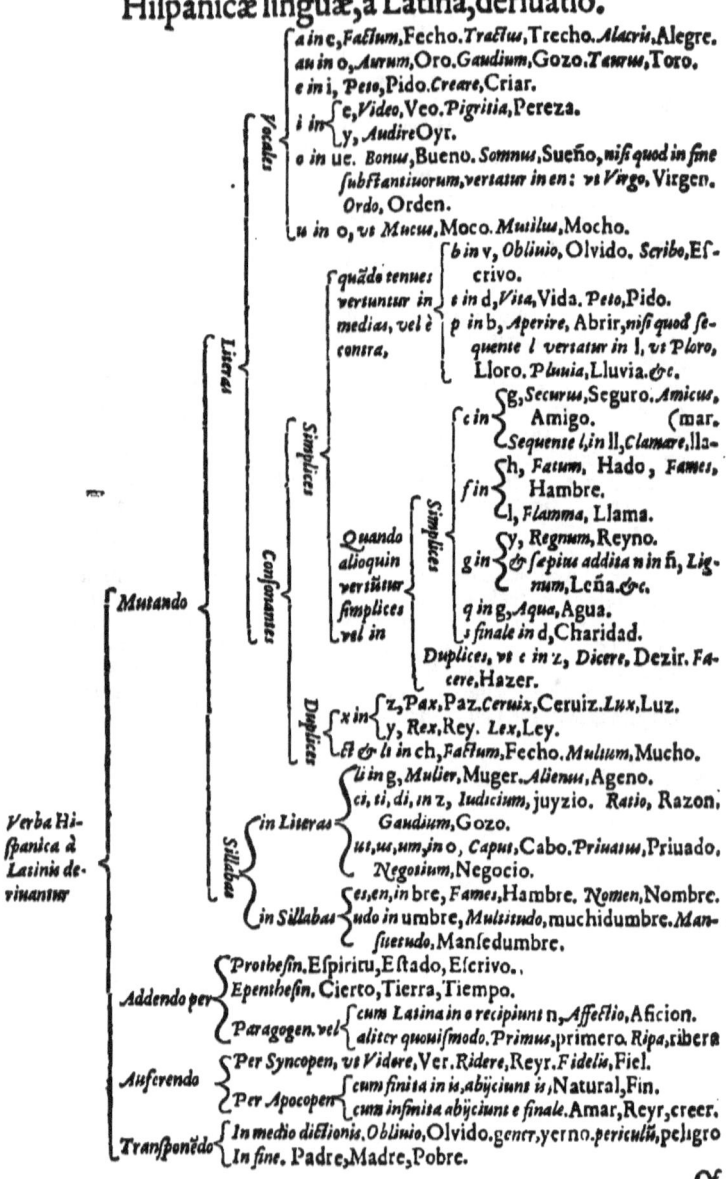

Of Construction and Concord.

Construction is the apt ioining of wordes in framing of a sentence. And bicause in the Spanish there is no such diuersitie in the termination of cases, as in the Latin; there is the lesse occasion ministred to deale at large with this part of Grammar: yet this toong being specially deriued from the Latin, and retaining so great affinitie with it, as the bastard daughter with the mother, it must of necessitie be ordered by many rules incident to the Latin. I will therefore follow that course which the best Latin Grammarians do obserue, as neere as my meane knowledge, and the propriete of the language wherwith I deale, wil giue me leaue. I do therefore diuide the *Syntaxis*, into these two parts: Concord, and Regiment.

Concord.

Concord is the agreement or vniformitie, betweene wordes or partes of speech in a sentence. There be three Concordes. The first betweene the nominatiue case and the verbe: The second betweene the substantiue and the adiectiue: The third betweene the antecedent and the relatiue.

THE FIRST CONCORD.

The first Concord is betweene the nominatiue case and the verbe thus: knowing your verbe, aske the question, *who? or what?* and the word that answereth, is the nominatiue case, which must agree with the verbe in number and person: as Yo escrivo, *I write*, Tu duermes, *Thou sleepest, &c.* And note that many nominatiue cases singular with a Coniunction comming betweene them, will haue a verbe plural, agreeing with the nominatiue case of the most woorthie person: accounting the first person more woorthie then the second, and the second more woorthy then the third: as Tu y yo comeremos oy en casa de Fulano, *You and I will dine to day at such a ones house.* Tu y Iuan yreys comigo a mi casa, *You and Iohn shall go with me to my house.* Furthermore, as concerning the vse of the persons, know ye, that the Spaniard accounteth it a matter of disgrace to speake to any man in the second person singular, except to their lackey, horsekeeper, or some man of vile and base account. To their seruants of better reckoning they speake in the second person plurall. as Direys a Fulano de mi parte, que me pague los deneros, que se me deuen, *Ye shall tell such a one from me that he pay me the monie which is owing me.* To all other they vse the third person singular or plurall as occasion requireth: as Huelgo me mucho de ver, que V.M. sta con salud, suplicandole que se sirva de mi, como de su servidor, que todo bien y honra le desseo, *I am glad to see your masterschip in good health, praying it so vse me as his seruants, that wish it, all good and honor that may be.*

THE

Of the Concords.

THE SECOND CONCORD.

The second, is betweene the substantiue and the adiectiue thus: hauing the adiectiue, aske the question, *who?* or *what?* and that which answereth, is the substantiue, with whom the adiectiue must agree in gender and number: for of the case there is no great rule to be giuen, since if the preposition and article be added to the substantiue or adiectiue it serueth for both: as Oy en dia, se hallan muchos, los quales mas ayna se enamoran de mugeres hermosas aunque liuianas, que de las Señoras honestas y virtuosas, *Now a daies many are found, that sooner loue faire women though they be light, than the honest and vertuous gentlewomen.* And note that for auoiding the harshnesse and gaping in sounde, when a a shoulde meete too neere, sointime they ioine the article of the masculine gender in the singular number, to a substantiue of the feminine: as El agua el alma, which notwithstanding in the plurall they make to agree: as Las almas, las aguas.

Note also that the participle, in declining the actiue of any verbe, as in the second preterperfect tense of the Indicatiue mood, or the preterpluperfect, the preterperfect tense, the preterpluperfect tense, or second future of the subiunctiue, neuer changeth gender or number, whatsoeuer the gender or number be of the nominatiue case to the verbe: as Estos Señores le avian dado licencia de yr se, pero las Señoras le an llamado otra vez, *These gentlemen had giuen him leaue to depart, but the gentlewomen called him againe.* But in the passiue they change number and gender, as also euerywhere else where they are vsed adiectiuely.

Many substantiues singular with a coniunction betweene them, haue an adiectiue plurall agreeing with the substantiue of the most worthy gender, the masculine being more worthy then the feminine, and the feminine more worthy then the neuter: as Mis dedos y mi pluma estan ya cansados de escrevir, *My fingers and my pen are already wearie of writing.* El fuego y la estopa, son muy peligrosos para juntarse, *Fire and towe are very dangerous to be put togisher.*

THE THIRD CONCORD.

The third betweene the antecedent and the relatiue thus: hauing the relatiue, aske the question *who?* or *what?* and the word answering is the antecedent, with whom the relatiue must agree in gender, number, and person: as En cargo te soy, que cada dia tantas mercedes me hazes, *I am beholding to thee, that doest me euery day so many pleasures.* Buen me puedo fiar de mis cartas, las quales me siruen de sieles secretarios, *I may well trust my papers, which serue me as faithfull secretaries.*

Note that many antecedents singular with a coniunction, wil haue a relatiue plurall, agreeing with the antecedent of the most worthy gender: as A tu padre y tu madre, los quales te criaron, mucha honrra, y acatamiento se deven, *To thy father and mother which brought thee vp, are due much honor and reuerence.*

In

Of Regiment.

In the relatiues Que and Quien the vse of the gender cannot be receiued, but the number and person must be obserued: this word Lo often vsed relatiuely, and yet hath no agræment with any antecedent: as Muchos se precian de Catholicos Christianos, que de veras no son, *Many vaunt themselues to be Catholike Christians, which in truth are noing so.* Fulano prometio de enseñarme la lengua Española, pero nolo mplio, *Such a one promised to teach me the Spanish toong, but he performed it not.* ough in this last it may seeme to haue relation to the whole sentence clause afore going.

Regiment.

Regiment is, when any part of speech requireth or gouerneth in construction, any case or moode to be set before him or after him, and it we will deale with the construction of substantiues.

NOVNES SVBSTANTIVES.

The English of the participle, of the present tense with a noune substantiue: which in Latine is expressed by the ablatiue case absolute, is Spanish the nominatiue case, as Escripta la carta, fuese luego para mensajero: *The letter being written he went streight to the messenger.* Venida Reyna, todos luego comencaron de alegrarse: *The Queene being come all sently beganne to reioyce.*

That which in English we vtter in this forme, *Iohns booke, Peters vse,* the Spaniard speaketh by the genitiue case, as, el Libro de Iuan, la sa de Pedro.

The length of time is put in the nominatiue case: as Detuuose tres is en Flandes. *He stayed three daies in Flaunders.* A part of time in the nominatiue case with the verbe he, as Tres dias a: *Three daies agoe.* Avra dos os, *two yeares past.*

From a place, is put in the genetiue, as viene de Londres. In a place at a place with en, the preposition as sta en Londres. To a place if it the name of a countrie or region is put in the datiue case, as Fuese pa-España, *He is gone to Spaine.* Fulano se parte oy para Flandes: *Such a one tth to day for Flaunders, or into Flaunders.* If it be the name of a towne, in e accusatiue, as yo me voy a Londres. The prayse or dispraise is put the genetiue.

REGIMENT OF ADIECTIVES.

Partitiues will haue a Genitiue case: as el vno de ellos, *One of them.* Iguno de aquellos, and sometime they elegantly in a *Prolepsis* leaue oute partitiue, as Las mugeres engañan a los hombres, dellas lastimanles con sus lagrimas fingidas; dellas, halagandoles con palabras lesonges: *Women deceiue men, some of them, greeuing them with their feyned teares; otrs fawning on them with flattering wordes.*

PRONOVNES.

Note, that neither these possessiues, mio, tuyo, suyo, neither their plurals, are vsed with substantiues, but in steed of the mi, tu, su, mis, tus, sus, and

Of Regiment.

and are set before the substantiues, as Mi señor te ruega, que le embies tu cauallo, y que yo le trayga a su casa: *My master prayeth you to send him your horse, and that I may lead him home to him.* Tus manos ensuzian mis ropas: *Thy handes foule my clothes*. But if the possessiue be set alone, ether as hauing reference to a Substantiue going before, or as answering a question, then mio, tuyo, suyo, are vsed, as El cavallo es de mi padre, pero la silla es tuya: *The horse is my fathers, but the saddle is yours.* Cuyas son estas armas? *whose weapons are these?* Son mias, *they are mine.*

The Accusatiue cases, Me, te, se, le, les, are vsed in sted of the datiues of the Latine, & are commonly set before the verbes, El Alcalde te manda, que le quiteys las armas. *The Constable commaundeth thee, to take away his weapons.*

PARTICIPLES.

Participles require such case as the verbes that they come of, as Dado a letras, esta carta sta escripta para mi, it is therefore conuenient to marke well the construction of the verbes.

VERBES ACTIVES AND NEVTERS.

Soy, when it signifieth possession or propertie, will haue a genitiue case, as este thesoro es del rey de España, *this treasure is the king of Spaynes.* When it signifieth abilitie in the partie of whom we speake it, it is put in the datiue: as Fulano es para mucho, *such a one is a man of great valour:* no creo que sea para tanto, *I doe not thinke h ma man of such valour.*

Verbs of accusing, condemning, warning, acquitting or such like, wil haue an accusatiue of the person, and a genitiue of the crime: as Aunq; el Diablo accuse a los hombres de muy graues delictos, toda via la sangre de nuestro Señor, limpiara a todos los fieles, de sus suziedades, y les dara libres de sus pecados: *Though the Diuell accuse men of very grieuous offences, yet the bloud of our Sauiour will cleanse the faithfull from their filthinesse, and free them from their sinnes.*

Verbes of Esteeming will haue a genitiue case: as Precia se de buen Christiano, with mucho poco tanto quanto, they haue the Preposition en, as Estiman le en mucho: with soy, tanto quanto mucho and poco, are put in the datiue case, as is before said.

Verbes of loading, filling, and the contrarie require a nominatiue or accusatiue of the person, or thinge sayd to be filled or loaden, and a genetiue of the thing wherewith: as Cargó lu nao de seda, *He loaded his ship with silke:* cargo sus espaldas de su alforsa, *He loaded his shoulder with his wallet.* So likewise verbes of arraying: as vistio a su hermana de verde, *he clothed his sister in greene.*

Verbes of a transitiue signification with nounes appellatiues, haue after them a nominatiue case: as El perezoso a penas vera buen fin de su negocio: *The slouthfull shall hardly see a good end of his businesse,* & many times an accusatiue, A y enterraron a mi abuelo. Los nuestros siguieron a los enemigos, hazia la puente, with nounes proper they haue alwaies an accusatiue, Iuan hirio a Pedro, Diego mato a Vasco. Los enemigos prendieron o tomaron a Don Alonso en campo raso, &c. with the pronounes primitiues

Of Regiments.

they haue often a double accusatiue case: as A mi me dieron libre, por cien escudos. *They freed me for an hundred crownes.*

Verbes of Gesture, going, resting, doing, commonly haue these accusatiues of the pronounes primitiue before them: Me, te, se, as yo me voy, tu te sientes, aquel se duerme.

Verbes put acquisitiuely with the signe *for* will haue a datiue of the person, and a nominatiue or accusatiue of the thing. Compro el sombrero para mi y el jubon para ti, with the signe *to* they haue a nominatiue of the thing, and an accusatiue of the person, Encaminadme estas cartas a tu padre. Mandó el rey su carta, a sus subditos, &c. Quien no da obediencia, a su rey, ya su ley no merece viuir, which the Pronoune primitiues they haue, Me te se: as Mostrarse lo hemos el recaudo. Darme has estos dineros.

THE INFINITIVE MOODE.

The signe *to* is a note of the Infinitiue, and generally if two verbes come together in a sentence: the second not hauing any Nominatiue case to answere the question, who or what; it shall be put in the Infinitiue moode; which after a Noune is vsed with de, the preposition: as Tengo mucho desseo de verle, *I desire greatly to see him.* After a Verbe it is vsed with para or a: as Vengo para holgarme con vos: *I come to be merie with thee.* Salia a combatir sin espada: *Hee went foorth to fight without his sworde.*

Note that the Infinitiue moode is often vsed as a Noune, Muestra se el hombre quien es, en su passearse, en su hablar, y en su mirar: *A man sheweth what he is, in his walking, in his speach, in his countenance.* And often with a nominatiue case and a preposition: as Basta esto para salir yo de este peligro.

VERBES PASSIVE.

The Passiues haue a Genitiue case: as Cuentase de los españoles: De los yngleses se dize. Iuan es muy amado de todos.

VERBS IMPERSONALS.

Verbs impersonals of the actiue voice haue commonly a double accusatiue case, as A mi me conviene, a ti te pertenece: a los franceses les es menester.

Impersonals of the passiue voice haue a genitiue: as Del rey Alexandre se lee.

ADVERBS AND CONIVNCTIONS.

Aduerbs commonly gouerne an indicatiue moode: saue that where Interrogatiues are changed into Indefinites they haue sometimes a subianctiue. as Como se haze esto? No se como se haga; quando se boluio tu padre? no se quando se aya buelto.

Aduerbs of forbidding will haue a subianctiue moode, as No lo diga VM. no haga assi.

Coniunctions

Of Regiment.

Coniunctions commonly couple like cases like moods and like tenses: and most commonly Causals, as Porque, &c. will haue an indicatiue moode: But Conditionals, as si, Aduersatiues, as Aunque, puesto que, comoque, although, Quando, although, que, when it signifieth *that*, and Paraque, *To the end that*, will haue a subiunctiue.

PRÆPOSITIONS.

Some prepositions are vsed onely in composition, as Des, and In signifyng a contrarietie, as Des dicha, injusto, Em, enforcing the sence. Re signifyng an iteration: Some in composition and apposition both, as en in composition enforcing the sence, con signifyng a consent or companie. In apposition, they are set before, either the infinitiues of verbs as is afore said, or the cases of nounes as appeareth in the former treatise of this part of speech; somtime they are neither set before a verbe of the infinitiue moode, nor noune, but vsed aduerbially.

Thus much I thought necessarie to admonish the Reader touching constrnction, bicause it varieth somewhat from the English manner of speech, not prosecuting more particularly the rules of our Latin Grammar; bicause in the rest, the course is so ordinarie, as if he marke the signification and vse of the præposition, he shall find no great difficultie in the language.

F I N I S.

BIBLIOTHECÆ HISPANICÆ PARS ALTERA.

CONTAINING A DICTIONARIE IN
SPANISH, ENGLISH, and LATINE:
Gathered out of diuers good
Authors: very profitable
for the studious of
the Spanish
toong.

By RICHARD PERCYVALL gent.

Enlarged with the Latine by the aduise
and conference of Master Thomas
D OYL EY Doctor in
Physicke.

Imprinted at London by Iohn Iackson,
for Richard Watkins.

1 5 9 1

To the Reader.

Beholde good Reader, the seconde part of my Librarie: without which this little worke woulde be maimed and mishapen: for since that hath the forme, and this the matter, vnlesse thou haue that from hence, which the other may set in order, decke, and polish, I shal seeme but slenderly to haue respected thy studies. But least thou stumble in the verie entrance: Thou must marke these three points. The Accent, certaine maymed and vnperfect words; The matshalling of the letters in the Alphabet. Of the Accent know this, that in the first booke where I giue the rule of Euphonia; bicause of some vncertaine words which no rule can containe, I referred many things to the Dictionarie. In such Nounes, whose pronuntiatiō varieth from the rule, I haue heere for the most part noted the accent, which I would haue thee vnderstand to be alwaies sharpe. In Verbes, although all infinitiue moodes make the last sharpe; yet thou shalt often find the accent vpon the last saue one, or the last saue two: not to the ende thou shouldest imagine that the sillable where the accent standeth, should belong in the infinitiue moode; but that thou knowe it must be so in the first person of the presens tense of the indicatiue. Those in io and uo, commonlie make short the last saue one of the indicatiue, vnlesse the line ouer it saie the contrarie; And all the rest which haue no accent, make it long, though they be deriued from such Latin Verbes as are short, as you may see in these, Imagíno Dissímulo. The words set by the infinitiue, whether they be perfect or no; shewe thee that those letters make a difference, betweene the infinitiue moode and the indicatiue; by adding or changing some letter: as of Amolar, the first of the indicatiue, is Amuélo: of Afligir, Aflíjo, & so of the rest. The Order of the letters may seeme somewhat vnorderly. But as it fell out it could be no otherwise; bicause that following Nebrissensis and Casas, I traced their steps. The Alphabet is thus set, A, B, ca, co, cu, ça, ce, ci, ço, çu, ch, D, E, F, G, H, I, Y, j, L, ll, M, N, ñ, O, P, Q, R, S, T, u, V, X, Z. The Spanish words gathered out of Nebrissensis, are not al in vse: for him selfe saith; he framed and coined some; yet I haue

EN tibi, lector, Bibliothecæ nostræ pars altera: sine qua opusculū hoc mancum, deforme. Cum enim illius forma, hujus materia propria sit; nisi tibi ex hac, quod illa disponat, poliat, exornet: studijs tuis malè certe consultum videbitur. Verùm ì ne in ipso limine impingas, tria tibi animaduertenda. Accentus, Voculæ quædam mancæ & inarticulatæ; Literarum in Alphabeto dispositio. De Accentu sic habeto; Me in priore illa, vbi de Euphonia præcepta tradidi, propter incerta quædā quæ nulla capit regula; multa ad Dictionarium rejecisse. In nominibus quæ à præcepto diuersam enūciationem sortiuntur, accentu hîc pleraq; notaui; quem acutum esse semper, velim intelligas. In verbis, licet omnia Infiniti modi vltimam acuant; sæpe tamen inuenies accentum penultimæ, vel antepenultimæ insidentem: non eo consilio, vt arbitrere, syllabam illam ab accentu occupatam, in ipso infinito producendam; sed vt intelligas, eam in prima præsentis indicatiui acuendam. In io & uo pleraque penultimā indicatiui corripiūt, nisi aliud doceat accētus insidens. Reliqua omnia, quibus nullus apex; eandem producunt; etsi à Latinis correptis deriuata; vt in his videre est, Imagíno, Dissímulo. Vocula illæ infinitis additæ siue perfectæ, siue imperfectæ: illis literis, primam præsentis indicatiui, ab infinitiuo distingui significant; literam aliquam vel addendo, vel mutando; vt ab Amolar prima indicatiui Amuélo, ab Affligir, Afflíjo, & sic de cæteris. Literarum ordo paulò videbitur inuersior: sed vt res tulit, aliter fieri non potuit. Nebrissensem enim & Casam sequuti, illorum vestigijs plurimùm institimus. Sic igitur Alphabetum tibi dispositum. A, B, ca, co, cu, ça, ce, ci, ço, çu, ch, D, E, F, G, H, I, vocalis, Y, j, L, ll, M, N, ñ, O, P, Q, R, S, T, u, V, X. Z. Verba etiam Hispanica, quæ è Nebrissensi, scito non vsquequaque omnia in vsu: cum & ipse apertè loquatur, à se nonnulla ficta & excusa. Apposui tamen omnia,

To the Reader.

ne me parum sana fide in illo versatum existimares. Crebras illas ejusdem verbi repetitiones, quæ illi frequentes, ad Latinæ dictionis sensum exprimendum; prudens vitavi. Hispanica enim lingua mihi explicanda, non Latina. Hoc amice lector præmonuisse sufficiat: & si quid peccatum in prima hac editione imprudentia fuerit; modò his per te expeditum iter, postea corrigetur. Cognosce mecum & agnosce; homines nos, & humanum, labi falli : quod si nulli hîc nævi essent, nullæ maculæ, extra Britanniæ fines deportandam prolem hanc nostram, & (quod prodigiosis partubus factitatum à Romanis, historiæ testes) igne cremandam, ipse ego autor & suasor essem. Vale, & nostris faue, vtere.

set downe all, least thou shouldest thinke I deale scarse faithfully with him: I haue purposely passed ouer his repetitions of the selfe same word, which he often vseth to expresse the sense of the Latin words; for I go about to explain the Spanish, not to teach the Latine. Let it suffice good Reader to admonish thee thus much; and if by ouersight, any thing haue escaped in this first impression; so this with thy good fauor, may haue speedy passage; it shall be amended hereafter. Know with me, and acknowledge, that we are men, and as men we may slip, and be deceiued; for if there were in this, no spots nor freckles, I my selfe would wish and perswade it, to be carried out of the boundes of this Realme, and there burned: as the histories witnesse, the Romans were woont to do with monstrous births. Farewell good Reader, fauour and vse vs.

R. P.

A DICTIONARIE IN SPANISH, ENGLISH, AND LATINE.

A To,towards,at. *Ad,apud,verſus.*
A,a, alas, *Ah.*
Aaron,an herbe called Cuccowpint, *Arum.*

A B
Abad,an Abbot,a prieſt, *Abbas, ſacerdos.*
Abadeſſa, Abbeſſe or Prioreſſe, *Abbatiſſa.*
Abadía, abbots dignitie,abbie, *Abbatia.*
Abadejo, a kind of flie called *Cantharis*, alſo a wagtaile, *Motacilla.*
Abadengo, pertaining to an abbot, *Ad abbatem pertinens.*
Abahar,to ſmoke or to fume, *Euaporo.*
Abalançar, to thruſt into the midſt of a companie or preſſe of people, *Inferre ſe in medium, injicere.*
Aballar, to remooue with much labour, *Amoliri.*
Abarca, a ſhoe of wood or rawe leather, *Pero,onis.*
Abarcado, ſhod with ſuch a ſhoe, *Peronatus.*
Abarcar, to claſpe in the armes, to imbrace,to introch, *Complecti, ambire, irreptare, graſſari.*
Abarraganada, a leman,a ſtrumpet, *Concubina, Pellex.*
Abarraganado, a leman keeper, a whoremaſter, *Concubinarius.*
Abarraganamiento, leman keeping, looſeneſſe of life, *Concubitus.*
Abarrajar, to do violence,to aſſaile forcibly, *Inuadere, vim facere.*
Abarrar, to daſh againſt the wall, *Illidere.*
Abarrancarſe, to fall from a ſteepe hill, *Præcipitare, præcipitem dare.*
Abarrancadero, a downe fall, a ſteepe hill or rocke, *Præcipitium.*
Abarrancado ganado, ſtanding on a ſteep hill, *In præcipitio hærens.*

Abarriſco, quite & cleane, *Penitus, prorſus.*
Abarraz, Staueſacre, *Staphiſagria.*
Abaſtar,to ſuffice, *Sufficere.*
Abaſtança, abaſto, ſufficiencie, ynough, *Abundantia, copia, ſaties.*
Abatirſe, to ſtoupe, to abaſe, *Deijcere, deturbare.*
Abatido, throwen downe, *Deiectus.*
Abatimiento, ſtouping, throwing downe, *Deiectio, dimiſſio.*
Abatidamente, baſely, *Abiectè, dimiſſè.*
Abaxar, to come downe, to throw down, *Deſcendere, deijcere.*
Abaxado, throwen downe, *Deiectus.*
Abaximiento, throwing downe, comming downe, *Deiectio, deſcenſus.*
Abeja, a Bee, *Apis.*
Abejéra, Balme, *Meliſſophillum.*
Abejonazo, a great Bee, *Apis magna.*
Abejon, a drone Bee, *Fucus.*
Abejuruco, a woodpecke, *Apiaſtra.*
Abenuz, Ebene tree, *Hebenus.*
Abertura, opening, cleft, or ryuing of any thing, *Apertura, rima, hiatus, fiſſura.*
Abeſtruz, an oſtritch, *Struthius.*
Abéto, a Firre tree, *Abies.*
Abezar, to teach, to accuſtome, *Docere, aſſueſacere, conſueſcere.*
Abezado, taught, accuſtomed, *Doctus, aſſiſtefactus, conſuetus.*
Abierto, open, *Apertus.*
Abil, able, fit, *Habilis, aptus.*
Abilidad, abilitie, fitnes, aptnes, *Habilitas, aptitudo.*
Abilitar, to fit, to enable, *Aptare.*
Abilmente, aptly, fitly, *Aptè, ſufficienter.*
Abiltar, to debaſe, to throwe downe, *Paruiſacere, deijcere.*
Abiltadamente, baſely, *Viliter, deiectè.*
Abiſmo, bottomleſſe pit, *Abyſſus.*
Abiſpa, a waſpe, *Veſpa.*

A   Abiſpillo,

A B

Abifpillo, rabadilla de aue, the rumpe of a bird, *Vropigium.*
Abifpon, a hornet, *Crabro.*
Abito, habite, apparel, attire, maners, *Habitus, vestimentum, vestus, mos.*
Abituado, nurtured, mannered, accustomed, *Moratus, assuetus.*
Abituar, to accustome, to instruct in maners or behauiour, *Assuefcere, consuescere.*
Ablandar, to soften, *Mollire.*
Ablandadura, softening, softnes, *Mollificatio, mollities.*
A bocados, by morsels, peece meale, *Morsicatim.*
Aboferear, to buffet, *Pugnis cædere.*
Abogado, an aduocate, a lawyer, *Aduocatus, iurisconsultus, causidicus.*
Abogar, to play the aduocate, to pleade, *Patrocinari, causam agere.*
Abogacia, pleading, counsell giuing, the profession of an aduocate, *Patrocinium, causæ dictio.*
Abolengo, *vide* Abolerio.
Abollonado, *vide* Abollado.
Abollado, dented in with blowes, beaten in, battered, *Incusus, contusus.*
Abollar, to dent in with blowes, to beate in, *Contundere, incudere.*
Abollonar, *idem.*
Abolladura, denting in with blowes, beating in, *Contusio.*
Abolório, Abolengo, a pedegræ, *Series auorum, stemma.*
Abominar, to detest, to abhor, *Abominari, execrari, detestari.*
Abominable, abominable, *Execrabilis.*
Abominacion, detesting, *Execratio, detestatio.*
Abonar, to gage, to put in suretie, to make good, *Prædes dare.*
Abonado, he that hath put in suretie, *Qui prædes dedit.*
Abono, making good, or vndertaking for another, *Vadimonium.*
Abonarse el tiempo, to be faire weather, *Tranquillare, serenare.*
Abonança, faire weather, *Serenitas.*
Abondar, to abound, *Abundare.*

Abondoso, abundante, abundant, abounding, *Abundans, copiosus.*
Abondosamente, abundantly, plentifully, *Copiosé, abundé.*
Abondamiento, abundance, plentie, *Copia, abundantia.*
Aborrecer, aborefco, to abhor, *Odio habere, abominari.*
Aborrecedor, he that abhorreth, *Osor.*
Aborrecible, hatefull, odious, *Odiosus, exosus.*
Abortado, an vntimely birth, *Abortiuus.*
Abortar, to bring forth an vntimely birth, *Abortire.*
Aborton, a colt foaled before the time, *Pullus abortiuus.*
Abortadura, vntimely deliuery or bringing forth, *Abortus, abortio.*
Abotonar, to button, to clafpe, to bud, *Fibulas nectere, & germinare.*
Abotonadura de plata o oro, a button or clafpe of siluer or gold, *Spinther.*
Abraçar, to imbrace, *Amplecti.*
Abraçado, imbraced, *Amplexus.*
Abrasar, to burne, *Adurere, vrere, in prunas redigere.*
Abrasamiento, burning, *Combustio.*
Abreuar, to make drinke, to water cattell, *Potare, adaquare.*
Abreuado, one that hath dronke, watered, *Potus, adaquatus.* (rium.
Abreuadero, a vale, a watering pit, *Aquarium.*
Abréuiar, to shorten, to abreuiate, *Compendium facere.*
Abreuiadura, shortening, abreuiating, cutting off, *Compendium.*
Abrigar, to warme against the funne, to fofter, to cherifh, *Apricari, fouere.*
Abrigado, a warme place, warmed, cherifhed, *Soli expositus, fotus, apricus.*
Abrigo, the South wind, fostering, cherifhing, the warme sun shine, *Africus, apricitas, focillatio.*
Abrigaño, a warme sunnie banke, or such like, *Locus apricus.*
Abril, April, *Aprilis mensis.*
Abrir, to open, to cleaue, *Aperire, resignare, hifcere.*

Abridor,

A C

Abridor, he that openeth, *Apertor.*
Abrochar, to lace a coate, *Stringere.*
Abrochadura, lacing of a coate, *Strictura.*
Abrogar, to abrogate, to abolish, *Abrogare.*
Abrojo, a bramble, a pricke, *Tribulus.*
Abrotono, Southernwood, *Abrotonum.*
Absoluer, to absolue, *Absoluere.*
Abstinentia, abstinence, *Abstinentia.*
Absynthio, wormwood, *Absynthium.*
Abubilla, a lapwing, *Vpupa.*
Abuelo, la, a grandfather, a grandmother, *Auus, auia.*
Abuelo segundo, tercero, a great grandfather, the great grandfathers father, *Proauus, abauus.*
Abuelos, auncestors, *Maiores.*
A buen tiempo, in good time, *Opportune.*
Abuhado, abuhetado, mumpesick, swolen about the face, *Parasynanche laborans.*
Abuhamiento, the mumps, *Parasynanche.*
Abundancia, *vide* Abondamiento.
Aburar, to burne, *Comburere.*
Aburado, burned, *Combustus.*
Aburrido, desperate, forlorne, *Desperans, spei perditæ.*
Aburrir, to despaire, *Desperare, spem abijcere.*
Abusar, to abuse, *Abuti.*
Abusion, abuse, *Abusio, abusus.*
Abutarda, a Bustard, *Otis.*

A C

Aca, hither, *Huc.*
Acabar, to end, to finish, to die, *Finire, perficere, mori.*
Acabado, ended, perfect, finished, *Perfectus*
Acabador, a finisher, *Perfector.*
Acabadamente, perfectly, *Perfecte.*
Acabamiento, ending, the end, *Finis, perfectio.*
Acácia, a kind of shrub, *Acacia.* (*ctio.*
A cada barrio, street by street, *Vicatim.*
A cada casa, house by house, in euery house, *In singulis ædibus.*
A cada, in, at, or by euery, *Per singulos.*
Acadarrado, reumatike, *Qui catarrho laborat, rheumaticus.*
Acaduz, *vide* Alcaduz.
Acaecer, to happen, *Contingere, accidere.*
Acaecimiento, hap, chaunce, *Casus.*

A C

Acallar, to still, to make quiet, *Silentium imponere.*
Acanales, by gutters, *Imbricatim.*
Acanalado, made with gutters, chamfured, *Imbricatus.*
Acañaverear, to pierce with canes, *Arundine consigere.*
Acaricear, to cocker, to make much of, *Indulgere, perhumaniter habere.*
Acarrear, to bring, *Aduehere, apportare.*
Acarreadura, bringing, carriage, *Aduectio.*
Acarréto, *vide* Acarreadura.
Acarreadizo, any thing brought or carried, *Aduectitius.*
Acatar, to reuerence, to honor, to behold, to regard, to looke too, to marke, *Obseruare, colere, aspicere, animaduertere.*
Acatamiento, reuerence, beholding, regard, marking, noting, *Obseruantia, cultus, aspectus, respectus.*
Acatadura, the countenance, *vultus, facies.*
Acaudalar, to sum vp, *In summam redigere.*
Acaudillar, to lead, to guide, *Ducere, imperare exercitui.*
Acaudillamiento, the leading or guiding of soldiors, *Ductus, imperium.*
Accion, an action, *Actio.*
Aclarar, to make cleere, to make manifest, to make quiet, *Serenare, clarificare, apertum facere, clarum facere.*
Aclaracion, making manifest, clearing, *Serenitas, claritas.*
Acodar, to leane on the elbow, to strike with the elbow, *Cubito niti, cubito percutere.*
Acodadura, leaning on the elbow, striking with the elbow, *Cubiti nixus, cubiti ictus.*
Acodar vides, to ioynt vines, to prune vines, *Geniculare.*
Acodadura, pruning of vines, *Geniculatio.*
Acoger, Acojo, to entertaine, to retire, *Excipere in ædes, recipere se.*
Acogimiento, entertainment, retiring, *Exceptio, receptus.*
Acometer, to assaile, to set vpon, to take in hand, *Aggredi, adoriri, inuadere.*
Acometedor, he that assaileth, that taketh

A 2

A C   A C

keth in hand, *Aggreſſor, inuaſor.*
Acometedora coſa, inuaſiue, *Inuaſorius.*
Acometimiento, aſſailing, aſſault, *Aggreſ-ſio, inuaſio.*
Acompañar, to accompany, to attend vpon, *Operam dare, comitari.*
Acompañamiento, *Comitatus.*
Acontecer, y Acontecimiento, *vide* Acaecer.
Acocear, to kicke, *Calcare, calcitrare, conculcare, peſſum dare.*
Acoceamiento, kicking, *Calcatio.*
Acoceador, he that ſpurneth, he that kicketh, *Calcator.*
Acordarſe, acuerdo, to remember, to awake, to determine, *Meminiſſe, recordari, ſtatuere.*
Acordar, to put in mind, to awake, to agree, *Memorare, admonere, concordare, conſonare.*
Acorde, agréeing, *Conſonantia, harmonia.*
Acoro, galingale, *acorum.*
Acorrallar, to cloſe vp, to driue into a corner, to pound vp, *In anguſtias redigere.*
Acorrer, to run, to helpe, to ſuccor, *Accurrere, auxiliari.*
Acorro, helpe, ſuccour, *Suppetiæ, auxilium.*
Accoſſar, to driue, to courſe, to baite the bear, or bull, *Agitare, agere, curſu agere.*
Acoſſador, he that driueth, he that courſeth, he that baiteth the bear, or bull, *Agitator, exagitator.*
Acoſtarſe, to leane on, to lie downe, to ſit at table, to leane towards, to go to bed, *Niti, accumbere, diſcumbere, cubare.*
Acoſtamiento, ſitting downe, lying, leaning, *Niſus, accubitus, cubitus.*
Acrecentar, ciento, to encreaſe, to augment, *Augere.*
Acrecentado, augmented, encreaſed, *Auctus.*
Acrecentamiento, encreaſe, augmenting, *Auctio, incrementum.*
Acuchillar, to cut with a ſword: to wound, to fight with another, *Gladio cædere, vulnerare, dimicare.*
A cuchilladas, with blowes, with cuts, *Cæſim.*

Acúciar, to ſharpen, *Acuere.*
Acúcia, ſharpnes of edge, *Acumen.*
Arucioſo, ſharpe, *Acutus.*
Aucioſamente, ſharpely, *Acutè.*
Acudir, to repaire vnto, to drawe néere, to aſſemble, to approch, *Accedere, conuenire.*
Acudimiento, approching, drawing near, *Acceſſio, appropinquatio.*
Acuerdo, a decree, an agréement, a determination, *Decretum, conſenſus.*
Acullá, there, thither, that way, *Illic, illuc, illac.*
Acumular, to heape vp, *Accumulare.*
Acuñar, to coine money, to cleaue with wedges, *Cudere, cuneis partire.*
Acuñador, a coyner, a cleauer with wedges, *Cuſor, & qui cuneis diuidit.*
Acuſar, to accuſe, *Accuſare.*
Acuſado, accuſed, *Accuſatus, reus.*
Acuſadora coſa, that blameth, that procureth blame, *Accuſatorius.*
Acuſacion, accuſation, blaming, *Accuſatio, criminatio.*

A Ç

Açacan, a waterbearer, a ſcullion, *Aquarius, lixa.*
Açada, a pickaxe, *Ligo.*
Açadon, a mattocke, a ſpade, *Runcina, pala.*
Açafran, ſaffron, *Crocum.*
Açafranado, colored with ſaffron, *Croceus.*
Açaguan, *vide* çaguan.
Açafranar, to colour with ſaffron, *Croco inficere.*
Açelga ſaluage, wilde beets, *Limonium.*
Acelga, beetes, *Beta.*
Acemite, flower of meale, *Simila.*
Acendrado, excellent, *Excellens, perfectus.*
Acento, accent, tune, *Accentus.*
Acentuar, to tune, to note the accent, *Accinere, accentu notare.*
Aceña, a water mill, *Molendinum aquaticũ.*
Aceñero, a miller, *Molendinarius.*
Acepillar, to ſhaue, to ſmooth, *Læuigare.*
Acepilladuras, the ſhauing, the pils, *Ramenta.*
Aceptar, to accept, *Accipere.*
Aceptable, acceptable, *Acceptabilis, Gratus.*
Aceptacion,

A ç

Aceptacion, acceptance, *Acceptatio.*
Acepto, accepted, *Gratum, acceptum.*
Acéquia, a trench, a pit, a ditch, *Fossa.*
Acerca, neere, *Circa, iuxta, prope.*
Acercarse, to come neere, to approch, *Accedere appropinquare.*
Acercamiénto, approching, comming neere, *Appropinquatio, accessio.*
Acertai cierto, to hit, to light on, *Rem acu tangere, signum figere.*
Acertamiento, hitting right, *Signi confixio.*
Acetre, a bucket of brasse, *Vrna ærea.*
Acetrería, faulconrie, *Accipetraria ars,* vide Cetreria.
Acetrero, a faulconer, *Accipetrarius.*
Aceuadarse la bestia, to be cloied with prouender, *Saturum esse, fastidire.*
Acevadado, cloyed with prouender, *Satur*
Acevadamiento, the cloyeng with prouender, *Saturatio, fastidium.*
Aceuilado, wretched, base, *Miser, homo infimæ sortis.*
Acezar, to breath, to sigh, *Anhelare, suspirare.*
Acezo, breathing, sighing, *Anhelatio, suspiratio.*
Acezoso, he which breatheth, panteth, or sigheth, *Anhelus, suspirans.*
Acíbar, aloes, *Aloes.*
Acicalar, to polish, to burnish, *Polire.*
Acicalado, polished, burnished, *Politus.*
Acicaladura, the polishing, the burnishing, *Politura, polities.*
Acidente, an accident, happening, *Accidens.*
Acidental, chancing, *Accidens.*
Acidia, sharpnes, *Amaror, acerbitas.*
Acipres, cypres trees, *Cupressus.*
Aciones, stirrop leathers, *Stapedarum lora.*
Acitára de Silla, the pannell or the sadble tree, *Stragulum lignum.*
Açofeyfa, a fruite called Juiuba, *Zizyphum.*
Açófar, molten brasse, *Aes fusile.*
Açomar, to prouoke, to stir vp, *Instigare, incitare.*
Açomamiento, prouoking, stirring vp, *Instigatio, irritatio.*

A ç

Açor, a hauke, a gose-hauke, *Phasianophonus.*
Açorado, fierce, wilde, *Efferus, ferus.*
Açorarse, to waxe fierce, to be wilde, *Efferari.*
Açote, a whip, a rod, *Flagellum, virga.*
Açotar, to whip, *Flagellare.*
Açotadizo, he that is whipped, *Verbero, Mastigia.*
Açotador, a whipper, *Flagellator.*
Açotamiento, whipping, *Flagellatio.*
Açotéa, a flat roofe couered with lead, or plaster, *Panimentum in summo ædium.*
Açucéna, lillie, *Lilium.*
Açúcar piedra, sugercandie, *Saccarum candificatum.*
Açúcar, suger, *Saccarum.*
Açucarado, sugered, *Saccaro conditus.*
Açuda, a trench, a great wheele to cast water, *Machina aquaria, fossa.*
Açucla, a little pickaxe, *Asciola.*
Açumbre, a kinde of measure, *Vas vinarium, Mensura quædam vini.*
Achacar, to excuse, to finde an excuse, to finde an errand, *Causam fingere, occasionem captare.*
Acháque, an errand, an excuse, *Causa, occasio, causatio.*
Achacozo, he that findeth errands or excuses, *Causabundus.*
Achicadura, making little, *Diminutio, curtatio.*
Achicar, to make little, *Minuere, contrahere.*
Achocar, achucco, to fel, to strike down, *Prosternere.*

A D

Adalid, a captaine, *Dux.*
Adarga, a buckler, a target, *Cetra.*
Adargado, a targetier, he that carieth a buckler, *Cetratus.*
Adargarse, to vse the target, or buckler, *Cetra armare, sive tegere.*
Adarues, battlements of wals, *Minæ, arii.*
Adarme, a dram in waight, *Drachma.*
Adelante, before, *Præ, ante.*
Adelantado, a lieutenant, *Præses.*
Adelantarse, to excell, to go before, *Præire, præcedere.*

Adelantar,

A D

Adelantar, **to appoint as cheefe,** *Præficere.*
Adelantamiento, **lieuetenantship, excel-**
ling, going before, *Præfectura,præitio,ex-*
cellentia.
Adelfa, **a baffadownbilly, or rather rose**
bay tree, *Rhododaphne.*
Adelgazar, **to make small, to make fine,**
Attenuare, extenuare,deducere.
Adelgazado, **made fine, made small,** *Atte-*
nuatus, deductus.
Adelgazamiento, **making small, making**
fine, *Attenuatio,deductio.*
Ademanes, **behauior, demeanor,** *Gestus.*
Adentellar, **to byte,** *Mordere.*
Adentelladas, **by bites,** *Mordicus.*
Adentro, **within,** *Intus, intrò.*
Aderecar, **resco, to prepare, to make rea-**
die, to make streight, *Apparo, præparo,*
dirigo.
Adereço, **preparation, making streight,**
Apparatus, directio.
Aderecamiento, **preparing, making**
streight, *Præparatio,directio.*
Adereçadamente, **redilie,** *Paratè.*
Adezoras, **suddenlie,** *subitò repentè.*
Adespecho, **in despight, despightfullie,**
Dispectè, inuito aliquo facere.
Adeudarse, **to grow in debt,** *Aes alienum*
contrahere.
Adeudado, **endebted,** *Obæratus.*
Adiues de bestia, **the quincie, or squinan-**
cie in a beast, also crooked pinnes that
they put in meate to kill dogs, *Angina,*
acicula retortæ.
Adiuinar, **see** Diuinar.
Administrar officio, **to beare office, to exe-**
cute an office, *Obire magistratum.*
Administracion, **bearing of an office,** *Ad-*
ministratio.
Administrador, **he that beareth office,** *Ad-*
ministrator.
Administrar la hazienda, **to gouerne a**
houshold: to dispose goods, *Rem fami-*
liarem gerere.
Administradora cosa, **that may be gouer-**
ned, *Administratorius.*
Adobar, **to mende, to sauce, to botch,**
Condire, & reconcinnare, sarcire.

A D

Adoba, **sauce, mending, botching,** *Condi-*
mentum, concinnatio.
Adobado, **saused, mended,** *Conditus, recon-*
cinnatus.
Adobe de barro, **morter,** *Lutum, later crudus*
Adolecer, **to grieue, to be sicke, to be so-**
rie, *Aegrotare, dolere, condolere.*
Adolentarse, **to be sicke, to be sory,** *Aegro-*
tare, dolere.
A Jonde, **whither,** *Quo?*
Adondequiera, **whithersoeuer,** *Quocunq;.*
Adoptar, **to adopt,** *Adoptare.*
Adopcion, **adoption,** *Adoptio.*
Adoptado, **adopted,** *Adoptatus.*
Adorar, **to worship,** *Adorare, supplicare.*
Adoracion, **worshipping,** *Adoratio, suppli-*
catio.
Adormecer, **to nap, to sleepe, to bring a**
sleepe, *Dormitare, obdormiscere, sopire.*
Adormir, **to fall on sleepe,** *Dormire.*
Adormido, **sleepie,** *Somnolentus.*
Adormecido, **sleepie,** *Sopitus.*
Adornar, **to decke, to trim, to adorne,** *Or-*
nare, adornare.
Adornamiento, **adorning, decking, trim-**
ming, *Adornatio, ornamentum.*
Adquirir, **adquiero, to get,** *Acquirere.*
Adquirido, **gotten,** *Acquisitus.*
Adquiridor, **a getter,** *Acquisitor.*
Adráda, **seldome,** *Rarò.*
Adréde, **of purpose,** *De industria.*
Adrianes, **corns in the feet or toes,** *Grana*
illa callosa in pedibus, & pedum digitis.
Aduana, **custome, the custome house,** *Te-*
lonium.
Aduar, **a billage of tents remoueable, as**
in Barbarie, *Villula.*
Adúfe, **a timbrell,** *Tympanum.*
Adufero, **a plaier on a timbrel,** *Tympanistes.*
Aduertir, vierto, **to marke,** *Aduertere.*
Aduerténcia, **marking,** *Aduersio, animad-*
uersio. (*care.*
Adulçar, **to make sweet, to sweeten,** *Edul-*
Aduenedizo, **a stranger, strange, happe-**
ning, chancing, *Aduentitius, extraneus,*
Aduena, contingens.
Aduersario, **an aduersarie,** *Aduersarius.*
Aduersidad, **aduersitie,** *Aduersitas.*

Adulterar,

A F

Adulterar, to commit adulterie, *Adulterare*
Adulterio, adulterie. *Adulterium.*
Adultero, an adulterer, *Adulter.*
Adulterino, counterfetted, *Adulterinus fictitius.*
A empuxones, with thrusts, with pushes, *Pulsatim.*
A escondidas, secretly, closely, *Secreto.*

A F

Afable, affable, *Affabilis.*
Afabilidad, affabilitie, *Affabilitas.*
Afan, labor, trauell, *Labor, ærumna.*
Afanar, to labor, to trauell, *Laborare, ærumna affici.*
Afanado, wearied with labor, toyled, *Aerumnosus, fatigatus.*
A fe, by the faith, *Medius fidius.*
Afear, to make foule, to reuile, to reproch *Dehonestare, deformare, deuenustare, conuitiari.*
Afeamiento, making foule, reuiling, *Deuenustatio.*
Afeador, he that maketh foule, that reuileth, *Deuenustator, conuitiator.*
Afectado, affected, *Affectatus.*
Afeytar, to paint the face, to florish, to giue a glasse to any thing, to trim the beard, to decke, *Comere, Tondere, ornare, Exornare, fucare.*
Afeytado, painted, trimmed, decked, colored, *Comptus, ornatus, fucatus.*
Afeyte, painting, color, glasse, or florish, *Fucus, ornatus, medicamen, splendor.*
Afeytador, a barber, a trimmer, a decker, *Tonsor, fucator, ornator.*
Afeytadera, a barbers shop, *Tonstrina.*
Aferes, trifling busines, *Nugæ.*
Aferrar, to gripe, to graple, *Prensare, apprehendere.*
Afilar, to sharpen, *Acuere.*
Afiladura, the edge of a weapon, *Acies, acumen.* (*ficere.*
Afinar, to make fine, to make perfect, *Perficere.*
Afinadura, making perfect, *Perfectio.*
Afirmar, to affirme, to strengthen, *Affirmare, firmare, asseuerare.*
Afirmacion, affirmation, strengthening,

A G

Affirmatio, asseueratio.
Afirmador, he that affirmeth, *Asseuerator.*
Afirmadamente, affirmatiuely, *Asseueratè.*
Afistolado, fistoled, *Fistolatus.*
Afligir, jo, to afflict, *Affligere.*
Afligimiento, affliction, *Afflictio.*
Afloxar, to let loose, to slacken, to weaken, to be discouraged, to vnbende a bowe, to be idle, *Laxare, retendere, desidere, torpere, ignauum esse, animum dimittere.*
Afloxadura, slacknes, weaknes, idlenes, *Ignauia, desidia, laxatio, dimissio animi.*
Aforro, furre, *Pellicium.*
Afrecho, bran, *Furfur.*
Afrentar, to reproch, *Crimen obijcere, exprobrare, dehonestare.*
Afrenta, shame, reproch, perill, danger, *Dehonestatio, crimen, periculum, discrimen.*
Afuziar, to put in hope, to trust, *Spem facere, confidere.*

A G

Agaçapado, squatted as a hare or conie, *Recumbens.*
Agacharse, to squat as a hare or conie, *Recumbere.*
Agachado, squatted, *Recumbens.*
Agalla, gaules, the kernels in the necke, the gill of a fish, *Galla, Tonsilla, Branchia.*
Agarar, to claspe, *Fibulare.*
Agatas, creeping as a cat, *Rependo gerun.*
Agarico, Agarike, *Agaricum.*
Ageno, strange, another mans, vnacquainted, *Alienus.*
Agenar el hijo, to cast off a sonne, *Abdicare*
Agenamiento, casting off a sonne, alienating, *Abdicatio, alienatio.*
Agenar, to alienate, *Alienare.*
Agerato, a kind of Agrimony, *Eupatorium mauoleine.*
Ageno ser de alguna cosa, to be vnacquainted with, *Alienum esse.*
Agonia, agonie, *Agonia.*
Agonizando, giuing vp the ghost, *Extremum spiritum trahendo.*
Agora, now, *Nunc, statim, iamiam.*
Agorar, guero, to gesse at, to diuine, *Augurari, ominari.*

Agorero,

A G   A G

Agorero, a soothsaier, a diuiner, *Aruspex.*
Agorería, soothsaying, *Augurium, auspicina.*
Agosto, August, *Augustus.*
Agostadero, a sommer house, *Aestiua, orum*
Agostar, to sommer, to dwell in a sommer house, *Aestiuare.*
Agotar, to empty, to draw out, *Exhaurire.*
Agouear, to humble, *Humiliare, submittere.*
Agro, sharpe, sower, *Acer.*
Agro, a field, *Ager.*
Agrura, sharpnes, sowernes, *Acritas, acerbitas.*
Agramente, sharply, sowerly, *Acerbè.*
Agraz, a sower grape, honie vnmade, oile vnclarified, Veriuice, *Omphacinum, mel omphacinum, oleum omphacinum, omphacium*
Agradar, to please, *Placere.*
Agradamiento, pleasing, *Placitum.*
Agradecer, to giue thanks, *Agere gratias.*
Agredecido, thankfull, *Gratus.*
Agradecimiento, giuing thanks, *Gratitudo, gratiarum actio.*
Agráviar, to greeue, to vexe, to molest, *Grauare, vexare.*
Agraviadamente, greeuously, *Grauatè.*
Agrimonio, Agrimonie, *Eupatorium.*
Agrávio, oppression, vexation, greeuance *Aggrauatio, iniuria, vexatio.*
Agua, water, *Aqua.*
Aguas biuas, the spring tides, *Aestus maris.*
Aguadéro, a water bearer, a scullion in a campe, *Aquarius, aquator, lixa.*
Aguador, vide Aquadero.
Aguado, watered, foundered as a horse, *Aquatus, dilutus.*
Aguar, to water, to put water in wine, *Aquare, diluere.*
Aguadaña, a sythe, *Falx.*
Aguaducho, a conduit, *Aqueductus.*
Aguamanil, a basen, *Peluis, malluuium.*
Aguamiel, meath, water and honie, *Aqua melle condita.*
Aguapie vino, the smaller wine, *Vinum acinaceum.*
Aguanoso, full of water, *Aquosus.*
Aquatocho, a spout, a syringe, *Sypho.*
Aguáitar, to wait for, to lie in wait, *Insidiari, captare.*

Aguaitador, he that lieth in wait, *Captator, insidiator.*
Aguaitamiento, lying in wait, *Insidiæ.*
Aguaitadora cosa, deceitfull, *Captatoria.*
Agudo, sharpe, sharpe of wit, *Acutus.*
Agudeza, sharpnes of wit, sharpnes, *acumen.*
Agudamente, sharply, *Acutè.*
Aguelo, abuelo, *Auus.*
Aguero, soothsaying, *Augurium, omen.*
Aguja, a needle, a pricke, *Acus, aculeus.*
Agujereado, full of holes, *Cancellatus.*
Agujero, a hole, *Foramen.* (tum.
Agujeta, a point of leather, *Ligula, strigmen-*
Agujetero, a point maker, *Strigmentarius.*
Aguija, a small pibble stone, *Calculus, glarea.*
Aguijeño, full of pibbles or grauell, *Glareosus.*
Aguijar, to pricke or driue forward, *Stimulare, agitare.*
Aguijador, he that pricketh forward, he that driueth on, *Stimulator, agitator.*
Aguijadura, driuing on, posting on, haste *Agitatio, festinatio.*
Aguijarse, to make haste, *properare, festinare.*
Aguijon, a pricke of iron, the sting of a bee, a goade, *Aculeus, stimulus.*
Aguijonear, to pricke forward, *Stimulare.*
Aguila, an eagle, *Aquila.*
Aguileño, of an eagle, *Aquilinus.*
Aguilocho, an eagles chicke, a yong eagle, *Aquilæ pullus.*
Aguinaldo, a reward, handsel, *Strenæ, arum*
A gusto, with liking, to the liking, *Gratè.*
Aguzar, to sharpen, *Acuere.*
Aguzado, sharpned, *Acutus.*
Aguzadera piedra, a whetstone, *Cos.*
Aguzanieve, a wagtaile, *Motacilla.*

A H

A hao, ho, *Heus.*
Ahechar, to sift, to purge, *Cernere, cribrare, purgare.*
Ahechaduras, chaffe, drosse, dust of corne, bran, *Purgamina, Furfures, pollen.*
Ahelear, to taste of gall, *Fel sapere.*
Ahijar, to adopt, to suckle a lambe, *Adoptare, subrumare.*

Ahijami-

A H

Ahijamiento, adopting, *Adoptatio.*
Ahijado, adopted, a Godson, suckled, *Adoptatius, suscipius, subrumius.*
Ahilado, waxed leane, waxed lanke, *Macilentus.*
Ahilarse, to waxe leane, to waxe lanke, *Macrescere.*
Ahilamiento, waxing leane or lanke, *Macredo, macritudo.*
Ahincar, to hasten, to be earnest, *Festinare, instare, insistere.*
Ahinco, haste, earnestnes, *Festinatio, instantia.*
Ahincadamente, hastily, earnestly, *Instanter, festinanter.*
Ahinojar, to kneele, *Genu flectere.*
Ahitado, rawe stomacked, *Crudus.*
Ahito, rawnes of stomacke, *Cruditas.*
Ahitarse, to be raw stomacked, *Crudescere.*
Ahocinarse el rio, to run in nookes, or to run with turnings or elbows, *In fauces & sinus coarctari, sinuari.*
Ahocinado, a crooked streame, *Sinuosus.*
Ahogar, to strangle, to choke, to drowne, *Suffocare, strangulare, extinguere, submergere.*
Ahogamiento, strangling, choaking, *Suffocatio, exsinctio.*
Ahogamiento de urina, the stone, the stranguriou, *Calculus, stranguria.*
Ahoyar, to dig a ditch, *Fodere scrobem.*
Ahoyadura, digging of a ditch, *Fossio scrobis*
Ahorcar, to hang up, *Suspendere.*
Ahorcado, hanged, *Suspensus.*
Ahorcadura, hanging, *Suspensio, suspendium.*
Ahornagarse la tierra, to be blasted or burnt, *Carbunculari.*
Ahorramiento, sauing of charge, sparing, *Parsimonia.*
Ahorrar, to saue charge, to spare, to deliuer, to make free, *Parcere sumptui, liberare*
Ahorradura, making free, sparing, sauing of charge, *Parsimonia.*
Ahotado, bold, boldened, *Audax, animatus.*
Ahuyentar, to driue away, to put to flight, *Fugare.*
Ahuyentado, put to flight, *Fugatus.*
Ahullar, to howle, to roare, *Vlulare.*

A I

Ahumar, to smoke, to make a smoather, *Fumare, fumigare.*
Ahumadas, smoake, *Fumi.*
Ahumado, smoakie, *Fumosus.*
Ahusada figura, shaped spindle wise, *In fusi morem fabricatus.*

A I vowell.

Ai, Ay, there, *Ibi, illic.*
Ay monasyllabum, there is, there are, *Est, sunt.*
Aia, a nurse, a mistres, *Nutrix, domina.*
Aio, a master, *Educator, Præceptor.*
Ayme, alas, *Hei.*
Ayna, quickly, hastily, *Cito, properè.*
Aire, pleasantnes, beautie, comelines, *Venustas, decor, pulchritudo.*
Airoso, pleasant, comely, beautifull, *Venustus, decorus, pulcher.*
Airado, angrie, *Iratus.*
Airamiento, anger, *Ira, indignatio.*
Airarse, to be angrie, *Irasci.* (*anima.*
Aire, the aire, winde, breath, *Aër, aura,*
Airoso, of the aire, *Aëreus.*
Aisar, to inclose with water, *Aqua intercludere.*
Aiuda, helpe, a glister, a purge, *Auxilium, clysterium, potio.*
Aiudador, a helper, *Auxiliator.*
Aiudar, to helpe, *Auxiliari.*
Aiuno, fast, *Ieiunium.*
Aiunar, to fast, *Ieiunare.*
Aiuntar, to ioine, to couple, *Iungere, coniungere, copulare.*
Aiuntamiento, ioining, coupling, *Iunctura, coniunctio, copulatio.*
Aiuntamiento con parienta, incest, *Incestus*
Aiuso, downwards, beneath, vnder, *Sub, subter, subtus.*
Ajo, garlicke, *Allium.*
Ajonge, a seed like fenell, *Sesamum.*
Ajonjoli, *idem.*

A L

Alamares, laced buttons, *Fibulæ ligatæ.*
Al, a el, to the, to, *Ad.*
Ala, a wing, a finne of a fish, the causes of a house, *Ala, pinna, protectum.*

B   Ala,

A L   A L

Ala, Elicampane, *Enula campana.*
Alar, of a wing, *Alaris.*
Alabança, praise, *Laus.*
Alabancioso, praising, boasting, bragging, *Iactabundus, gloriosus.*
Alabar, to praise, to boast, to vaunt, *Laudare, iactare.*
Alabarda, an halberd, *Bipennis.*
Alabastro, Alabaster, *Alabastrum.*
Alache, hering, *Halec.*
Alacran, a Scorpion, *Scorpio.*
Alaçor, an herbe wherwith they dy Carnation, bastarde Saffron, *Crocum sylvestre.*
Aladar, the arme pits, or the arme holes,
Alado, winged, *Alatus.* (*Ala, Axilla.*
Alambre, Copper, *Aes.*
Alambique, Alquitara, a Limbecke, a Stillitorie, *Sublimatorium, Turbo.*
Alameda, a popler groue, *Populetum.*
Alamo blanco, popler, *Populus.*
Alamo negro, blacke popler, Alder, *Populus nigra, alnus.*
Alançada, an acre of ground, *Iugeris.*
Alano, a Mastiue dog, *Molossus.*
Alarde, a muster, *Censius, recensus, lustratio.*
Alarde hazer, to muster, *Recensere.*
Alargar, to prolong, to let go, *Differre, proferre, laxare.*
Alargas de tiempo, driuing off, prolonging, *Dilatio, mora.*
Alaridos, cries, shoutes, *Vlulatus, vociferationes.*
Alaridos dar, to crie out, *Vociferari.*
Alarife, a master Carpenter, Surueior, *Architector, ædilis.*
Alarifadgo, Surueiorship of buildings, the office of a master Carpenter, *Aedilitas, architectura.*
Alasazon, at that time, then, *Tunc.*
Alastrar, to balast a ship, *Saburrare.*
Alastrarse el animal, to be laden, *Onerari, sterni.*
Alaton, Latton, a kinde of mettall so called, *Orichalcum.*
Alazena, *vide* Alhazena.
Albacea de testamento, an executor, *Executor.*

Albahaca, Basill, *Basilicum.*
Albahaquilla, a kind of small Basill, *Basilicum minus.*
Albahaquilla saluage, wild Basill, *Acinus.*
Albañar, a sinke, a gutter, *Cloaca.*
Albañi de casas, a Tiler, a Plaisterer, *Imbricator, Latomus, cementarius.*
Albañeria, tiling, Tilers art, Masons craft, *Tegularis ars, comentaria, latomia.*
Albarda, a packsaddle, *Clitella.*
Albardar, to saddle with a packsaddle, *Clitella sternere.*
Albardero, a pannell maker, *Clitellarius.*
Albardon cavallo o mulo, a horse or mule that carieth a packsaddle, *Equus clitellarius.*
Albarrada, a stone wall, a bulwarke, *Maceria, agger, vallum.*
Albarran, a batcheler, vnmaried, *Cælebs.*
Albarrania, single life, *Cælibatus.*
Albarrana, a turret on a wall, *Turris.*
Albarrana cebolla, a kinde of sea Onions, *Scylla, æ.*
Albatoça, a kinde of boate, *Emphrata nauis.*
Albéytar, a Farrier, a Horseleach, *Veterinarius.*
Albeyteria, Farriers art, *Veterinaria.*
Alberca, a poole or pond, *Stagnum.*
Albogue, a pipe or flute, *Calamus.*
Alboguero, a piper, *Fistulator.*
Albor, the dawning, the breake of day, *Aurora.*
Alborbolas, a noise of ioy, *Iubilus.*
Alborbolas hazer, to reioice, *Iubilare.*
Alborear, *vide* Amanecer.
Alboroço, alborote, alboroto, a tumult, stur, hurly burly, sedition, *Tumultus, seditio.*
Alborotadora cosa, seditious, *Seditiosus, tumultuarius.*
Alboroçar, alborotar, to raise a tumult, to raise a sedition, *Tumultuari.*
Albornoz, a soldiors cassocke, *Sagum militare.*
Albricias, a reward for good news, *Strenæ.*
Albur, a Mullet, *Mugil.*
Alcaçaba, a castel or strong house, *Arx.*
Alcáçar, a pallace, a house of stregth, *Arx.*
Alcacer

Alcacer de ceuada, greene barly, *Hordeum viride.*
Alcaduz, the scoope in a water wheele, a pipe of a conduit, *Haustrum, tubus.*
Alcahuete, a bawde, *Lena.*
Alcahuetería, bawdry, *Lenocinium.*
Alcayde de fortaleza, a captain of a fort, *Præses.*
Alcadía, the captainship of a fort, *Præsidiatus.*
Alcayde mayor de justicia, the sheriffe, *Prætor.*
Alcaydía, iusticeship, *Prætura.*
Alcayta, a hooke, *Vncus.*
Alcalde, a sheriffe, or cunstable, *Curator pacis.*
Alcalde de las alçadas, collector of subsedies, *Recuperator.*
Alcançar, to obtain, to ouertake, to reach, to get, to compasse, *Contingere, attingere, consequi, assequi.*
Alcance, ouertaking, obteining, pursuing, reaching, *Assequutio, adeptio, consecutio.*
Alcanfor, camphire, *Caphura.*
Alcándara, a perch for a hawke, *Pertica.*
Alcanzía, bals made of earth, and filled with ashes, *Pilæ desultoriæ.*
Alcaparra, capers, *Capparis.*
Alcaparral, a bed of capers, *Capparetum.*
Alcarauea, carrowaies, *Carum.*
Alcarchófa, an artochock, *Acanthus, cynara.*
Alcarchofado terriopelo, wrought veluet, *Bombicinum cynaratum.*
Alcarías, cottages, *Tesqua.*
Alcatára, *vide* Alquitara.
Alcartaz para especias, a spice bag, a coffin for spice, *Cucullus, charta emporetica.*
Alcarita, a rug for a bed, *Stragulum gausapinum*
Alcatraces, a kinde of foule like a seamew that feedeth on fish, *Auis quædam Indica.*
Alcauála, subsedie, common reuenues, *Census, vectigal.*
Alcaualero, a customer, a collector of subsedies, *Censor.*
Alcauci, de cardo que se come, the head of a kinde of thistle like an artichocke, which is eaten in Spaine, *Acanthus.*

Alchimilla, Starwurt, *Aster atticus.*
Alcóba, a closet, a close roome for a bed, *Conclaue, angulus siue recessus lecto aptus.*
Alcohol stybium, *Antimomium.*
Alcoholar, to smeere or dawbe, *Illinere.*
Alconcillo de brasil, red inke, *Purpurissum.*
Alcornoque, corke, *Suber.*
Alcorque, a pantofle, *Crepida.*
Alcotan, a hawke called an hobby, *Nisus.*
Alcriuite, brimstone, *Sulfur.*
Alcuña, a stocke, Progenies, *stemma.*
Alcuza, *vide* Azeytera.
Alçadura, slacking, lifting vp, taking vp, raising, breaking of the ground, *Cessatio, eleuatio sublatio, profectio soli.*
Alçar baruecho, to plow vp ground, *Scindere solum.*
Alçar de obra, to leaue worke, *Cessare, manum amouere.*
Alçar, to lift vp, to rise as a subiect against his prince, *Eleuare, rebellare.*
Aldáua de puerta, the ring or hamer of a doore, a bar, *Annulus, repagulum, malleolus.*
Aldéa, a village, *Pagus.*
Aldeano, he that dwelleth in a village, *Paganus.*
Aldeguela, a little village, *Villula.*
Aleda o hiez de colmena, the dregs of the hony, & of the hony combs, *Propolis*
Alegre, mery, pleasant, *Alacris, hilaris.*
Alegria, ioye, mirth, also a kinde of seede, *Hilaritas, sesamum.*
Alegrarse, to be mery, to be ioyfull, *Gaudere, exhilarare.*
Alegremente, merely, ioyfully, cheerfully, *Hilariter.*
Alentar liento, to breath, *Anhelare.*
Aleluya, cockow meate, *Oxys.*
Alerta, ready, prepared, *Paratus.*
Alerze, ceder, *Cedrus.*
Alezna, an awle, *Subula.*
Aleta, a little winge, *Alula, axilla.*
Aléve, treason, treacherie, *Prodiʦio.*
Alevoso, a traitor, *Proditor.*
Alexado, departed, set far off, *Longè absens*
Alexarse, to depart, to go far off, *Abire.*
Alexixa, a kinde of pudding made of wheate, *Farciminis genus.*

B 2   Alexu,

A L   A L

Alexu, a kind of bisket made with honie, *Panis biscoctus melle conditus.*
Alfabega, *vide* Albahaca.
Alfámar, a couerlet, *Stragulum laneum.*
Alfayate, a botcher, *Sarcinator.*
Alfalfa, three leaued grasse, clauer grasse, *Medica.*
Alfarge de molino de azeyte, an oile Mill, *trapetum.*
Alfaxor, *vide* alexu.
Alfenique, suger pellets, *Saccari gluten.*
Alférez, an ancient bearer, *Signifer.*
Albî, diuining, prophecying, a token of good or ill lucke, *Augurium, omen.*
Alfidel a pin, *Acicula.*
Alfiler, *idem.*
Alfocigo, fistickenuts, *Pistacea nux.*
Alforja, a wallet, *Mantica.*
Alforza de vestido, a plaite in a garment, a tucke, *Sinus.*
Alga marina, rocks or sea weede, *Alga.*
Algalia, ciuet, *Ciuettum oloris genus.*
Algarada, a stur, a tumult, *Tumultus.*
Algaravia, the moores language, *Lingua punica.*
Algarve, a den, a hole, a pit, *Specus, caverna.*
Algarrova, Carobes, or S. Iohns bread Siliqua.
Algebra, bone setting, *Ossium luxatorum compactio.*
Algebrista, a bonesetter, *Ossium luxatorum compactor.*
Algibe, a cesterne, a prison vnder ground, a dungeon, *Cisterna, ergastulum.*
Algo, somwhat, *Aliquid.*
Algodon, Cotton, *Gossipium.*
Algorfa o soberado, a loft, a storie, *Tabulatum.*
Alguazil, Shiriffe, Bailiffe, Chiefe executioner, *præfector officialis.*
Alguaziladgo, the shirifwike, the bailifwike, *Præfectura.*
Alguarismo, Arithmetike, *Arithmetica.*
Alguien, some bodie, *Aliquis.*
Alguirnalda, a garland, *Corona, Serta, orum.*
Alguno, some bodie, *Aliquis.*
Alguna vez, sometimes, *Aliquando.*
Algun tanto, somewhat, *Aliquantulum.*

Alhaja, housholdstuffe, *Supellex.*
Alhadida, burnt brasse, *Aes combustum.*
Alhaxeme, a Barber, *Tonsor.*
Alhambra, a Carpet, *Tapetum.*
Alhaqueque, an Haralde, *Caduceator in lingua Arabica.*
Alharequientos, that make a great noise, *Vociferatores.*
Alhazena, a small basket, a hole in a wal to set things in, an Ambrie, *Reconditorium, repositorium.*
Alheli, White violets, *Alba viola.*
Alheña, Pruet, *Ligustrum.*
Alhilel, a pinne, *Acicula.*
Alholi, a place appointed to keepe salt, a barne, *Horreum, granarium.*
Alholvas, Fenegreeke, *Fænum græcum.*
Alhombra, *vide* Alhambra.
Alhóndiga, a barne or garner for corne, *Horreum.*
Alhondiguero, he that keepeth a barne or garner, *Horrearius.*
Alhondon, the bottome of any thing, *Fundum.*
Alhostigo, alhocigo, Pistacke tree, *Pistacea nux.*
Alhostiga, the fruit of Pistacke tree, *Pistacea nux.*
Alhurreca de la mar, the salt fome that commeth out of the rootes of canes, *Adarca, adarces.*
Alhuzema, Lauander, *Lauandula.*
Aliar, to confederate, to allie himselfe, *Confœderare.*
Aliado, allied, confederate, *Affinis, confœderatus.*
Aliança, alliance, *Confœderatio.*
Aliçacee o canca, foundatiō, *Fundamentum*
Aliento, brcth, *Anhelitus, spiritus.*
Alimaña, a beast, *Animal, brutum.*
Alimentar, to nourish, to maintaine, *Alere.*
Alimento, meat, victuals, *Alimentum.*
Alimpiar, to make cleane, to brush, to wipe, to cleanse by sacrifice, *Mundare, purgare, expiare, abstergere.*
Alimpiadura, purging, cleansing, *Expurgatio, expiatio.*

Alimpia-

A L   A L

Alimpiadero, a ſtrainer to cleanſe ſwine, *Emunctorium vas.*
Alimpiaduras, dregs, *Purgamenta.*
Alindar, to limit, *Limitare.*
Alinde, a kinde of ſpectacles, *Perſpicilla.*
Aliñar, to fit, to make fit, *Aptare, parare.*
Aliño o atavio, fitting, *Aptatio.*
Aliox, Marble, *Marmor.*
Aliſar, to make ſmooth, *Leuigare.*
Aliſadura, ſmoothing, *Leuigatio.*
Aliſo, a kinde of willow, *Salix.*
Aliſma, a kinde of Planten, *Plantaginis genus.*
Aliſtar, to make a roll of names, *Catalogum facere.*
Aliviar, to lighten, to eaſe, *Subleuare.*
Alivio, eaſe, lifting vp, *Subleuatio.*
Aljama, o alçama, a Synagog, *Synagoga, congregatio.*
Aljava, a quiuer, *Pharetra.*
Aljonge, the gum of a kinde of Thiſtle, *Viſcum è carduo ſuario.*
Aljongera, a Sow Thiſtle, *Vernilago.*
Aljófar, a pearle, the ſeede of pearle, *Margarita.*
Aljoſifar, ladrillado, pauing tile painted, *Aſarotum.*
Aljonjoli, ajonjoli, a white graine wherof tile is made, *Seſamum.*
Aljuban moriſco, a mooriſh Caſſocke, *Veſtis punica.*
Allá, there, thither, *Illic, illuc.*
Allanar, to make plaine, *Complanare.*
Allanadura, making plaine, *Complanatio.*
Allegar, to gather together, to come near, to arriue, *Accedere, appellere, aggregare.*
Allegamiento, arriuing, comming neare, gathering, *Acceſſio, appulſio, aggregatio, clientela.*
Allegadizo, gathered, *Congregatus, aggregatus.*
Allegado en vando, a client, one that followeth a faction, *Cliens.*
Allende, beyond, *Vltra.*
Allende y aquende, this way and that way, *Vltro citróq;*
Alli, there, thither, *Ibi, illuc.*

Alma, the ſoule, the mind, the ſpirit, *Anima, mens, animus.*
Almáciga, Maſtix, *Maſtix.*
Almaden, a mine of mettall, *Vena metalli.*
Almadana o marra, a paring ſhouel, *Marræ, arum.*
Almadraque, a bolſter or a pillow, *Culcitra*
Almadrava, fiſhing for Tunies, *Cetarium, rij.*
Almagrar, to marke with oker, *Rubrica tingere.*
Almagre, red oker, redding, *Rubrica, ochra.*
Almagrado, marked with oker, *Rubricatus*
Almayzar, a wiping cloth of haire, *Sudarium ſetabeum.*
Almanach, an Almanacke or Prognoſtication, *Ephemeris.*
Almário, an armorie, an ambrie, *Armarium, repoſitorium, reconditorium.*
Almariete Alhazena pequeña, *Armariolum.*
Almarraxa, an ewer of glaſſe, *Guttus vitreus.*
Almárraga, a kind of headſtall for a horſe trimmed, gilt, and imbrodered, or the ſcum of Lead, *Capitalis genus, Lythargyris.*
Almazen, an armorie, a trunke, a cupbord, a conduit head, *Armamentarium, colluuiarium, ciſta.*
Almea, red Storax, *Naſcapthum.*
Almear de feno, a Hey loft, *Fænile.*
Almeja, a cockle, *Corhlea.*
Almena, a pinacle of a tower, *Pinna.*
Almenára de fuegos, fires made in the night, Beacons, *Ignes noctu̇rni.*
Almenára de açofar, a candleſticke of braſſe with many ſockets, *Lucerna polymixos.*
Almendro, an Almond tree, *Amygdalus.*
Almendra, an Almond, *Amygdalum.*
Almendral, a garden of Almond trees, *Amygdaletum.*
Almendrada, Almond milke, *Amygdalinum lac.*
Almete, an helmet, *Caſſis, idis.*
Almez, Lote tree, *Lotus.*
Almiar, a Hay rocke, *Fæni congeries.*
Almidon, Sterch, *Amylum.*

Almillas.

A L   A L

Almilla, a waltcoat, *Tunicula, indusium laneum.*

Almirante, an Admirall, *Nauarchus.*

Almiralle, a king in the Arabians language, *Rex.*

Almirez, a brasen morter, *Mortariũ æreum.*

Almiron, Endiue, *Intubus.*

Almizque, Muske, *Muscus, Zibethum.*

Almizquera, a Muskcat, *Oderatus mus.*

Almívar, Suger made liquide, *Saccarum liquidum.*

Almocafre, a dibbe to set herbs, *Pastinum.*

Almodrote, a hotchpot of garlicke and cheese, *Moretum.*

Almofrez, a great male made in fashion like a pillowbeere, *Culcitraria fascia.*

Almofía, a dish, *Discus.*

Almogavar, an aduenturer in war, a light harnessed soldior, *Velites.*

Almohada, a pillow, *Puluinus.*

Almohaça, a curry combe, *Strigilis.*

Almohazar, to curry, *Strigilare, strigili mundare.*

Almojávana, a cake of flower and cheese, *Circulus, moretum.*

Almonéda, open sale, *Auctio, sectio.*

Almonedear, to set to sale, *Auctionari.*

Almorranas, Piles, the disease so called, *Hemorrois.*

Amorramiento, ful of Piles, *Hemorroicus.*

Almoradux, Matoram, *Sambucus.*

Almotacen, a common Crier, *Præco.*

Almotacenadgo, a Criers office, *Præconis minus.*

Almoxarife, a customer, *Telones, publicanus.*

Almoxarifadgo, the customership, custome, *Telonium.*

Almorzar, to breake fast, *Ientare.*

Almuerzo, breakfast, *Ientaculum.*

Almud o Celemin, a bushell, *Modius.*

Almuédano de moros, a Crier, *Præco.*

Almuñécar, a place where they sell raisons, *Mercatus vuarum passarum.*

Alna, a yarde, an ell, *Vlna.*

Alocado, frantike, become foolish, *Demens, mente captus.*

Alojar, to lodge, *Diuertere.*

Alojamiento, lodging, *Diuersorium.*

Alomas, for the most part, *Vt plurimum.*

Alondra, a larke, *Alauda.* (*pinnæ.*

Alones, the pinions of the wings, *Alarum*

Alongar, to prolong, to be absent, *Protrahere, abesse.*

Alongamiento, prolonging, absence, *Protractio, absentia.*

Alofa, an Alose or shad, *Aristosus.*

Aloxa, Metheglin, *Aqua mulsa.*

Alpargata, a shoo made of linen, *Carbatine, arium.*

Alpechin, Sirup in Oliues, a fruit of a tree like Oliues, *Amurca, æ.*

Al presente, at the present time, *Impræsentiarum.*

Alpiste, Foxtailes, *Cauda vulpis.*

Alquetifa, a Couerlet or Rug for a bed, *Stragulum, gausapinum.*

Alquería, a farme, *Aedes conductitiæ, ager conductitius.*

Alquerque, Table play, *Calculorum ludus.*

Alquicer morisco, a Cassocke, *Sagum punicum.*

Alquilar, to let to farme, to hire, *Locare, conducere.*

Alquilador, he that hireth or letteth, *Locator, conductor.*

Alquiler o arrendamiento, hiring, letting *Locatio, conductio.*

Alquiladizo, letten, hired. *Conductitius.*

Alquimista, an Alchimist, *Alchymistes.*

Alquinal morisco, a handkercher, *Sudarium linteum.*

Alquitara o alcatara, a stillatorie, *Sublimatorium.*

Alquirira, Dragagant, *Tragacanthum.*

Alquitran, Naphtha, *Bitumen.*

Alrededor, round about, *Circum.*

Alreves, contrary, *Contrarió.*

Alsine, Chickweed, *Alsine.*

Altabaxo, a downright blow, *Telo in alium sublato ferire.*

Altabaque, a basket, *Calathus.*

Altar, an Altar, *Altaré.*

Altanero, a Falcon, *Falco.*

Alterado, troubled, *Perturbatus.*

Alterar, to trouble, to change, *Mutare, perturbare.*

                              Alteza,

Alteza, highnes, loftines, highnes in estate, *Celsitudo, altitudo.*
Altivo, lofty, proud, stately, *Celsus, excelsus, superbus.*
Altiveza, loftines, statelines, highnes, *Superbia, celsitudo.*
Alto, high, the loft in a house, a storie in a house, *Altus, celsus, Solarium, Tabulatum.*
Alto hazer, to keepe aloofe, *Eminus stare.*
Altramuzes, Lupines, *Lupinus.*
Altraves, athwart, acrosse, *Ex obliquo.*
Altura, height, the top of a hill, *Altitudo, fastigium.*
Alumbrar, to lighten, *Illuminare, illustrare.*
Alumbre, A lume, *Alumen.*
Alumbrado con alumbre, dressed with Alume, *Alumine infectus.*
Alumbrado, lightened, *Illustratus, illumina-*
Alunado, Lunatike, *Lunaticus.* (*tus.*
Alúziar, to make bright, *Illustrare.*
Alva, the morning, day breake, the morning watch, *Vigilia matutina, aurora.*
Alvayalde, Ceruse, *Cerussa.*
Alvalá, the handwriting, an acquittance, *Apocha, æ.*
Alvanega, a kind of coife, *Reticulum.*
Alvar, that which is soon ripe, soone sodden, *Præcox.*
Alvardillo, a little packsaddle, *Clitellula.*
Alvarjones, Pease, *Pisa.*
Alvarazos, Morphew, *Alphus.*
Alvarino, a dun or swart colour, *Fuscus.*
Alvarcoque, apricocke, *Armeniacum malum.*
Alvedrar, to iudge, to deeme, *Arbitrari.*
Alvedrío, freewill, *Arbitrium.*
Alvérchigas, *vide* Alvarcoque.
Alvergar, to lodge, *Divertere, hospitio suscipere.*
Alverguería, a lodging, *Diversorium.*
Alverjana, a kinde of weede in corn, *Herba inter arista crescens.*
Alvin, a bloud stone that stoppeth bloud, *Lapis sanguinarius.*
Alvina, the beating of the tide, the raging of the tide, *Æstus.*
Alvo, *vide* Blanco.
Alvura, *vide* Blancura.

A M

Ama, a mistresse, a nurse, *Patrona, domina, nutrix.*
Amable, louely, amiable, *Amabilis.*
Amablemente, amiablie, louingly, *Amabiliter.*
Amado, loued, *Amatus.*
Amador, a louer, *Amator.*
Amadora cosa, perteining to loue, *Amatorius.*
Amagar, to make offer of giuing or striking, *Intentare, minari.*
Amaestrar, to teach, *Docere.*
Amaynar, to strike saile, *Vela contrahere.*
Amamantar, to giue sucke, *Lactare.*
Amamantamiento, giuing sucke, *Lactatio.*
Amancebado, womanish, he that haunteth women, a loose liuer, *Fornicator, machus.*
Aman derecha, on the right hand, *A manu dextra.*
Aman yzquierda, on the left hand, *A leua manu.*
Amanecer, to waxe day, the morning, *Lucescere, diluculum.*
Amaneciendo, betimes, earely in the morning, *Aurora, diluculo.*
Amañar, *vide* Aliñar.
Amanojado, the hands ioined togither, *Conclusæ manus.*
Amansar, to make gentle, to pacifie, to tame, *Domare, mansuefacere, cicurare, placare.*
Amante, a louer, louing, *Amans, amator.*
Amapolas, wilde poppie, *Papauer erraticum.*
Amar, to loue, *Amare.* (*cum.*
Amargar, to be sharpe, or bitter, *Amarico, as.*
Amargo, sharpe, bitter, *Amarus, acerbus.*
Amargura, bitternes, *Amaror, acerbitas.*
Amarillo, pale, wan, pale as gold, *Pallidus.*
Amarillez, palenes, *Pallor.* (*lidus.*
Amarillecerse, to be pale, *Pallescere.*
Amarrar, to fasten, to moaze a ship, *Religare, depangere.*
Amarra, a corde, or cable tto fasten, *Retinaculum.*

Amassar,

Amaſſar, to moulde dowe, to bake, *Subigere, pinſare.*
Amaſſador, a baker, *Piſtor.*
Amaſſadura, moulding, baking, *Subactio.*
Amaſſadera, a woman baker, *Piſtrix.*
Ambargris, ambargriſe, *Ambar.*
Ambar, ambar, *Electrum.*
Amblar, to amble, *Gradior.*
Amblador, an ambler, *Gradarius equus.*
Ambos a dos, both two, *Ambo.*
Ambroſia, a kinde of woꝛmewoode, *Ambroſia.*
Amelezinar, to cure, *Mederi.*
Amelonado, ſoftned, *Mollificatus.*
Amedrentar, to affray, *Terrere.*
Amenazas, thꝛeates, *Minæ arum.*
Amenazador, a thꝛeatner, *Minax.*
Amenazar, to thꝛeaten, *Minari.*
Amenazando, with thꝛeats, *Minaciter.*
Amenguar, to leſſen, to diminiſh, to diſcredite, *Minuere, dehoneſtare.*
Amenguado, diminiſhed, diſcredited, diſcredited, *Imminutus, dehoneſtatus.*
Amentar, amiento, to ſling, *Amento.*
Amenudo, often, thicke, *Sæpe, crebrò.*
Ameos, Ameos, *Ammi.*
Ametalado, fained, double faced, *Fictus, dubiæ fidei.*
Amiento, a ſtringe of a ſling, *Habena, amentum.*
Amieſgado, a ſtrawberie, *Fragum.*
Amiga, a louer, a friend, *Amica.*
Amigo, a friend, a louer, *Amicus.*
Amigable, friendly, louely, *Amicus, a, comis.*
Amigar, to curry fauoꝛ, to get friendſhip, *Amicitiam inire.*
Amiſtad, friendſhip, goodwil, *Amicitia, beneuolentia.*
Amo, a maſter, a ſchoolmaſter, *Pædagogus, dominus.*
Amohatrar, to grow in debt, to boꝛrow of one foꝛ the paiment of another, *AEs alienum contrahere, vorſura ſoluere.*
Amohinar, to chafe, to fret, *Succenſere, ſtomachari.*
Amojonar, to ſet bounds, *Limites ponere.*
Amollentar, to ſoften, *Mollire.*
Amollentadura, ſoftening, *Mollities.*

Amolar, muelo, to ſharpen, to grinde, to foꝛge, *Acuere, molire.*
Amoladuras, the droſſe of yꝛon, *Scobi ferri.*
Amonio, an herbe ſo called, *Amonium.*
Amoneſtar, to warne, *Admonere.*
Amoneſtador, a warner, *Admonitor.*
Amoneſtacion, warning, *Monitio.*
Amontonar, to heape vp, *Accumulare.*
Amontonado, heaped vp, *Aggeſtus.*
Amontonamiento, heaping vp, a heape, *Accumulatio, acerruus.*
Amontones, by heapes, *Aceruatim.*
Amor, loue, *Amor.*
Amor de hortelano, cloeuers, *Aparine.*
Amoroſa, amoꝛous, louely, *Amorabundus, beneuolus.*
Amoroſamente, amoꝛouſly, *Amanter, beneuolè.*
Amoradux, maioꝛm, *Sambucus.*
Amordazar, to bite, *Admordere.*
Amordazador, a biter, *Mordax.*
Amordazamiento, byting, nipping, *Mordacitas.*
Amordazando, bitingly, *Mordaciter.*
Amortecerſe, to ſowne, *Exanimari.*
Amortecimiento, ſowning, *Exanimatio.*
Amortecido, fallen in a ſowne, *Exanimatus.*
Amortiguar, to moꝛtifie, *Mortificare.*
Amortiguamiento, moꝛtification, *Mortificatio.*
Amoſcador, a fan of feathers, *Flabellum.*
Amotinador, a mutinous fellow, a ſeditious perſon, *Tumultuoſus, ſeditioſus.*
Amparar, to pꝛotect, to defend, *Protegere, tueri.*
Amparo, defence, pꝛotection, *Protectio, tutela.*
Ampolla, a ſwelling, a bubble, a dꝛinking glaſſe, *Ampulla, bulla.*
Ampollera, a ſmall bubble, *Bullula.*
Ampollarſe, to riſe in bliſters, *Ampullari.*
Anade, a ducke, oꝛ dꝛake, *Anas.*
Anadino, a duckling, *Anaticulus.*
Anadon, a great ducke, *Anas.*
Anadear, to wallowe like a ducke, *In anatis morem gradi.*

Anagyris,

Anagyris, beane, trefoile, *Anagyris.*
Anales, chronicles, *Annales.*
Anapelo, woolfes bane *Lupi strangulator.*
Anca, the hips, a horses buttocke, *Nates clunis.*
Ancusa, a kinde of buglosse, *Anchusa.*
Ancla, an anker, *Anchora.*
Ançarotes, the gum of a certaine tree, *Sarcocolla.*
Anciano, ancient, *Senex, antiquus, vetus.*
Anciania, ancientnes, *Antiquitas.*
Ancho, broad, large, *Amplus, latus.*
Anchura, breadth, largenes, *Latitudo, Amplitudo.*
Anchamente, largely, *Latè, ampliter.*
Anchova, hering frie, *Halecula.*
Andado, gon, a son in law, *Profectus, priuignus.*
Andamio, a scaffold, a gallerie, *Ambulachrum.*
Andariega, a gadding gossip, *Ambulatrix.*
Andar, to go, *Ire, gradi, ambulare.*
Andadura, going, walking, *Ambulatio.*
Andadora cosa, wandring, *Vagabundus, ambulatorius.*
Andador, pregonero, a crier, *Præco.*
Andas, a horse litter, a chaire to carrie one in, a beere, *Lectica, carpentum, capulus, pheretrum.*
Andancio, a walking place, *Ambulacrum.*
Anden, a walke, *Ambulatio.*
Andrajo, a rag, *Pannus, panni segmentum.*
Andrinas, plums, prunes, vide Ciruelas.
Anduares, villages, *Attegiæ.*
Anegar, to drown, *Submergere, naufragium facere.*
Anegamiento, drowning, *Submersio, naufragium.*
Anfiteatro, the theater, *Amphitheatrum.*
Angarillas, a hurdle to draw any thing on, *Vectabulum cratitium.*
Angel, an angell, *Angelus.*
Angelica, Angelica, *Angelica, Smyrnium.*
Angosto, streight, narrow, *Angustus.*
Angostura, streightnes, narrownes, *Angustia.*
Angostar, to make narrow, *Angustare.*
Anguilla, an eele, *Anguilla.*

Angurias, a kinde of pompion, *Peponum genus.*
Angustia, sorrow, greefe, *Angustia.*
Angustiado, greeued, *Anxius.*
Angustiar, to make sorrowfull, *Angere.*
Anidar, to make a nest, *Nidificare.*
Anillo, a ring, *Annulus.*
Animal, a liuing creature, a beast, *Animal.*
Animalejo, a little creature, a little beast, *Animalculum.*
Animales ceñidos, flies, and wormes, and such others, which the Latines call *Insecta animalia.*
Anima, a soule, *Anima.*
Animar, to encourage, *Animare.*
Anime, a kinde of perfume, *Cancanum.*
Animoso, coragious, *Animosus, magnanimus.*
Animosidad, corage, *Magnanimitas.*
Aniñado, become a childe, childish, *Factus puer, puerilis.*
Aniñadamente, childishly, *Pueriliter.*
Anis, matalahuga, anis, *Anisum.*
Anoche, pesternight, *Heri vesperi.*
Anochecer, the euening, to waxe night, *Aduesperascere.*
Anocheciendo, the euening, *Crepusculum vespertinum.*
Anoria, a well or engine to draw water, *Machina aquaria.*
Ansar, a goose, *Anser.*
Ansarino pollo, a gosseling, *Pullus anserinus.*
Ansaron, a great goose, *Anser.*
Ansereria, a place to keepe geese in, *Chenotrophium.*
Antaño, the last yeere, *Annus superior.*
Ante, before, *Ante, præ.*
Antesque, before that, *Antequam.*
Antes, rather, *Potius.*
Antecessor, an ancestor, *Antecessor.*
Antecedente, one that goeth before, *Antecedens.*
Anteceder, to go before, *Antecedere, præcedere.*
Antenado, a son in law, *Priuignus.*
Antena de nave, the saile yarde, *Antenna.*
Antepecho, a curate, *Thorax.*

C Anteponer

A ñ

Anteponer, pongo, to prefer, *Præferre, præponere.*
Antepuerta, a hatch of a doore, *Ianuæ velum.*
Anterior, the former, *Anterior.*
Anticipar, to preuent, *Anticipare.*
Anticipacion, preuenting, *Anticipatio.*
Antier, the other day, *Nudius tertius.*
Antifaz, a vaile, a maske, *Velamen, larua.*
Antiguo, old ancient, *Antiquus.*
Antiguidad, antiquitie, *Antiquitas.*
Antiguamente, of old, anciently, *Antiquè.*
Antiguar, to abolish, *Antiquare.*
Antiguamiento, the abolishing, *Antiquatio*
Antiguor, ancientnes, *Antiquitas.*
Antiparas, bootes, buskins, *Ocreæ.*
Antojos, spectacles, lust, desire, longing of a woman with childe, *Perspicilla, libido, appetitus.*
Antojarse, to long for, to lust for, to desire, to seeme, *Libere, picare, videri.*
Antojadizo, lustfull, *Libidinosus, cupidus.*
Antorcha, a torche, *Cereum.*
Antruejo, shrouetide, *Quadragesima, carnisprinium.* (*nire.*
Antúviar, to preuent, to excell, *Præue-*
Antúvio, preuenting, *Præuentio.*
Anxia, congoxa, greefe, cares, *Angor, anxietas.*
Anzuelo, an angle, a fishhooke, *Hamus.*
Anzelado, full of fishhookes, *Hamatus.*

A ñ

Añadir, to ad, *Addere.*
Añadidura, adding, *Additio.*
Añafil de moros, a moorish trumpet, *Tuba punica.*
Añagaza, a stale, a call for birds, *Illex.*
Añal, yeerely, *Annalis, annuarius.*
Añazas, faires, *Nundinæ.*
Añejo, old, ancient, *Vetus, annosus.*
Añejar, to waxe olde, *Senescere.*
Añino, lambes wooll, *Vellus agninum.*
Añil, azure, *Glastum.*
Añilado, coloured with azure, *Glastatus.*
Año, a yeere, *Annus.*
Añojo, a calfe of a yeere olde, *Viculus vnius anni.*

A P

Añublarse el cielo, to waxe cloudie, *Nubilare.*
Añublo de trigo, rust of wheate, *Rubigo.*
Añublado, rustie wheate, *Rubiginosus.*

A O

Aócar ahueco, to make hollow, *Cauare, excauare.*
Aojar, to bewitch with the eie, *Fascinare.*
Aojadura, bewitching, *Fascinatio.*
Aorça, with a quarter winde, *Vento alterum puppis latus feriente.*
A osadas, boldly, I warrant you, assuredly, *Audacter, confidenter.*

A P

Apacentar, to feed, *Pascere.*
Apacentamiento, feeding, *Pastio, pastus.*
Apagar, to quench, *Restinguere.*
Apagamiento, quenching, *Restinctio.*
Apalear, to beate with a cudgell, *Baculo cædere.*
Apaleado, cudgelled, *Fuste cæsus.* (*ripere.*
Apañar, arrebatar, to catch, to snatch, *Ar-*
Aparar, aparejar, to prepare, *Parare.*
Aparato, aparejo, preparation, *Apparatus.*
Aparador, a cupboord, *Abacus.*
Aparcero, quiñonero, he that parteth, a deuider, a partner, *Diuisor, particeps.*
Apartar, to deuide, to seuer, to part, to make difference, to depart, *Diuidere, partire, discedere.*
Apartamiento, seuering, departing, diuorce, *Diuisio, discessio, diuortium.*
Apartadamente, seuerally, *Distinctè, diuisim.*
Apasionado, sicke, greeued, passioned, *Æger.*
Apassionar, to greeue, to be passioned, *Ægrescere, molestia affici.*
Apazible, quiet, peaceable, *Placabilis.*
Apazibilidad, quietnes, peaceablenes, *Placabilitas.*
Apaziblemente, peaceablie, *Placabiliter.*
Apaziguar, to pacifie, *Placare.*
Apearse, to alight off a horse, *Descendere.*
Apeamiento, a lighting off a horse, *Descensus.*

Apedaços,

A P

A pedaços, peece meale, *Carptim.*
Apedrear, to ſtone to death, to ſpoile with hayle, *Lapidare, grandine, concutere.*
Apegar, to cleaue to, to ſticke to, to ioine, to glue togither, *Hærere adhærere, conglutinare.*
Apegamiento, ſticking to, cleauing to, *Adhæſio, conglutinatio.*
Apelar, to appeale, *Prouocare.*
Apelacion, appealing, *Prouocatio.*
Apelo, y apelo aiuſo, downe the heare, *Pilus ſecundus.*
Apellido de guerra, the watchword, *Symbolum, teſſera.*
Apellido, a ſurname, *Cognomen.*
Apellidar, to crie in warre, to name, *Symbolum cancre, appellare.*
Apenas, ſcarſely, hardly, with much a do, *Vix, ægrè.*
Apercebir, cibo, to forewarne, to preſſe out for a ſoldior, *Præmonere, euocare.*
Apercibimiento, forewarning, preſſing, preparing, *M... itus, euocatio, præparatio.*
Apeſarado, ſorrowfull, grœued, *Grauis, æger.*
Apeſgar, to way downe, to preſſe downe, *Grauare, degrauare, deprimere.*
Apeſgamiento, preſſing downe, *Depreſſio.*
Apetecer, to deſire, *Appetere, cupere.*
Apetito, appetite, *Appetitus.*
Apiadar, to pittie, *Miſereri.*
Apiñado, cerrado, cloſe togither, *Coniunctus, vnitus.*
Apio, ſmalledge, *Apium.*
Apitonado cauallo, fierce, hot, *Furibundus, ferus.*
Apitonamiento, fierceneſs, furiouſneſs, *Ferocitas.*
Aplacar, to appeaſe, *Placare.*
Aplazer, to pleaſe, *Placere.*
Aplazar, to ſummon, *Citare.*
Aplazible, pleaſant, *Placidus, iucundus.*
Aplomado, heauie, leaded, *Plumbeus.*
Apodar, to quip, to taunt, to nip, *Taxare.*
Apodamiento, quipping, taunting, *Taxatio.*
Apodos, quippes, taunts, *Dicteria.*

A P

Apoyar, to ſucke a dug, to prop vp, *Lalo, Lus, ſuffulcire.*
Apolillar, to eate with mothes, *Tinea corrumpere.*
Apolillado, motheaten, *Tinea corruptus.*
Apoplexia, the falling euill, *Apoplexia.*
Aporcar o arrimar tierra, to make ridges, *Porcare.*
Aporcadura, the making of ridges, *Porcatio.*
Aporfia, a vie, ſtriuingly, *Certatim.*
Aporrear, to cudgell, *Fuſte cædere.*
Aporreadura, cudgelling, *Fuſtigatio.*
Aportillado, opened, broken open, *Apertus.*
Apoſentarſe, to lodge, *Diuertere.*
Apoſentamiento, a lodging, *Diuorſorium, hoſpitium.*
Apoſentado, lodged, a gheſt, *Hoſpes.*
Apoſento, a chamber, a lodging, *Cubiculum.*
Apoſentador, an harbenger, *Præcurator, menſor.*
Apoſtemarſe, to grow to an impoſtume, *Abſcedere, corrumpi.*
Apoſtema, an impoſtume, *Apoſtema, abſceſſus.*
Apoſtemacion, *idem.*
Apóſtol, an apoſtle, *Apoſtolus.*
Apoſpelo, pelo arriba, againſt the haire, *Pilus aduerſus.*
Apréciar, to prize, *Æſtimare.*
Apreciadura, prizing, *Æſtimatio.*
Apreciador, a prizer, *Æſtimator.*
Aprémiar, to force, to compell, *Cogere.*
Apremiadura, force, compulſion, *Coactio.*
Apreſſurarſe, to make haſt, *Feſtinare.*
Apreſſurado, haſtie, *Feſtinus.*
Apreſſuradamente, haſtelie, *Feſtinanter.*
Apreſtar, to make readie, *Parare.*
Apretar, to bind, to ſtreighten, to ſtrein, to gripe, *Premere, ſtringere, comprimere.*
Apretamiento, griping, ſtreining, *Preſſio, aſtrictio, compreſſio.*
Apretadamente, ſtreightly, violentlie, *Compreſſim, ſtrictè, violenter.*
A prieſſa, haſtely, *Properè.*
Aprieto, a ſtreight, *Anguſtia.*

C 2   Apriſco,

A Q

Aprisco, a shœpehouse, *Ouile.*
Aprópriar, to appropriate, to liken, to compare, *Proprium facere, assimilare.*
Apropriacion, a comparison, *Assimilatio.*
Aprovar pruevo, to allow, *Probare.*
Aprovechar, to profit, *Prodesse.*
Aprovacion, allowing, *Probatio, comprobatio.*
Aprovechamiento, profiting, *Profectus.*
A pruevas, by proof, *Probaté.*
Apuesta, a gage, a wager, *Depositum.*
Apuesta cosa, decked, trimmed, *Ornatus.*
Apuñar, to buffet, *Pugnis cadere.*
Apuntar, to note, to point out, *Notare, signare.*
Apuntalar, to prop up, *Fulcire.*
Apuntalado, propped up, *Fultus.*
Apuntillar, to spurne, *Pede aduerso ferire.*
Apurar, to purifie, to streine, to enforce, *Purificare, stringere, urgere.*

A Q

Aquedar, to staie, *Manere, sistere, cohibere.*
Aquedador, a staier, *Cohibitor.*
Aquende, on this side, *Cis, citra.*
Aquel, he, *Ille.*
Aquella, shœ, *Illa.*
Aquello, it, *Illud.*
Aquesso, this, *Hoc.*
Aqueste, this, *Hic.*
Aquexar, to hasten, to make haste, *Properare, festinare, stimulare, maturare.*
Aquexamiento, haste, spœde, *Festinatio, stimulatio, maturatio.*
Aquexadamente, hastely, spœdely, *Maturé.*
Aquexado, hastened, *Stimulatus, maturus.*
Aqui, hœre, *Hic.*
Aquila, an eagle, *Aquila.*

A R

Ara, an altar, *Ara.*
Arádo, a plow, *Aratrum.*
Arado camera, a crooked plowe, *Aratrum curuum.*
Arada, plowed ground, *Arata terra.*
Arador, a plowman, a handworme, *Arator, Teredo.*

A R

Arar, to plow, *Arare.*
Arambre, copper, *AEs.*
Aranzel, a proclamation in paper, *Edictum.*
Araña, a spyder, *Aranea.* (*sue.*
Arañenta cosa, full of spyders, *Arachnoarañuelo*, a snare, a grin to catch birds, *Decipula.*
Arbitrio, iudgement, an award, *Arbitrium, iudicium.*
Arbitrar, to thinke, to awarde, *Arbitrari, censere.*
Arbitrario, arbitrarie, *Arbitrarius.*
Arbitrador, an arbitrator, *Arbitrator.*
Arbitro, an arbitrator, *Arbiter.*
Arbol, a tree, *Arbor.*
Arbolillo, a little tree, *Arbustum.*
Arboleda, a groue, *Lucus, sylua.*
Arboleçer, to growe up to a tree, *Arborescere.*
Arbol de parayso, *vide* Alheña.
Arca, a chest, a deske, *Arca, scrinium.*
Arcabuz, an harquebusse, *Tormentum, Bombarda.*
Arcaduz, a conduit pipe, *Fistula, vide,* Alcaduz.
Arcangel, an archangell, *Archangelus.*
Arco, an arche, a vault, a bowe, *Arcus, fornix.*
Archero, an archer, *Sagittarius.*
Archiuo, a treasurie of euidences or of records, *Archinum.*
Arcediano, an archdeacon, *Archidiaconus.*
Arcedianadgo, an archedeaconship, *Archidiaconatus.* (*chipresbiter.*
Arcipreste de yglesia, a chiefe priest, *Ar-*
Arçobispo, an archbishop, *Archiepiscopus.*
Arçobispado, an archbishopricke, *Archiepiscopatus.*
Arda, a squirrell, *vide* Harda.
Arder, to burne, *Vrere, ardere, flagrare.*
Ardimiento, heate, burning, *Ardor.*
Ardientemente, hotlie, *Ardenter.*
Ardid de guerra, a strategeme, a policie of war, *Stratagema.*
Ardiente, burning, hot, *Ardens.*
Ardite, a pœce of money worth three maravedis, *Monetæ species.*

Ardor,

A R

Ardor, heat, burning, *Ardor*,
Arena, arenal, sand, *Arena, sabulum*.
Arenoso, sandie, *Arenosus*.
Arenisca tierra, sandie ground, *Arenarius*.
Arenque, an hering, *Halec*.
A respeto, in respect, *Prae*.
A restin, the scratches in a horses pasterns, *Scabies in equorum suffragine*.
Arñl, the bishop at Chesse, *Episcopus scaccarius*.
Argadija, the frame of any thing, *Fabrica*.
Argadillo, a reele to winde yarne, *Alabrum, rhombus*.
Argamassa, embossed worke, *Opus signinū*.
Arguella, a wallet, *Mantica*.
Argolla de hierro, a ring of iron, *Annulus ferreus*.
Arguyrguyo, to argue, to dispute, *Arguere, disputare*.
Argullo, sharpnes, *Argutia*.
Argulloso, sharpe, *Argutus*.
Argullosamente, sharply, *Argutè*.
Argumentar, to dispute, *Argumentari*.
Argumento, an argument, *Argumentum*.
Argumentador, a disputer, *Argumentator*.
Arithmetica, Arithmetike, *Arithmetica*.
Aristolochia, Hartwurt, *Aristolochia*.
Armado, armed, *Armatus*.
Armada, a fleete, *Classis*.
Armadura, armor, *Armatura*.
Armandijas, snares or traps to catch birds or beasts, *Decipula, Tendicula*.
Armar çancadilla, to trip, *Supplantare*.
Armar, to arme, to prepare, to set a snare, *Armare, praeparare, tendere*.
Armar engeño, to bend, to leuell, *Tendere*.
Armas, armor, armes, weapons, *Arma, insignia gentilitia, tela*.
Armario, an armorie, an ambrie, *Armarium*.
Armatoste, a top, a grin, a snare, a racke for a crosse bow, *Crepundia, ineptia, decipula, vertibulum arcuarium*.
Armazon, a bedsted, *Fulcrum*.
Armero, an armorer, *Armamentarius*.
Armella de hierro, a ring of iron, *Annulus ferreus*.
Armin, Ermines, *Pellicium armillinum*.

A R

Armiños, the beasts that beare the furre Ermines, *Armillini mures*.
Armoniaque, Armoniake, *Armoniacum*.
Armuelles, orache, *Atriplex*.
Arqueta, arquita, arquilla, a little chest, *Arcula*.
Arquitetura, building, *Architectura*.
Arnes, harnesse, *Arma*.
Arrabal, the suburbs, *Suburbium*.
Arracadas, earings, *Inaures*.
Arracife, a rocke or shelfe in the sea, *Scopulus, vadum*.
Arráygar, to take roote, to settle, *Radicare, radices agere*.
Arraygadura, taking roote, *Radicatio*.
Arrayhan, Myrtle, *Myrtus*.
Arrayhanal, a groue of Myrtles, *Myrtetum*.
Arrancado, pulled vp, *Euulsus*.
Arrancar, to plucke vp, *Euellere, extirpare, refigere*.
Arrancadura, plucking vp, *Euulsio, extirpatio, eradicatio*.
Arras, the earnest peny, a token, *Arrha, Arrhabo*.
Arrasar medida, to strike a bushell or other measure, *Hostire*.
Arrasadura, the striking of a bushell or other measure, *Hostimentum*.
Arrastrar, to drag, to draw, *Trahere, rapiare*
Arrastradura, dragging, drawing, *Tractio*.
Arrear, to array, to prepare, *Parare, apparare*.
Arrebañar, to gather togither, *Congregare, congerere*.
Arrebañadura, gathering togither, *Congestio, congeries*.
Arrebatar, to catch, to snatch, *Rapere, diripere, abripere*.
Arrebatamiento, catching, snatching, *Raptus*.
Arrebatado, catched, *Raptus, a*.
Arrebatadamente, suddenly, *Raptim*.
Arrebatina, catching, a skirmish, a sudden affray, *Rapina, tumultus, pugna tumultuaria*.
Arreboles, red strakes in the element, *Rubedo caeli surgente sole vel occidente*.

Arrechar,

A R   A R

Arrechar, to lift vp, to set vpright, pro-
perly pertaining to the priuie mem-
ber, *Arrigere.*
Arrechadura, the standing stiffe, &c. *Arre-*
ctio, tentigo.
Arredrar, to driue away, *Arcere.*
Arregostado, tasting, the liking of the tast
of any thing, *Gustus, gustatus.*
Arrejada, the plow staffe, *Rulla.*
Arrellanar, to settle, to sit with maiestie,
Vultu & gestu compositis sedere.
Arrelde, a two pound waight and a halfe,
Bilibris.
Arremangar, to bind vp, to tucke vp, *Suc-*
cingere, suffarcinare.
Arremeter, to inuade, to set vpon, to as-
saile, *Adoriri, inuadere.*
Arremetida, an assault, a salie, *Inuasio, im-*
petus, eruptio.
Arremolinar, to whirle about, *Turbinis*
more circumagere.
Arrendar, to rain vp a horse, to let for
rent, to hire for rent, to take by great,
Frænare, locare, conducere, redimere.
Arrendamiento, letting, ferming, taking
by great, *Locatio, conductio, redemptio.*
Arrendador, a lettor, a hirer, *Locator, con-*
ductor.
Arreo, a row, on a row, *Serie, ordine.*
Arrepastar, to fæde, *Pascere.*
Arrepentirse, piento, to repent, *Pænitere.*
Arrepentimiento, repentance, *Pænitentia.*
Arrepentido, repentant, *Pænitens.*
Arrepiso, repenting, repentant, *Pænitens.*
Arrexaque, a bird called a marten, a fork,
an æle speare, a quarrell of a crosse-
bow, *Cypselus, tridens, fuscina, catapultiarii.*
Arréziar de dolencia, to recouer, *Connalef-*
cere.
Arriba, aboue, vpwards, *Super, supra, sur-*
sum.
Arribar, to arriue, *Appellere.*
Arribado, arriued, *Appulsus.*
Arriar, to fall backe as the ship that let-
teth go his cable, *Recipere se, reijci.*
Arrimar, to set vp against, to leane a-
gainst, to sticke to, *Admouere, adhærere,*
inniti, adniti.

Arrimadura, leaning to, standing vp by,
Admotio, adnixus, reclinatio.
Arrimo, any thing to leane on, *Reclinato-*
rium.
Arrinconado, thrust vp in a corner, *In an-*
gulum coactus.
Arriscar, to indanger, *Discrimen adire.*
Arriscado, endangered, *Periculo obnoxius.*
Arrobas, a kinde of measure, xxb. li.
Mensura genus, 25. li.
Arrobado, measured by that measure,
Mensus.
Arrodillar, to kneele, *Genu flectere.*
Arrodilladura, kneeling, *Genu flectio.*
Arrocinado cavallo, an ill fauored Iade,
Cantherius fœdus.
Arrogancia, arrogance, *Arrogantia.*
Arrogante, arrogant, *Arrogans.*
Arroyar, o tornar, o arar lo sembrado, to
plow the ground, *Proscindere solum.*
Arroyos, water brookes, *Riuuli.*
Arroyarse el rio, to run along, *Fluere, vol-*
ui, labi.
Arrojar, to throw or cast, to presse into,
to throng in, *Iacere, iaculari, inferre se in*
medium.
Arrollar, to roll, *Voluere, convoluere.*
Arrope de mosto cozido, new wine sod-
den, *Mellatium, mustum.* (*moron.*
Arrope de moros, sirup of mulberies, *Dia-*
Arropar, to cloath, *Vestire.*
Arrostrar, to face, to come face to face, *Co-*
ram affari.
Arroz, Rice, *Oryza.*
Arruga o plegadura, a wrinkle, a plaite,
Ruga, sinus. (*nuosus.*
Arrugado, wrinkled, plaited, *Rugosus, si-*
Arruynar, to throw downe, *Euertere.*
Arruynado, throwen downe, *Euersus.*
Arrullar el niño, to lull a childe, *Sopire.*
Arrullarse la paloma o tortola, to cric as
the stockdoue or turtle, *Gemere.*
Arsenico, Orpiment, *Auripigmentum.*
Arte, art, science, cunning, craft, deceit,
Ars, dolus, techna, scientia, astutia.
Artero, cunning, craftie, deceitfull, *Dolo-*
sus, astutus.
Artero, an artificer, *Artifex.*

Artejo,

A R

Artejo,the ioint of the finger,*Articulus*.
Artemisa,Mugwort,*Arthemisia*.
Artesa,a maund to put bread in, *Vasculum panarium*.
Artesano,a craftsman,*Artifex*.
Artesilla,a little boll,a vessell,*Vasculum*.
Artesones, the workes of Plaisterers on the roofes of houses, or seelings wrought,*Opus gypsatum*.
Articulo,a part,a point of time, an article of the faith, an article in a noune, *Articulus*.
Artificio, workmanship, cunning, *Artificium*.
Artificioso,cunning,*Artificiosus*.
Artificialmente, cunningly, *Affabrè, artificiosè*.
Artimaña,deceit,*Dolus,techna*.
Artillería, artillerie, ordinance, *Machinæ bellicæ,tormenta*.
Artillero,master of the ordinance,a gunner,*Machinarius*.
Artista,an artificer,*Artifex*.
Arveja,pease,*Eruilia,pisæ*.
Arzilla,a kinde of clay,*Argilla*.
Arzon, the pomell of a saddle, the arson of a saddle, *Pomelum,postilena*.

A S

As,an ace in the dice,*As*.
Asa, an handle, occasion, opportunitie, *Ansa,occasio,opportunitas*.
Asar,to rost, *Assare*.
A sabiendas, wittingly, of purpose,*De industria*.
Asarabacar, a kinde of Narde, a kinde of foale foote, *Asarum,vulgago*.
Ascalonia cebolla,a scallion or little oinion,*Cepa,ascalonia*.
Asco,aver asco,loathing,to loath,*Fastidium,horrere,fastidire*.
Ascoroso,he that loatheth,*Fastidiosus*.
Ascua,hot coales,*Pruna*.
Asgar,*vide* Asir.
Asga,opportunitie,*Ansa,occasio*.
Asendrado, troden as a path, *Vsitatus,tritus*.
Asion,*vide* Aciones.
Asir,to take hold of, to cleaue to,to sticke

to,*Prendere,præhendere,ahærere*.
Asido,cleauing to,*Prendens,adhærens*.
Asilla,opportunitie,*Occasio,opportunitas*.
Asma,shortnes of breth,*Asthma*.
Asmatico, he that hath a short breath, *Asthmaticus*.
Asmar,to esteeme,to imagine,*Existimare, imaginatione comprehendere*.
Asna,asno,a shee Asse,a hee Asse,*Asinus*.
Asnal,pertaining to an Asse,*Asininus*.
Asnarizo,an Asse driuer,*Agaso*.
Asnero,an Asse keeper,*Asinarius*.
Asnico,a little Asse,*Asinus paruus*.
Aspa,a reele for threed,*Alabrum*.
Aspado,reeled,*Alabratus*.
Aspar,to reele threed,*Alabrare*.
Aspeluzar, to haue the haire stiffe with feare,*Horrere,horrescere*.
Aspero,sharpe,rough,raggie,stony way,*Asper*.
Aspereza, sharpnes,roughnes,*Asperitas*.
Asperear,to make sharpe,to make rough,*Exasperare*.
Asqueroso,lothsome, *Fastidiosus*.
Assadero,a spit,*Veru*.
Assadura de animal,the entrailes,*Exta*.
Assado,rosted,*Assatus,Torridus*.
Assaltar, to assaile, to set vpon, *Inuadere, adoriri*.
Assar,to roste,*Assare,torrere*.
Assaz,ynough,*Satis*.
Assaetado,shot through, *Sagitta confixus*.
Assarabacar,our Ladies gloues, *Asarum*.
Asseado,neate,curious,handsome,*Cultus, comptus*.
Assechar,to wait,to lie in wait,to intrap *Captare,insidiari*.
Assechança,lying in wait,*Insidiæ*.
Assechador,he that lieth in wait,*Insidiator*
Assechadora cosa,deceitfull,*Insidiosus*.
Assechando tomar, to take by lying in wait,*Excipere,intercipere*.
Assendereado,rare,excellent, *Rarus,excellens*.
Assentar, siento,to place or set, to sit,*Locare,sedere,discumbere*.
Assentarse, to sit downe, to sinke to the bottome,*Sedere,discumbere,sidere*.

Assentarse

A S

Aſſentarſe ſobre las piernas a cuclillas, to rucke downe, to cower downe, *Coſſim ſedere.*
Aſſentamiento, placing, ſitting, pitching of a campe, *Seſſio, diſcubitus, caſtrametatio.*
Aſſentar real, to pitch a campe, *Caſtrametari.*
Aſſentador de real, he that pitcheth a campe, *Metator, menſor.*
Aſſenſio, wormwood, *Abſynthium.*
Aſſerrar, to ſaw in ſunder, *Serrare.*
Aſſerrador, a ſawyer, *Serrator.*
Aſſerraduras, ſaw duſt, *Scobs.*
Aſſervar, to keepe, to watch, *Obſeruare.*
Aſſeſtar tiro, to aime, *Collimare, dirigere.*
Aſſeſtadura, aiming, *Directio.*
Aſſeſſor, an aſſociate on the bench, *Aſſeſſor*
Aſſiento de edificio, the ſcituation, the dregs, *ſedes, ſedimentum.*
Aſſiento hazer, to ſink downward, *Sidere.*
Aſſi, ſo, *Sic, ita.*
Aſſi como, euen as, like as, *Tanquam, quemadmodum.*
Aſſignar, to appoint, to aſſigne, *Aſſignare.*
Aſſignacion, aſſignment, appointing, *Aſſignatio.*
Aſſiſtente, an aſſiſtant, *Aſſiſtens.*
Aſſolver, to abſolue, *Abſoluere.*
Aſſolucion, abſolution, *Abſolutio.*
Aſſolado, ſet againſt the ſunne, *Soli expoſitus.*
Aſſolear, to drie againſt the ſunne, *Soli exponere.*
Aſſoladura, making waſte, *Deſolatio.*
Aſſolar, to make deſolate, to ſpoile, *Deſolare, vaſtare.*
Aſſoltar ſuelto, to looſe, *Soluere.*
Aſſomar, to peere vp, to appeere, to looke vp, *Apparere, caput erigere.*
Aſſomada cabeça, heauie headed, giddie headed, *Grauedine laborans.*
Aſſombrado, afraid, *Territus, attonitus.*
Aſſombrar, to afray, *Terrere.*
Aſſonadas, by ſounds, *Sonitu.*
Aſſonador, a tuner, *Commodulator.*
Aſſonar ſueno, to ſound, to ſing with, *Conſonare, commodulare.*
Aſſoſſegar ſiego, to appeaſe, *Sedare.*

A T

Aſſoſſegado, appeaſed, *Sedatus.*
Aſſulcar arado, to make a furrow, *Sulcare.*
Aſſulcado en dos partes, diuided by a furrow, *Sulcatus.*
Aſſuelto, abſolued, *Abſolutus.*
Aſta, the ſtaffe of a launce, *Haſta.*
Aſtil, the ſtaffe of a ſpeare, *Haſtile.*
Aſtillado, ſet on a ſtaffe, *Haſtatus.*
Aſtilla, a ſtub, a ſingle quarter of timber, a ſtalke, *Stipula, aſſula, caulis.*
Aſtilejo, a conſtellation called Orion, *Orion.*
Aſtillero, a docke to build ſhips in, *Nauale*
A aſtillas, by ſmall quarters of timber, *Aſſulatim.*
Aſtrología, Aſtrologie, *Aſtrologia.*
Aſtrologo, an Aſtronomer, an Aſtrologer, *Aſtrologus.*
Aſtrologal, Aſtronomical, Aſtrological, *Aſtrologicus.*
Aſtroſo, vnfortunate, vnluckie, *Infælix, infauſto ſidere natus.*
Aſtuto, ſubtill, craftie, deceitfull, *Aſtutus, verſutus.*
Aſtutamente, deceitfully, craftily, *Aſtutè.*
Aſtucia, deceit, *Aſtutia.*

A T

Atabal o pandero, a taber, *Tympanum.*
Atabalero, a taborer, *Tympaniſtes.*
Atacar, to ty, to truſſe vp, *Alligare, ſtringere.*
Atacadura, tying or truſſing vp, *Structura*
Atado, tied, bound, *Impeditus, ligatus.*
Atadura, tying, binding, *Ligamentum, ligatio.*
Ataharre, a crupper, *Caudale.*
Atahona, an Aſſe mill, *Mola aſinaria.*
Atahorma, a kinde of birds of pray, *Pygargus.*
Ataitor, a cupboord, *Abacus.*
Atajar los enemigos, to cut off the enimie *Intercludere.*
Atajo de enemigos, cutting off, *Intercluſio.*
Atajar deſcubriendo tierra, to foray the country, to diſcouer the country, *Depopulari, ſpeculari.*
Atajador, a ſcout, *Speculator.*

Atajado,

Atajado, circumcifed, *Circumcifus.*
Atajo, the difcouerie made by a fcout, *Speculatio.*
Atajar, to circumcife, *Circumcidere.*
Atajar camino, to ſtop the paſſage, *Viam intercludere.*
Atajar pleyto, to cut off a ſute, to finiſh a ſute, *Decidere.*
Atajo de pleyto, cutting off of a ſute, *Decifio.*
Ataladrar, to bore through, *Terebrare.*
Atalaya, a watch tower, *Specula.*
Atalaymiento, watching, *Speculatio.*
Atambor, *vide* Atabal.
Atañer, to pertaine, *Attinere.*
Atanor, a conduit pipe, *Tubus, fiſtula.*
Atanquia para arrancar pelos, pincers, *Vulſella, forceps.*
Atapar, to ſtop, to couer, *Obſtruere, operire, tegere.*
Atar, to tie, to binde, *Ligare, obligare.*
Ataraçana, a docke for ſhips, *Nauale.*
Atafcado, ſticking in the mire, *In luto hæſitans.*
Ataviar, to make fit, to attire, *Aptare, ornare.*
Ataviado, fitted, attired, *Aptatus, ornatus.*
Ataud, a tombe, a beere for dead men, a coffine, *Monumentum pheretrum.*
Atauxia, damaſking of a knife or ſword, *Scutulatio, variegatio.*
Atemorizar, to affray, *Terrere.*
Atencion, attention, *Attentio.*
Atender, to attend, *Attendere.*
Atento, attentiue, *Attentus.*
Atenerſe en voto a otro, tengo, to aſſent, *Aſſentire.*
Atentar tiento, to aſſay, to touch, to ſearch, *Tentare, tangere.*
Atenazar, to plucke with pincers, *Forcipare.*
Atenazadas, with plucks of pincers, *Forcipatim.*
Aterecerſe, to waxe ſtiffe with cold, *Rigere.*
Aterecimiento, ſtifneſs with cold, *Rigor.*
Aterido, ſtiffe, *Rigidus.*
Atirirſe, *vide* Aterecerſe.

Aterrar, to throw to the earth, *In terram proſternere.*
Ateforar, to heape vp monie, *Congerere nummos.*
Ateſtar, to fill, to ſtuffe full, *Farcire, implere.*
Ateſtado, filled, ſtuffed, *Impletus, refertus.*
Athanaſia, Tanſie, *Athanaſia, Tanacetum.*
A tiempo, in good time, *Oportunè.*
A tiento, by geſſe, by groping, *Coniecturando, tentando.*
Atincar, Borax, *Chyſocolla.*
Atinar, to geſſe, *Coniecturare, coniicere.*
A tino, by geſſe, *Coniecturando, coniiciendo.*
Atizar, to kindle, to lighten fire, *Irritare, incendere, accendere.*
Atizador, he that kindleth fire, *Incenſor, inflammator.*
Atochado, fooliſh, frantike, *Stolidus, attonitus.*
Atocha, a kind of ſhrub to make frailes, *Sparti virgulæ.*
Atollar, to ſtick in the mire, *In luto hæſitare.*
Atolladal, atolladero o lamedal, a mire, a puddle, *Cænum, volutabrum.*
Atormecerſe, to be aſtonied, *Stupere, torpere.*
Atormecido, aſtonied, *Stupidus.* (re.
Atormecimiento, aſtoniſhment, *Stupor, torpor.*
Atorçonada beſtia, that hath the griping in the belly, *Tormine laborans.*
Atordido, aſtonied, *Stupidus, attonitus.*
Atormentar, to torment, *Torquere, cruciare.*
Atormentado, tormented, *Tortus.*
Atormentador, a tormentor, *Tortor.*
Atoſſigado, poiſoned, *Toxicatus.*
Atraer, traygo, to draw, *Trahere, attrahere.*
Atrahimiento, drawing to, *Attractio.*
Atrahillar, to draw in a ſlip or leaſh, *Loro ducere, numella ducere.*
Atrancar la puerta, to bar the doore, *Peſſulum obdere.*
Atramuzes, *vide* Altramuzes.
Atras, behinde, *Ponè, retrò.*
Atras mano, behind hand, *Retrorſum.*
Atraveſar, to croſſe, *Tranſuertere.*
Atraveſado, croſſed, *Tranſuerſus.*
Atreguado loco, frantike by fits, *Per interualla inſanus.*

Areverſe,

A u

Atreuerſe, to be bold, *Audere, confidere.*
Atreuimiento, boldnes, *Audacia, confidentia.*
Atreuido, bold, *Audax, confidens.*
Atriaca, treakle, *Theriacum.*
Atriaquero, he that maketh oꝛ ſelleth treakle, *Pharmacopola.*
Atribuyr, buyo, to attribute, *Attribuere.*
Atribuirſe, to arrogate, *Aſſumere, arrogare.*
Atribulado, troubled, *Vexatus.*
Atronado, *vide.* Atochado.
Atronar trueno, to thunder, to aſtoniſh, *Tonare, ſtupefacere.*
Atronamiento, aſtoniſhment, *Attonitus.*
Atruendo, a noiſe, *Strepitus.*
A tuerto, by wꝛong, wꝛongfully, *Iniquè.*
Atufar, to be in a rage, to be in a ſudden choller, *Fremere, Succenſere, iraſci.*
Atun, a Tunny, *Thynnus.*
Aturdir, to aſtoniſh, *Stupefacere.*
Aturdido, aſtoniſhed, *Attouitus ſtupefactus.*

A u

Auditorio, an auditoꝛy, *Auditorium.*
Auditor, an hearer, *Auditor.*
Audiencia, audience, hearing, *Audientia.*
Aullar, to howle, *Vlulare.*
Aullido, howling, *Vlulatus.*
Aumentar, to encreaſe, *Augere.*
Aumento, encreaſe, *Augmentum.*
Aun, yet, hetherto, *Tamen, adhuc.*
Aunque, although, *Quamuis.*
Auſentarſe, to be abſent, *Abeſſe.*
Auſente, abſent, *Abſens.*
Autentico, authentike, *Authenticus.*
Autillo, an owle, *Bubo.*
Autor, an authoꝛ, *Autor.*
Autoridad, authoꝛitie, *Autoritas.*
Autorizar, to authoꝛiſe, *Autorisate confirmare.*

A V

Avanicos, fannes which women beare in their hands, *Ventilabrum.*
Avalorios, garniſhing with bugles, *Ornamentum braclearium vitrearum.*
Avaricia, auarice, couetouſnes, *Auaritia.*
Avariento, couetous, *Auarus.*

A V

Avarraz, ſtauefacre, *Staphiſagria.*
Ave, a bird, *Auis.*
Averamia, a teale, *Species quędam anatis.*
Avellana, a haſell nut, *Nux auellana.*
Avellana de la India, Mirabolaine, *Mirabolani.*
Avellano, a haſell tree, *Corylus.*
Avellanedo, a haſell groue, *Coryletum.*
Avellacar, to make vile, to reuile, *Vili facere, conuitiari, dehoneſtare.*
Aventura, aduenture, hap, *Caſus, fors.*
Aventurarſe, to aduenture, *Audere.*
Avena, Avena vana, otes, wilde otes, *Auena.*
Avenado, ſod with otes, madde, braineſicke, *Cerebroſus, auenatius.*
Avenedizo, *vide* Advenedizo.
Aventajarſe, to excell, to take aduantage, *Primas obtinere, lucrari.*
Aventajado, excellent, *Primarius.*
Avenir vengo, to agree, to be friends, *Conuenire.*
Avenencia, agreement, *Conuenientia, compoſitio.*
Avenir el rio, to ouerflow, *Inundare.*
Avenidas, a floud, *Diluuium.*
Aveñolas, the eielid, *Palpebræ.*
Aventar, viento, to make winde, to fan coꝛne, *Ventilare.*
Aventadero, a fan to make winde, *Ventilabrum.*
Aventarſe el ganado, to run headlong as ſheepe do that are afraid, *Conſternari.*
Aventamiento, the running headlong, *Conſternatio, præcipitatio.*
Averiguar, to verifie, to pꝛoue, *Verificare.*
Averiguamiento, verifieng, *Verificatio.*
Averiguacion, verifieng, *Verificatio.*
Aver, he, avia, vue, avre, to haue, *Habere.*
Averes, goods, *Bona.*
Avieſſo, a contrary waie, alſo frowarde, ouerthwarting, *Deuium, Peruerſus.*
A vezes, ſometimes, *Aliquando.*
Avezindar, to dwell by, to make free of a towne, *Iuxta habitare, priuilegio donare.*
Avilenteza, opoꝛtunity, *Oportunitas.*
Avinagrado, made ſharpe, *Acetoſus.*
Aviſado, aduiſed, *Monitus, admonitus.*

Avizo,

A H

Aviſo, aduiſe, *Significatio, monitio.*
Aviſar, to aduiſe, *Monere, admonere.*

A X

Axaqueca, a kinde of paine in the heade, *Dolor capitis.*
Axedrea, winter ſauorie, *Satureia.*
Axedrez, cheſſe, *Scacchius luſus.*
Axenuz, nigella Romana, *Melanthium.*
Axi, red pepper, *Piper rubeum.*
Aximezes, iutties in a houſe, *Proiecta.*
Axorca, a braſelet, fetters, *Armilla, compedes,* (*tea.*
Axuar, linnen for houſhold, *Supellex linea.*

A Z

Azagaya, a moores weapon, *Telum punicum.*
Azahar, the flowers of orenges, *Flos citreus.*
Azaleja, a towell, *Linteum.*
Azarote, ſarcocoll, *Sarcocolla.*
Azar, an ill token, an ill ſigne, *Malum omen.*
Azar en el dado, hazard, *Luſus quidam aleæ.*
Azarcon, burnt leade, *Plumbum combuſtum.*
Azavache, ieate, *Gagates lapis.*
Azcona, a kind of dart, *Acontias.*
Azebo, hollie, *Agrifolium.*
Azebuche, a wilde oliue, *Oleaſter.*
Azebuchal, an oliue groue, *Oleaſtrum.*
Azedo, ſower, *Acidus.*
Azedia, a ſole fiſh, *Soleola.*
Azedia, ſharpnes, ſowernes of ſtomack, hartburning, *Aceroſitas, ſtomachi acor.*
Azedura, ſowernes, *Acetoſitas.*
Azedarſe, to be ſower, *Acteſcere.*
Azedéra, ſorrell, *Oxalis.* (*teria.*
Azeche, a kind of blacke minerall, *Melanteria.*
Azeytuno, an oliue tree, *Olea, oliua.*
Azeytuna, an oliue bery, *Olea.*
Azeytuna en cortido, an oliue in ſyrope, *Olea conditanea.*
Azeyte, oyle, *Oleum.*
Azeytera, a veſſell of oyle, *Olearium vas.*
Azeytero, he that ſelleth or maketh oile, *Olearius.*
Azemila, a mule, *Mulus.*
Azemilero, a muleter, *Mulio.*

A I

Azemilar, perteining to a mule, *Mularis.*
Azero, ſteele, *Chalybs.*
Azerar, to ſteele, *Chalybe indurare.*
Aziago, a diſmall day, *Dies ater.*
Azige, inke, *Atramentum.*
Azicates de eſpuelas, the ſide irons of ſpurs, *Calcarium coſtæ.*
Azogue, quicke ſiluer, *Argentum viuum.*
Azogado, one that is ouercome with the aire of quicke ſiluer, by metaphor, a fearefull wretch, a poore quaking wretch, *Timidus, pauidus.*
Azre, a maple, *Acer.*
Azul, blew, azure, *Ceruleus color.*
Azulejo, pauement, *Pauimentum.*
Azumbar, *vide* Almea.

B A

BAchara, our ladies gloues, *Baccharis.*
Bacalaos, a kinde of newlande fiſh, *Piſcis borealis genus.*
Bacia, a bole, *Trulla.*
Bacin, a baſen, a trey, *Peluis, trulla.*
Bacinete, a peece to piſſe in, *Pelluuium.*
Baço, the ſpleene, *Splen.*
Baço, dun, browne, *Fuſcus.*
Bachiller, a batcheler, *Baccalaureus.*
Badajo de campana, a clapper of a bell, by metaphor, a dolt, an aſſehead, *Crepitaculum ſtolidus, malleus campanæ.*
Badajadas, iangeling of bels, *Campanarum tinnitus.*
Badeha, a kinde of melons, *Anguria.*
Badil de hogar, a fire ſhouell, *Batbillum.*
Bagaje, baggage, *Quiſquiliæ, impedimenta exercitus.*
Baga de laurel, the bayberrie, *Bacca lauri.*
Bahari, a kinde of hauke, *Accipiter.*
Bahear, to fume, to ſmoke, *Exhalare, euaporare.*
Baho, Baſo, bapor, *Vapor, halitus.*
Bajeles, veſſels, *Vaſa.*
Baya de mar, a baie, a creeke, *Sinus, ſtatio.*
Bayben, a bob, a blow, *Ictus, alapa, colaphus.*
Baylar, to daunce, *Tripudiare.*
Bayle, a daunce, *Tripudium.*

D 2 Baylador,

B A

Baylador, a dauncer, *Tripudiator, saltator.*
Bajo de vientre, the bottome of the belly, *Abdomen.*
Bala, a bullet, *Pila plumbea tormentaria.*
Baladron, a prater, *Blattero.*
Baladronear, to prate, *Blatterare.*
Balagos, haycockes, *Fæni congeries.*
Balança, a balance, *Trutina, lanx.*
Balar, to bleate, *Balare.*
Balcon, a bay window, *Fenestra prominens.*
Baldado, of free cost, *Gratuitus.*
Baldio, any thing that is common, *Publicus.*
Baldon, a scoffe, a taunt, *Opprobrium, conuitium, scomma.*
Baldonar, to scoffe, to reproch, *Conuitiari, expobrare, subsannare.*
Baldres, white leather, a sheepskin, *Melota.* (*Balatus.*
Balido de oveja, the bleating of sheepe,
Balija, a wallet, *Mantica.*
Balitar, to bleate as a fawne, *Glocitare.*
Balitado, bleating, *Glocitatus.*
Ballesta, a crossebowe, *Balista.*
Ballestero, a crossebowe maker, a crossebowe man, *Balistarius.*
Ballestar, to shoote in a crossebowe, *Sagittare.*
Balsa, a boate, a poole of water, *Cymba, stagnum.*
Balsamo, baulme, *Balsamus.*
Baluarte, a bulwarke, *Agger.*
Balumen, a volume, *Volumen.*
Baltrueto, a gadding fellow, a roging fellowe, *Vagabundus, erro.*
Bambancar, to stammer, *Titubare, nutare.*
Bambaneando, stammeringlie, *Titubanter.*
Bancal, a bench, *Subsellium.*
Banco, a stoole, a bench, a shelue in the sea, *Sedile, subsellium, vadum, dorsum.*
Banduxo, a pudding, *Farium.*
Bañar, to bathe, *Balneare.*
Baño, a bathe, the vessell to bathe in, *Balnea, balneatio.*
Bañador, a bathe keeper, *Balneator.*
Banquero, a bankor, an exchanger of money, *Argentarius.*

B A

Baquilla, a little cowe, a kinde of beetle with horns, *Vacca, innenca, genus scarabeorum.*
Baque, a fall, a losse, *Casus, damnum.*
Baraça, brotle, let, trouble, *Impedimentum turba.*
Barahunda, a tumult, a turmoyle, *Tumultus.*
Barahustes, turned posts, *Postes tornatiles.*
Barajar, to brabble, to shuffle cardes, *Litigare, chartas miscere.*
Baratija hazer, to buy pedlery wares, *Emere quæ postea distrahantur.*
Baraja, a brabble, a packe of cards, *Lis, chartarum fasciculus.*
Barahuster, to crosse launces, *Hastis transuersis concurrere.*
Barato, good cheape, *Vili, paulò.*
Baratar, to sell cheape, to deceiue, *Vili vendere, decipere, fallere.*
Baraton, a broker, *Instilor.*
Barbaro, barberouse, *Barbarus.*
Barbaria Barbariedad, barbarousnes, *Barbaries.*
Barba, *vide* Barva.
Barbo, a barbell, *Barbus.*
Barbullar, to deceiue, to cosen, *Fallere, imponere, fucum facere.*
Barca, a boate, a barcke, a skiffe, *Cymba scapha.*
Bardar, to lay iopces of timber on a mud wall, *Parieti cæmentitio signa transuersa imponere.*
Bardaxo, a bardasso, *Cynædus, ganymedes.*
Barjuleta, a pocket, a little wallet, *Manticula, pera.*
Barniz, barnish, *Vernix.*
Barnizado, barnished, *Vernice illinitus.*
Barquero, a bargeman, a pilote, *Nauicularius, portitor.*
Barquiño, bellowes, *Follis.*
Barra, a bar of pron, a shelue in the sea, *Massa ferrea, vadum.*
Barragan, a big stout fellow, *Iuuenis.*
Barragana, a great ramping wench, a roile, *Adolescentula.*
Barranco, a bancke of earth, a breach of the earth betweene two hils, *Anfractus.*
Barredera red, a tramell, *Verriculum.*

Barrena,

Barrena, a wimble, an augur, *Terebra*.
Barrenar, to boare through, *Terebrare*.
Barreno, a hole bored, *Terebratum foramen*.
Barreña, a great earthen pan, *Sinum fictile*.
Barrer, to sweep, to brush, *Verrere, scopare*.
Barredero, he that sweepeth, *Scopator*.
Barredero de horno, a malkin, *Verforium, penicillum*.
Barreduras, dust and filth that is swept, *Scobs*.
Barrera, a barrier, a clay pit, *Pergula, argilletum*.
Barrial, a plot of clay, *Argilletum*.
Barriga, the paunch, the belly, the womb, the priuie parts, *Venter, vulua, penis*.
Barrigudo, gorbelly, *Ventriculofus*.
Baril, a barrell, *Dolium*.
Barrio, a streete, a warde, *Vicus*.
Barro, claie, wheales, pimples in the face, *Argilla, pustulæ*.
Barroso, he that hath a rich face, any thing claiele or full of claie, *Argillofus, Papulofa facies*.
Barruntar, to winde out, to suspect, *Odorari, suspicari*.
Barrunte, suspicion, *Suspectio*.
Barva, the chin, the beard, *Mentum, barba*.
Barva de Aaron, cockow pint, *Arus*.
Barva de cabron, gotes beard, *Tragopogus*.
Barvado, bearded, *Barbatus*.
Barvar, to haue a beard springing, *Pubescere*.
Barvacana, a yarde about a house, *Pomerium*.
Barvasco, longwort, or cowslip, *Verbascum*.
Barvechar, alçando, to break vp the ground, *Proscindere solum*.
Barvechar vinando, to eare grounde the second time, *Iterare solum*.
Barvechar terciando, to eare the ground the third time, *Tertiare solum*.
Barvecho, plowed grounde, *Veruactum*.
Barvechazon, the time of plowing, *Arasio*
Barveria, a barbars shop, *Tonstrina*.
Barvero, a barbour, *Tonsor*.
Barvudo, he that hath a long beard, *Barbatus*.

Basa de coluna, the foote of a pillar, *Basis*.
Basilisco, a serpent called a basilisae, *Basiliscus*.
Basquiña, a cassocke without sleues, a kirtle, *Subminia*.
Bastar, to suffice, *Sufficere*.
Bastaje, a porter, *Baiulus*.
Bastante, sufficient, *Sufficiens*. (*enter*.
Bastantemente, sufficiently, *Satis, sufficienter*.
Bastardo, a bastard, also wine so called, *Nothus, spurius*.
Bastardia, bastardie, *Illegitimum stemma*.
Bastecer, to fortifie, to victuall, to furnish, *Munire, commeatu innare*.
Bastimento, fortification, victuall, furniture, *Commeatus, munitio*.
Bastida, a tower, a fort, *Turris, castellum*.
Basto, thicke, course, *Crassus*.
Baston, a club, a staffe, *Fustis*.
Batalla, a troupe, a company of souldiors, the battell, an armie, *Cohors, agmen, pugna, exercitus*.
Batallar, to fight, *Prælium inire, confligere*.
Batallolas, the space in a galley betweene the oares for souldiors to stande in, *Tranftra*.
Batan de paños, a fuller of clothes, *Fullo*.
Batanado, fulled, *Fullatus*.
Batanar paños, to full clothes, *Fullare*.
Batel de nave, a ship boat, a skiffe, *Scapha*.
Batiente de puerta, the dornes of a dore, *Antæ*.
Batihoja, a goldbeater, *Bractearius*.
Batirhoja, to beate gold, *Bracteare*.
Batir, to beate, to strike, to thresh corne, *Percutere, triturare*.
Batir los dientes regañando, to gnash the teeth, *Infrendere*.
Bava, slauer, spittle, *Saliua*.
Bavadero, a muckender, a bib, *Saliuarium*.
Bavaza, spittle, slauer, *Saliua*.
Bavear, to slauer, *Saliua conspergere*.
Bavoso, slauering, a snaile, *Saliuofus, limax*.
Bavera, a pœce of armor called a beuer, a bib, *Buccula saliuarium*.
Bausan, y Pausan, he that standeth gaping in beholding any thing, *Qui hiante ore rem aliquam miratur*.

Bautismo,

B A

Bautifmo, Baptifme, *Baptifmus.*
Bautifar, to baptife, *Baptizare.*
Bautifta, he that baptifeth, *Baptifta.*
Bautifterio, the funt, *Baptifterium.*
Baxada, a going downe, *Defcenfio, defcenfus.*
Baxas, quicke fands, fhelues, *Breuia, fyrtes.*
Baxo, lowe, humble, bafe, vile, *Humilis, imus, infimus.*
Baxo, vnder, vnderneath, *Subter, fubtus.*
Baxilla, a garnifh of plate, *Vafcula argente.*
Baxeza, bafenes, *Humilitas, pufillanimitas.*
Baxura, bafenes, *Vilitas, pufillanimitas.*
Bdelio, the liquor of a certaine tree fo called, *Bdellium.*

B E

Beca para rodear el cuello, a kind of tippet which fchollers vfe to weare, *Focale.*
Beço, a lip, *Labium.*
Beçudo, great lipped, *Labeo.*
Bedel, a bedle ſtone, *Bethillus.*
Befas, iniurie, wrong, difpleafure, *Iniuria, moleſtia.*
Behetrias, a confufed noife, a fudden tumult, *Tumultus, confufio fonorum.*
Beldad, beautie, *Forma, pulchritudo.*
Belleza, beautie, *Beldad.*
Bellamente, beautifully, *Bellè, pulchrè.*
Bello, faire, beautifull, *Bellus, pulcher.*
Bellon, moneda de bellon, bafe money, copper money, *Moneta area.*
Bellota, an acorne, *Glans.*
Bellotero, he that gathereth acornes, *Glandarius.*
Bellotero arbol, a tree that beareth acornes, *Glandifera.*
Ben blanco y roxo, a kind of nut, *Nux vnguentaria.*
Bendezir, digo, to bleffe, *Benedicere.*
Bendicion, bleffing, *Benedictio.*
Benedicho, bleffed, *Benedictus.*
Beneficio, a benefite, a curteſſe, a good turne, *Beneficium, munus, officium.*
Beneficiado, he that hath receaued a benefite, grounds or fruites well tilled, or well husbanded, *Beneficiarius, & ager bene cultus.*

B A

Beneficiar, to do a good turne, to cherifhe any kind of fruite, *Benefacere, excolere agrum, vel fruges.*
Benigno, gentle, bountifull, courteous, *Benignus.*
Benignidad, bountie, gentlenes, *Benignitas.*
Benjuy, herbe lafer, *Laferpitium.*
Beodo, dronken, *Ebrius.*
Beodez, drunkennes, *Ebrietas.*
Berberis, barbaries, *Crefpinus, oxyacantha.*
Berça, coleworts, *Colis, crambe, braſſica.*
Berça peruna, wild mercurie, *Cynocrambe.*
Bercera, perteining to coleworts, *Braſſicarius.*
Berengena, a kinde of fruite, *Melongena.*
Beril, a berill ſtone, *Berillus.*
Bermejo, red, *Rubens.*
Bermejito, ruddie, fomewhat red, *Subrubidus.*
Bermejura, rednes, *Rubedo.*
Bermejerfe, to waxe red, *Rubefcere.*
Bermellon, vermillion, *Minium.*
Bernia veſtidura, an irifh rug, *Veſtis hibernica.*
Berrazas, water creſſes, *Naſturtium.*
Berriondez de puerca, when a fow is briming, *Subatio.*
Berraco, a boze, a nut with a green hufke, *Verres, nux imantura.*
Berro, water creſſes, *Naſturtium.*
Berruga, a warte, *Verruca.*
Berrugofo, full of warts, *Verrucofus.*
Berrueco, hillocks, *Verruca.*
Berrocal, a place full of hillocks, *Verrucetum.*
Befar, to kiſſe, *Ofculari.*
Befo, a kiſſe, *Ofculum.*
Beſtia, a beaſt, *Beſtia, bellua.*
Beſtial, beaſtly, *Belluinus.*
Beſtion o reparo, a kinde of forte, *Vallum, arx.*
Beta, *vide* Veta.
Betonica, betonie, *Betonica.*
Beton de colmena, a compoſition found in bee hiues like vnto waxe, *Propolis.*
Betun, bitumen, *Bitumen.*
Betuminar con Betun, to glue *Bituminare.*
Bevedero,

Bevedero, a trough for beasts to drink in, *Aquarium.*
Bever, to drinke, *Bibere.*
Bever al cabo, to drinke all, *Ebibere.* Beuer a porfia, to drinke a vie, to carowse, *Perpotare, certatim bibere.*
Bevedor, a drinker, *Potator.*
Bevida, drink, a potion, a drunken match, *Potus, potio, compotatio.*
Bexiga, a bladder, a bubble, *Vesica, bulla.*
Bexuco, a kinde of withe, *Vimen.*
Bezar, *vide* Abezar.
Bezado, *vide* Abezado.
Bezero, he that keepeth turne, *Vicissitudinarius.*
Bezerra yerva, calues snowt, *Antirrhinon.*
Bezerro, a calfe, *Vitulus.*
Bezo, custome, fashion, vse, *Vsus, mos.*

B I

Biblia, the Byble, *Biblia.*
Bieldo, a fan, or a scoupe to throwe corne with against the winde to wynow it, *Ventilabrum.*
Bien, well, *Bene.*
Bienes, goods, *Bona.*
Bienaventurado, happy, *Fœlix.*
Bienaventurança, happines, *Fœlicitas.*
Biendezir, to blesse, *Benedicere.*
Bien granada, oke of Jerusalem, *Betrys.*
Bien hablado, affable, well spoken, *Affabilis, facundus.*
Bien hazer, to do well, *Benefacere.*
Bien hecho, a benefit, wel done, *Beneficium, benefactum.*
Bienhechor, he that bestoweth a benefit, *Benefactor.*
Bienhechora cosa, bountifull, *Beneficus.*
Bienquerer, to wish well to, to beare good will, *Bene velle.*
Bienquisto, well beloued, *Beneuolus, charus.*
Bienquerencia, good will, *Beneuolentia.*
Bienquista y amigablemente, friendly, *Beneuolè.*
Bigor o mostaza de barva, the mustachos of the beard, *Mostax.*
Bila, a ranke, *Ordo, series.*
Billon, moneda de billon, Bullion, *Aes*

confusaneum.
Bilma, the filme, *Cutis, cortex.*
Bimbrera, a willow bed, *Salicetum.*
Birlos, kayls, *Lusus quidam puerilis.*
Bisabuclo, a great grandfather, *Proauus.*
Bisabuela, a great grandmother, *Proauia.*
Bisnaga, *vide.* Visnaga. (*nepos.*
Bisnieto, the child of the grandchild, *Pro-*
Bisperas, the euening, *Vespertinæ horæ.*
Bispera de fiesta, the eue of a feast, *Vigiliæ.*
Bisperadas, euensong, *Vespertinæ preces.*
Bissiesto, a leape yeere, *Bisextilis annus.*
Bistorta yerva, bistort, *Bistorta.*
Bitor, a Bittor, *Glottis.*
Bivar, a warren, a place to keepe hens, geese, or foule in, a fish poole, *Viuarium, auiarium, piscina.*
Biuda, a widow, *Vidua.*
Biudo, a widower, *Viduus.*
Biudez, widowhood, *Viduitas.*
Bivaro, a badger or brocke, *Fiber, castor.*
Bivienda, liuelyhood, liuing, *Victus.*
Bivo, liuely, ful of life, aliue, *Viuus, viuidus.*
Biviente, liuing, *Viuens.*
Bivir, to liue, *Viuere.*
Bivora, a viper, *Vipera.*
Bivoresno, a yong viper, *Catulus viperinus.*
Bixa, an herbe wherewith the Indians paint themselues, *Herba qua se pingunt Indi.*
Bizarro, braue, gallant, *Alacris, elegans.*
Bizarría, brauerie, gallantnes, *Elegantia, alacritas.*

B L

Blanca, a peece of money being the 68 part of a riall of plate, *Monetæ genus.*
Blanco, white, *Albus.* dexar en blanco, to leaue any thing vnspoken of, *Omittere, præterire.*
Blancura, whitenes, *Albedo.*
Blancor, *Idem.*
Blanco, a marke, a white to shoote at, *Signum, scopus.*
Blanchete, a little beagle of Malta, *Catellus Melitensis.*
Blanquear, to be white, to make white, *Candescere.*

Blanqueadura

B O

Blanqueadura de pared, the whiting of a wall, *Dealbatio*.
Blanquezino, whitish, *Subalbidus, albidus*.
Blanquibol. Ceruse, *Cerusa*.
Blando, soft, gentle, flattering, *Blandus, lenis, mollis*.
Blandura, softnes, gentlenes, flatterie, *Lenitudo, blanditiæ, mollities*.
Blandamente, softly, gently, *Leniter, molliter*.
Blandear, to florish a sword, to bend, to bow, *Vibrare, lentare*.
Blandon de cera, a waxe candle, *Cereus*.
Blassemar, to blaspheme, *Blasphemare*.
Blassemia, blasphemie, *Blasphemia*.
Blassemador, a blasphmer, *Blasphemus*.
Bledo, Blits, *Blitum*.

B O

Bobeda, a vault, *Fornix*.
Boca, a mouth, *Os, oris*.
Bocaci, Buckeram, *Brandium*.
Bocal de pozo, the mouth of a well, *Os putei*.
Bocado, a morsell, a bit, *Buccella, morsus, offa*.
Bocezo, gaping, *Oscitatio*.
Bocezar, to gape, *Oscitare*.
Boço de la barva, the mosse of the beard, *Pubes, lanugo*.
Boçal, a muffler, a muzzle, *Focale*.
Boçal, ignorant, *Imperitus*.
Bochorno, a close hot weather, *Æstus*.
Bodas, a mariage, *Nuptiæ*.
Bodega, a seller, *Cella vinaria*.
Bodegon, an alehouse, an Inne, *Taberna, caupona*.
Bodeguero, a tapster, *Cellarius*.
Bodegonero, an alehouse haunter, an alehouse keeper, *Caupo, Ganeo*.
Bodóques, pellets of clay, *Pilæ ex argilla*.
Boses, the lights, *Pulmones*.
Bofetada, a buffet, *Alapa*.
Boga, the rowing, *Remorum impulsio*.
Bogar, to rowe, *Remis impellere*.
Bohordar, to imbroder, *Laborare, limbo ornare*.
Boja, compassing about, *Circuisio*.
Bojar, to compasse about, *Circuire*.

B O

Boya, a boy, a corke for a net or angle, *Tragula, suber*.
Boyada, a heard of cattle, *Armentum*.
Boyero, a neatheard, *Bubulcus*.
Boyuno, pertaining to neat, *Bouinus*.
Bola, a bowle, a football, *Globus, pila pedalis*.
Bolapie, to go fluttring with the wings currendo alas concutere.
Bolar, to flie, to surprize, *Volare, prehendere, opprimere*.
Bolcar, to fall downe, *Concidere*.
Bolea de pelota, the flying of a bal or pellet, *Volitatus pilæ*.
Boletines, little morsels of an orenge, little round stones, *Pillulæ, glarea*.
Bolina, the sheat, a cord so called in a ship, *Funis nauticus*.
Bolsa, a purse, *Crumena, loculus*.
Bolarmenico, Bolearminack, *Armeniaca terra*.
Bolsico, a little purse, *Locellus*. (*silire*.
Boltear, to tumble, to leape, *Volutare, sub-*
Boltejador, a tumbler, *Subsultor*.
Boltejar, to tumble, *Subsilire*.
Bolver, buelvo, to turne, to returne, to restore, *Redire, vertere, reuersi*.
Bolvible, turning, *Volubilis*.
Bolvimiento, a turning, a roling, *Volubilitas*.
Bollicio, *vide* Alboroto.
Bollicioso, seditious, *Seditiosus*.
Bolliciar, to moue sedition, *Tumultuari*.
Bollo de pan, a lofe, *Panis, orbis*.
Bollo de golpe, the swelling of a stripe, *Tuber, vibex*.
Bollon de cinta, the studs of a girdle, *Bulla*
Bollonado, studded, *Bullatus*.
Boltezuela, a short turne, *Subita conuersio*.
Bomba, a pumpe, *Cochlea, sentina nauis*.
Bonança, faire weather, a calme, *Serenitas tranquillitas*.
Bondad, goodnes, *Bonitas*. (*scitus*.
Bonito, good, proper of bodie, pretie, *Bellus*
Bonéte, a cap, the top saile, *Pileus suppariï*.
Boñiga, a cow turd, *Stercus bouinum*.
Boñuelo Almojavana, a cake, *Placenta*.
Boquear, *vide* Bocezar.
Boquirotto, foule mouthed, *Conuitiator*.

Borbolear,

Borbolear, to bubble, to ſæthe, *Ebullire.*
Borbollones, bubbles with ſæthing, *Bullulæ.*
Borcellar de caxa, the brim of a cheſt, *Labrum.*
Bordar, boſlar, to imbroder, to edge, *Laborare, limbo ornare.*
Bordador, an imbroderer, an edger, *Phrygio, limborarius.*
Borde, a border of imbroderie, a baſtard, the brim, the edge of any thing, *Spurius, limbus, labrum, ora.*
Bordon, a ſtaffe, *Baculus.*
Bordonero, a baſe fellow, *Infimæ ſortis homo.*
Borne, the bending of a ſtaffe or timber by beathing in the fire, *Lentatio.*
Bornear, to bend timber by beathing in the fire, *Lentare.*
Borni, a kind of hauke, *Accipiter.*
Borracho, y borrachez, *vide* Beodo.
Borraja, borage, *Borago.*
Borrar, to blot, *Obliterare.*
Borras, dregs of wine, oile, or ointments *Fex, magma, fraces.*
Borrador, a blotter, a blotting paper, the firſt draught of any note, *Obliterator, autographum primarium.*
Borraſca, a tempeſt, *Tormentum, tempeſtas.*
Borrax, *vide* Atincar.
Borrégo, a lambe of a yeere old, *Agnus anniculus.*
Borrico, an aſſe colt, *Pullus aſininus.*
Borron, a blot, *Litura.*
Borujo, *vide* Burujo.
Borzegui, a buſkin, *Cothurnus.*
Borzeguinero, a buſkin maker, *Sutor cothurnarius.*
Borzeguineria, a buſkin makers ſhop, *Cothurnaria ſutrina.*
Boſlar, *vide* Bordar.
Boſladura, imbroderie, *Limboraria ars.*
Boſlado, imbrodered, *Laboratus.*
Boſque, a wood, a groue, a coppeſſe, *Sylua, ſaltus, nemus.*
Boſſar, to vomit, *Vomere.*
Boſtezar, to gape, *Oſcitare.*
Boſtezo, gaping, *Oſcitatio.*
Bota de vino, a bottle, *Vtriculus.*

Bota, a bœte, *Ocrea.*
Botana, an iſſue in the legs, &c. *Fiſtula, fontenilla.* (*pellere.*
Botar, to put forth, to thruſt forth, *Expellere.*
Botarſe el color, to vaniſh, to be dim of colour, *Hebeſcere, vaneſcere.* (*pila.*
Bote de pelota, the ſtroke of a ball, *Pulſus*
Bote, a boxe, *Pixis.*
Botecica, a little boxe or little bottle, *Pixula.* (*pœia.*
Botica, an apothecaries ſhop, *Pharmacopœia.*
Boticario, an apothecarie, *Pharmacopola.*
Botija, a bottle, *Vtriculus.*
Botilla, a bottle, *idem.*
Botillero, a butler, *Cellarius, promus.*
Botilleria, a butterie, *Cellarium, promptuarium.*
Botin, a bootie, *Manubiæ, exuuiæ, præda.*
Botinero, he that keepeth the bootie, *Præfectus prædæ.*
Boto, dull in edge, dull in wit, *Hebes, obtuſus, tardus.*
Boton, a button, a bud, a ſearing iron, a boile, an impoſtume, *Fibula, nodus, cauterium, vlcus, apoſtema.*
Bóveda, *vide* Bobeda.
Bovear, to be fooliſh, *Deſipere.*
Bovo, a foole, *Stultus, inſipiens, morio.*
Boveria, follie, *Stultitia.*
Box, boxe tree, *Buxus.*
Boxedal, a groue of boxes, *Buxetum.*
Boz, the voice, *Vox.*
Bozes dar, to crie out, *Vociferari.*
Bozear, to cry out, *Vociferari.* (*rator.*
Bozinglero, one that crieth out, *Vociferator.*
Bozina, a trumpet, a ſhæpeheards pipe, a purple fiſh, *Buccina, purpura, murex.*
Bozinero, a piper, *Buccinator.*

B R

Braçada, an el, *Vlna.*
Braçales, poulbrons, *Brachiale.*
Braço, an arme, the leg of a creuiſh, *Brachium.*
Braccear, to ſhake the armes, *Lacertos excutere.*
Bracero, he that caſteth out the armes, *Brachiorum vibrator.*

E Bragado,

Bragado, an oxe with a white leg, breeched, *Bos caligatus, caligatus.*
Bragas, breeches, *Caligæ, femoralia.*
Bragueta, a codpeece, *Perizoma.*
Braguero, perteining to the breeches, *Bracchale.*
Bramar, to roze as a lion, to make anie fretting noise, *Mugire, rugire, fremere.*
Bramido, rozing, lowing, *Mugitus, rugitus, fremitus.*
Brasa, a cole, *Pruna.*
Brasero, a chafindish, *Ignitabulum.*
Brasil, brasill, the red colour made with brasill, *Acanthinum lignum, purpura.*
Bravear, to braue it, *Ferocire, efferari.*
Bravo, wilde, fierce, cruell, braue, *Ferox, ferus, crudelis, elegans.*
Bravamente, wildely, fiercely, brauelie, *Ferociter, efferatè, eleganter.*
Braveza, fierceness, wildnes, brauerie, *Ferocitas, feritas, elegantia.*
Brear, to calke a ship, *Seuo incrustare.*
Breço, twigs to make cole, *Virgulta. orum,* also furses, *Erica.*
Brega, strife, *Lis.*
Breña, o mata, a bush, a shrub, a thorne, a brier, *Frutex, fruticetum, tribulus, acanthus.*
Breton de berça, the buds, or knobs of a colewort, *Coliculus.*
Bretonica, betony, *Betonica.*
Breva, a fig soone ripe, *Ficus præcox.*
Breval, a figge tree, the figs whereof are soone ripe, *Ficus arbor.*
Breve, short, breefe, *Breuis.*
Brevemente, shortly, breefely, *Breuiter.*
Brevedad, breuity, shortnes, *Breuitas.*
Breviario, an epitome, a breefe, *Epitome, compendium.*
Brezna, a chip, *Assula, astula.*
Brida andar a la brida, to ride a great horse, *Equo vehi.*
Brimbillada, marmelad, *Cidoniatum.*
Brinco, a iercke, a leape, *Saltus, subsultus.*
Brio, wilfulnes, liuelines, headines, *Morositas, peruicacia, alacritas.*
Brioso, wilfull, liuelie, *Pernicax, morosus, alacris.*

Brisar la cuna, to rocke the cradel, *Motitare.*
Brocal de pozo, the brincke of a well, *Labrum putei.*
Brocado, cloth of gold, *Auro intextus.*
Broca, a shoomakers tacke naile, *Clauiculus calcearius.*
Brocha, a claspe, *Fibula.*
Broma, a worme that eateth holes in the ships, *Vermis oblongus, qui naues perforat.*
Bronze, brasse, *AEs.*
Borquel, a target, *Pelta, vmbo.*
Broquelado, armed with a target, *Peltatus.*
Broslado, *vide* Bordado.
Brotar, to bud, to break out as the hands, *Vlcerare, germinare.*
Brozno, rough, *Bruscus, asper.*
Bruces, groueling with the face betweene the hands, *Pronus manibus innitens.*
Bruno, browne, *Pullus.*
Bruneto, blacke, sad colour, *Subniger.*
Bruñir, to burnish, *Polire.*
Brusco, knee holine, *Ruscus.*
Brusear, to heate a ships sīde with roede burning, *Rusco nauigia calefacere.*
Bruto, brutal, brutish, *Brutum.*
Bruxa, bruxo, a hagge, *Strix, lamia.*
Bruxula para tirar, the stringe of any engine to shoote with, *Libramentum.*

B V

Buarro, an owle, *Bubo.*
Buchete, the cheeke, and a pop with the mouth, *Bucca, popisma.*
Buche de animal, the mawe of a beast, *Ventriculus.*
Bucy, an oxe *Bos.*
Bucy nuevo o novillo, a steere, *Iuuencus.*
Bucytre, a vulture, *Vultur.*
Bucytrera, a place to kill vultures, *Vulturinum.*
Buelo, flight, *Volatus.* (uersus.
Buelto, turned, tumbled, tossed, *Versus, in-*
Buelta, a returne, turning away, turning round, *Reditus, conuersio, auersio.*
Bueno, good, *Bonus.*
Buenamente, well, *Bene.*

Buétagos,

Buétagos o bofes, the lightes, alſo the tripes or belly of a beaſt, *Pulmones, ilia.*
Bufalo, a buffle, *Bubalus.* (*lare.*
Bufar, to puffe, to blow as a horſe, *Anhe-*
Bufete, a ſtanding table, *Menſula.*
Bufido, the puffing and blowing of a horſe, *Anhelatio.*
Bugerias, trifles, *Nugæ.*
Buho, an owle, *Bubo.*
Buhonero, a pedler, *Diſtractor, propola.*
Bujarroncar, to commit ſinne againſt nature, *Ordinem naturæ inuertere.* (*Sodomita.*
Bujarron, he that ſinneth againſt nature,
Bula, the popes bull, *Bulla, diploma.*
Bular la frente, to burne the forehead, *Inurere frontem.*
Bulbo, wild onion, *Bulbus.*
Bullidura, ſpringing vp, boiling vp, *Scatebra.*
Bullir, to ſpring vp, to boile vp, *Ebullire.*
Bullicio, *vide* Alboroço.
Bullon, an iriſh ſkeine, *Sica.* (*pus, ſpecies.*
Bulto, ſhape, the bulke of the bodie, *Cor-*
Buñuelos, pancakes, *Laganum.*
Burbuja, a little bubble, *Bullula.*
Burbugear, to bubble, *Bullare.* (*Burdo.*
Burdegano hijo de cavallo y aſna, a mule,
Burdel, the ſtewes, *Lupanar, proſtibulum.*
Buril, a grauing toole, *Cælum.*
Burlar, to ieſte, to mocke, to deceaue, *Iocari, fallere, Ludere.* (*ſio, deceptio.*
Burla, a ieſt, a mock, a deceit, *Irriſio, illu-*
Burlador, a ieſter, a mocker, a deceiuer, *Irriſor, illuſor, deceptor.*
Burlon, a ieſter, *Irriſor, iocator.*
Burujo, the ſtone of grapes, of an oliue, the core of any fruite, *Acinus, volux.*
Buſcar, to ſæke, *Quærere.*
Buſca, ſearch, ſæking, *Quæſitio, inquiſitio.*
Buva boja, a botch, a boile, the french pockes, *Vlcus, morbi gallici vlcera, bubo.*
Buxeta, a boxe, *Pixis.*

C A

Cabal, a portion, *Rata portio.*
Cabaña, a cabbin, a cottage, *Tiguriñ.*
Cabañuela, a little cottage, *Tiguriolum.*

Cabe, nære to, *Iuxta, prope.*
Cabeça, a head, *Caput.*
Cabeçado, a headſtall, new footings of bœtes, *Capital, ocrearum pedes.*
Cabe, imperſonale, it is held, it is conteined, it happeneth, *Cadit, capitur, accidit.*
Cabeçudo, headſtrong, great headed, *Pertinax, capito.*
Cabeçal, a pillow, a bolſter, *Ceruical.*
Cabeçera de cama, a beds heade, *Caput lecti.*
Cabecera de meſa, the vpper ende of the table, *Caput menſæ.*
Cabeça abaxo, headlong, *Præceps.*
Cabezcaydo, hanging downe the heade, *Cernuus.*
Cabeçada, a blowe with the head, *Ictus capitis.*
Cabeçon de camiça, the necke bande of a ſhirt, *Limbus ad collum.*
Cabecear, to nod, to ſhake the head, *Nutare.*
Cabeceamiento, the nodding, ſhaking the head, *Nutatio.*
Cabeça de perro, dogs head, *Cynocephalum.*
Cabeço, o cerro, a hill, *Collis, Tumulus.*
Cabello, heare, *Capillus.*
Cabelladura, the buſh of heare, *Capillitium, coma.*
Cabelléra, a falſe heare, or peruke, *Coma ſuppoſititia.*
Cabellado, long heared, *Capillatus.*
Caber en lugar, to be conteined, *Contineri.*
Cabero, the laſt, *Vltimus.*
Cabeſtro, an halter, *Capiſtrum.*
Cabeſtrar, to halter, *Capiſtrare.*
Cabeſtrage, haltering, *Capiſtratio.*
Cabeſtrero, a rope maker, *Capiſtrarius.*
Cabido, conteined, receiued, *Receptus, contentus.* (*lium.*
Cabildo, a ſenate, a counſell, *Senatus, conci-*
Cabildo de ygleſia, a chapter houſe, *Capitulum.*
Caboʒan ende, *Finis, terminus.*
Cabo de cuchillo, the hafte of a knife, *Capulus.*
Cabo de tierra, a cape, a headland, *Caput, promontorium.*

Cabra,

C A

Cabra montesina, a wilde goate, *Caprea.*
Cabra, a goate, *Capra.*
Cabrito, a kid, *Capreolus, hædus.*
Cabrahigo, wild figs, *Caprificus.*
Cabrahigar, to ripen figs, *Caprificare.*
Cabrero, cabrerizo, a goatehearb, *Caprarius.*
Cabrillos, a constellacion called the goats *Vergiliæ.*
Cabrio, cabrial, rafters or quarters set in thwo parts, to lift vp, or set an ende any high things, as a mast, &c. *Tignus, assula.*
Cabrituno, perteining to a kid, *Caprinus.*
Cabron, a ram goate, *Caper.*
Cabruno, of a goate, *Caprinus.*
Cacarear, to cackle as a hen, *Cucurire.*
Caça, birding, fowling, hunting, fishing, *Venatio, aucupium, piscatio.*
Caçar, to hunt, to hauke, to fish, to fowle, *Venari, aucupare, piscari.*
Caçador, a hunter, hauker, fisher, or fowler, *Venator, auceps, piscator.*
Caçadora cosa, perteining to hunting, hawking, fishing, or fowling, *Venaticus aucupatorius, piscatorius.*
Cacique, a prince of the Indians, *Rex apud Indos.*
Caço de hierro, a fleshooke, also a pipkin, *Creagra, olla.*
Caçon, a fish of whose skin water glue is made, *Icthiocolla.*
Caçolilla, a little skillet, *Ollula.*
Caçuela, a pipkin, *Ollula.*
Caçorro, couetous, *Parcus, auarus.*
Cacher en pedaços, to cleaue in pœces, *Diffindere.*
Cachete, a flicke in the cheeke, a whirret, *Alapa.*
Cachetado, he that hath a flicke, he that hath a whirret, *Alapa, percussus.*
Cachorro, a whelpe, *Catulus.*
Cacho, a crust, a pœce, a lumpe, *Frustum.*
Cachonda perra, a bitch swelping, *Catuliens.*
Cadañero, of euery yeere, *Annuus.*
Cada, dos, tres, o quatro, años, euery second, euery third, euery fourth yeere,

C A

Secundus, tertius, quartus quisque annus.
Cada dia, euery day, *singulis diebus, quotidie.*
Cada dos y cada tres dias, euery second or third day, *Secundus, tertius quisque dies.*
Cada qual, euery one, *Singuli, vnusquisque, quilibet.*
Cada uno, euery one, *Vnusquisque.*
Cada bueno, euery good man, *Optimus quisque.*
Cada ruyn, euery bad man, *Pessimus quisq̃.*
Cadahalso, a scaffold whereon execution is done, *Suggestum.*
Cadera de muger, the hips, *Coxendix,* Silla de caderas, a chaire with a backe, *Cathedra.*
Caduco, weake, *Caducus*
Caer, caygo, caes, to fall, *Cadere, ruere.*
Caedizo, ruynouse, falling, *Deciduus, ruinosus.*
Cafila, a knot of knaues, a packe of knaues, *Coniurasio.*
Cagar, to empt the belly, *Cacare.*
Cagajon o cagado, the dung of a man, *Stercus, merda.*
Cagarruto, sheeps dung, or goats dung, *Stercus ouillum, siue caprinum.*
Cayado, o cayada, a shephearbs staffe, *Pedum.*
Cayda, a fall, *Ruina, casus.*
Cayda, cruxia, a kinde of crane, *Grus.*
Caymiento, falling, *Casus, ruina.*
Cayman, a crocodile, *Crocodilus.*
Cal, lime, *Calx.*
Cala, a glister, a suppositorie, a surgians searching toole, a search, *Pessum, balanus, specillum, scrutinium.*
Calabaça, a gourd, a bottle of a gourd, *Cucurbita.*
Calaboço de hierro, an iron toole, *Runcina lignatoria.*
Calaboço, a kinde of prison, or place of execution, where condemned persons were cast downe headlong, *Scalæ gemoniæ.* (*tari.*
Calar, to search, to pierce, *Penetrare, scrutari.*
Calador, a searching toole, *Specillum.*
Calafetear naos, to calke ships, *Senoilli-nire.*

Calamar,

C A

Calamar, a cuttle, *Lolligo*.
Calambre, stiffnesse of the sinewes, the crampe, *Neruorum rigor, spasmus*.
Calamenta, wilde peniriall, cats mint, *Calamintha*.
Calamon, a kinde of bird, *Porphyrio*.
Calándria, a thrush, *Turdus*.
Calauerna, a skull, *Cranium*.
Calcañar, the heele, *Calx pedis*.
Calcar y recalcar, to tread vnder the feet, to kicke, to stuffe, *Calcare, recalcare, farcire, refarcire*.
Calçado, hosed, *Caligatus*. Calçado de botas, booted, *Ocreatus*.
Calçado de alcorques, in pantoples, *Crepidatus*. Calçado de chinelas, he that weareth soles of wood, *Soleatus*.
Calçado de guantes, gloued, *Manicatus*.
Calçado de çapatos, shod, *Calceatus*.
Calças, hose, *Caligæ*.
Calçada, a causeway, *Via strata*.
Calcetas, linnen nether stocks, *Caligæ linteæ, tibialia lintea*.
Calzar, to shoo, *Calceare*, to trig a wheele, *Sufflaminare*.
Calcetero, a hoser, *Sartor caligarius*.
Calçon, breeches, *Braccha*.
Caldera, a kettle, *Ahenum*.
Calderon, a caldron, *Cacabus*.
Calderero, a brasier, *Faber ærarius*.
Caldereria, a brasiers shop, *Officina æraria*.
Calderilla, a little kettle, *Ahenulum*.
Calderuela, *idem*.
Caldo, broth, *Iusculum, ius*.
Calendario, a calender, a roll, a catalog, *Calendarium*.
Calentarse, caliento, to warme himselfe, *Calere, calefcere*.
Calentamiento, warming, *Calefactio*.
Calentar, caliento, to warme, to heat, *Calefacere*.
Calentador de cama, a warming panne, *Calfactorium*.
Calentura, heat, *Æstus*, an ague, *Febris*.
Calenturoso, sicke of an ague, *Febricitans*.
Calera, a lime kill, *Calcaria*.
Calero, a lime maker, *Calcarius*.
Caleta, a suppositorie, a little creeke in the sea, *Balanus, Sinus*.

C A

Calidad, qualitie, *Qualitas*.
Caliente, warme, warming, *Calens, calidus*.
Calilla, a suppositorie, a creeke in the sea, *Balanus, Sinus*.
Calma, a calme, *Tranquillitas*.
Caloftre, the ill milke that is drawen out of a womans brest, *Colostrum : lac*.
Calongia, a canonship, *Canonicatus*.
Calor, heat, *Calor, æstus*.
Calura, heat, *Calor, æstus*.
Caluroso, hot, heating, *Calidus, æstuosus*.
Caluña, a cauill, *Calumnia*.
Caluñador, a cauiller, *Calumniator*.
Caluñar, to cauill, *Calumniari*.
Calua, baldnesse, *Caluities*.
Caluez, baldnesse, *Caluities*.
Caluo, balde, *Caluus*.
Callar, to holde ones peace, *Tacere*.
Callado, kept secret, *Tacitus, secret, Taciturnus*.
Calandico, quiet, soft and faire, *Sensim, pedetentim*.
Calle, y calleja, a path, a way, a street, *Callis, semita*.
Callo, brawne, the thicke skinne of the hand, *Callum*.
Calloso, thicke skinne, hard fleshed, *Callosus*.
Callescer, to waxe hard skind, *Callescere*.
Cama, a bed, a bedsted, *Lectus, torus*, also a cockle fish, *Hiatula*.
Cama de arado, the furrow, *Sulcus*.
Camara, a chamber, a close stoole, a purgation, the laske, the ordure, *Cubiculum, alui excrementum, ventris profluuium, merda*.
Camaranchon, a rude chamber vndrest, *Cubiculum male compositum*.
Camarero, a chamberlaine, *Cubicularius*.
Camaron, a lopster, *Gammarus*.
Cambiar, to change, *Commutare*.
Cambio, exchange, change, *Commutatio*.
Cambiador, an exchanger, *Permutator*.
Cambronera mata, brambles, *Ramnus*.
Camedreos, germander, *Quercula minor, chamædris*.
Camelo, a camell, *Camelus*.
Camelero,

Camelero, a camell keeper, *Camelarius.*
Cameleria, the office of a camell keeper, *Camelaria.*
Camiça, a shirt, a smocke, *Camisia, indusiū.*
Camiçada, an assault, *Inuasio.*
Caminar, to go a iourney, *Iter facere.*
Caminador, a traueller, *Viator.*
Camino, a way, a path, *Via, iter, semita.*
Camino de sanctiago en el cielo, *Lactea via.*
Camodar, to sell, to set to sale, *Vendere, venum exponere.*
Campana, a bell, *Campana.*
Campanaria, a tower of belles, *Turris campanaria.*
Campanilla yerva, withie winde, *Smilax.*
Campanero, he that ringeth belles, *Campanarum pulsator.*
Campear, to pitch a campe, *Castra metari.*
Campo, a field, *Campus.*
Campesino, of the field, *Campestris, agrestis.*
Campero, he that keepeth the field, *Campariūs.*
Campestre, rude, of the field, *Campestris.*
Camueça, a kinde of peppin, *Malorum genus.*
Can, a dogge, *Canis.*
Can sobre que cargan vigas, the post in a house that we call the somer, *Atlas.*
Canal, a gutter, *Canalis, imbrex.*
Canalado, chamfured, *Imbricatus.*
Cano, hoare headed, *Canus.*
Canas, hoar haires, *Cani orum.*
Canasta, a great maund or basket, *Cophinus.*
Canastilla, a little basket, *Qualus.*
Cancer, the constellation cancer, *Cancer.*
Cancion, a song, *Cantus, cantio.*
Cancionero, a song booke, *Cantionum liber.*
Candádo, a bolt, a button, *Pessulum, fibula.*
Candéda, the flowre of chestnuts, *Iulus.*
Candéla, a candle, *Candela.*
Candelero, a candlesticke, *Candelabrum.*
Candial trigo, faire red wheat, *Triticum subrubeum.*
Candioca, a vessell of Crꝫt, *Cadus cretensis.*
Candil, a lampe, a candle, *Candela, lampas, lucerna.*

Candilejos de Iudios, new lamps of the Iewes, *Lucernæ.*
Canéla, cinamom, *Cinamomum.*
Canez, baldnesse, *Canicies.*
Cangilon vaso de barro, an earthen vessel to carry water, *Congius.*
Cangrejo, a crab or creuish, *Cancer.*
Canilla de braço, the boane of the arme, *Vlna.*
Canina, dogges durt, *Stercus caninum.*
Canoa, the boats of the Indians, *Cymba apud Indos.*
Canon, a rule, *Norma, canon.*
Canonista, a canonist, *Canonistes.*
Canonigo, a canon, *Canonicus.*
Canonizar, to canonise, *In diuorum numerum referre.*
Canonizado, canonised, *In diuorum numerum relatus.*
Canonizacion, canonising, *Relatio in diuorum numerum.*
Cansar, to weary, *Fatigare.*
Cansado, weried, *Defessus.*
Cansancio, wearinesse, *Lassitudo.*
Cántaro, a pitcher, *Cantharus.*
Cantar, to sing as a bird, *Cantare, canere vt quæuis auis.*
Canteria, a quarrie, *Lapidicina.*
Cantero, he that diggeth stones, a mason, *Latomus.* (*excussor.*
Cantero de escoda, a free mason, *Lapicida.*
Cantidad, quantity, *Quantitas.*
Canto, a stone, *Lapis, saxum,* depth, *Profunditas,* thicknesse, *Crassities,* the side, *Latus,* a song, *Cantus,* the singing of birds, *Clangor vel garritus auium.*
Canton, the corner of a street, *Angulus.*
Cantor, a singer, *Cantor.*
Cantonada dar, to giue the slippe at a corner of a street, *In vici angulo se subducere alicui.*
Cantonera puta, a common strumpet, *Triuiale scortum.*
Cantuesso, stechado, *Stechados.*
Cantusar, to deceiue, *Fallere.*
Caña, a cane, *Calamus, arundo.*
Caña fistola, an apothicarie drugge, *Casia fistula.*

Cañada,

Cañada, a way to driue sheepe, *Actus pecudum.*
Cañaheja, ferula, alfo hemlocke, *Cycuta.*
Cañarroya, pellitorie of the wall, *Perdicium, parietaria.*
Cañal de pefcador, an angle rod, *Arundo pifcatoria.*
Cañama, fubfidie men, *Claßis tributariorum*
Cañamo, hempe, *Cannabis.*
Cañamon, hempe feed, *Semen cannabinum.*
Cañamazo, cloth of hempe feede, *Linteum cannabinum.*
Cañaveral de Cañas, a plot of ground fet with reedes or canes, *Arundinetum.*
Cañilla de braço, the bone of the arme, *Vlna.*
Canilla de cuba o tinaja, the faufet wherein they put the fpigot, *Canalicula.*
Caño o Albañar, a finke or kennell, *Cloaca, canalis.*
Cañon, a quill, *Calamus, caulis pennæ.*
Cañuto, a reed to make a pipe, *Calamus.*
Cañutillos, the fpace betweene knots in a cane, *Internodia.*
Canzel, a portall, *Porticus, portula.*
Capacete, a helmet, *Galea.*
Capacho, a bird that fingeth in the night *Cucuma.*
Capacho de molino, the hopper of the mill, the fraile whereinto they put oliues to be preffed, *Fifcus, fifcina.*
Capacho, a maund or great bafket, *Fifcus*
Capar, to geld, *Caftrare.*
Capado, gelded, *Caftratus, ennuchus.*
Capadura, gelding, *Caftratio.*
Caparrofa, Copperefle, *Chalcanthum.*
Capear, to take away the cloke, to waue with the cloke, *Pallio exuere, fignum pallio dare.*
Capelo de Cardinal, a Cardinals hat, *Galerus.*
Capellan, a prieft, a chaplaine, *Sacerdos.*
Capilla, a chappell, the cape of a cloke, *Sacellum, cucullus.*
Capillejo de muger, a caule, *Capillitium.*
Capirote, a haukes hood, *Capitium.*
Capirotada de ajos y quefo, a cheefe cake, *Moretum.*

Capifcol, a chanter in the quier, *Mefochocapitan, a captaine, Dux.* (*rius.*
Capitanía, a captainfhip, *Centurionatus.*
Capitanear, to be a captaine, *Ducere exercitum vel milites.*
Capitel de coluna, the head of a pfller, *Capitellum.*
Capitulo, a chapter, a chapter houfe, *Caput, capitulum.*
Capon, a capon, a filip, *Capo, talitrum.*
Caponera, a coope for capons, *Caponarium.*
Capote veftido ruftico, a cloke, *Capitium.*
Capulla de la feda, the ball that a filke worme maketh, *Bombylis, inuolucrum bombycinum.*
Capullo de miembro viril, the forefkin of the yard, *Præputium.*
Capuz, a mourning hood, *Cucullus funebris.*
Cara, the face, the countenance, *Vultus, facies.*
Cara a cara, face to face, *Coram.*
Carabo, a kind of barke or boate, *Nauigij genus.*
Caracol, a fnaile, a cockle, a paire of winding ftaiers, *Limax, teftudo, cochlea.*
Carámbano de yelo, a great flake of ice, *Gelicidium.*
Caramillo, brabbles, *Rixæ.*
Carater, a figure, *Caracter.*
Caratula carantoña, a bifarde, a mafke, *perfona, larua.*
Caratulado, bifarded, *Perfonatus, laruatus.*
Caravela, a carauell, *Nauigij genus.*
Caravo, *Nauigij genus.*
Carbon, carvon, a cole, *Carbo.*
Carboncol, a carbunkle ftone, *Carbunculus*
Carcax o liniavera, a quiuer, *Pharetra.*
Carcajada de rifa, extreame laughter, *Cachinnus.*
Carcajadas dar, to laugh extreamly, *Cachinnari.*
Carcavo del vientre, the panch, the bottome of the belly, *Barathrum.*
Carcava de muerto, a tombe, a pit, *Buftum.*
Carcavera puta, a ftrumpet bfing in church yards, *Bufluaria meretrix.*
Carcoma de madera, the woorme in timber, *Caries.*

Carcomido,

C A   C A

Carcomido, wormie eaten, *Cariofus*.
Cárcel, a prison, *Carcer*.
Carcelero, a Iailor, *Carceris custos*.
Carcelage, fees of the prison, *Stips carcellaria*.
Cardas, cards to card with, *Carptoria*.
Cardar, to card, *Carminare, carpere*.
Cardador, a carder, *Carminator*.
Cardadura, carding, *Carminatio*.
Cardenillo que se haze de cobre, the rust of copper, *Erugo*.
Cardeno, blacke and blew colour much like old brasse, *Luridus, liuidus*.
Cardenillo color, cardeno, somwhat blew, *Subliuidus*.
Cardenal de golpe, the blew wale of a stripe, *Vibex*.
Cardenal de ojo, the blacknes vnder the eie, *Suggillatio*.
Cardenal, a cardinall, *Cardinalis*.
Cardenaladgo, cardinalship, *Cardinalatus*.
Cardencha, a teasell, *Cardo fullonum*.
Cardo corredor, sea holly, *Eryngium*.
Cardo, a thistle, *Carduus*.
Cardohuso, wilde bastard saffron, wilde holy thistle, *Atractylis*.
Cardusar, to card, *Carminare*.
Carena, the keele of a ship, *Carina*.
Carescer, to want, *Carere*.
Carestia, careza, dearth, scantnes, *Caritas*.
Cargo, a burden, a waight, a charge, *Onus*
Cargado, charged, burdened, *Oneratus, onustus*.
Cargar, to burden, to charge, *Onerare*.
Caricia, making much of, *Indulgentia*.
Caridad, loue, charitie, pity, almes, *Charitas, amor, eleemosyna*.
Caritativo, charitable, pitifull, *Misericors*.
Cariluengo, long faced, *Qui facie est oblonga*.
Carlina, a kind of herbe, *Chamæleon*.
Carmel, a kind of herbe, *Lychnites*.
Carmenar, to picke wooll, to tease wooll, *Carminare*.
Carmenador, a teasor, *Carminator*.
Carmenadura, teasing, *Carminatio*.
Carmesi, crimsen, *Murex*.
Carnacha, a carcase, *Cadauer*.

Carnaval o carnestollendas, Shrouetide, *Carnispriuium*.
Carnal, carnall, fleshly, *Carnalis, carneus*.
Carnalidad, carnalitie, fleshlines, *Carnalitas*.
Carne, en carnes, flesh, naked, *Caro, nudus*.
Carnero, mutton, a weather, *Caro veruecina, veruex*.
Carne de membrillo, the meat of a quince also marmalade, *Cidoniatum*.
Carnicero, a butcher, a hangman, *Carnifex, lanius*.
Carniceria, a slaughter, a place of torment, *Strages, carnificina*.
Carniceria, the shambles, *Carnificina, Macellum*.
Carnicol, the pasterne bone, *Talus*.
Carnosidad, fleshlines, *Carnositas*.
Carnoso, carnudo, fleshie, full of flesh, *Carosus*.
Caro, deere, *Charus*.
Carpa, a carpe, *Carpa*.
Carpe, a tree so called, *Carpinus*.
Carpintero, a carpenter, *Faber lignarius*.
Carpinteria, a carpenters craft, *Ars lignaria, fabri lignarij ars*.
Carpintear, to play the carpenter, *Dolare*.
Carraca, a carike, *Genus nauigij*.
Carrança, the nails in a dogs coller, *Murex milli*.
Carrasco, a kind of holme, *Ilex*.
Carascal, a groue of holmes, *Ilicetum*.
Carrera, a carrere, a course, a race for horses to run, *Cursus, fuga*.
Carreta, a cart, *Plaustrum*.
Carreton, a little cart, *Plostellum*.
Carretada, a cart lode, *Plaustri vectura*.
Carretero, a carter, *Plaustrarius*.
Carril de carreta, a cart wheele, *Orbita plaustri*.
Carrillo como rodaja, a pulley, *Vertebra*.
Carrillo, the cheeke, *Bucca*.
Carrillado, swolen cheeked, *Qui buccas tumidas habet*.
Carrizo, sedge, *Carex*.
Carrizal, the place where sedge groweth, *Carectum*.
Carro, a cart, a charret, a wagon, *Carrus, currus, petoritum*.

Carro,

C A

Carro con andas, a hoꝛſlitter, *Rheda.*
Carrucha, a carroch, a coche, *Currus.*
Carta, a letter, *Charta, litere.*
Carta de pago, an acquittance, *Apocha.*
Cartilla, an abcee to teach childꝛen, *Abecedarium.*
Cartamo, baſtard ſaffron, *Cnicum.*
Cartapacio, a noting booke, a noting paper, *Libells exceptorij.*
Cártel ſe deſaſío, letters of defiance, *Literæ prouocatoriæ.*
Cartabon de Carpintero, a Carpenters ſquire, *Gnomon.*
Caruage, cariage, *Onus, vectura.*
Carvon, a cole, *Carbo.*
Carvoncol, *vide* Carboncol.
Carvonero, a collier, *Carbonarius.*
Caſa, a houſe, the familie, *Domus, ædes, familia.*
Caſar, a place where a houſe ſtood, *Tofium.*
Caſar, to marrie, *Vxorem ducere, nubere.*
Caſado, married, *Maritus, coniux.*
Caſadera moça, marriageable, *Nubilis.*
Caſamiento, marriage, the dower, *Nuptiædos.*
Caſamentero, a marriage maker, *Conciliator matrimonij.*
Caſcajo, grauell and ſtone, *Glarea, calculus, arenula.*
Caſcajal, a grauell pit, *Locus glareoſus.*
Caſcar, to ſhake, to bꝛeake, *Quaſere, quaſſare, frangere.*
Caſca truegas, a truce bꝛeaker, *Fœdifragus.*
Caſcabel, a little bell, a rattle, *Tintinnabulum.*
Caſcabellillo, *Diminut. à* Caſcabel.
Cáſcara, a ſhell, a caſe, the parings, *Cruſta, teſta, putamina.*
Caſco, the ſherds of an earthen pot, the ſkull, *Teſta, cranium.*
Caſero, muger caſera, pertaining to the houſe, a woman that keepeth home, *Domeſticus, domeſtica.*
Caſero, a ſoiourner, *Hoſpes, inquilinus.*
Cáſi, as though, almoſt, about, *Quaſi, propè, circiter.*
Caſia, the fruit Caſſia, *Caſia.*
Caſilla pagiza, a little cottage, *Tugurium.*

C A

Caſo, chance, foꝛtune, lucke, a caſe of law, *Caſus, fortuna ſors.*
Caſpa de cabeça, Dandꝛo, *Furfures capitis.*
Caſpoſo, full of dandꝛo, *Furfuroſus.*
Caſquete, a head peece, *Caſſis.*
Caſquillo de ſaeta, an arrow head, *Aculeus.*
Caſſacion, cancelling, diſanulling, *Antiquatio.*
Caſſar, to ſtrike out, to cancell, to diſanull, *Cancellare, antiquare, expungere.*
Caſſador, he that cancelleth, *Cancellator, antiquator.*
Caſta, a race, a linage, a bꝛeed, *Genus.*
Caſto, chaſt, *Caſtus.*
Caſtamente, chaſtly, *Caſtè.*
Caſtaña, a cheſtnut, a cheſtnut tree, *Caſtanea.*
Caſtañal, a groue of cheſtnut trees, *Caſtanetum.*
Caſtañuclas, the cracking of the fingers, *Digitorum crepitus.*
Caſtidad, chaſtitie, *Caſtitas.*
Caſtigar, to chaſtiſe, to chide, to coꝛrect, *Caſtigare, corrigere, iurgare.*
Caſtigador, a chaſtiſer, a coꝛrectoꝛ, *Caſtigator, obiurgator, correctòr.*
Caſtigo, chaſtiſement, coꝛrection, puniſhment, *Animaduerſio, correctio.*
Caſtillo, a caſtell, *Caſtellum.*
Caſtillejo juego de niños, a rattle, *Crepitaculum.*
Caſtiza, of a good race, *Boni generis.*
Caſtor, a bꝛocke, a badger, *Caſtor, fiber.*
Caſtrar, to geld, *Caſtrare.*
Caſtradura, gelding, *Caſtratio.*
Caſtrazon, time to gelde, time to make honie, *Tempus caſtrationi operiunum, mellatio.*
Canſtradera, the cutting, oꝛ gelding knife *Caſtratorium inſtrumentum.*
Caſtrado, gelded, *Caſtratus.*
Caſulla, a cope foꝛ a prieſt, *Læna.*
Cataſol, a daiſic, *Cellis.*
Catarraña ave, a ſheldꝛake, *Catarracta.*
Catarata de ojos, the cataract in the eie, *Cataracta oculorum.*
Catarro, rheume, *Catarrhus, rheuma.*

F   Cativerio,

C A

Cativério, **captiuitie**, *Captiuitas.*
Cativo, a captiue, a wretch, *Captiuus, miser.*
Católico, catholicke, *Catholicus.*
Cátreda, a chaire, *Cathedra.*
Catredatico, a graduate, a reader in schooles, *Cathedrarius.*
Catredal, perteining to the chaire, *Ad cathedram pertinens.*
Cativar, to take prisoner, *Captiuare.*
Catividad, captiuitie, *Captiuitas.*
Catorze, fourteene, *Quatuordecim.*
Catorze vezes, fourteene times, *Decies & quater.*
Catorzeno, the fourteenth, *Decimus quartus.*
Catorze tanto, fourteene times asmuch, *Decies & quater tantum.*
Caucion, a caution, *Cautio.*
Caudal, a mans stocke, the maine, a principall matter, *Res familiaris, fors, res capitalis.*
Caudillo, a captaine, *Dux.*
Causa, a cause, *Causa.*
Causar, to giue a cause, to excuse, *Causari, causam dicere, excusare.*
Causador, an excuser, *Causator, excusator.*
Causon, a burning feuer, *Febris continua.*
Cautela, a sleight, a subteltie, *Astutia.*
Cauteloso, wilie, suttle, *Astutus.*
Cautelosamente, wililie, suttelly, *Astutè.*
Cauterio, searing or a marke with a hot yron, *Cauterium.*
Cauterizado, seared, or marked with a hot yron, or cauterised, *Cauterio notatus.*
Cava, the ditch or trench of a fort, *Fossa.*
Cavadiza cosa, a hollow place, *Fossilis.*
Cavadura, digging, *Fossura.*
Cavador, a digger, *Cauator.*
Cavar, to dig, *Fodere, cauare.*
Cavallería, horsemen in war, *Equitatus.*
Cavallero, a horseman, a gentleman, *Eques, Generosus.*
Cavallete de tejada, the ridge of a house, *Cacumen, culmen domus.*
Cavallería, gentilitie, *Generositas.*
Cavalgadura, riding, *Equitatio.*
Cavalgar, to ride, to get on horsebacke,

C A

Equitare, conscendere equum.
Cavallo, a horse, *Equus.*
Cavallo emparamentado, a horse saddled, *Equus ephippiatus.*
Cavallo de brida, a great horse, *Equus desultorius.*
Cavallar, perteining to a horse, *Equinus.*
Cavallejo, a nag, *Mannus.*
Cavalleriza, a stable, *Stabulum.*
Cavallerizo, a horseman, a horsekeeper, *Equorum curator.*
Cavallero de espuelas doradas, a knight of the order, *Eques auratus.* (Porca.
Cavallillo, the ridge betweene furrowes,
Cavallillo entre era y era, the banke betweene the quarters in a garden, *Forus.*
Cavazon, digging, *Cauatio, fossio, pastinatio.*
Caverna, a caue, *Cauerna.*
Cavernoso, full of caues, *Cauernosus.*
Cavilacion, cauelling, wrangling, *Calumniatio.* (lumniosus.
Caviloso, full of cauils, a wrangler, *Ca-*
Cavilar, to cauill, to wrangle, *Calumniari.*
Caxa, a chest, a deske, a little cupboorde, a pennard, a sheath, the stock of a gun, *Arca, capsa, scrinium, theca pennaria.*
Caxcar, *vide* Cascar.
Caxcabel, caxcara, caxquillo, caxquete, *vide* Cascabel.
Caxero, a pedler, *Circumforaneus mercator.*
Caxon de arca, the till of a chest, *Loculus.*
Cazcarias, tanglings about thicking feete, *Tricæ.*

C L

Clamor, a crie, *Clamor.*
Clamoroso, clamorous, *Clamosus.*
Clara de huevo, the white of an egge, *Albugo oui.*
Claro, light, cleere, plaine, easie to be perceiued, *Lucidus, clarus, conspicuus, euidens.*
Clarificar, to clarifie, to make cleere, *Clarificare.*
Clarecer, to waxe cleere, *Clarescere.*
Claridad, cleerenes, plainnes, *Claritas, perspicuitas.*
Claramente, cleerely, plainely, euidently, *Clarè, conspicuè, euidenter.*

Clares,

C O

Clarea, claric, drinke of hony and wine *Mulsum.*
Clarion, a kinde of musicall instrument, *Instrumentum musicum.*
Clavar, to naile, *Clauum figere.*
Clavadura, nailing, *Claui fixura.*
Clavazon, the setting of nailes, *Clauamentum.*
Clavija, the key of virginals, the pin of a lute, *Clauicula.*
Clavicordios, virginals, *Clauecymbalum.*
Clavo, a nayle, *Clauus.*
Clavo de governalle, the rudder, *Clauus, temo.*
Clave, the stone on the top of a vault, *In summa fornice lapis prominens.*
Clavo, the spice called cloues, *Garyophilli.*
Clavo de gerofle, *idem.*
Clavellinas, gilliflowers, *Gariophilatus.*
Clavero, a key bearer, *Clauiger.*
Clematide, perwincle, *Clematis.*
Clemencia, gentlenes, *Clementia.*
Clemente, gentle, *Clemens.*
Clementemente, gently, *Clementer.*
Clerigo, a priest, *Clericus, sacerdos.*
Clerezia, the clergie, a conuocation, *Clerus.*
Cloque, garfio de nave, a hooke of a ship, *Harpago.* (*citare.*
Cloquear, to clocke as the hen doth, *Glocitare.*
Clueca gallina, a clocke hen, *Glocitans gallina, vel incumbans.*
Cluquillas, cowring downe, *Cossim sedere.*

C O

Cobarde, a coward, *Ignauus, iners, pusillanimis.*
Coberdia, cowardlines, *Ignauia, pusillanimitas.* (*lecti.*
Cobertor de cama, a couerlet, *Stragulum*
Cobertor, a couer, *Opertorium, operimentum.*
Cobertura, a couering, *Tegmen.*
Cobertera, a couer, *operimentum.*
Cobijar, to couer, *Operire, tegere.*
Cobrar, to recouer, *Recipere, recuperare.*
Cobre, copper, *AEs cyprium.*
Cobre de cebollas, a rope of onions, *Restis*
Cobre de bestias, a houell, *Mandra.*

C O

Cobrir, cubro, to couer, *Tegere.*
Cobro, receite, recouery, a place of safe keeping, *Receptus, recuperatio, receptaculum.*
Cocadriz, a cocatrice, *Basiliscus.*
Cocar, to gape at, to mocke, *Subsannare.*
Coce, a kicke, *Calcis ictus.*
Cocear, to kicke, *Calcare.*
Coceador, a kicker, *Calcator.*
Cochino, a sucking pig, *Porcellus.*
Cocho, sod, *Coctus.*
Coche, a coache, *Carpentum, vehiculum.*
Cochinillas, cuchinilla, *Musca infectoria.*
Cocle, grapple, *Harpago, Manus ferrea.*
Coco, a worme that eateth vines, a weeuell, *Gurgulio.*
Cocuyo, a glow worme, *Noctiluca.*
Codal, of a cubite, a grin, *Cubitalis, Decipule genus.*
Codales de carpintero, a measure of a cubite, *Mensura cubitalis.*
Codada, a blow with the elbow, *Ictus cubiti.*
Codear, to strike with the elbowe, *Cubito ferire.*
Codera, a scab on the elbowe, *Cubiti scabies.*
Codiciar, to couet, *Cupere, concupiscere, optare.*
Codicia, couetousnes, *Cupiditas, auaritia.*
Codicioso, couetousnes, *Auarus.*
Codicillo de testamento, a codicill, *Codicillum.*
Codo, an elbow, a cubite, *Cubitus.*
Codorniz, a quaile, *Coturnix.*
Cofia, a coife, a caule, *Reticulum.*
Cofin, a basket, *Cophinus, fiscus.*
Cofrade, a brother, *Confrater.*
Cofradia, a brotherhood, *Confraternitas.*
Cofre, a coffer, *Scrinium, capsa, arca.*
Coger, jo, to gather, to plucke vp, to take vp, *Colligere, discerpere, exigere.*
Cogedor, a gatherer, *Collector, exactor.*
Cogedizo, gathered, *Collectiuus.*
Cogollo, a hoode, a bud of a tree, *Cucullus, germen.*
Cogolmado, heaped vp, *Accumulatus.*
Cogollado, hooded, *Cucullatus.*

F 2　　　Cogote,

Cogote, the pole of the head, *Occiput.*
Cogujada, a larke, *Cassita.*
Cogombrillo, o cohombrillo, a cucumber, *Cucumis.*
Cohechar, to plowe grounde, to take bribes, to gather goods togither, *Arare, munera capere, opes corradere.*
Cahechazon, plowing, *Aratio.*
Cohecho de juez, bribes, *Repetunda.*
Cohollicos, smal colewortes, *Cauliculæ.*
Cohombrillo y cogombrillo, a cucumber, *Cucumis.*
Cohombro, a cucumber, *Cucumis.*
Cohombral, a bed of cucumbers, *Cucumerarium.*
Cohonder, to confound, to corrupt, *Confundere, corrumpere.*
Cohondimiento, confounding, *Confusio.*
Coyunda de yugo, the bowe of a yoke, *Iugum.*
Coyuntura, ioining, meeting, opportunitie, *Oportunitas, iunctura.*
Cojon, the stones or collions, *Coleus, testis.*
Cojudo, he that hath great collions, *Coleatus.*
Cola, a taile, pitch, glue, *Cauda, pix, gluten.*
Cola de cavallo, shauegrasse, horsetayle, *Equisetum.*
Col, *vide* Berça.
Cola, *vide* Caçon.
Colacion, a collacion, *Symposium.*
Colar beneficio, to bestowe a benefit, *Conferre, beneficium.*
Colar, to streine, *Colare.*
Coladero, a strainer, a colender, *Colum.*
Colar paños, to whiten clothes, to wash in bucke, *Lixiuio lauare.*
Colada de paños, whiting of clothes, a bucke of clothes, *Lixiuiarium.*
Colambre, a dicker of leather, *Decenarium coriorum.*
Colateral, collaterall, *Collateralis.*
Colcedra de plumas, a fetherbed, *Plumacium, culcitra.*
Colcha de cama, a quilt, *Stragulum.*
Colchon, colcedra de cama, a fetherbed, *Culcitra plumea.* (*tare.*
Colear, to wagge the taile, *Caudam moti-*

Colera, choler, *Bilis.*
Colérico, cholerike, *Biliosus.*
Colegio, a collegde, *Collegium.*
Colegial, perteining to a college, *Collegialis.*
Coleta, the haire rounded, *Coma.*
Coleto, a shirt band, a leather ierkin, *Collare, indusij limbus ad collum, & tunicula coriacea.*
Colgajo de uvas, a bunch of grapes, *Vua pensiles.*
Colgajo y colgadizo, that which hangeth, *Pendulus.*
Colgadura, hanging, *Appensio, suspensio, suspendium.*
Colgadizo, that which hangeth, *Pendulus.*
Colgado, hanged, *Suspensus, appensus.*
Colgar, cuelgo, to hang, *Pendere.*
Colica passion, the collike, *Colica passio.*
Colico, he that hath the collike, *Colicus.*
Colino, a cabbage, *Coliculi.*
Collaço, he that sucketh the same milke, *Collactaneus.*
Collacion, a banket, *Symposium,* a ward in a citie, *Regio, tribus.*
Collado, a ridge of an hill, *Collis.*
Collar de vestido, the coller of a garment, *Collare.*
Collar, a cheine, a coller, a skarfe, *Collare, torques.*
Colmar, to heape up, *Cumulare.*
Colmadura, heaping up, *Cumulatio.*
Colmo, the heape, *Cumulus.*
Colmena, a hiue, *Alueus, alnear.*
Colmenar, a place for bee hiues, *Apiarium.*
Colmenero, he that keepeth bees, *Apiarius.*
Colmillo, a tuske, *Dens columellaris, fulmen.*
Colodrillo, the poll of the head, *Occipitium.*
Colodra, a horne to drench beasts, *Cornu veterinarium.*
Coloquintida, colloquintida, *Colocynthis.*
Color, colour, *Color.*
Colorado, coloured, red, *Coloratus, rubeus.*
Columpiar, to swing in a halter, *Pendulum se fune agitare, & ciere.*
Columpio, swinging in a halter, *Agitatio huiusmodi.*

Coluna,

C O

Coluna, a pillar, *Columna.*
Colufion, collufion, *Collufio.*
Comadre, a goffip, *Commater.*
Comadreja, a weazell, *Muſtela,*
Comarca, the borders, *Confinium.*
Comarcano, bordering, *Confinis.*
Comba, a kinde of ſcope to caſt water, *Hauſtrum.*
Combatir, to fight, *Pugnare.*
Combate, a combate, a battell, an aſſault, *Pugna, Prælium, Innaſio.*
Combatible, aſſaultable, *Oppugnabile.*
Combidar, to inuite, to bid to a feaſt, *Inuitare.*
Combidado, bidden, inuited, a gueſt, *Inuitatus, hoſpes.*
Combite, a banket, *Conuiuium.*
Combleça de caſada, a concubine, *Concubina, pellex.*
Combleço, a riuall, *Riualis.*
Comedir, comido, to premeditate, *Præmeditari.*
Comedio, put in arbitrement, *Arbitrarius,* ſet in the midſt, *In medio poſitus,* in the meane while, *Interim.*
Comedido, premeditated, *Præmeditatus,* diſcreet, *Diſcretus,* manerly, *Vrbanus.*
Comedimiento, premeditation, diſcretion, *Diſcretio,* good maners, behauiour, *Præmeditatio, morum ciuilitas, vrbanitas.*
Comedor, a great eater, *Edax.*
Comedera coſa, any thing to be eaten, *Edulis.*
Comer, to eat, *Comedere,* to dine, *Prandere.*
Començar, mienço, to beginne, *Incipere.*
Comendar, to commend, *Commendare.*
Comendador, a lieutenant, *Cōmendatarius.*
Comenſal, a fellow gueſt, *Contubernalis.*
Cometa, a comet, a blazing ſtarre, *Cometa.*
Cometer, to commit, to ſet vpon, to endeuour, *Committere, Aggredi, inuadere, conari.*
Cometimiento, ſetting vpon, committing, *Aggreſſio, commiſſio.*
Cometidor, a committer, *Commiſſor.*
Comezon, the itch, a tetter, *Prurigo.*
Comida, meat, dinner, alſo a drinking betore mealcs, *Eſca, cibus, prandium, compotatio.*
Comienço, a beginning, *Principium.*
Comigo, with me, *Mecum.*
Comilon, *vide* Comedor,
Comino, cumin, *Cuminum.*
Comiſſario, a commiſſioner, *Commiſſionarius.*
Comiſſion, a commiſſion, *Commiſſio.*
Comiſſura, ioyning together, *Coniunctio.*
Comitre de galera, the maiſters mate. *Comes magiſtri.*
Como, as, ſeeing, that, *Vt, ſicut, cum.*
Comodidad, commodity, *Commoditas.*
Comoquiera, howſoeuer, *Quomodocunque.*
Compadecerſe, to haue com paſſion, *Compati.*
Compadre, a goſſip, *Compater.*
Compadrazgo, goſſipſhip, *Compaternitas.*
Compañero, a fellow, a companion, *Socius, comes.*
Compañas, a multitude, *Multitudo.*
Compañia, fellowſhip, companie, *Societas.*
Compañones, the ſtones or colhons, *Teſticuli.*
Comparar, to compare, *Comparare.*
Compañones de perro, ſtander graſſe, dogge colhons, *Teſticuli canis.*
Comparacion, comparison, *Comparatio.*
Compas, a compaſſe, *Circinus.*
Compaſſar, to meaſure with a compaſſe, *Circuire, circinare.*
Compaſſion, compaſſion, *Compaſſio.*
Compenſar, to recompence, *Compenſare.*
Competer, pito, to be meet for, to agree with, to ſue with, *Competit imperſonale, competere.*
Competidor, a competitor, *Competitor.*
Competicion, ſute for the ſame matter, *Competitio.*
Complazer, to pleaſe, *Placere.*
Compleſſion, complexion, *Complexio.*
Completas, complynes, a piece of popiſh ſeruice, *Precationes nocturnæ.*
Complir, to performe, *Complere, ſupplere.*
Complimiento, performance, *Complementum.*
Componer pongo, to make, *Componere.*

Componedor,

Componedor, a maker, Compositor.
Composicion, making, Compositio.
Compra, buying, Emptio,
Comprador, a buyer, Emptor.
Comprar, to buy, Emere.
Compradizo, bought, Emptitius.
Comprometer, to promise with, Compromittere.
Compromissio, promising, Compromissio.
Compromissor, a suretie, Compromissor, fideyussor.
Compuerta de fortaleza, a portcullesse, Cataracta.
Comulgar, to communicate, to receiue the communion, Communicare.
Comun, common, Communis.
Comunemente, commonly, Communiter, plerumque.
Comunal, common, meane, indifferent well, Communis, mediocris.
Con, with, Cum.
Concejo, councell, Concilium.
Concegil, common, publike, Communis publicus.
Concebimiento, conception, Conceptio.
Concebir, cibo, to conceiue, Concipere.
Concertarse, cierto, to agree, Conuenire, conciliare.
Concertador, a mediator, Conciliator.
Concha, a cockle fish, the shell of a fish, any shell fish, Concha.
Conchilla, idem.
Conciencia, conscience, Conscientia.
Concierto, agreement, Conuentio.
Concilio, a councell, Concilium.
Conciliar, to procure, to winne, Conciliare.
Conciliador, a winner, a procurer, Conciliator.
Concluyr, cluyo, to conclude, Concludere.
Conclusion, an end, a conclusion, Conclusio.
Concordable, agreeable, Concors, consonus.
Concordar, cuerdo, to agree, Conuenire, consonare.
Concórdia, concord, Concordia, consonantia.
Concordemente, agreeingly, Concorditer.
Concorde, agreeing, Concors.

Conde, a countie, an earle, Comes.
Condessa, a countesse, Comitissa.
Condado, an earldome, a countie, Comitatus.
Condestable, a constable, Ethnarches.
Condenar, to condemne, Damnare.
Condenacion, condemning, Damnatio.
Condenado, condemned, Damnatus.
Condicion, condition, qualitie, Conditio, qualitas.
Condicional, conditionall, Conditionalis.
Condicionalmente, conditionally, Conditionaliter.
Conducho, accustomed, Consuetus.
Conduzir, duzgo, to lead, Ducere.
Conduzido, ledde, Ductus.
Concejo, a cunny, Cuniculus.
Conejero, a warrener, Cunicularius venator.
Confederar, to confederate, to make a league, Confœderare.
Confederados, confederate, leaguers, Confœderati.
Conferir, to compare, Conferre, comparare.
Confacionador, a confectioner, Confector.
Confacionadura, confection, Confectio.
Confessar, fiesso, to confesse, Confiteri.
Confession, confession, Confessio.
Confessor, a confessor, Confessor.
Confesso, a conuert to the christian religion, Confessus, prosilyta.
Confiar, to trust, Confidere, fidere, credere.
Confiança, trust, Fiducia, confidentia.
Confiando, boldly, confidently, Confidenter.
Confiador, he that trusteth, Depositor, qui fidem habet.
Confirmar, to confirme, Confirmare.
Confirmacion, confirmation, Confirmatio.
Confirmar en mal, to make obstinate, Obdurare.
Confirmado, confirmed, Confirmatus.
Confiscar, to confiscate, Publicare, confiscare.
Confiscacion, forfeiture, confiscating, Confiscatio, publicatio.
Confites, comfets, iunkets, Bellaria, confecta.

Confitero,

Confitero, a **comfit maker**, *Dulciarius pistor*.
Confitura, **making comfets**, *Confectio*.
Conformar, **to conforme**, *Conformare*.
Conformidad, **likenes, conformitie**, *Conformitas*.
Conformacion, **conforming**, *Conformatio*.
Conforme, **like**, *Conformis*.
Confundir, **to confound**, *Confundere*.
Confusion, **confusion**, *Confusio*.
Confusamente, **confusedly**, *Confuse*.
Confuso, **confused, confounded, astonished**, *Confusus, attonitus*.
Confutar, **to confute**, *Confutare, refutare*.
Congelar, **to congeale**, *Congelare*.
Congelado, **congealed**, *Congelatus*.
Congoxa, **care, anguish**, *Cura, anxietas*.
Congoxoso, **full of care**, *Anxius*.
Congoxosamente, **carefully**, *Anxie*.
Congoxar a otro, **to vexe, to trouble**, *Angere*.
Congrio, **a cunger eele**, *Conger*.
Conjecturar, **to coniecture**, *Coniicere*.
Conjectura, **gesse, coniecture**, *Coniectura*.
Conjugacion de verbo, **a coniugation**, *Coniugatio*.
Conjunction, **coniunction**, *Coniunctio*.
Conjurar, **to conspire, to coniure**, *Coniurare*.
Conusco, **with vs**, *Nobiscum*.
Conocidor de pleyto, **an arbitrator, a iudge**, *Iudex, arbiter*.
Conocer nosco, **to know, to acknowledge**, *Cognoscere, agnoscere*.
Conocimiento, **knowledge, acknowledging**, *Cognitio, agnitio, notitia*.
Conocible, **that may be knowen**, *Cognoscibilis*.
Conocido, **knowen**, *Cognitus, agnitus*.
Conociente, **knowing**, *Cognoscens*.
Conocimiento de paga, **an acquittance**, *Apocha*.
Conortar, **to comfort**, *Consolari*.
Coño, **a womans priuitie**, *Cunnus*.
Conquistar, **to conquer**, *Debellare*.
Conquista, **a conquest**, *Debellatio*.
Consagrar, **to consecrate**, *Consecrare*.
Consagrado, **consecrated**, *Consecratus*.

Consagracion, **consecrating**, *Consecratio*.
Con sazon y tiempo, **in season**, *Opportune*.
Conseja fingida, **a nouell, a fable, a tale**, *Fabula*.
Consejar, **to counsell, to aduise**, *Consulere*.
Consejero, **a counsellor**, *Consiliarius*.
Consejo, **counsell, aduise**, *Consilium*.
Conseguir, **sigo, to attaine, to follow**, *Consequi, assequi*.
Conseguimiento, **attaining, following**, *Assecutio, consecutio*.
Consiguiente, **following**, *Consequens*.
Consiguientemente, **consequently**, *Consequenter*.
Consequencia, **the sequele**, *Sequela*.
Consentir, **siento, to consent**, *Consentire*.
Consentimiento, **consent**, *Consensus*.
Conserva, **a consort in shipping, a conserue**, *Consors, fructus conditaneus*.
Conservador, **he that keepeth**, *Conseruator*.
Conservar, **siervo, to keepe**, *Conseruare, seruare*.
Considerar, **to consider**, *Considerare*.
Consideracion, **consideration**, *Consideratio*.
Considerado, **considerate**, *Consideratus*.
Consideradamente, **considerately**, *Considerate*.
Consigo, **with him**, *Secum*.
Consistorio, **a consistorie**, *Consistorium*.
Consolar, **suelo, to comfort**, *Consolari*.
Consolacion, **comfort**, *Consolatio, solatium*.
Consolador, **a comforter**, *Consolator*.
Consoladora cosa, **comfortable**, *Consolatorius*.
Consonancia, **a consort in voices**, *Consonantia, harmonia*.
Consonante, **agreeing, a consonant**, *Consonans, consonus*.
Consonar, **sueno, to sound togither, to agree**, *Consonare*.
Conspirar, **to conspire**, *Coniurare, conspirare*.
Constante, **constant**, *Constans*.
Constancia, **constancie**, *Constantia*.
Constantemente, **constantly**, *Constanter*.
Constituir, **tuyo, to appoint, to establish**, *Constituere*.
Constitucion, **establishing, appointing**, *Constitutio*.

Constellacion,

Conſtelacion, conſtellation, *Conſtellatio.*
Conſuegros, fathers in law, *Conſocer.*
Conſuelda, comfozie, *Conſolida, ſymphytum.*
Conſultar, to conſult, *Conſilium capere.*
Conſul, a conſull, *Conſul.*
Conſulado, the conſulſhip, *Conſulatus.*
Conſular, pertaining to the conſull, he that was conſull, *Conſularis.*
Conſumacion, ending, conſummation, *Perfectio, conſummatio.*
Conſumir, to conſume, *Conſumere.*
Conſuno, together, *Simul, vnà, pariter.*
Contador, an accounter, a receiuer of the Exchequer, *Computator, quæſtor.*
Contado, a repozt, *Fabula, rumor.*
Contaduría, the office of a receiuer, *Quæ-ſtura.*
Contagion, infection, contagion, *Infectio, contagio.*
Contal de cuentos, a ſet of counters, *Linea calculorum.*
Contante, a counter, *Calculus.*
Contar, cuento, to account, to reckon, to caſt account, to tell, to number, to recount, *Computare, calkulare, narrare, numerare, referre.*
Contaminar, to defile, *Contaminare.*
Comtemplar, to contemplate, *Contemplari.*
Contemplacion, contemplation, *Contemplatio.*
Contender, tiendo, to contend, *Contendere.*
Contendedor, a contender, a ſtriuer, *Certator.*
Contencion, contention, *Contentio.*
Contenciofo, contentious, *Contentioſus.*
Contenerſe, to rule himſelfe, to containe himſelfe, *Continere.*
Contento, content, *Contentus.*
Contentarſe, to be contented oz to be pleaſed, *Placere ſibi, ſatisfieri.*
Contentar, to pleaſe, to ſatiſfie, *Placere, ſatiſfacere.*
Contentamiento, contentment, *Satiſfactio*
Contera, the chape of a ſwozd oz dagger, *Theca roſtrum.*
Contienda, contention, a ſtrife, *Contentio, lis.*
Contigo, with thœ, *Tecum.*

Contino, alwaies, *Semper, continuè, perpetuò.*
Continencia, continentie, *Continentia.*
Continente, the geſture, the countenance *Geſtus, vultus.*
Continentemente, continently, *Continenter.*
Continuar, to continue, *Continuare.*
Continuo, continuall, *Continuus.*
Continuamente, continually, *Aſſiduè.*
Contoneo, moouing, ſtirring, ietting, *Motio, motitatio, iactatio.*
Contorno, round about, *Circum.*
Contra, againſt, oueragainſt, *Contra.*
Contradezir, to gainſay, *Contradicere.*
Contradicion, gainſaying, *Contradictio.*
Contradezidor, a gainſaier, *Contradictor.*
Contradezidora coſa, gainſaying, *Contradictrius.*
Contrahazer, to counterfet, *Imitari, aſſimilare, adulterare.*
Contrahazedor, a counterfetter, *Imitator, adulterator.*
Contrahazimiento, counterfetting, *Imitatio, adulteratio.*
Contrahecho, counterfetted, *Imitatus, adulteratus, adulterinus.*
Contramina, a countermine, *Cuniculus aduerſus.*
Contraminar, to countermine, *Cuniculum aduerſum agere.*
Contramuro, a counterſcarfe, *Antimurale.*
Contrapeſar, to counterpeaſe, *Rependere.*
Contrapeſo, counterpoiſe, *Repenſum.*
Contrapóliça, the counterpane of a chartipartie, *Antigraphum.*
Contraponer, to ſet againſt, *Opponere.*
Contraponedor, he that ſetteth againſt, *Oppoſitor.*
Contrapoſicion, ſetting againſt, *Oppoſitio.*
Contrariar, to contrarie, *Aduerſari.*
Contrariedad, contrarietie, *Contrarietas.*
Contrario, contrarie, *Contrarius.*
Contraſte, contention, *Contentio, lis.*
Contraſtar, to contend, *Contendere.*
Contratar, to contract, *Contrectare, communicare.*
Contratacion, contracting, bargaining, *Contrectatio.*

Contrato,

Copilar, to compile, to gather out of bookes, *Compilare, colligere.*
Copo, the flax of a diſtaffe, *Penſum.*
Coquillo, a woorme that eateth vines, *Vermis qui rodit vineas.*
Coraçon, the hart, *Cor.*
Coraça, a corſlet, a coate of maile, *Paludamentum, lorica.*
Coracina, a curat, *Thorax.* (*cerem.*
Coraçoncillo, S. Iohns wurt, *Hyperi-*
Coradela, the intrails, *Præcordia.*
Corage, courage, *Animus.*
Coral, corall, *Coralium.*
Coraxa entre dos muros, a ſcarfe between walls, *Musculus.*
Córcoba, a bunche in the backe, *Gibbus.*
Corcobado, crooked, crookbacked, *Gibboſus.*
Córcobos, the lifting of a horſe to caſt a man out of the ſaddle, *Calcitratio, ſubſulſus.*
Corcha, corcke, *Suber.*
Corchete de veſtidura, a claſpe, a hooke, by metaphor a catchpole, a ſergeant, *Vncus, lictor.*
Corcho de colmena, a beehiue of corcke, *Aluear ſuberinum.*
Cordel, y cordon, a rope, a halter, a ſtring, *Funis, chorda.*
Cordéra, a lambe, *Agnus.*
Corderillo, a little lambe, *Agniculus.*
Cordojo, a hart griefe, *Cordolium.*
Corma, a little paire of ſtockes, *Cippulus.*
Cornado, a crowne in money, *Aureus coronatus.*
Cornamuſa, a cornamuſe, a horneppppe, *Fiſtula.* (*petere.*
Cornear, to puſh with the hornes, *Cornu*
Corneador, a puſher with the hornes, *Cornupeta.*
Corneja, a dawe, *Cornix.*
Cornerina, an onix ſtone, *Onix.*
Corneta, a cornet, an inſtrument of muſicke, *Fiſtula.*
Cornezuela, a little horne, *Diminutuum à cornu.*
Cordonada, a blow with a ſtringe, a laſh with a whip, *Iſtus chordæ.*
G   Cornicabra,

Cornicabra, the tree whereof turpentine commeth, *Terebinthus.*
Cornudo, a cokold, *Cornutus.*
Coro, de coro, a quier, by hart, the turning of the saile, *Chorus, Memoriter, veli transuersio.*
Coroça, a painted paper set on the heade of a witch, *Mitra scelerata.*
Corona, a crowne, a garland, a myter, *Corona, mitra.*
Coronar, to crowne, *Coronare.*
Coronacion, crowning, *Coronatio.*
Corónica, a chronicle, *Chronica, historia.*
Coronista, a chronicler, *Chronista, historicus.*
Corporal, of the bodie, *Corporeus.*
Corpulencia, greatnes of body, *Corpulentia.*
Corral de gallinas, a court to keepe poultrie, *Cors.*
Corral, a court, a yard, a quadrangle, *Cors, Area.*
Corrallillo, a little court or yard, *Areola.*
Correa de cuero, a strap, a band, a girdle, *Chorda, cingulum, corrigia.*
Correcion, correction, *Correctio.*
Corredera, a race for horses, *Stadium, hippodromus.*
Corrediza, a sliding knot, *Nodus currens.*
Corredor, a curtain, a gallerie, a post that runneth, a vauntcurrior, an heralde, a broaker, *Cortina, solarium, præcursor, cursor, caduceator, institor.*
Corregir, rijo, to correct, to amende, *Corrigere.*
Corregidor, a iustice, a bailiffe, a constable, *Prætor.*
Corregimiento, a iusticeship, *Prætura.*
Correndilla, a race for horses, *Hippodromus.*
Corregudo, knot grasse, *Polygonon.*
Correo, a post, a carrier, a bag for money, *Cursor, tabellarius, bursa.*
Correr, to run, to flow, to make ashamed, to hunt the bull, *currere, fluere, pudefacere, confundere, agitare.*
Correria, running, *Cursura, cursus.*
Corretage, brokage money, *Stips institoria, proxeneticum.*
Correspondiente, correspondent, *Correspondens.*
Corrillo de gente, a companie standing round, *Corona, circulus.*
Corrida, a courfe, a running ouer, *Cursus, curriculum.*
Corrido, offended, ashamed, *insensus, Confusus.*
Corridamente, swiftly, angerly, *Cursim, infensè.*
Corriente, running, *Fluens, confluus.*
Corro de toro, hunting the bull, *Agitatio sauri.*
Corrihuela, knotgrasse, *Polygonon.*
Corromper, to corrupt, *Corrumpere.*
Corrompimiento, corruption, *Corruptio.*
Cortar, to cut, *Scindere.*
Cortadura, cutting, *Sectio.*
Cortadora cola, that may be cut, *Incisiuus.*
Cortador, a cutter, *Scissor, sector, putator.*
Cortapisa de saya, the fur or lining about the skirts of a coate, *Fimbria.*
Corte, the court, *Aula regia.*
Cortesana, a courtisan, *Scortum.*
Cortesano, a courtier, *Aulicus.*
Cortes, curteous, gentle, *Clemens, urbanus, comis.*
Cortesia, curtesie, *Comitas.*
Cortesmente, courteouslie, *Comiter.*
Corteza, the barke, the rinde, a crust, *Cortex, codex, crusta.*
Corto, short, weake hearted, *Breuis, ignauus.*
Cortedad, shortnes, *Breuitas.*
Cortina, a courteine, *Cortina.*
Cortinal, a yard of a house, or a court belonging to a house, *Area.*
Cortijos, a fielde of errable lande, also a dairie house, *Arua.*
Corva de la pierna, the ham, *Genu curuatura, poples.*
Corvo, crooked, *Curuus.*
Corusca, an owle, *Bubo.*
Corvadura, crookednes, *Curuatura.*
Corza, a roe bucke, *Caprea.*
Cosa, a thing, *Res.*

Coscoja.

C O

Coſcoja, the trææ whereon dieis grayne groweth, *Coccus infectorius.*
Coſcojar, a groue of thoſe treæs, *Coccorum ſylua.*
Coſecha, profit, frute, reuennes, harueſt, grape gathering, gathering of frute, gathering of honꝑ, *Prouentus, fructus, meſſis, fructus cuiuſuis perceptio.*
Coſer cueſo, to ſowe, *Suere.*
Coſido, ſowed togither, *Conſutus.*
Coſedura, the ſowing togither, *Sutura.*
Coſmografia, coſmographie, *Coſmographia.*
Coſmografo, a coſmografer, *Coſmographus.*
Coſquillas, tickling, *Titillatio.*
Coſſario, a rouer, a pyrate, *Pirata.*
Coſſelete, a corſelet, *Paludamentum.*
Coſſo, the bull baiting place, *Arena tauris agitandis.*
Coſta, coſte, *Sumptus.*
Coſtado, the ſide, *Latus, coſta.*
Coſtal, a bag, a wallet, a bugget, a cloake bag, *Saccus.*
Coſtar, to coſt, *Conſtare.*
Coſtilla, a rib, coſt, charges, *Coſta, ſumptus, impenſa.*
Coſtoſo, coſtly, *Sumptuoſus.*
Coſtra, a cruſt, or barke, or ſkin, as on a wounde, *Cruſta, cortex.*
Coſtreñir, to compell, to conſtreine, *Cogere.*
Coſtreñimiento, compelling, conſtreining, *Coactio, impulſio.*
Coſtribar recalcando, to ſtuffe, to thruſt vp togither, to tire with lying vpon, to wearie with lying on, *Farcire, ſatigare.*
Coſtumbre, cuſtome, faſhion, flowers, *Conſuetudo, Menſtruum.*
Coſtura, a ſeame, a ſowing, a mending, *Sumentum.*
Coſturero, a botcher, a mender, *Sarcinator.*
Cota de malla, a ſhirt of male, *Lorica.*
Cotejar, to coate, to confer, to compare, *Comparare, conferre.*
Cotejamiento, coating, comparing, *Collatio, comparatio.*
Cotidiano, daily, *Cotidianus.* (rum.
Coto, a parke, a warren, *Vivarium dama-*

C R

Cotral, cattle drawen from the hearde, *Bos reijculus.*
Coxear, to halt, *Claudicare.*
Coxin, a cuſhion, *Puluinus.*
Coxo, lame, *Claudus.*
Coxixos, grœfes, *Dolores.*
Coxedad, lamenes, *Claudicatio.*
Coxquear, to hault, *Claudicare.*
Coxquillas, *vide* coſquillas,
Cozer cuezo, to ſeeth, *Coquere.*
Cozedura, ſeething, *Coctio.* (tius.
Cozedizo, ſodden, or to be ſodden, *Cocti-*
Cozido, ſodden, *Coctus, elixus.*
Cozimiento, dreſſing, ſeething, *Coctio.*
Cozina, a kitchin, *Coquina.*
Cozinero, a cooke, *Coquinarius.*
Cozinar, to play the cooke, *Coquum agere.*

C R

Creſcer, to grow, *Creſcere.*
Creſciente de mar, the flud, *Aeſtus maris.*
Creſcimiento, growing, encreaſe, *Incrementum.*
Creſcido, growen, *Auctus, ſuccretus.*
Creer, to beleeue, *Credere.*
Creéncia, beleefe, credit, *Fides, credulitas, litere cum mandatis.*
Creyble, credible, *Credibilis.*
Creynte hazer en creynte, to make to beleeue, *Facere, vt credat quis,*
Crencha, the partition of the haire, *Coma diuiſo.*
Creſpa, the tuffe of haire, a tuffe of feathers, *Criſta, criſpa.*
Creſpo, curle headed, *Criſpus.*
Criar, to create, to bring vp, to nouriſh, to grow, *Creare, educare, alere, creſcere.*
Criança, bringing vp, good manners, *Educatio, mores.*
Criador, a bringer vp, a nurſe a creator, *Educator, nutricius, creator.*
Criado, a ſeruant, a nurſe childe, *Famulus, alumnus.*
Criatura mal parida, borne out of time, *Abortus.*
Crica de muger, a perruke, *Criſta, coma ſuppoſitiia.*
Crimen, a fault, *Crimen.*

C R

Criminalmente, faultely, *Criminosè.*
Criminoso, full of faults, *Criminosus.*
Criminosamente, faultely, *Criminosè.*
Crines, the haire, *Crines.*
Crinado, that hath haire, *Crinitus.*
Crisma, oyntment, annointing, *Vnctio.*
Crismar, to annoint, *Vngere.*
Crisol, a melting pot of a goldsmith, *Catinus.*
Cristal, chrystall, *Chrystallus.*
Cristalino, of chrystall, *Chrystalinus.*
Cristo, Chrift, *Chriftus.*
Cristiano, a christian, *Christianus.*
Cristiandad, christendome, christianitie, *Christianismus, orthodoxia.*
Cristel, a glister, *Clifter.*
Crivar, to sift, *Cribrare.*
Criva çaranda, a siue to sift, *Cribrum.*
Crudo, rawe, cruell, bluddie, *Crudus, crudelis.*
Crudeza, rawnes, *Cruditas.*
Crueldad, crueltie, *Crudelitas.*
Cruel, cruell, *Crudelis.*
Cruelmente, cruelly, *Crudeliter.*
Crucificar, to crucifie, *Crucifigere.*
Crucificado, crucified, *Crucifixus.*
Crueza, crueltie, *Crudelitas.*
Cruxía, the planks in a gally for men to passe on, a kinde of crane, *Tranftra, gruum genus.*
Cruxiendo, cracking, *Crependo.*
Cruz, a crosse, *Crux.*
Cruzado, a piece of money so called, *Monetæ genus.*
Cruzero en edeficio, a kinde of quartered building, *Structura quadriuialis.*
Cruzar, to crosse, *Cruce notare.*

C V

Cuajar, to crud, to congeale, *Coagulare congelare.*
Cuajamiento, crudding, congealing, *Coagulatio, congelatio.*
Cuajo, the crudde or congealing, also a runnet for cheese, *Coagulum.*
Cuba, a cup, *Cuppa, crater.*
Cubero, a cup maker, *Cupparius.*
Cubilete, a goblet, *Cratercuum.*

C V

Cubebas, a kinde of poisoned hearbe, *Carpesium.*
Cubierta, a couer, *Operimentum.*
Cubierto, couered, *Opertus, tectus.*
Cubillo, *vide* Abadejo.
Cubo, a small water mill, *Molendinum aquaticum.*
Cubrir, to couer, *Tegere.*
Cuchára, a spoone, a ladle, a flesh hooke, *Cochlear, cochleare, creagra.*
Cucharada, a spoonefull, a ladlefull, *Cochlearium, quod in pleno cochleari continetur.*
Cuchillo, a sword, a knife, *Ensis, cultellus.*
Cuchillada, a gash with a sword, a cut, *Ictus ensis.*
Cucita, the voice they vse when they set on a little dogge to any thing, *Vox animantis canem.*
Cuclillo, a cuckoo, *Cuculus.*
Cuello, the necke, *Collum.*
Cuellos, ruffes, *Collare.*
Cuenca, pila, a cisterne, a pot of water, *Cifterna, olla.*
Cuenca de ojo, the corner of the eye, *Oculi angulus.*
Cuenda para atar, a string, *Lorum.*
Cuenta, an account, *Ratio, calculus.*
Cuento, a number, a poale, ten hundred thousand, a post to beare vp a wall, a tale, an historie, *Numerus, contus, millies mille, Fulcrum, historia, narratio.*
Cuerdo, wise, discreet, *Prudens.*
Cuerdamente, wisely, discreetly, *Prudenter.*
Cuerda, a cord, a rope, the raine of a bridle, the string of an instrument, *Funis, restis, lorum, habena, chorda.*
Cuerno, an horne, the wing in battell, *Cornu.*
Cuero, a leather ierkin, *Tunicula coriacea.*
Cuero, leather, the skinne, a bottle of wine, *Corium, cutis, vter.*
Cuerpo, a body, *Corpus.*
Cuervo, a crow, *Coruus.*
Cuesta arriba, vp the hill, *Acclinis.*
Cuesta abaxo, downe the hill, *Decliuis.*
Cueva, a caue, *Cauca.*
Cuevano de vimbres, a wicker basket, *Cophinus vimineus.*

Cugujada,

C V

Cugujada, *vide* Cogujada, copada.
Cuexco de fruta, mugeres cuexcas, the ſtone, the coare, malicious women, *Acinus, volua, mulieres malicioſæ, contumaces.*
Cugulla, a cole, *Cucullus.*
Cüyo, whoſe, *Cuius.*
Cuydado, care, *Cura.*
Cuydadoſo, carefull, *Anxius.*
Cuita, carefulneſſe, anguiſh, miſerie, *Cura, anxietas, miſeria.*
Cuitado, carefull, vexed, perplexed, miſerable, *Anxius, miſer.*
Culantro, coriander, *Coriander.*
Cular, the gut of the fundament, *Inteſtinum rectum.*
Culantrillo y culantro de pozo, maiden haire, *Capillus veneris.*
Culebra, a ſnake, a ſerpent, *Coluber, ſerpens.*
Culebrilla, the itch, a tetter, *Lichen, impetigo.*
Culo, the arſe, *Anus, podex.*
Culpa, a fault, blame, *Culpa.*
Culpar, to blame, *Culpare.*
Culpademente, faultely, *Culpatè.*
Cultivar, to till, to trim, to nouriſh in a garden, *Colere.*
Cumbre, the top, *Culmen.*
Cumplir, to accompliſh, *Complere.*
Cumple, it muſt, it is conuenient, *Oportet.*
Cumpledero, full of faire ſpeech, full of curteſie, *Blandus.*
Cundir, to creepe, to ſpred by little & little, *Serpere.*
Cuna, a cradle, *Cuna, arum.*
Cuñado, a brother in law, *Lenir.*
Cuña, a wedge, *Cuneus.*
Cuño, coine, *Moneta.*
Cura, care, cure of the ſicke, a curate, *Cura, curator animarum.*
Curar, to cure, to take cure of, to haue in cure, *Curare.*
Curador, a gouernor, a tutor, a gardein, *Curator, tutor.*
Curaderia, a tutorſhip, a gardeinſhip, *Curatura.*
Curioſo, curious, *Curioſus.*
Cutioſidad, curioſitie, *Curioſitas.*

Ç A

Curſado, commonly vſed, *Vulgo vſitatum.*
Curtir cueros, to tanne, *Macerare coria.*
Curtir, to ſteepe, *Macerare.*
Curtidura, ſteeping, tanning, *Maceratio.*
Curtidor, a tanner, *Coriarius, alutarius.*
Curuxa, a night crow, *Noctua, nicticorax.*
Cutir, to ſhake, *Quatere, concutere.*

Ç A

çaborda, ſtarbord, *Ad dextram nauis.*
çabullido, drenched, diued, *Merſus.*
çabullir, to drench, to diue, *Mergere.*
çaſari granada, the principall pomegranat, *Apirinum pomum granatum.*
çaſio en lengua, rude in any tongue, *Idiomaticus.*
çafires, ſaphyres, *Sapphyrus.*
çaga, the end, *Finis, extremitas.*
çaguero, the laſt, *Extremus.*
çaguan, a porch, *Porticus.*
çahereño, wilde, coy, diſdaineful, *Efferus, faſtuoſus, faſtidioſus.*
çaherir, hiero, to vpbraid, *Exprobare.*
çaherimiento, vpbraiding, *Exprobratio.*
çahinas, hony ſops made of bread, hony and water, *Iuſculum mellitum.*
çahondar, to diue to the bottome, *Subſidere.*
çahumerio, a perfume, *Incenſorium.*
çahon, a kinde of hoſe or breeches, *Caliga.*
çahorda, a pigges ſtie, *Hara.* (ditia.
çalſmas, curteſie, fained kindneſſe, *Blanditia.*
çamarra, çamarron, a leather pelt, *Rheno.*
çamarilla, an hearbe called ſhepheards purſſe, *Burſa paſtoris.*
çonahorias, carrats, *Paſtinaca.*
çanca de pierna, a ſmall leg, *Tibia.*
çancadilla armar, to trip, *Supplantare.*
çancajoſo, crooklegged, *Varus.*
çancarron, a dead horſſe legge, *Equi mortui perna.*
çanco, ſtilts, *Pertica grallatoria.*
çancudos, gnats with long legges, *Culicis genus.*
çanquear, to goe ſtalking, *Deuaricavi.*
çanqueamiento, ſtalking, *Deuaricatio.*
çanqueador, a ſtalking fellow, *Deuaricator.*

çapatero,

Ç E

çapatero, a shoomaker, *Calcearius sutor, cerdo.*
çapato, a shoo, *Calceus.*
çapatería, a shoomakers craft, *Sutoria calcearia.*
çapato sobre pilar, a stay to lay a sommer on in building, *Mutilus.*
çapuzar, to diue, to ducke, *Submergere.*
çaqueçami, a beame, *Laquear.*
çaraças, crooked pinnes to choake one with *Aciculæ retortæ.*
çaraguelles, gascoigne hose, *Femoralia.*
çaranda, a siue to sift, *Cribrum.*
çarandar, to sift meale, *Cribrare.*
çaratan, the canker, *Cancer morbus.*
çarçaparrilla, rough byndweed, *Smilax aspera.*
çarça, a brier, *Rubus.*
çarçal, a brier bush, *Rubetum.*
çarça mora, a blackberie, *Morum rubeum.*
çarça perruna, dogge brier, *Canis rubus.*
çarcear, to trauerse the ground, *Circummeare, circumuersari.*
çarcillos, earings, *Inaures.*
çarpas, daggles of durt, spots of durt, *Luti conspersio.*
çarposo, daggled with durt, spotted with durt, *Collutulatus, luto conspersus.*
çarzo de vergas, a hurdle, *Crates.*
çatico, a luncheon of course bread, *Frustum panis.*
çavila, aloe, *Semper viuum.*

C E

Ceatica, the sciatica, *Ischia.*
Cebolla, an onion, a chibboll, *Cepe.*
Cebollino, onion seed, *Semen ceparum.*
Cecear, to lispe, *Balbutire.*
Ceceoso, lisping, *Balbus.*
Cecina, poudered flesh, *Caro salita.*
Cecinar, to pouder flesh, *Salire carnem quamlibet.*
Cedaço, a siue to sift corne, a searce, *Cribrū.*
Cedacillo, a little siue to sift, *Cribulum.*
Cedicio, weake, filthy, *Infirmus, turpis.*
Cedo, quickly, *Citò.*
Cedro, cedar, *Cedrus.*
Cedula, a scedule, *Schedula.*

C E

Cegar ciego, to make blinde, to fill vp a ditch, *Cæcare, cæcutire, scrobem implere.*
Cegajosa, purblinde, *Luscus.*
Cegagez, purblindnes, dimnes of sight, *Elusciatio, oculorum hebetudo.*
Cegagear, to be purblinde, *Luscum esse, cæcutire.*
Ceguedad, blindnes, *Cæcitas.*
Ceguera, dimnes of sight, *Oculorum hebetudo.*
Ceguta, hemlocks, *Cicuta.*
Ceja, the eiebowes, the space betweene the eiebrowes, *Supercilium, intercilium.*
Cejunto, beetle browed, *Toruus.*
Celada, an ambush, a sallet for the head, *Insidiæ, galea.*
Celar, to hide, to couer, to be ielous, *Celare, zelare.*
Celda, a cell, a cabbin in a ship, *Cella, prætoriolum.*
Celebrar, to celebrate, *Celebrare.*
Celebracion, celebrating, *Celebratio.*
Celebro, the braine, *Cerebrum.*
Celemin, a kind of measure, a bushel, *Modius.*
Celestial, heauenly, *Cælestis.*
Celestialmente, heauenly, *Cælitùs, diuinitùs.*
Celedonia, Celandine, *Chelidonia.*
Celicio, a shirt of haire, *Cilicium.*
Celoso, ielous, *Zelotypus.*
Celos, ielousie, *Zelotypia.*
Cementar, cimiento, to lay a foundation, to ioine togither with lime, *Fundare, cementare.*
Cementador, he that laieth a foundation, *Cementator.*
Cementerio, a churchyard, *Cœmiterium.*
Cena, a supper, *Cœna.*
Cenar, to sup, *Cœnare.*
Cenador, a dining chamber, *Cœnaculum.*
Cenadero, a parlour, *Cœnatorium.*
Cenceño, single, vnleuened, *Syncerus, azymus.*
Cencerro, a bel for a cow, *Tintinnabulum.*
Cendal, a fine rag of linnen, *Segmentum linteum.*
Cendrar, to imbosse, *Pustulare.*
Cendrado, imbossed worke, *Pustulatum signinum.*

Cenedal,

Cenedal, a mirie plot, *Canum.*
Ceniza, aſhes, *Cinis.*
Ceniziento, full of aſhes, *Cinericius.*
Cenogiles, garters, *Subligacula.*
Cenſo, a taxe, *Cenſus.*
Cenſor, a cenſo2, a taxo2, *Cenſor.*
Cenſura, the cenſo2ſhip o2 iudgement, *Cenſura.*
Centaurea, centaurie, *Centaurium.*
Centauro, a centaure, *Centaurus.*
Centella, a ſparkle, *Scintilla.*
Centellar, to ſparkle, *Scintillare.*
Centeno, rie, *Typha.*
Centinela, the ſwatch o2 guard, *Excubiæ.*
Centolla, a kind of ſhell fiſh, *Teſtudo celſina.*
Centurion, a captaine of an hund2ed, *Centurio.*
Centuria, a companie of an hund2ed, *Centuria.*
Centurionadgo, a captainſhip, *Centuriatus*
Centro, the center, *Centrum.*
Ceñir, ciño, to girde, *Cingere.*
Ceñido animal, *Inſecta animalia.*
Ceñidura, girding, *Cinctura.*
Ceñidero, a girdle, *Cingulum.*
Cepa, a vine, the b2anch of a vine, the plants of a vine, a hedge, a ſnare, a pitfall, *Vitis, planta vitium, ſeps, pedica, decipula.*
Cepa cavallo, ground thiſtle, *Chamæleon.*
Cepillar, to ſmooth, to make plaine, *Læuigare.*
Cepillo, a plaine, *Læuigatorium.*
Cepilladuras, ſhauings, *Segmenta.*
Cepo, the ſtocks, *Cippus.*
Cera, ſware, *Cera,* (*tum.*
Cerapez, a kinde of ointment, *Ceramen-*
Cerbiguillo, the necke of a bull, any fat necke o2 ioule, *Ceruix præpinguis.*
Cerca, neare, about, *Circa, circum, ad, apud, iuxta, prope.*
Cercano, neere, *Propinquus.*
Cerca de lo vltimo, the laſt ſaue one, *Penultimus.*
Cercanidad, nearnes, *Propinquitas.*
Cerca, the trench about a fo2t, an incloſure, *Vallum, foſſa.*

Cerco, ſiege, a compaſſe, *Obſidio, murus, circuitus.*
Cercado, incloſed, hedged, *Obſeſſus, ſepius.*
Cercar, to compaſſe, *Circundare.*
Cercarſe, to come neare, *Appropinquare.*
Cercenar, to cut round, *Circumcidere.*
Cerceta, a coote, *Fulica.* (*preolus.*
Cercillo de vid, the tend2els of a vine, *Ca-*
Cerco, a companie of men, *Circulus, corona.*
Cerdas de beſtia, the haire, *Crines.*
Ceremonia, a ceremonie, *Cæremonia.*
Cerezo, a cherie tree, *Ceraſus.*
Cereza, a cherie, *Ceraſum.*
Cereza tieſta, a hard cherie, *Ceraſum duracinum.*
Cerillas, lip ſalue, *Vnguentum labiorum.*
Cernada, the aſhes of a bucke, *Cinis lixiuiarius.*
Cernejas, the haire of a beaſt, *Iuba, pilus.*
Cernicalo, a caſtrell, *Tinnunculus.*
Cernir, cierno, to ſift meale, *Cernere, cribrare*
Cernidura, ſifting of meale, *Cribratio.*
Cerniduras, b2an, the duſt ſifted out, *Furfures, purgamenta.*
Cerote, a ſeere cloth, *Ceratum, cerotum.*
Cerrado el cielo, cloudie, ouercaſt with cloudes, *Cælum nubilum.*
Cerraja, milke thiſtles, a locke, *Sonchus, ſera.*
Cerrajero, a lockſmith, *Faber ſerarius.*
Cerradura, the bolt of a locke, a bolt o2 bar, a hedge, *Sera, peſſulum, clauſtrum, ſepimentum.*
Cerrar, cierro, to locke, to ſhut, to bolt, to hedge, *Obſerare, claudere, peſſulum obdere, ſepire.*
Cerrado camino, a rough way, *Inuius.*
Cerrar, cierro, to cloſe vp, *Occludere, coire vt vulnus.*
Cerrion, a great flake of iſe, freſh cheeſe, *Gelicidium, caſeus recens.*
Cerrados años, old yeeres, *Senectus.*
Cerro, a hill, a hillocke, taſke of wooll o2 flaxe, *Collis, tumulus, penſum.*
Cerro entre las eſpaldas, the ſpace betweene the ſhoulders, *Interſcapulum.*
Cerrojo, a locke, *Sera.*
Certero, a ſure ſhooter, *Qui metam attingit.*
Certidumbre,

Certidumbre,certaintie,*Certitudo.*
Certificar,to certifie, *Certificare.*
Cervatillo,a fawne of a stag,*Hinnulus.*
Cerveza,beere,*Ceruisia.*
Cerviz,the necke,*Ceruix.*
Cervigudo,thicke necked,*Ceruicosus.*
Cervuno, pertaining to a hart,or pertai=
ning to a stag,*Ceruinus.*
Cesped,a turfe,*Cespes.*
Cessar,to cease,*Cessare.*
Cessacion,ceasing,leauing off,*Cessatio.*
Cesta,a chest,a basket,*Cista,qualus.*
Cestero, a chest maker, a basket maker,
Cistellarius.
Cestilla, a little basket,*Cistella,fiscella.*
Cesto, coger agua en cesto, a basket, to
take vp water in a basket,to labour in
vaine,*Corbis.*
Cetreria,falconrie, *vide* Acetreria.
Cetrino,a pale yellow colour,*Citrinus.*
Cetro,a scepter,*Sceptrum.*
Cevada, barly,*Ordeum.*
Cevadizo,of barly,*Ordeaceus.*
Cevadera,the saile of the boltspret,*Velum*
antennale,dolon.
Cevada de cavallos,prouender, *Ordeum e-*
quinum.
Cevar,to feed, to bait, to cram, *Cibare,ob-*
escare,saginare.
Cevado,fed,baited,crammed, *Saginatus.*
Cevo,meat,bait,*Cibus,esca.*
Cevil,common,base,vile,shameful, *Pub-*
licus,humilis,vilis,pudendus.
Cevon,fat,*Obesus.*
Cexar,*vide* Cessar.

C I

Ciar,to stop, to retire, *Recipere se, retroire.*
Cicatero,a cutpurse,*Crumenifeca.*
Cicion de calentura, the fit of an ague,
Accessio febris.
Cicorea,cichorie,*Cicoreum.*
Cidra, a citron tree, also the fruit of the
same,*Citrus.*
Cidron, the stinke of a rotten fig, *Putidi*
ficus fætor.
Cidral,a tree of citrons, *Malus citrea.*
Ciegamente,blindly,*Cæciter.*

Ciego,blinde,*Cæcus.*
Cielo,the heauen, weather,*Cælum.*
Cien nudillos,knotgrasse,*Geniculata.*
Cien cabeças, hundred headed thistle,
Centum capita.
Cieno,mud,mire,*Cænum,limus.*
Ciento,an hundred,*Centum.*
Cien vezes,an hundred times,*Centies.*
Cientenal,an hundred yeeres old,*Centen-*
nis.
Cientopies, a woorme with many feete,
Scolopendra.
Cierço,the north winde,*boreas.*
Cierne, the blossoms of grapes, *Flos vua-*
rium.
Cietnir,to sift,*Cernere,cribrare.*
Cierto,sure,certaine,*Certus.*
Ciertamente,surely,certainly,*Certè.*
Cierva,a hinde,*Cerua.*
Ciervo,a hart,*Ceruus.*
Cifra,a cipher,*Cifra.*
Cigarra, a grashopper,a cricket,*Cicada.*
Ciguena, a storke, also an instrument to
measure depth with,*Ciconia.*
Cigonino, a yong storke, *Pullus ciconi-*
nus.
Cigoñal,a brewers crane to draw water,
Pertica putealis.
Cilicio,haircloth,*Cilicium.*
Cilindro,a diall,*Cylindrus.*
Cilla,a garnet,a binne,*Horreum,cella.*
Cillero, a celler,a pantrie, a celler keeper,
Cellarium,cellarius.
Cimera, the crest of an helmet, *Chimera,*
crista.
Cimiento, the foundation, *Fundamentum.*
Cimitarra, a falchion, a Turkie sword,
Acinacis.
Cinco,fiue, *Quinque,quintus.*
Cinco en rama, fiue leafed grasse, cinke=
foile, *Quinquefolium.*
Cinquenta,fiftie, *Quinquaginta.*
Cinquesma,whitsontide,*Pentecoste.*
Cincha, a girse, the iron that bindeth a
whœle,*Cingulum,orbita ferrea,canthus.*
Cinchar,to gird,*Cingere.*
Cincho para queso, a cheesefat, or hoope
to make a cheese in,*Fiscina.*

Cinchadura,

Cinchadura, girding, *Cinctura.*
Cinquepul de los Iudios, certaine Iewish sacrifices, *Nudipedalia.*
Cinta, a girdle, a point, a garter, *Cingulus, ligula, ligamen.*
Cipres, cypresse, *Cupressus.*
Cipresal, a groue of cypresse, *Cupressetum.*
Circulo, a circle, *Circulus.*
Circular, perteining to a circle, *Circularis.*
Circularmente, roundly, like a circle, Circulariter.
Circuncidar, to circumcise, *Circuncidere.*
Circuncidado, circumcised, *Circuncisus.*
Cirio, a waxe candle, *Cereus.*
Cirial, the candlesticke, *Ceroferarium.*
Ciruelo, a plum tree, *Prunus.*
Ciruela, a plum, *Prunum.*
Cirugiano, a chyrurgion, *Chirurgus.*
Cirugía, chyrurgerie, *Chirurgia.*
Cisco de hogar, the sparkels of fire, *Fauilla.*
Ciscado, afraid, *Territus.*
Cisma, a schisme, *Schisma.*
Cismatico, a schismatike, *Schismaticus.*
Cisne, a swan, *Cygnus.*
Cisterna, a cesterne, *Cisterna.*
Citar, to cite, *Citare.*
Citacion, citing, *Citatio.*
Citola, a citterne, the clapper of a mill, *Cithara, molendini lingula.*
Citolero, he that plaieth on a citterne, *Cytharædus.*
Civdad, a citie, *Civitas.*
Civdadano, a citizen, *Civis.*
Civera, corne, *Frumentum.*
Civil, ciuill, *Ciuilis.*
Civilidad, ciuilitie, *Ciuilitas.*
Civilmente, ciuillie, *Ciuiliter.*
Cizerca, tiches, *Cicercula.*

Ç O

çoçobras, ouerturning, crossing of fortune, *Fortunæ inuersio.*
çoca, a place for a faire, *Locus nundinarum.*
çocodouer, a port in Toledo, *Portus Toletanus.*
çopo, maimed, *Mancus.*
çorita, *vide* çurita.

Ç U

çueco, a shoe of wood, *Soccus.*
çufre, brymstone, *Sulfur.*
çumaque, an hearbe vsed to tan leather in stede of barke, *Nausea, rhus.*
çumo, iuice, *Succus.*
çumillo o jarrillo, an herbe called dragon, *Aros.*
çumoso, full of iuice, *Succosus.*
çumaya, a night crow, *Noctua.*
çurana palomo a stockdoue, *Palumba.*
çurita, a yoong stockdoue, *Pullus Palumbinus.*
çurrar cueros, to tan leather, *Macerare.*
çurrador, a tanner, *Coriarius.*
çurrear, to hum as a bee, or flie, *Susurrare.*
çurron, a budget of leather, *Pera.*
çurroncillo, a little budget, *Perula.*
çurrana, a wilde pigeon, *Columba fera.*
çurriaga, a strap of leather to hurle a dart, *Amentum.*
çutano, such a one, *Quidam.*
çuzon, a stincking herbe, *Herba fœtida.*

Ch A

Chaça, a chase at tennise, *Meta, terminus.*
Chafaldete, a cord in a ship, *Funis genus.*
Chafallos, patches, *Panni veteres & detriti, assumenta panni.*
Chambrana de puerta, the garnishing of gates or doores, *Antepagmentum.*
Chamelote, chamlet, *Capripilia.*
Chamuscar, to burne, to singe with fire, *Adurere, amburere.*
Chamusquina, singeing with fire, *Ambustio.*
Chancelar, to cancell, *Antiquare.*
Chanciller, a chauncellor, *Cancellarius.*
Chancillería, a chauncellourshippe, the chauncerie, *Cancellaria.*
Chantre de yglezia, the chauntrie in a church, *Præcentor.*
Chantría, the chauntership, *Præcentoris munus.*
Chapa, a plate of mettall, *Bractea, Lamina.*
Chapado, plated, *Bracteatus.*
Chapar, to plate, *Bracteare.*

H Chapas,

Chapas, an iustrument of muficke made of two plates, *Instrumentum muficum, cro-talum, crepitaculum.*
Chapear, to make a ringing noise, *Tinnire, crepitare.*
Chapido, the noise of plates, the ringing of plates, *Tinnitus.*
Chapin de muger, a slipper, *Solea.*
Chapinero, a seller of slippers, *Solearius,* (*cina.*
Chapinería, a shop of slippers, *Solearia offi-*
Chapitel, a pinacle, *Pinnaculum.*
Charco, a poole, a ditch, *Stagnum, lacus, sossa.*
Charlatar, to babble, to prate, *Garrire.*
Chaton, studs, *Bullæ.*
Cherubin, a cherubin, *Cherubim.*
Chibo o cabrito, a kid, *Hœdus.*
Chibo mayor, the hee goate, *Hircus, caper.*
Chibital, a heard of goates, *Hædile.*
Chico, little, *Paruus.*
Chicharro, *vide* Cigarra.
Chicorea, cicorie, *Cicoreum.*
Chichon, a blister, a pinswell, *Pustula.*
Chifflar, to whistle, *Sibilare.*
Chiffle, a whistle, *Sibilatio, fistula.*
Chillar, o rechinar, to make a shrill crie, *Stridere.*
Chillido, a shrill cry or noise, *Stridor.*
Chiminea, a chimney, *Caminus.*
China, a little stone, a counter, *Scrupulus, lapillus, calculus.*
Chinche, a worme that in hot countries lieth about beds, & biteth venemously, *Dimex.*
Chinela, a slipper, *Crepida.*
Chiriar, to sing as a swallow, *Garrire.*
Chirimias, a kinde of instrument of musicke, *Instrumentum muficum.*
Chirivía, parseneps, also a birde called a wagtaile, *Sifer, motacilla.*
Chirridos, chirping of birds, *Garritus.*
Chisme, *vide* Chinche.
Chismería, trifles, *Nugæ.*
Chisma, a schisme, *Schisma.*
Chismero, a schismatike, also a prater of trifles, *Schismaticus, Nugigerulus.*
Chistes, iestes, *Ioci, ludi.*
Chivato, a hee goate, *Caper.*

Chocallos, little bels, little iewels, *Tinsinnabula, gemmæ.*
Chocarrerías, iestes, gibes, *Lusus, dictéria.*
Chocarrear, to ieste, to gibe, *Ludere.*
Chocarrero, a iester, giber, *Mimus.*
Choça, a cottage, *Tigurium.*
Choqueçuela, the bone in the knee, *Patella, mola.*
Chorrico, a kinde of pudding, *Farciminis genus.*
Chorro, a brooke, *Riuus, torrens.*
Chorrear, to run as a brooke, *Fluere.*
Chotacabras, birds like guls that sucke goates, *Caprimulgus.*
Chocar, to sucke, *Sugere.*
Chozno, a nephewe of the thirde degree, *Trinepos.*
Chueca, the hollownes of a ioint where the bone plaieth, *Vertebra.*
Chupar, to sucke, *Sugere.*
Chupadura, sucking, *Exuctus.*
Chusma, a company of poore base people, *Multitudo iners.*

D A

Dadivas, giftes, *Dona.*
Dadivoso, liberall, *Liberalis.*
Dadivosamente, liberally, *Liberaliter.*
Dadivosidad, liberalitie, *Liberalitas.*
Dado, a die, giuen, *Alea, Datus.*
Daga, a dagger, *Pugio.*
Dama, a ladie, *Domina, amica.*
Dança, a daunce, *Tripudium.*
Dançar, to daunce, *Saltare.*
Dañar, to hurt, *Nocere, lædere.*
Daño, losse, hurt, *Damnum.*
Dançador, a dauncer, *Saltator.*
Dañoso, hurtfull, *Damnosus, nociuus.*
Dar, to giue, to strike, to hit, to yeelde, *Dare, ferire, percutere, dedere.*
Daragoncia, an herbe called dragons, *Dragontis.*
Dardo, a darte, *Iaculum.*
Datil, a date, *Dactylus.*
Datiuo caso, the datiue case, *Datiuus.*

De

D E

De, of, from, out of, *De, e, ex, ab.*
De ay, from thence, *Ifthinc.*
De alli, from that place, *Illinc.*
De accullá, from yonder place, *Illinc.*
De aqui, from hence, *Hinc.*
De aqui a poco, within short space, *Paulo post.*
Dean, a Deane, *Decanus.*
Deanadgo, a Deanrie, *Decanatus.*
Deaqui adelante, from henceforth, *Deinde, dehinc.*
Debalde, vile, nothing woorth, freely, for nought, *Vilis, gratis, gratuitus, gratis.*
Debate, debate, contention, *Lis, contentio, certamen.*
Debatir, to striue, *Litigare, certare.*
Debastia, a generation of kings, *Prosapia.*
Debaxo, vnder, below, *Sub, subter, subtus.*
Debil, weake, *Debilis.*
Debilitadamente, weakely, *Debiliter.*
Debilitado, weakened, *Debilitatus.*
Debilitar, to weaken, *Debilitare.* (tro.
De buena gana, of good will, *Libenter vl-*
Debuxo, the arte of drawing, the arte of portrating, *Delineatio.*
Debuxar, to portraite, to drawe, *delineare.*
Debuxado, a drawer, *Delineator.*
De cada parte, from euery side, *Vndequaque.*
De camino, by the way, *Obiter.*
Decendir, to come downe, *Descendere.*
Decendimiento, comming downe, bringing downe, *Descensus, deductio.*
Decendencia, posteritie, *Posteritas.*
Decendientes, posteritie, *Nepotes.*
Decessor, a predecessor, *Qui magistratu cessit, prædecessor, decessor.*
Decession, a predecessorship, *Decessio.*
Dechado, a patterne, *Typus.*
Decimo, the tenth, *Decimus.*
Decision, deciding, determining, *Determinatio.*
Declamar, to declaime, *Declamare.*
Declamador, a declaimer, *Declamator.*
Declamacion, a declamation, *Declamatio.*

Declarar, to declare, *Declarare.*
Declaracion, a declaration, *Declaratio.*
Declarador, a declarer, *Declarator.*
De coraçon, from the hart, *Ex animo.*
De coro, without booke, by hart, *Memoriter.*
Decoro, comely, seemely, *Decorus.*
Decorar, to make comely, *Decorare.*
De corrillo en corrillo, from one companie of men to another, *Circulatim.*
De dentro, from within, *Ab intus.*
Dedicar, to dedicate, *Dedicare.*
Dedicacion, dedicating, *Dedicatio.*
Dedil o dedal, a thimble, *Digitale.*
Dedo, a finger, a toe, *Digitus.*
Dedo pulgar, the thumbe, *Pollex.*
Dedo menique, the little finger, *Digitus minimus.*
De donde, from whence, *Vnde.*
De donde quiera, from whencesoeuer, *Vndecunque.*
Deesa, a goddesse, *Dea.*
Defender, to defend, to protect, to forbid, *Defendere, protegere, interdicere.*
Defencion, defence, protection, *Defensio, protectio.*
Defendedor, a defender, *Defensor.*
Defendido, defended, forbidden, *Defensus, interdictus.*
Defensora, a defendresse, *Patrona.*
Defeto, defect, *Defectus.*
Defetuoso, faultie, *Deficiens.*
Defuera, without, *Foris.*
Defunto, dead, *Defunctus, vita functus.*
Dejenerar, to degenerate, *Degenerare.*
Degollar, guello, to kil, to behead, *Iugulare, decollare.*
Degolladura de cuello, the throate boll, *Iugulus.*
Degollamiento, beheading, killing, *Iugulatio.*
De hecho, indeed, *Reuera.*
Degradar, to disgrace, *Degradare, gradu priuare.*
Dehender, to cleaue in sunder, *Diffindere.*
Dehesa concegil, a common of pasture, *Ager compascuus.* (*fissio.*
Dehendimiento, cleauing asunder, *Dif-*

H 2   Dehesa

Dehefa privada, a priuate pasture, *Pascua*
Dejarretar, to hough a beast, *Subneruare*.
De improviso, on the sudden, vnwares, *De improuiso*.
Del, of him, *De illo*.
Dela, of iyir, *De illa*.
Delantal, an apron, *Ventrale*.
Delante, before, *Ante*.
Delantera de casa o cama, a settle, *Subsellium*.
Delegado, sent on an ambassage, *Delegatus*.
Delegar, to send to any place, to appoint, *Delegare*.
Delegacion, the appointing, *Delegatio*.
Deleytar, to delight, *Delectare*.
Deleyte, delight, pleasure, *Delectatio, voluptas*.
Deleytoso, pleasant, delectable, delightfull, *Voluptuosus, delectabilis, amœnus*.
De lexos, from far, *A longè, eminus, procul*.
Deletrear, to spell, *Syllabicare*.
Deleznar, to make slipperie, *Lubricare, labi*.
Deleznable, slipperie, *Lubricus*.
Delez namiento, slipperinesse, *Lubricitas*.
Deleznadero, a slipperie place, *Lubricum*.
Delfin o golfin, a dolphin, *Delphin*.
Delgado, fine, slender, small, *Tenuis, subtilis, gracilis*.
Delgadez, finenes, slendernes, *Tenuitas, gracilitas*.
Delgazar, to make fine, to make small, *Extenuare*.
Deliberar, to deliberate, to take aduise, to purpose, *Deliberare, consulere, decernere*.
Deliberacion, deliberation, aduise, purpose, *deliberatio, consultatio, destinatio, propositum*.
Delibrar, to deliuer, to set free, to set at libertie, *Liberare, manumittere, emancipare*.
Delibramiento, deliuering, setting free, *Liberatio*.
Delibrado, deliuered, made free, set at libertie, *Liberatus, emancipatus, manumissus*.
Delicado, delicate, deintie, *Delicatus, deliciosus, lautus*.
Delicadeza, deintines, delicatenes, *Delisia, lautitia*.

De ligero, lightly, *Leuiter*.
Delito, a fault, *Delictum*.
Del todo, altogither, *Penitus, prorsus*.
Delustrar, to make foule, *Fœdare*.
Demandar, to demand, to require, to aske to beg, *Postulare, poscere, petere, mendicare*.
Demanda, a demand, a suite, an asking, a requiring, *Postulatio, efflagitatio, petitio*.
Demandador, a demander, suter, begger, plantife in an action, *Postulator, efflagitator, mendicus, actor*.
Demandadora cosa, a thing demanded or sued for, *Postulatitius, petitorius*.
Demandado en juyzio, the defendant, *Reus*.
De manera, so as, *Ita vt*.
Demasiado, too much, superfluous, *Superfluus*.
Demasiadamente, superfluously, exceedingly, *Superfluè*.
Demasia, superfluitie, ouermuch, *Nimium, superfluitas*.
Demediar, to diuide in two, *Dimidiare*.
Demediado, diuided in two, *Dimidiatus*.
Dementras, in the meane time, *Interim*.
Demonio, the diuell, an euill spirit, *Dæmon*.
Demoniado, possessed with the diuel, *Dæmoniacus*.
Demostrar, muestro, to shew, to point out, *Demonstrare*.
Demuestra, shewing, pointing out, *Indicium, ostensio*.
Demudar, to change, *Mutare*.
Dende, from, sithence, since, *Deinde, inde, exinde*.
Dende entonces, since that time, *Postea*.
Denegar, to denie, *Negare*.
Denostar, nuesto, to reuile, *Conuiciari, dehonestare*.
Denuesto, reuiling, railing, despising, *Conuitium, dehonestatio, vituperatio*.
Denodado, bold, forward, quicke, rash, *Audax, confidens, agilis, temerarius*.
Denuedo, boldnes, frowardnes, *Confidentia, agilitas*.
Dental de arado, the plough share, *Dentale*.

Dentado,

Dentado, toothed, Dentatus.
Dentadura, tuskes, Brochitas.
Dentar, to file a fize, to make the teeth of a saw, Spicare, limare serram vel falcem.
Dentellada, biting, Morsus.
Dentera, the teeth being on edge, Dentium stupor.
Dentecer, to grow as teeth, Dentescere.
Denton, that hath sharpe teeth, also a sharpe toothed fish, Dentatus, dentex.
Dentro, within, Intus.
Dentro de si, betweene themselues, Inter se.
Dentudo, that hath great teeth, Brochus.
Denunciar, to denounce, to shew, to take witnes, Denunciare, renunciare, contestari.
Denunciacion, denouncing, shewing, Denunciatio.
Denunciado, denounced, shewed, Denunciatus.
Denuevo, afresh, of new, Ab integro, denuo.
Deñar, to vouchsafe, to thinke woorthy, Dignari.
De parte de fuera, of the outside, Forinsecus.
Deposito, in trust, Depositum.
Depositar, to leaue in trust, Deponere.
Deposicion, leauing in trust, Depositio.
Depositario, left in trust, Depositarius.
Depravado, depraued, Deprauatus.
Deprender, to learne, Discere.
De punta, with the point, Cuspidatim.
De rayz, from the roote, Radicitus.
Derecho, right, straight, iust, euen, lawe, fees of a lawyer, Rectum, iustum, æquum, ius, stips.
Derecha mano, the right hand, Dextera.
Derechura, rightnes, straightnes, Æquitas.
Derecho de entrambas manos, a plaier on both hands, Ambidexter.
De repente, suddenly, Subito, repente.
Derrabar, to curtall, Caudam truncare.
Derrabado, curtalled, Cauda auntactus,
Derrabadura, curtalling, Caudæ truncatio.
Derramar, to shed, to spill, to scatter, Diffundere, effundere, dispergere.

Derramamiento, shedding, spilling, scattering, Diffusio, effusio, dispersio.
Derramadamente, scatteringly, Sparsim.
Derrengar, to breake the reines of the backe, Delumbare.
Derrengado, broken backed, Delumbatus.
Derrengadura, breaking of the backe, Delumbatio.
Derretir, rieto, to thawe, to melt, to rot, Regelare, liquefcere, tabefcere.
Derretido, melted; thawed, Liquefactus, regelatus.
Derretimiento, thawing, rotting, melting, Regelatio, liquefactio, tabes.
Derredor, about, Circum.
Derribado, throwen downe, Demolitus.
Derribar, to plucke downe, to throwe downe, Demoliri, diruere.
Derrocar, rueco, to throw downe, Demoliri, deijcere.
Derrostrar, to fall on the face, In faciem incidere.
Derrota, a course, a way, Cursus, iter.
Derrumbadero, a downfall, Præcipitium.
Desabahar, to ceafe fuming or smoking, Vaporem continere.
Desabezar, to vnteach, Dedocere.
Desabituar, to vnaccustome, Desuefacere.
Desabituacion, vnaccustoming, Desuetudo.
Desabollar, to beate out the batterings in a peece of armor or plate, Crenas exterere.
Desabotonar, to vnbutton, Condylos soluere.
Desabotonadura, vnbuttoning, Condylorum solutio.
Desabrido, vnsauorie, of an euill taste, Insipidus.
Desabrigar, to set in the cold, Frigori exponere.
Desabrimiento, vnsauorinesse, Insulsitas.
Desabrochado, vnlaced, Diffibulatus, recinctus.
Desacompañar, to leaue companie, to separate, Dissociare, disiungere.
Desacompañado, alone, Solus.
Desacompañamiento, lonenesse, Solitudo.
Desacordar,

D E D E

Deſacordar, to forget, to diſagree, to diſ-
ſent, *Obliuiſci, diſcordare, diſſentire.*

Deſacuerdo, forgetfulnes, diſcord, diſ-
ſention, *Obliuio, diſcordia, diſſentio.*

Deſacordado, forgetfull, diſagreeing, *Ob-
liuioſus, diſſentiens.*

Deſacorde, diſagreeing, *Diſſentiens, diſſo-
nus, diſcors.*

Deſacordamente, diſagreeingly, *Diſcor-
diter.*

Deſacoſtumbrar, to diſaccuſtome, *Deſueſcere, deſuefacere.*

Deſafiar, to defie, to challenge, *Prouocare,
laceſſere.*

Deſañador, a challenger, *Prouocator, laceſ-
ſitor.*

Deſafúziar, to deſpaire, to diſtruſt, *Deſperare, diffidere.*

Deſaforrado, ill clad, ill apparelled, *Malè
veſtitus.*

Deſafueros, wrongs, iniuries, *Iniuriæ.*

Deſagradecer, to be vnthankfull, *Ingratum eſſe.*

Deſagradecido, vnthankfull, *Ingratus.*

Deſagradecimiento, vnthankfulnes, *Ingratitudo.*

Deſaguadero, a conduit, *Aquæductus.*

Deſayudar, to leaue without helpe, *Non
iuuare.*

Deſalforjar, to put out of a wallet, *Eman-
ticulari.*

Deſalabado, diſpraiſed, *Illaudabilis.*

Deſalabar, to diſpraiſe, *Vituperare.*

Deſalbardar, to vnſaddle an aſſe, *Clitella
exonerare.*

Deſalentado, breathleſſe, *Anhelus, Exanimis.*

Deſaliñar, to ouerturne, to ouerthrowe,
Reſupinare, peruertere.

Deſaliñado, ouerturned, fooliſh, vnfit,
Reſupinus, ineptus.

Deſaliño, giddines of the head, fooliſh-
nes, vnfitnes, *Perturbatio, ineptiæ, ineptitudo.*

Deſalmado, without life, without ſoule
Exanimis.

Deſamar, to hate, *Odiſſe, odio habere.*

Deſamparar, to forſake, to leaue, to caſt
off, *Deſerere.*

Deſamparado, left, forſaken, *Deſertus.*

Deſamparo, leauing, forſaking, *Deſertio.*

Deſamparador, he that leaueth, he that
forſaketh, *Deſertor.*

Deſañudar, to vnknit, *Enodare.*

Deſañudado, vnknit, *Enodatus.*

Deſañudadura, vnknitting, *Enodatio.*

Deſapegar, to vnlooſe, *Soluere.*

Deſaplazible, vnpleaſant, *Iniucundus.*

Deſapercebido, vnaduiſed, *Improuidus.*

Deſapercebidamente, vnaduiſedly, *Im-
prouidè.*

Deſapiedado, vnmercifull, *Inclemens.*

Deſaprouechar, to hinder, *Obeſſe, incommo-
dare.*

Deſaprouechado, hindred, *Incommodatus.*

Deſaprouechadamente, vnprofitably, *In-
commodè.*

Deſapriſionar, to let out of priſon, *Carcere
emittere.*

Deſapuntar, to rip vp, *Diſſuere.* (nis.

Deſapoderado, heady, headſtrong, *Infræ-*

Deſarmar, to vnarme, to ſhoot off, *Exar-
mare, exbaliſtare.*

Deſarmado, vnarmed, *Inermis.*

Deſarmadura, vnarming, *Exarmatura.*

Deſarraigar, to plucke vp by the root, *E-
radicare.*

Deſarraigamiento, plucking vp by the
root, *Eradicatio.*

Deſarrugadura, ſmoothing, *Erugatio.*

Deſarrugar, to make ſmooth, *Erugare.*

Deſaſnarſe, to ſpeake wiſer then of cuſtome, *Loqui ſolito acutius.*

Deſaſtre, misfortune, *Infortunium.*

Daſaſtrado, vnfortunate, deadly, *Infælix,
Exitialis.*

Deſatar, to looſe, to vntie, to diſſolue,
Soluere.

Deſataradura, looſing, vntying, *Solutio.*

Deſatauiado, vnfitted, vnhandſome, *Ineptus, incompoſitus.*

Deſatavio, vnhandſomneſſe, *Inconcinnitas.*

Deſatacar, to vntie, to vnbinde, *Soluere.*

Deſatapar, to open, to vnſtop, *Deoperculare*

Deſatapadura, opening, *Deoperculatio.*

Deſatinar, to ſtammer, to ſtumble, to
miſſe, *Titubare, vacillare, errare.*

Deſatinado,

D E   D E

Defatinado, ſtammering, ſtumbling, raſh, inconſiderate, rauing, *Titubans, vacillans, temerarius, inconſideratus.*

Defatino, ſtumbling, raſhneſſe, inconſiderateneſſe, folly, *Titubatio, temeritas, ineptiæ.*

Defatinadamente, raſhly, inconſideratelie, rauingly, fooliſhly, *Temerè, ineptè.*

Defatraueſſar, to take away any thing that lieth croſſe the way, *traſuerſa tollere.*

Defavenir, to diſagree, *Diſcordare.*

Desbalidas ouejas, ſtraying ſheepe, *Palanues.*

Desballeſtar, to ſhoot off a croſbow, *Exbaliſtare.*

Desbaratar, to put to flight, *Profligare.*

Desbarato, putting to flight, *Profligatio.*

Desbaratado, put to flight, *Profligatus.*

Desbaratador, he that putteth to flight, *Profligator.*

Desbarbado, beardleſſe, *Imberbis.*

Desbaſtar, to pare or ſhaue downe, *Dedolare, Lauigare.*

Desbaſtadura, the paring or ſhauing downe, *Dedolatio.*

Desbocado, headſtrong, alſo laviſh of ſpeech, *Effrænis, garrulus.*

Deſcabeçar, to behead, *Obtruncare.*

Deſcabeçado, beheaded, *Obtruncatus.*

Deſcabeçamiento, beheading, *Obtruncatio.*

Deſcabellado, pilled, bald, *Caluus.*

Deſcabeſtrar, to vnhalter, *Excapiſtrare.*

Deſcabullirſe, to ſlip away, *Elabi.*

Deſcaecer de la memoria, to ſlip out of memorie, *Excidere, obliuiſci.*

Deſcaecimiento, ſlipping out of memorie, *Obliuio.*

Deſcalçar, to vnſhoo, *Diſcalceare.*

Deſcalçado, vnſhod, *Diſcalceatus.* (brare.

Deſcalabrar, to breake ones head, *Excere*

Deſcalabrado, he that hath a broken head, a foole, *Excerebratus, cerebroſus, inſipiens.*

Deſcalabradura, the breaking of the head, *Excerebratio.*

Deſcaminar, to be out of the way, *Errare.*

Deſcaminado, out of the way, *Errans, Deuius.*

Deſcampar lluvia, to be faire weather, *Serenare.*

Deſcanſar, to reſt, *Quieſcere.*

Deſcanſo, reſt, *Quies.*

Deſcanſado, reſting, *Quieſcens.*

Deſcanſadamente, quietly, *Quietè.*

Deſcaperuzado, bareheaded, the cap off, *Aperto capite.*

Deſcapillar, to take away the cloake, *Pallio exuere.*

Deſcaradamente, ſhameleſlie, *Impudenter.*

Deſcarado, ſhameleſſe, *Impudens.*

Deſcargar, to vnburthen, to vncharge, *Exonerare.*

Deſcargo, vnburthening, vncharging, *Exoneratio.*

Deſcarillar, to teare the cheekes in ſunder, *Malas dirumpere.*

Deſcarilladura, tearing of the cheekes in ſunder, *Malarum diſſolutio.*

Deſcaſarſe, to deuorce, to breake off a marriage, *Diuortium facere, repudium facere.*

Deſcaſamiento, diuorce, procuring a diuorce, *Diuortium, repudium.*

Deſcavalgar, to alight off a horſſe, *Ex equo deſcendere.*

Deſcavalgadura, alighting off a horſſe, *Ex equo deſcenſus.*

Deſcaxar, to take out of the ſhale, *Enucleare.*

Deſcaxcamiento, follie, *Stultitia.*

Deſcercar, to raiſe a ſiege, *Obſidione liberare.*

Deſcercador, he that raiſeth a ſiege, *Ab obſidione liberator.*

Deſcerco, the raiſing of a ſiege, *Ab obſidione liberatio.*

Deſceñir, to vngird, *Diſcingere.*

Deſcerrajar, to vnlocke, *Reſerare.*

Deſceruigado, the necke ſtricken off, *Excernicatus.*

Deſcimentado, vndermined, digged vp, *Subrutus.*

Deſclauar, to vnnaile, *Clauum refigere.*

Deſcubrir, to diſcouer, *Retegere.*

Deſcocar, to make cleane, to take out wormes, *Vermes educere,*

Deſcolgar,

Descolgar, to take downe that which hangeth, *Detrahere.*
Descolgado, vnhanged, taken downe, *Detractus.*
Descocorar, to kill with a blowe in the necke, *Collum frangere.*
Descoger, to vnfolde, *Euoluere.*
Descolorado, without colour, *Decolor.*
Descolorar, to make without colour, *Decolorare.*
Descoloramiento, vncolouring, *Decoloratio.*
Descomedido, discourteous, vnmanerlie, *Inciuilis, inurbanus.*
Descomedimiento, discourtesie, *Inhumanitas, inurbanitas.*
Descompadrar, to breake off kindred, *Affinitatem soluere.*
Descomulgar, to excommunicate, *Excommunicare.*
Descomunion, excommunication, *Excommunicatio.*
Descomunal, vnmeasurable, *Immodicus.*
Desconcertar, to disagree, to breake a match, to set at variance, *Discordare, perturbare, confundere.*
Desconcierto, disagreement, trouble, confusion, *Discordia, perturbatio, confusio.*
Desconcertadamente, disorderly, disagreeingly, *Confusè, discorditer.*
Descontar, to abate in an account, *Subducere.*
Descuento, the rebatement, the allowance, *Subductio.*
Desconocido, vnthankefull, forgetfull, *Ingratus, obliuiosus.*
Desconocimiento, vnthankfulnesse, forgetfulnesse, *Ingratitudo, obliuio.*
Desconocidamente, vnthankefullie, *Ingratè.*
Desconfiar, to mistrust, *Diffidere.*
Desconfiança, distrust, *Diffidentia.*
Desconformar, to disagree, *Discordare.*
Desconfortar, to discomfort, *Exanimare.*
Descomedir, ido, to be vnmanerly, *Inurbanum esse.*
Desconvenir, *vide* Desconcertar.
Desconveniencia, *vide* Desconcierto.

Desconocer, to forget, to be vnthankefull, *Obliuisci, ingratum esse.*
Desconsolar, *vide* Desconfortar.
Desconsolado, discomforted, *Exanimatus.*
Desconsuelo, discomfort, *Exanimatio.*
Desconversar, to leaue company, *Societatem abrumpere.*
Descorazinarse, to be slothfull, to be dul, to be without heart, to be without spirit, *Excordem esse, inertem esse.*
Descorazinado, heartlesse, dull, sluggish, slow, *Iners, excors.*
Descorazinamiento, heartlesnesse, sloth, sluggishnesse, *Inertia, vecordia.*
Descortez, discourteous, *Inhumanus, inurbanus.*
Descortezia, discourtesie, *Inhumanitas, inurbanitas.*
Descortezmente, vncourteously, *Inhumaniter, inciuiliter.*
Descorchar o descortezar, to vnbarke, to plucke off the skin, *Decorticare, delibrare.*
Descortezadura, barking of trees, rinding of trees, *Decorticatio, Delibratio.*
Descoser, to rip vp, *Diffuere.*
Descostumbre o desuso, want of vse, *Desuetudo.*
Descosido, ripped vp, *Diffusus.*
Descrecer, to decrease, *Diminui, decrescere.*
Descreer, not to beleeue, *Diffidere.*
Descrecimiento, decreasing, *Diminutio.*
Descrinar, to take off the haire, *Crines auellere.*
Descreuir, scriuo, to write out, to describe, *Describere.*
Descripcion, writing out, description, *Descriptio.*
Descuento, satisfaction, *Satisfactio.*
Desculpar, to excuse, *Excusare.*
Desculpa, an excuse, *Excusatio.*
Descuydado, negligent, rechlesse, *Negligens, incurius.*
Descuydo, negligence, carelesnesse, *Negligentia, incuria.*
Descuydadamente, negligently, carelesly, *Negligenter, securè.*
Descubierto, open, discouered, *Apertus, retectus.*

Descubrir,

Defcubrir, to open, to difcouer, *Retegere, Aperire.*
Defcubridor, a difcouerer, *Index, retector.*
Defcubrimiento, difcouery, reuealing, *Retectio, Reuelatio.*
Defde niño, from the childehood, *A pueritia.*
Defde aqui a pocos dias, fhortly, *Breui.*
Defden, difdeine, *Dedignatio.*
Defdeñarfe, to difdeine, *Dedignari.*
Defdeñofo, difdeinfull, *Dedignabundus.*
Defdentado, without teeth, toothlelle, *Edentulus.*
Defdezir, to gainfay, to vnfay, *Palinodiam canere.*
Defdicha, misfortune, *Infalicitas, infortunium.*
Defdichado, vnfortunate, *Infælix.*
Defdichadamente, vnfortunately, *Infæliciter.*
Defdon, vncomlineffe, vnpleafantneffe, *Infulfitas, indecentia.*
Defdonado, vnpleafant in talke, *Infacetus, infulfus.*
Defdonadamente, vnpleafantlie, *Infacete, infulte.*
Defechado, cast off, *Defertus.*
Defecho, cafting off, *Defertio.*
Defechar, to cast off, *Deferere.*
Defelar, yelo, to thaw, *Regelare.*
Defembarrar, to open, *Aperire.*
Defembaraçar, to rid out of trouble, to rid out of incumbrance, *Expedire.*
Defembaraço, freeing from trouble, *Expeditio.*
Defembarcar, to take out of a barke, to take land, *Ex cymba defcendere.*
Defembocar, to come out of the mouth of a riuer or hauen, *Exgurgitare, E portu excedere.*
Defembriagar, to make fober one that is drunke, *Ebrietatem tollere.*
Defemboluer, to roll out, to vnroll, to let loofe, *Euolucre, diffoluere.*
Defemboltura, dexteritie, readineffe, *Strenuitas, dexteritas.*
Defembuelto, luftie, readie, quicke, *Strenuus, dexter, agilis.*

Defembofcar, to go out of the wood, *Sylua exire.*
Defembravecer, to make tame, *Manfuefacere.*
Defembravecimiento, making tame, quietneffe, *Manfuetudo.*
Defembuchar, to draw out, *Egurgitare.*
Defempachar, *vide* Defembaraçar.
Defempacho, *vide* Defembaraço.
Defempalagar, to rid the mouth, *Palatum abftergere, faftidium tollere.*
Defemparejar, to feparate, *Separare, difiungere.*
Defempegar, to feuer that which cleaueth to, *Relinere.*
Defempeñar, to redeeme a gage, *Pignus foluere.*
Defemperezar, to make luftie, to fhake off floth, *Segnitiem excutere.*
Defempoluar, to beate out duft, *Puluerem decutere.*
Defemprefiar, to be deliuered of childe, *Parere.*
Defempulgar arco, to vnbende a bowe, *Retendere.*
Defempulgadura, vnbending of a bowe, *Retenfio.*
Defencadenar, to vnchaine, *Catena foluere.*
Defencabeftrar, to vnhalter, *Excapiftrare.*
Defencantar, to vnwitch, *Recantare.*
Defencapotar orejas, to fet vp the eares, *Aures arrigere.*
Defencapotadura de orejas, the fetting vp of the eares, *Aurium arrectio.*
Defencapotar los ojos, to behold ftedfaftly, *Intueri, obtueri.*
Defencapotar la bavera, to fet vp the beuer, *Attollere bucculam.*
Defencafar hueffos, to put out of iointe, *Luxare.*
Defencafado, put out of ioynt, *Luxatus.*
Defencafadura, o defencafamiento, the being out of ioint, *Luxatio.*
Defenconar, to purge poifon, *Venenum expellere.*
Defenfamar, to defame, *Infamare.*
Defenfamado, infamous, *Infamis.*

I   Defenfrenar,

Defenfrenar, to vnbridle, *Effrænare*.
Defenfrenado, vnbridled, *Effrænis*.
Defenfrenamiento, vnrulines, *Effrænatio*.
Defengañar, to open a deceit, to perceiue a deceit, to leaue to be deceiued, *Fraudes retegere*.
Defengrudar, to vnglue, *Reglutinare*.
Defengrudamiento, vngluing, *Reglutinatio*.
Defenhadar, to take away lothfomnes, *Faſtidium tollere*.
Defenhado, the taking away of lothfomnes, *Faſtidy ſublatio*.
Defenhetrar, to deliuer out of a fnare, *Extricare*.
Defenfenar, to take out of the bofome, *Exinuare*.
Defenfañar, to appeafe wrath, *Placare*.
Defenfeñar, to vnteach, *Dedocere*.
Defenlazar, to loofe, to vntie, *Soluere*.
Defenquadernar libros, to vnbind books, *Libros diſſuere*.
Defenredar, to take out of a net, *E rete ſoluere*.
Defenfayar, to put off a caſſocke, *Tuniculam exuere*.
Defenterrar, to dig vp out of the earth, *Effodere*.
Defenterramiento, digging out of the earth, *Effoſſio*.
Defentonar, to founde out of tune, *Diſſonare*.
Defentonado en canto, a difcorde, *Diſſonantia*.
Defentrañar, to plucke out the bowels *Exenterare*. (*care*.
Deferedar, to difenherite, *Exhæredare, abdicare*.
Deferencia, difenhereting, *Exhæredatio, abdicatio*.
Deferedado, difenherited, *Exhæres, abdicatus*.
Defefperado, defperate, *Deſperans*.
Defefperacion, defpaire, *Deſperatio*.
Defefperar, to defpaire, *Deſperare*.
Defefperado, defperate, *Deſperans*.
Desfallecer, to faint, to fowne, *Deficere*.
Desfallecimiento, fainting, fowneing, *Defectus, defectio*.

Desfamar, to defame, *Infamare*.
Desfavorecer, to diflike, to put out of fauour, *Explodere*.
Desfavor, difſauor, difgrace, *Diſplicentia*.
Desfavorecedor, he that difliketh, he that difgraceth, *Improbator*.
Desfavorecido, difgraced, out of fauour, *Diſplicens, deformatus*.
Desfigurar, to deforme, to diffigure, *Deformare*.
Desflemar, to purge, to fcum a pot, *Deſpumare*.
Desflorar, to deflowre, *Deflorare*.
Desforme, illfauored, *Deformis*.
Desformidad, deformitie, *Deformitas*.
Desformar, *vide* desfigurar.
Desfogar, fuego, to coole, *Refrigerare*.
Desfrutar, to gather frute, *Fructus colligere*.
Desfundar, to beate out the head of a but or other veſſel, *Dolij caput pertundere, excutere*.
Defgajar, to cleaue a funder, to ſlit, to fplent, *Diffindere*.
Defgarro, brauing, bragging, *Iactatio*.
Defgarron, a bragging fellowe, *Iactabundus*.
Defgovernar, to mifgouerne, to diforder, *Male rem gerere*.
Defgoznar, to take off hinges, *Cardines auellere*.
Defgranar, to threſh, *Triturare*.
Defguarnecer, to vngarniſh, *Ornatum tollere*.
Defguſtar, to diflike, *Diſplicere*. (*lere*.
Defguſto, diflike, vnpleafantnes, *Diſplicentia*.
Defgracia, difgrace, vnpleafantnes, vncomelines, *Illepiditas, indecentia*.
Defgraciado, vnpleafant, vncomely, difgraced, *Illepidus*.
Difgraciadamente, vnpleafantly, without grace, *Illepidè, inſulſè*.
Defhazer, to vndoo, to vnmake, *Factum infectum reddere, diſſoluere, perdere*.
Defhazimiento, vndooing, vnmaking, *Diſſolutio*.
Defhecho, vndone, *Infectus, perditus*.
Defherrar beſtia hierro, to vnſhoo a horſe, *Soleam refigere*.

Defherrado,

Deherrado, vnſhod, *Exſoleatus.*
Deſhilar, to vntwiſt, *Retexere.*
Deſhiladura, vntwiſting, *Retexus.*
Deſhincar, to plucke vp, to plucke out a naile, *Refigere.*
Deſhincadura, plucking out, *Refixio.*
Deſhinchar, to aſwage the ſwelling, *Deturgere.*
Deſholejar, to pare, to flea, to vnbarke, *Deglubere, delibrare.*
Deſhollinar, to wipe away ſout, *Exfuliginare, fuliginem decutere.*
Deſhojar, to take of leaues, *Frondare.*
Deſhojador, he that taketh off leaues, *Frondator.*
Deſhojadura, pulling of leaues, *Frondatio.*
Deſhuſiar, to diſtruſt, to deſpaire, *Diffidere.*
Desjarretar la beſtia, *vide* Dejaretar.
Deſygual, vnequall, *Impar.*
Deſygualdad, inequalitie, *Imparitas.*
Deſygualarſe, to be vnequall, *Diſconuenire, imparem eſſe.*
Deſierto, forſaken, *Deſertus.*
Deſierto, a deſart, a wildernes, *Solitudo, eremus. (tum.*
Deſiño, deſeigne, purpoſe, *Propoſitũ, decre-*
Deſlatar, deſparar, to ſhoote off, *Emittere.*
Deſlate, ſhooting off, a iſt, a fond ſpeech, *Emiſſio, ineptie.*
Deſlavar, the waſhing off, *Elutio.*
Deſlavadura, to waſhe off, *Eluere.*
Deſleal, diſloyall, *Infidus.*
Deſlealdad, diſloyaltie, *Infidelitas.*
Deſleirſe, to be diſſolued, to crum breade, *Diſſolui, dilui, tabeſcere.*
Deſleidura, diſſoluing, *Diſſolutio, dilutio, tabes.*
Deſlechugar vides, to lop vines, to prune vines, *Frondare.*
Deſlechugador, he that pruneth vines, *Frondator.*
Deſlendrar, to take out nets, *Lentes tollere.*
Deſlenguado, without toong, he that can not rule his toong, a prater, *elinguis, linguax, futilis.*
Deſligar, to vnbinde, *Soluere.*

Deſlindar heredades, to mark out groūd, to bound, *Limitare.*
Deſlindadura, the marking or bounding, *Limitatio.*
Deſlindador, he that marketh, he that boundeth, *Limitator.*
Deſlizarſe, to ſlip, to ſlide, *Labi.*
Deſlizadero, a ſlipperie place, *Lubricum.*
Deſloar, to diſpraiſe, *Vituperare.*
Deſlomado, broken backed, *Delumbatus, elumbis.*
Deſlomar, to breake the backe, *Delumbare.*
Deſlomadura, breaking of the back, *Delumbatio.*
Deſlumbrar, to ſhadow, to darken, *Obumbrare.*
Deſluzir, to take away the glaſſe of anie colour, to darken, *Obſcurare.*
Deſluzido, darkened, *Obſcurus.*
Deſmayar, to diſmay, to ſown, *Examinare, Examinari.*
Deſmayo, diſmay, ſowning, *Examinatio.*
Deſmajolados capatos, ſhoes vnbuckled ſhoes downe at the heeles, *Calcei ſemiexuti.*
Deſmallar, to vnmaile, *Deloricare.*
Deſmalladura, vnmailing, *Deloricatio.*
Deſmanarſe, to ſtray, to go aſtray, *Aberrare, palare.*
Deſmanar de la mañada, to ſeuer from the flocke, *Separare, ſegregare.*
Deſmandarſe, to go aſtray, to miſgouerne himſelfe, to go out of order, *Exorbitare, confundere, aberrare, palare, malè ſe gerere.*
Deſmandado, diſordered, *Errans, immoderatus.*
Deſmarañar, to vntwine, to vnfolde, to vntangle, *Extricare, explicare.*
Deſmarhojar, to prune a vine, *Frondare.*
Deſmedrar, to faile, to faint, to empaire, to decreaſe, *Deficere, decreſcere, diminuere.*
Deſmejorar, to make worſe, *Deterere.*
Deſmejorado, made worſe, *Deterior.*
Deſmelonado, vntrimmed, filthy, ſlouenly, *Incomptus.*
Deſmembrar, miembro, to diſmember, *Deartuare.*

I 2   Deſmem-

Desmembradura, dismembring, *Dilaceratio.*
Desmemoriado, forgetfull, *Obliuiosus, Immemor.*
Desmenuzando, braying by peeces, *Minutius contusio.*
Desmenuzar, to diminish, to braie, to pound, *Diminuere, comminuere.*
Desmenuzado, broken, braied, pounded, *Diminutus, comminutus.*
Desmentir, to confute, *Refutare.*
Desmeollar, to take out the kernell, to take out the braines, *Medullam, cerebrum vel acinum educere.*
Desmeollamiento, taking out of the kernell, taking out of the braines, *Enucleatio, Excerebratio.*
Desmesurado, vnmeasurable, *Immodicus.*
Desmesura, want of measure, *Immodestia.*
Desmesuradamente, vnmeasurably, *Immodicè.*
Desmesurarse, to bee vnreasonable, to bee vnruly, *Immodestè se gerere.*
Desmerecer, to deserue ill, *Male mereri.*
Desmerecimiento, ill desert, *Malum meritum.*
Desmolerse, to be weake, to be tired, *Defatigari, tabescere.*
Desmoler, to digest meate, *Concoquere cibum.*
Desmoledura, the digesting of meate, *Concoctio cibi.*
Desmochar, to maime, to cutte off, *Mutilare.*
Desmochadura, maiming, cutting off, *Mutilatio.*
Desmochado, maimed, without hornes, *Mutilus.*
Desmontar, to grub vp trees, *Extirpare, runcare.*
Desmontadura, grubbing of trees, *Runcatio. (ere.*
Desmoronar, to pull downe a wall, *Diruere.*
Desnarigar, to cut off the nostrels, *Nares mutilare.*
Desnarigado, cut nosed, *Naribus mutilus.*
Desnatar, to skim a creame bole, *despumare lac.*

Desnaturalizar, to banish, *Proscribere.*
Desnaturalizado, banished, *Proscriptus.*
Desnegar, to recant, to deny, *Negare.*
Desnegamiento, denying, recanting, *Denegatio.*
Desnervar, to cut off sinewes, *Eneruare.*
Desnudar, to vncloth, to make naked, *Nudare.*
Desnudez, nakednes, *Nuditas.*
Desobedecer, to disobey, *Non parere.*
Desobediente, disobedient, *Inobediens.*
Desobedientemente, disobediently, *Inobedienter.*
Desobligar, to vnbinde, *Obligatione soluere.*
Desocupar, to leaue, *Deserere.*
Desocupado, left, *Desertus.*
Desollar suello, to skin, to pul off the skin, *Cutem detrahere.*
Desovillar, to vntwist, to vnwinde thred, *Retexere, euoluere.*
Desonesto, filthie, dishonest, *Inhonestus, turpis.*
Desonestidad, filthines, dishonestie, *Turpitudo.*
Deshonestar, to dishonest, *Dehonestare, inhonestè agere.*
Deshonrrar, to dishonor, *Inhonestare.*
Deshonrrado, dishonored, *Dehonestatus, inglorius.*
Deshonrra, dishonor, *Dedecus, ignominia.*
Desordenado, disordered, *Inordinatus.*
Desordenar, to disorder, *Ordinem confundere.*
Desordenadamente, disorderlie, *Inordinatè.*
Desorden, disorder, *Confusio ordinis.*
Desorejar, to cutte off the eares, *Auribus mutilare.*
Desorejado, the eares cutte off, *Auribus truncus.*
Desospedado, that keepeth no hospitalitie, *Inhospitalis.*
Desospedamiento, keeping of no hospitalitie, *Inhospitalitas.*
Desovada gallina, a henne that hath laid all her egges, *Effeta.*
Desossar, vesso, to take out bones, *Exossare.*
Desossado, without bones, *Exossatus.*

Despachar,

Despachar, to dispatch, *Absoluere negotium, Expedire.*
Despacho, expedition, dispatch, *Negotij absolutio, expeditio.* (*tus.*
Despachado, dispatched, *Absolutus, expedi-*
Despagarse, to be displeased, *Displicere.*
Despagamiento, displeasure, *Displicentia.*
Despajar trigo, to winnow corne, *Exacerare.*
Despajadura, winnowing of corne, *Exaceratio.*
Despalmar, to giue a blow on the cheeke, *Alapam dare.*
Despampanar las vides, to cut leaues off a vine, *Pampinare,*
Despampanadura, cutting leaues off a vine, *Pampinatio.*
Despampanador, a cutter of leaues from a vine, *Pampinator.*
Desparejar, to separate, *Seiungere.*
Desparar, to shoot off, *Exballistare.*
Desparate, foolishnesse, *Ineptiæ.*
Despartyr ruydo, to part a fray, *Partire, pugnæ se interponere, pacare seditionem.*
Despartidor de ruydo, a parter of a fray, *Qui pugnæ se interponit.*
Despavesar o despauilar, to snuffe a candle, *Emungere.*
Despavesadura, the snuffing of a candle, *Emunctio.*
Despavilador, snuffers, *Emunctoria.*
Despavilar, *vide* Despavesar.
Despearse, to be surbated, *Subterrere pedes.*
Despeadura, surbating, *Subtritio pedum.*
Despeado, surbated, *Subtritus pedibus.*
Despeçonar, to take away the stalke or stem of fruit, *Caulem detrahere.*
Despechar, to draw drie by tributes, *Exhaurire.*
Despechado, drawen drie by tributes, empouerished, driuen out of heart, *Exhaustus.*
Despechugar, to take out the flesh off the brest of a bird, *Expapillare.*
Despechugadura, taking out the flesh off the brest of a bird, *Expapillatio.*
Despedaçar, to rent in pieces, to teare in pieces, *Lacerare, discerpere.*

Despedaçado, torne in pieces, *Discerptus.*
Despedaçadura, tearing in pieces, *Discerptio.*
Despedir, to dispatch, to send away, *Dimittere, expedire.*
Despedida, dispatch, departure, *Expeditio, discessus.*
Despedido, dispatched, *Dimissus.*
Despedrar, despedregar, to pull out stones, *Elapidare.*
Despegar, to seuer that which cleaueth or sticketh, *Separare, seiungere.*
Despegadura, the seuering, *Separatio.*
Despejar, to dispatch, *Dimittere.*
Despeynar, to ruffle the haire, *Comam vibrare.*
Despeluzar, to haue the haire standing an end, *Horrere.*
Despernar, *vide* Desjarretar. (*dere.*
Despender, to spend, to dispend, *Impen-*
Despendedor, he that spendeth, *Expensor.*
Despensa, expence, charges in money, a seller, *Viaticum, impensa, sumptus, promptuarium.*
Despensero, a butler, a steward, *Promus obsonator.*
Despeñar, to throwe downe headlong, *Præcipitare.*
Despeñado, throwen downe headlong, *Præcipitatus.*
Despeñadero, a downfall, a steepe rocke, *Præcipitium.*
Desperar, to despaire, *Desperare.*
Desperacion, despaire, *Desperatio.*
Despepitar, *vide* Despeñar.
Desperdiciar, to scatter, to spend unthriftily, *Disperdere.*
Desperdiciado, spent unthriftily, *Disperditus.*
Desperdiciadura, spending unthriftily, *Disperditio.*
Despertar, pierto, to awaken, to raise, *Expergefacere, excitare.*
Despertador, he that awaketh, or raiseth, *Expergefactor, excitator.*
Despesar, to grieue, *Displicere, dolere.*
Despierto, awakened, *Experrectus, excitatus.*

Despiojar,

D E

Defpiojar, to take lice, to louʒe, *Expediculare*.
Defplazer, to difpleafe, *Difplicere*.
Defplazible, difpleafing, *Difplicens*.
Defplegar, to vnfolde, to make plaine, to take away pleits, *Explicare, displicare*.
Defplegadura, taking away pleits, making plaine, *Explicatio*.
Defplomado, liuely, vnleaded, *Alacris, acutus, fine plumbo*.
Defplumado, vnfeathered, pluckt, *Implumis*.
Defplumar, to plucke off feathers, *Deplumare*.
Defplumadura, plucking off feathers, *Deplumatio*.
Defpoblar, to vnpeople, to make defolate, *Depopulari*.
Defpoblado, vnpeopled, defolate, *Depopulatus*.
Defpoblacion, vnpeopling, making defolate, *Depopulatio*.
Defpojar, to fpoile, to vnarme, *Spoliare*.
Defpojado, fpoiled, vnarmed, *Difpoliatus*.
Defpojador, a fpoiler, he that vnarmeth, *Difpoliator*.
Defpojos, fpoiles, *Spolia*.
Defpoluorizar, to beat to duft, *In puluerem redigere*.
Defpofar, to betroth, *Defpondere*.
Defpofados, the betrothed, *Sponfus, vel fponfa*.
Defpoforios, the time of betrothing, *Sponfalia*.
Defpreciar, to defpife, *Paruifacere*.
Defpreciado, defpifed, *Contemptus*.
Defpreciador, a defpifer, *Contemptor*.
Defpreciadamente, difpightfully, *Contemptim*.
Defprecio, difpight, difpifing, *Contemptus*.
Defproveido, vnprouided, *Improuidus*.
Defpuchar, to draw out, *Exhaurire*.
Defpues, after, after that, afterwardes, *Poft, poftea, deinde*.
Defpuntar, to make blunt, *Obtundere*.
Defpuntado, made blunt, *Obtufus*.
Defquartizar, to quarter, *In quatuor partes, diffecare*.

D E

Defquiciar, to lift out of the hookes, *Cardine auellere*.
Defreglado, a ficke man that keepeth no diet, *Immoderatus*.
Defronchar, to heale fcabs, *Sanare*.
Deffabrido, *vide* Defabrido.
Deffaynar, to take out the fat, *Pinguedinem elicere*.
Deffear, to defire, to wifh, *Optare, cupere, expetere*.
Deffeo, defire, wifh, *Expetitio, optatum, optio*.
Deffeable, to be defired, *Defiderabilis, optabilis*.
Deffeablemente, defiroufly, *Optabiliter, defyderabiliter*.
Deffeofamente, defiroufly, *Optabiliter, cupide*.
Deffeofo, defirous, *Cupidus*.
Deffemejar, to be vnlike, *Diffimilem effe*.
Deffemejante, vnlike, *Diffimilis*.
Deffemejantemente, of another fafhion, *Diffimiliter*.
Deffervir, to miflike, *Difplicere*.
Deffollar, fuello, to paunche, *Exenterare euifcerare*.
Deffolladura, paunching, *Euifceratio*.
Deffollejar, to barke a tree, *Delibrare*.
Deffollinar, *vide* Defhollinar.
Deftajo en la obra, tafke worke, *Redemptio operis*.
Deftechar, to vntile a houfe, *Detegere*.
Deftechadura, vntiling, *Detectio*.
Deftellar, to drop, to diftill, *Diftillare*.
Deftelladura, dropping, diftilling, *Diftillatio*.
Deftemplado, vntemperate, *Intemperans*.
Deftemplança, intemperaunce, *intemperies*.
Deftempladamente, intemperately, *Intemperanter*.
Deftemplar hierro, to coole yron, *Refrigerare*.
Defterrar tierro, to banifh, *Profcribere*.
Defterronada tierra, clods of earth broken, balled ground, or rolled ground, *Terra vel gleba occata*.
Deftierro, banifhment, *Exilium*.
Defterrado, banifhed, *Exul*.

Deftetar.

D E   D E

Deſletar, to ſweate, *Ablactare.*
Deſtino, deſtinie, *Fatum.*
Deſtinar, to purpoſe, *Decernere, ſtatuere.*
Deſtiñar las colmenas, to make cleane hiues, *Purgare aluearia.*
Deſtorcer, to vnwreath, *Detorquere.*
Deſtravar, to vnplat, to vndo, *Seiungere, ſecernere.*
Deſtravado, vnplatted, *Secretus, ſeiunctus.*
Deſtral, an axe, *Securis.*
Deſtraleja, a hatchet, *Securicula.*
Deſtreza, dexteritie, *Dexteritas.*
Deſtroçar, to put to the worſt, to put to flight, *Profligare.*
Deſtroço, putting to the worſt, putting to flight, *Profligatio.*
Deſtroncar, to breake off, *Truncare.*
Deſtruir, uyo, to deſtroy, to waſte, *Deſtruere, vaſtare, excindere.*
Deſtruidor, a deſtroier, *Diſtructor, exciſor, vaſtator.*
Deſtrucion, deſtruction, *Diſtructio, vaſtatio excidium.*
Deſuñir, to ſeuer, to ſeperate, *Diſiungere.*
Deſuñido, ſeuered, ſeperated, *Diſiunctus.*
Deſuſarſe, to be out of vſe, *Obſoleſcere, deſueſcere.*
Deſuſado, vnuſed, vnuſuall, *Obſoletus.*
Deſuſo, want of vſe, *Deſuetudo.*
Deſvaynar, to draw out of the ſheath, to vnſheath, *Euaginare, ſtringere.*
Deſvaynadura, drawing out of the ſheath, *Euaginatio.*
Devaynado, drawen out of the ſheath, *Strictus.*
Deſvanecer, deſmayar, to vaniſh, *Euaneſcere.*
Deſvanecimiento, vaniſhing, ſowning, *Euaneſcens, deficiens.*
Deſvanecido, in a ſowne, vaniſhed, *Euanidus, deficiens.*
Deſvanecimiento de cabeça, ſwimming in the head, giddineſſe in the head, *Vertigo.*
Deſvan de caſa, a garret or cockloft, *Solarium.*
Deſvariar, to dote, to raue, to tell trifling tales, *Delirare, deſipere, inepire.*

Deſvario, dotage, ſenceleſſe talke, *Deliratio, ineptiæ, delirium.*
Deſvariado, a dotard, a talker without ſence, *Delirus, inſipiens.*
Deſvariadamente, dotingly, fondly, *Delirè, inſipienter.*
Deſventura, miſadventure, misfortune, *Infortunium.*
Deſventurado, vnfortunate, *Infælix.*
Deſventuradamente, vnfortunately, *Infæliciter.*
Deſvergonçado, ſhameleſſe, impudent, *Impudens.*
Deſvergonçarſe, to be ſhameleſſe, to be impudent, *Depudere.*
Deſverguença, impundencie, ſhameleſneſs, *Impudentia.* (denter.
Deſvergonçadamente, ſhameleſly, *Impudenter.*
Deſvelarſe, to ouerwatch, *Peruigilare.*
Deſvelado, ouerwatched, *Peruigil.*
Deſviarſe, to goe out of the way, *Deuiare, excrbitare.*
Deſvio, miſſing the way, *Diuerſio, aberratio.*
Deſvirgar, to deflowre, *Deflorare, Stuprare.*
Deſvirgamiento, deflowring, *Deuirginatio, Stupratio.*
Detener, to holde, to ſtay, *Detinere.*
Detenimiento, holding, ſtaying, *Detentio, retentio.*
Determinar, to determine, *Determinare, conſtituere.*
Determinacion, determination, *Determinatio, conſtitutio.*
Detiene bucy, cammocke, reſt harrow, ſo hin, *O nonys.*
De todo punto, altogether, *Omnino, prorſus.* (ſue.
Detras, after, *Poſt, pone.*
De traves, acroſſe, *Ex tranſuerſo.*
Deuda, det, *Aes alienum, debitum.*
Deudor, a debter, *Debitor, obæratus.*
Devanar, to winde vp, to roll vp, *Glomerare.*
Devanéar, to raue, to talke fooliſhly, *Delirare, deſipere.*
Devanaderas, bottomes of thred, clues of thred, *Glomeratoria.*
Devengar, to reuenge, *Vindicare.*

Devedar,

D E

Devedar, to forbid, *Vetare.*
Dever, to owe, *Debere.*
De veras, indeed, *Reipsa, reuera.*
Devido, due, *Debitus.*
Devidamente, duely, *Debitè.*
Deviedo, forbidding, *Vetatio.*
Devieſſo, a kinde of ſwelling or ſore, *Vlceris genus, panus.*
Deviſa, a deuiſe, *Inuentum.*
Deviſar, to perceiue, to eſpie, *Aſpicere.*
Devoto, deuout, *Deuotus.*
Devocion, deuotion, *Deuotio.*
Devotamente, deuoutly, *Deuotè.*
Dexar, to leaue, to let go, to forſake, *Dimittere, linquere, deſerere.*
Dexado, left, forſaken, *Relictus, deſertus.*
Dexo *vide* Cabo.
Dezeno, the tenth, *Decimus.*
Dezir digo, to ſpeake, to ſay, to indite, *Dicere, loqui, dictare.* (*tator, dicax.*
Dezidor, a ſpeaker, an inditer, *Dictor, di-*
Deziembre, December, *December.*
Dezmar, to tithe, *Decumare.*
Dezmero, a tither, *Decumator.*

D I

Dia, a day, *Dies.*
Dias ha, ſome day paſt, *Iam diu.*
Dia ferial, a holyday. *Dies feſtus.*
Diablo, a diuell, *Diabolus.*
Diabolico, diuelliſh, *Diabolicus.*
Diacono, a deacon, *Diaconus.*
Diaconadgo, a deaconſhip, *Diaconatus.*
Diadema, a crowne, a diademe, *Diadema.*
Diamante, a diamond, *Adamas.*
Diametro, the diameter, *Diameter.*
Diaquilon, a kind of drug, *Diachylon.*
Diaſpero, a iaſper ſtone, *Hiaſpis.*
Diſciplina, diſcipline, learning, correction, penance, *Diſciplina, doctrina, caſtigatio, pænitentia.* (*ſtigatus.*
Diſciplinado, taught, corrected, *Doctus, ca-*
Diſciplinar, to teach, to correct, *Docere, caſtigare.*
Diſcipulo, a ſcholler, *Diſcipulus.*
Dicha, lucke, fortune, hap, chance, *Caſus, fortuna, euentus.* (*natus.*
Dichoſo, fortunate, happy, luckie, *Fortu-*

D I

Dicho, a ſaying, *Dictum, dictus.*
Dichoſamente, happily, luckily, *Fauſtè, fortunatè.*
Dientes delanteros, the foreteeth, *Dentes primores.*
Diente, a tooth, *ens.*
Dieſtra mano, the right hand, *Dextera.*
Dieſtro, cunning, ſkilfull, perfect, *Dexter, ſtrenuus.*
Dieta, a daies iourney, diet, *Diarium, victus, diæta.*
Diez, ten, *Decem.*
Diezmo, the tenth, the tything, *Decimus, decima.*
Difamar, to defame, *Defamare.*
Diferir, fiero, to defer, *Differre.*
Diferencia, difference, *Differentia, diſcrimen.*
Diferente, different, *Differens.*
Diferentemente, diuerſly, *Differenter.*
Dificil, hard, *Difficilis.*
Dificilmente, hardly, difficultly, *Difficulter.*
Dificultad, difficultie, *Difficultas.*
Dificultar, to make hard, *Difficultatem inducere.*
Dificultoſamente, difficultly, hardly, *Difficulter, ægrè.*
Dificultoſo, hard, difficult, *Difficilis.*
Difinir, to define, *Definire.*
Difinicion, a definition, a deſcription, *Definitio.*
Difuſamente, diffuſedly, *Diffuſè.*
Difunto, dead, *Vita functus.*
Digerir, to digeſt, *Digerere, concoquere.*
Digeſtion, digeſtion, *Digeſtio, concoctio.*
Digeſtos, bookes of the ciuill lawe ſo called, *Digeſti.*
Digno, worthie, *Dignus.*
Dignidad, dignitie, worthineſſe, *Dignitas.*
Dignamente, worthily, *Dignè.*
Dilatar, to deferre, to prolong, *Differre, protelare.*
Dilacion, deferring, prolonging, *Dilatio, protelatio.*
Diligente, diligent, *Diligens.*
Diligentemente, diligently, *Diligenter.*
Diligencia, diligence, *Diligentia.*

Diluvio.

Diluvio, a deluge o2 flud, *Diluuium.*
Diminucion, diminishing, *Diminutio.*
Diminuido, diminished, *Diminutus.*
Diminuyr, nuyo, to diminish, *Diminuere.*
Dinero, monie, *Pecunia.*
Dinerofo, full of monie, *Pecuniofus.*
Diocefis, a dioces, *Diæcefis.*
Dios, God, *Deus.*
Diofa, a goddeffe, *Dea.*
Diputar, to depute, *Deputare.*
Difcorde, difagreeing, *Difcors.*
Difcordar, to difagree, to be at difcord, *Difcordare.*
Difcordia, difcor?, *Difcordia.*
Difcretamente, difcreetly, *Difcretè.*
Difcreto, difcreet, *Difcretus, prudens.*
Difcrecion, difcretion, *Difcretio, prudentia.*
Difcurrir, to difcourfe, *Difputare.*
Diffamar, *vide* Difamar.
Disfavor, *vide* Desfavor.
Disfavorecido, *vide* Desfavorecido.
Disforme, difformed, difagreeing in shape, *Deformis.*
Disfraçado, masked, muffled, *Perfonatus, laruatus.*
Disfrez, the masking, the muffling, *Perfona, larua.*
Disfraçadamente, closely, secretly, with a maske, *Secretè, capite obuoluto.*
Diflate, *vide* Deflate.
Difparar, to shoote off, *Emittere.*
Difparate, *vide* Deflate y Desvarío,
Difpenfar, to difpence, *Indulgere, foluere à legibus.*
Difpenfacion, difpenfation, *Indulgentia, folutio.*
Difponer, to difpofe, to o2der, *Difponere.*
Difpoficion, difpofition, o2der, health, *Difpofitio, fanitas.*
Difpuefto, bien difpuefto, difpofed, wel in health, *Difpofitus, fanus.*
Difputo, difputing, *Difputatio.*
Difputar, to difpute, *Difputare.*
Difputacion, difputing, *Difputatio.*
Difputador, a difputer, *Difputator.*
Difpuficion, difpofition, *Sanitas.*
Diffimular, to diffemble, *Diffimulare.*
Diffimulacion, diffimulation, *Diffimulatio.*

Diffimuladamente, diffemblingly, *Diffimulanter.*
Diffimulador, a diffembler, *Diffimulator.*
Diffimulado, diffembled, *Diffimulatus.*
Diffimulando, diffemblingly, *Diffimulanter*
Diffipar, to fcatter, *Diffipare.*
Diffipacion, fcattering, *Diffipatio.*
Diffipador, a fcatterer, *Diffipator.*
Diffencion, diffention, *Diffentio.*
Diffolucion, diffolning, *Diffolutio, luxus.*
Diffoluto, diffolued, diffolute, *Diffolutus.*
Diffonante, difagreeing, *Diffonus.*
Diffonancia, the difagreeing, *Diffonantia.*
Diffonar, to difagroe, *Diffonare.*
Diftancia, diftance, *Diftantia.*
Diftante, diftant, *Diftans.*
Diftinguir, to diftinguish, *Diftinguere.*
Diftinction, diftinction, *Diftinctio.*
Diftintamente, diftinctly, *Diftinctè.*
Diftinto, diftinct, diuided, *Diftinctus.*
Diftillar, to diftill, *Diftillare.*
Diftillacion, diftillation, *Diftillatio.*
Diftillada, diftilled, *Diftillatus.*
Diftribuir, uyo, to diuide, to diftribute, *Diftribuere.*
Diftribucion, diuifion, diftribution, *Diftributio.*
Difturbar, to difturbe, *Turbare.*
Ditado, a title, *Titulus.*
Ditamo, ditamie, *Dictamus.*
Diverfamente, diuerfly, *Diuersè.*
Diverfo, diuerfe, *Diuerfus.*
Diverfidad, difference, diuerfitie, *Diuerfitas*
Divertir, to turne afide, *Diuertere.*
Dividir, to diuide, *Diuidere.*
Dividido, diuided, *Diuifus.*
Divino, diuine, holy, a foothfaier, *Diuinus, fanctus, diuinater.*
Divinacion, diuining, foothfaying, *Diuinatio.*
Divinamente, diuinely, *Diuinè.*
Divinar, to diuine, to p2opheste, *Diuinare.*
Divinidad, diuinitie, *Diuinitas.*
Divifible, diuifible, *Diuifibilis.*
Divifion, diuifion, *Diuifio.*
Divorcio, diuo2ce, *Diuortium.*
Divulgar, to publifh, *Diuulgare.*
Diziembre, December, *December.*

K Dobla,

D O

Dobla, a piece of monie, *Monetæ genus.*
Doblado, doubled, *Duplex.*
Dobladamente, doubly, *Dupliciter.*
Doblar, to double, *Duplicare.*
Dobladura, doubling, *Duplicatio.*
Doble, double, *Duplum.*
Doblegar, to double, to bend twifold, *Lentare, flectere.*
Doblegadura, bending, *Flexus, flexio, lentatio.*
Doblegado, doubled, bent twifold, *Flexus.*
Doblegable, that may be doubled, that may be bent twifold, *Flexibilis.*
Doblez, the lining of a garment, *Pannus subditicius.*
Docil, fit to be taught, *Docilis.*
Dogal o cordel, a cord, a rope, a smithes instrument to hold horses by the nose, a grin to hold a horse, *Funis, restis, chorda, laqueus.*
Dolar, to hew, *Dolare.*
Dolado, hewed, *Dolatus.*
Dolencia, griefe, sicknes, a disease, ache, *Dolor, morbus.*
Doler, to grieue, to be sorie, *Dolere.*
Doliente, sicke, *Aegrotus.*
Dolor, griefe, *Dolor.*
Doloroso, sorowfull, grieued, *Dolens.*
Dolorosamente, sorowfully, greuously, *Ingenti cum dolore.*
Domar, to tame, *Mansuefacere, domare.*
Domadura, taming, *Domitura.*
Domador, a tamer, *Domitor.*
Domestico, of the house, tame, *Domesticus, mansuetus.*
Domesticamente, tamely, gently, *Mansuetè.*
Domestiqueza, tamenesse, gentlenesse, *Mansuetudo.*
Domesticar, to make tame, to make gentle, *Mansuefacere.*
Domingo, sunday, *Dies dominicus.*
Don, sir, also a gift, a reward, *Dominus, donum.*
Donacion, a gift, *Donatio.*
Donar, to giue, *Donare.*

Donador, a giuer, *Donator.*
Donayre, a iest, a wittie saying, *Facetia, lepidè.*
Donosamente, pleasantly, wittily, *Facetè, lepidè.*
Donoso, merrie, pleasant, wittie, *Facetus, lepidus.*
Donde, whither, where, *Quò, ubi.*
Dondequiera, wheresoeuer, *Vbicunque, quocunque.*
Doña, mistres, madam, *Domina.*
Donzella, a maid, a virgin, *Virgo.*
Dorada, a kind of fish, *Piscis genus.*
Doradilla, a kind of fish, also finely gilt, also an herbe called stone ferne or finger ferne, *Deauratus, Asplenium.*
Doradura, the gilding, *Deauratio.*
Dorado, gilt, *Deauratus.*
Dorador, a gilder, *Deaurator.*
Dorar, to gild, *Deaurare.*
Dormidera, poppie, *Papauer.*
Dormilon, a sluggard, *Dormitator.*
Dormir duermo, to sleepe, *Dormire.*
Dormidor, a sleeper, *Dormitor.*
Dormitorio, a dorture, a place to sleepe in, *Dormitorium.*
Dornajo, a pigs trough, *Aqualiculus.*
Dos, two, *Duo.*
Dos tanto, twise as much, *Bis tantum.*
Dos vezes, twise, *Bis.*
Dos añal, of two yeeres, *Bimus.*
Dotar, to endowe, *Dotare.*
Dotal, belonging to the dower, *Dotalis.*
Dote, dower, *Dos.*
Dotado, endowed, *Dotatus.*
Dotor, a doctor, *Doctor.*
Dotrina, learning, *Doctrina.*
Dotrinado, taught, *Doctus.*
Dotrinar, to teach, to instruct, *Docere.*
Doze, twelue, *Duodecim.*
Dozena, a dosen, *Duodenarium.*
Dozeno, the twelft, *Duodecimus.*
Dozeñal, of twelue yeeres olde, *Duodecim annorum.*
Dozientos, two hundred, *Ducenti.*

D R

Drago, dragon, a dragon, *Draco.*
Draguntia, dragons, *Dracontia.*

Drasgo

D V

Drafgo de cafa, Robin goodfellowe, *Incubus.*
Drama, a drain, *Drachma.*
Dromedario, a dromedarie, *Camelus.*

D V

Ducado, a ducket, a dukedome, *Ducalis aureus, ducatus.*
Ducho, accustomed, acquainted, *Assuetus.*
Duda, dout, *Dubium.*
Dudar, to doubt, *Dubitare.*
Dudoso, doubtfull, *Dubius.*
Dodosamente, doubtfully, *Dubiè.*
Duelo, griefe, mourning, *Dolor.*
Duendo, tame, *Mansuetus.* (*bus.*
Duende de casa, Robin goodfellow, *Incu-*
Dueño, a master, *Dominus.*
Dueña, a mistres, *Domina.*
Dulce, sweete, *Dulcis.*
Dulcemente, sweetely, *Dulciter.*
Dulçor, sweetenes, *Dulcedo.*
Dulçura, sweetenes, *Dulcedo.*
Duque, a duke, *Dux.*
Duquesa, a duchesse, *Duxcissa.*
Durable, durable, *Diuturnus, perennis.*
Duramente, hardly, *Dur iter.*
Duro, hard, cruell, niggardly, *Durus.*
Durar, to endure, to harden, *Diuturnare, indurare.*
Duracion, enduring, hardening, *Diuturnatio induratio.*
Durante, during, *Durans.* (*num.*
Durazno, a kind of peach, *Persicum duraci-*
Dureza, hardnes, *Duritia.*

E A

E. And, when the next word beginneth with I. *Et.*
Ea, go to, oh, holla, *Eia, age?*
Ea pues, go to then, *Agedum.*

E B

Ebeno, a blacke kinde of woode, *Hebenus.*

E C

Ecelentia, excellencie, *Excellentia.*
Ecelente, excellent, *Excellens.*

Ecesso, excesse, *Excessus.*
Eceptuar, to except, *Excipere.*
Ecepto, except, *Excepto.*
Ecepcion, an exception, *Exceptio.*
Eclipse, an eclipse, *Eclipsis.*
Eclipsar, to be eclipsed, *Pati eclipsin.*
Echar, to cast, to throw, to powre out, to lay, to lie, *Iacere, conijcere, effundere, iacere.*
Echar plumas, to put out feathers, *Plumescere.*
Echar renuevos, to bud out, *Germinare.*
Echadizo, cast out, *Proiectitius.*
Echacuervo, a scarcrow, a bragging fellow, *Iactabundus, cornifuga.*
Echar el cuervo, to make a vain bragging or prating, *Iactare.*
Eco, an eccho, *Eccho.*

E D

Edad, age, *Aetas.*
Edificar, to build, *Aedificare.*
Edificacion, building, *Aedificatio.*
Edificador, a builder, *Aedificator.*
Edificado, built, *Aedificatus.*
Edificio, building, *Aedificium.*
Edito, an edit, a proclamation, *Edictum.*
Edito publicar, to proclaime, *Edicere.*

E F

Efeminar, to effeminate, *Effæminare.*
Efecto, effect, *Effectus.*
Efectuar, to effect, *Efficere.*
Eficaz, effectual, *Efficax.*
Eficazmente, effectually, *Efficaciter.*
Eficacia, efficacie, *Efficacia.*

E G

Egloga, an egloge, *Egloga.*

E L

El, he, the, *Hic, ille.*
Ella, shee, *Hæc, illa.*
El qual, el que, he which, *Ille qui.*
Elada, a frost, *Pruina, gelu.*
Elado, frosen, *Rigidus, gelidus.*
Elar, yelo, to freese, *Rigescere, congelare.*
Eleboro, bearfoote, *Helleborus.*
Elecion, choyse, *Electio.*

Elefante,

Elefante, an elephant, *Elephas.*
Elefancia, a kinde of leprosie, *Elephantiasis.*
Elefantino, perteining to an elephant, *Elephantinus.*
Elegia, a mournefull song, *Elegia.*
Elegido, chosen, *Electus.*
Elegancia, finenes, *Elegantia.*
Elegante, fine, *Elegans.*
Elegantemente, finely, *Eleganter.*
Elegir lijo, to chose, *Eligere.*
Elemental, perteining to the elements, *Elementaris.*
Elemento, the element, *Elementum.*
Elevar, to lift vp, *Eleuare.*
Elitropia, marigolds, *Heliotropium.*
Eloquencia, eloquence, *Eloquentia.*
Eloquente, eloquent, *Eloquens.*
Eloquentemente, eloquently, *Eloquenter.*

E M

Emancipar, to set at libertie, to make free, *Emancipare.*
Emancipacion, setting at libertie, *Emancipatio.*
Embaçar, to make browne, *Fuscare.*
Embaçarse, to be astonied, to maruaile, *Stupere, admirari.*
Embaçador, he that maketh browne, *Fuscator.*
Embaçadura, the making browne, astonishment, *Fuscatio, stupor.*
Embaydor, a deceiuer, a cosener, *Fallax, impostor.*
Embaymiento, deceite, cosenage, *Fallacia, Deceptio.*
Embayr, to deceaue, to cosen, to make a man beleeue an vntruth, to make giddie, *In fraudem inducere, fallere, decipere, seducere, imponere, vertigine corripere.*
Embaraçar, to let, to stop, to entangle, *Impedire, implicare.*
Embaraçado, letted, stopped, entangled, *Impeditus, implicatus.*
Embaraço, let, stop, entangling, *Impedimentum, obstaculum.*
Embargar, to arrest, to stop, to staie, *Sequestrare, sistere, obstare.*
Embargo, arresting, stopping, staying, *Sequestratio, obstaculum.* (*linere.*
Embarrar, to daube with claie, *Argilla obEmbarrador,* he that daubeth, *Gypsator.*
Embarradura, dawbing, *Argillæ incrustatio.*
Embarcar, to embarke, *Conscendere nauem.*
Embarcadura, embarking, *Nauis conscensio.*
Embarbascar, to make fishe drunke, to make a man giddie in the head, *Vertigine corripere, vertiginosum facere.*
Embargante no embargante, notwithstanding, *Tamen, attamen.*
Embarnizar, to varnish, *Vernice illinire.*
Embarnizadura, a varnishing, *Vernicis delibutio, illinitio,* (*inijcere.*
Embaucar, to caste into a hole, *In Foramen*
Embaucador, he that casteth a ball into a hole, *Iniector in foramen.*
Embaucamiento, casting into hole, *Iniectio in foramen.*
Embaxada, an embassage, *Legatio.*
Embaxador, an embassador, *Legatus.*
Embeodar, to make drunke, *Inebriare.*
Embevecerse, to be astonied, to be amased, *Stupescere.*
Embevecido, astonied, *Stupens, stupidus.*
Embever, to drinke in, to sup vp, to draw in, *Imbibere.*
Embevido, drunke, supped vp, *Imbibitus, absorpus.*
Embermejar, to make red, *Rubefacere.*
Embermejecerse, to waxe red, *Rubere.*
Embiar, to send, *Mittere.*
Embiadizo, sent, *Demissitius.*
Embiado, sent, *Missus.* (*tio.*
Embidia, enuie, emulation, *Inuidia, æmulaEmbidia* aver, to enuie, to emulate, *Aemulari, inuidere.*
Embidioso, enuious, *Inuidiosus.*
Embite, vieng at any game, *Iteratio.*
Embiudarse, to become a widow, *Viduari.*
Emblanquecerse, to make white, to make pale, *Albescere, dealbare.* (*albatio.*
Emblanquecimiento, making white, *DeEmbocar, vide* Embaucar.
Embolsar, to purse vp, *In crumenam cödere.*
Emboltorio, a packe, a furdell of foule clothes, *Fasciculus, sarcina, innolucrum.*
Embolver,

Empolver, to rolle vp, to wrap vp, *Inuoluere, glomerare.*
Embolvedor, a roller, a wrapper vp, *Inuolutor, glomerator.*
Embolvimiento, rolling, wrapping vp, *Inuolutio.*
Emboltorio de letras, a packet, *Fasciculus.*
Emborrachar, to make drunke, *Inebriare.*
Emboscarse, to go into a wood, *In syluam se recipere.*
Emboscada, an ambush, *Insidiæ.*
Embotador, a duller, *Obtusor.*
Embotamiento, dulling, *Hebetatio, retusio.*
Embotar, to make dull, *Obtundere, Retundere.*
Embotado, dulled, *Obtusus.*
Embovecerse, to become a foole, *Desipere.*
Embovecido, become a foole, *Insipiens.*
Embovecimiento, folly, foolishnesse, *Stupor, stultitia.*
Embraçar, to make fit for the arme, *Brachio aptare.*
Embraçadura, fitting to or for the arme, *Brachij aptatio.* (circ.
Embravecerse, to be fierce, *Efferari, Ferocire.*
Embravecimiento, fiercenesse, *Ferocia.*
Embriagarse, to be drunke, *Inebriari.*
Embriago, a drunkard, *Ebriosus.*
Embriagado, drunken, *Ebrius.*
Embriaguez, drunkennesse, *Ebrietas.*
Embrocar, to powre in, *Inuergere.*
Embrocadura, powring in, *Infusio.*
Embrutecerse, to waxe rude, to waxe brute, *Obrutescere.*
Embudar, to tunne vp, *In infusorium indere.*
Embudo, a tunnell, *Infusorium.*
Embuelto, wrapped vp, rolled vp, intangled, *Inuolutus.*
Embuste, cosenage, deceit, *Fraus, dolus, impostura.*
Embutir, to stuffe, *Farcire.*
Embutido, stuffed, *Refertus.*
Emelga, a ridge, *Candetum.*
Emendar miendo, to amend, *Emendare.*
Emendador, an amender, *Emendator.*
Emendadura, amendment, *Emendatio.*
Emendado, amended, *Emendatus.*
Emendadamente, perfectly, *Emendatè.*

Emienda, amendment, *Emendatio.*
Emispherio, the hemisphere, *Hemisphærium.*
Emina, a kind of measure, *Hemina.*
Emmaderar, to timber, *Contignare.*
Emmaderamiento, timber worke, *Contignatio.*
Emmagrecerse, to waxe leane, *Macrescere.*
Emmarañar, to winde vp, to roll vp, *Conglomerare, intricare.*
Emmarañado, wound vp, rolled vp, *Conglomeratus, inuolutus, intricatus.*
Emmarchitarse, to wither, to pine, *Tabescere, marcescere.*
Emmascarar, to maske, *Personam induere.*
Emmascarado, masked, *Laruatus, personatus.*
Emmocecerse, to waxe a boy, *Pubescere.*
Emmohecerse, to waxe mouldie, to waxe mustie, *Situ obduci.*
Emmotada, steepe vp, *Acclinis.*
Emmotadura, steepenesse, *Acclinitas.*
Emmudecerse, to be dum, *Mutum esse.*
Empachar, to let, to hinder, to trouble, *Obstare, obsistere, turbare.*
Empachadamente, troublesomely, *Turbatè.*
Empacho, trouble, let, hinderance, rudenes, *Turba, obstaculum, inurbanitas.*
Empachado, troubled, letted, rude, *Turbatus, prohibitus, inurbanus.*
Empadronar, to register in the number of such as are no gentlemen, *Censere.*
Empadronado, registred, *Census.*
Empalagar, to loath, to make the mouth out of taste, *Fastidium parere.*
Empalagado, loathing, *Fastidiosus.*
Empalagamiento, loathsomnesse, *Fastidium.*
Empalar, to set on a pole or stake, *In perticam ponere.*
Empanada, a pastie, *Artocrea.*
Empandar, to bend, to bow, *Lentare.*
Emparedar, to shut in a wall, *Muro includere.*
Empapar, to embrew, *Inficere.*
Emparejar, to compare, *Comparare.*
Emparejadura, comparing, *Comparatio.*

Empeçar,

Empeçar, pieço, to begin, *Incipere*.
Empeciente, harmfull, *Noxius*.
Empecer, to hurt, to hinder, *Infestare, impedire*.
Empecimiento, hurt, hinderance, *Infestatio, impedimentum, noxa*.
Empedernido, stonie, *Lapideus*. (cere.
Empedernecerse, to waxe stonie, *Lapidescere*.
Empedrar, to paue, *Pauimentare*.
Empedrador, a pauier, *Pauimentator*.
Empedrado, paued, stoned, *Pauimentatus*.
Empegar, to pitch, *Picare*.
Empegado, pitched, *Picatus*.
Empegadura, pitching, *Picatio*. (*tagra*.
Empeyne, the tetter, the itch, *Impetigo, mē-*
Empeyne, the horne in a horse leg neare the inside by the knee, also liuerwurt, *Lichen*.
Empeynoso, full of tetters, *Impetiginosus*.
Empellejar, to couer with skin, *Cutem inducere*. (*ductus*.
Empellejado, couered with skin, *Cute in-*
Empellar, empuxar, to thrust, *Impellere*.
Empellon, empuxon, a thrust, *Impulsus*.
Empeñar, to gage, to pledge, *Oppignerare*.
Empeñado, gaged, pledged, *Oppigneratus*.
Empeño, a gage, a pledge, *Pignus*.
Empeorar, to make woorsse, to empaire, *Deterius fieri*.
Empeoramiento, empairing, *Degeneratio, defectio*.
Empeorado, empaired, *Deficiens, deterior*.
Emperador, an emperour, *Imperator*.
Emperatriz, an empresse, *Imperatrix*.
Emperial, perteining to the empire, *Imperialis*.
Emperchar, to set on a pearch or on a string, *Pertice affigere*.
Emperezar, to be slothfull, *Pigrescere*.
Empero, yet, *Tamen*.
Emperrado, become a dogge, dogged, *Cani similem esse*.
Emperradamente, doggedly, *Canino more*.
Empicotar, to set on the pillory, *Palo affigere*.
Empicotadura, setting on the pillory, *Ad palum affixio*. (*fixus*.
Empicotado, set on the pillorie, *Palo af-*

Empinar, to lift vp, to stand on tippe toe, *Attollere, erigere*.
Empinado, lifted vp, *Sublatus, erectus*.
Empinadura, lifting vp, *Sublatio, eleuatio*.
Emplastrar, to plaister, *Emplastrare*.
Emplastradura, plaistering, *Fomentatio*.
Emplastro, a plaister, *Fomentum*.
Emplazar, to cite, to summon, *Citare*.
Emplazador, a summoner, a citer, *Citator, lictor*.
Emplazamiento, summoning, citing, *Citatio*.
Emplear, to imploy, *Insumere*.
Empleado, employed, *Insumptus*.
Empleyta o emplenta, a mat, a hurdle, *Storea, craticula*.
Emplumar, to feather, *Plumis tegere*.
Emplumado, feathered, *Plumis tectus*.
Emplumecer, to haue feathers, *Plumescere*.
Empobrecer, to be poore, *Depauperari*.
Empoderar, to obteine, to winne, *In potestate habere, adipisci*.
Empolvorar, to beat to dust, *In pulueren redigere*.
Empolvorado, beaten to dust, *In pulueren redactus*.
Empolvoramiento, beating to dust, *Pulueratio*.
Empollar, to breed chicke, *Pullescere*.
Empollado, an egge that hath a chicke, *Pullescens*.
Empolla, a blister, *Ampulla, pustula*.
Empolvar, to cast dust on, *Puluerem inijcere*.
Empos, after, *Post*.
Emponçoñar, to poison, *Veneno inficere*.
Emponçoñado, poisoned, *Venenatus*.
Empozar, to put into a ditch, *In fossam dimittere*.
Emprentar, to print, *Imprimere*.
Emprenta, print, *Impressio*.
Empreñar, to get with childe, *Fæcundare, concipere, prægnantem facere*.
Emprender, to take vpon him, *Suscipere*.
Emprensar, to presse, *Imprimere*.
Emprensado, pressed, *Impressus*.
Empresa, an enterprise, *Captum, Incæptum*.

Emprestar,

E N

Empreſtar, to borrow, to lend, *Mutuà accipere & dare.*
Empreſtado tomar, to borrow, *Mutuari.*
Empreſtido, borrowed, lent, *Mutuus.*
Empringar, to baſte, to drop with hoat bacon greaſe, *Feruente axungia delinere.*
Empulgar arco, to bend a bow, *Tendere.*
Empulgadura, bending of a bow, *Tenſio.*
Empulgueras, the nocks of a bow, *Crenæ.*
Empuñadura, the haft or handle, *Capulus.*
Empuñar, to gripe in the fiſt, *Pugno premere.*
Empuxar, to puſh, to thruſt, *Impellere.*
Empuxado, thruſt, puſhed, *Impulſus.*
Empuxando, with thruſt, *Pulſaum.*
Empuxon, a thruſt, *Impulſus.*
Emputecer, to become a harlot, *Proſtare, proſtituere ſe.*
Emulo, he that enuieth, *Aemulus.*

E N

En, in, by, of, *In, e, de.*
Epagenar, to alienate, *Abalienare.*
Enagenamiento, alienating, *Abalienatio.*
Enaguaçar, to water, *Aquare.*
Enalbardar, to ſet on a packſaddle, *Clitella onerare.*
Enamorado, enamored, *Amans, amator.*
Enamorar, to enamorate, *Amare.*
Enamoramiento, loue, enamoring, *Amor.*
Enano, a dwarfe, *Nanus.* (*dere.*
Enarcar, to put in a cheſt, *In arcam recondere.*
Enarcado, put in a cheſt, *In arca reconditum.*
Enaſpar el cuerpo, to reame, to reach, *Pandiculare, exporrigere ſe, extendere.*
Enaſtar lança, to point a lance, *Ferrum præfigere.*
Enaſtado, headed with iron, *Ferro præfixus.*
Enaſtadura, pointing of a lance, *Ferri præfixio.*
Enaziado, a runnagate, *Perfuga, Transfuga.*
Encabellado, long haired, *Capillatus, comatus.*
Encabellecerſe, to haue long haire, *Comare.*
Encabeſtrar, to halter, *Capiſtrare.*

E N

Encabeſtrado, haltred, *Capiſtratus.*
Encadenar, to chaine, *Catenare.*
Encadenado, chained, *Catenatus.*
Encadenadura, chaining, *Catenatio.*
Encalabriar, to pierce into the braines, *In cerebrum penetrare.*
Encalar, to lime, to plaiſter a houſe, *Calce illinire.*
Encaladura, the liming, the plaiſtering of an houſe, *Calcis obductio.*
Encallar la naue, to ſtrike on ground, *Nauem illidere.* (*uia.*
Encalladura, ſtriking on ground, *Illiſio nauia.*
Encallecer, to waxe hard as brawne, *Calleſcere.*
Encallecido, growen hard, *Calloſus.*
Encalmado, calmed, *Tranquillus.*
Encalvar, to make balde, *Caluum facere.*
Encalvecerſe, to waxe bald, *Caluum fieri.*
Encambio, change, *Commutatio.*
Encaminar, to direct, *In viam reducere.*
Encaminadura, direction, *Directio, in viam reductio.*
Encandilado, dazled with ſudden light, *Præſtrictus.*
Encanecerſe, to waxe hoare, *Caneſcere.*
Encañonarſe las aves, to be hard feathered, *Plumeſcere.*
Encantar, to inchant, *Incantare, faſcinare.*
Encantado, inchanted, *Incantatus.*
Encantador, an enchanter, *Incantator, præſtigiator.*
Encantamiento, an inchauntment, a charme, *Incantatio, carmen.*
Encapacetado, armed with a helmet, *Galeatus.*
Encapado, cloaked, *Palliatus.*
Encapachar, to put in a maund, *In cophinum condere.*
Encapotado de orejas, flag eared, *Flaccidus.*
Encapotar los ojos, to twinkle the eies, *Conniuere.*
Encapotado de ojos, fat eie browed, *Toruus, ſuperciliofus.*
Encapotadura, lowring, *Toruitas.*
Encaramar, to raiſe vp to a top, *Faſtigiare.*
Encaramadura, raiſing vp to a top, *Faſtigium.*

Encaramado,

Encaramado, raiſed, *Erectus.*
Encarcoxado, he that carieth a quiuer, *Pharetratus.*
Encarcelar, to impriſon, *Incarcerare.*
Encarcelado, impriſoned, *Incarceratus.*
Encarnar, to become fleſh, *Incarnari, carnem aſſumere.*
Encarnacion, incarnation, *Incarnatio.*
Encarniçar, to torment, *Carnificare, torquere*
Encarniçamiento, tormenting, *Cruciatus, tormentum.*
Encarniçador, a tormentor, *Cruciator.*
Encarecer, to augment, to amplifie, to extoll, *Amplificare, magnifacere.*
Encargar, to charge, *Mandare, onerare.*
Encartar, to baniſh, *Proſcribere.*
Encartado, baniſhed, *Proſcriptus.*
Encartacion, baniſhing, *Proſcriptio.*
Encaſtellar, to ſhut in a caſtle, *In arcem includere.*
Encaſtellado, ſhut in a caſtle, *Incluſus.*
Encaxar, to put into a boxe, *In pixidem condere.*
Encaxe, encaxadura, putting in a boxe, *Pixidatio.*
Encella, a cheſt, a ſatchell, *Fiſcella, pera.*
Encenagar, to durt, *Oblimare, cæno polluere.*
Encenagado, durtie, *Oblimatus.*
Encenagamiento, raying with durt, *Oblimatio.*
Encenizar, to ſtraw with aſhes, *Cinere conſpergere.*
Encender ciento, to kindle, to ſet on fire, *Incendere.*
Encendimiento, kindling, ſetting on fire, *Incendium, inflammatio.*
Encendidamente, hotly, *Inflammanter.*
Encenderſe, to burne, to be kindled, *Ardere, incendi.*
Encendido, kindled, *Incenſus.*
Encenſio, frankincenſe, *Thus.*
Encenſios, wormwood, *Abſynthium.*
Encenſiar, to cenſe, *Thurificare.*
Encenſario, a cenſer, *Thuribulum.*
Encenſar, to taxe, *Cenſere.*
Encenſar tierra para plantar, to ſet graſſing ſtockes, *Emphyteuſin dare.*
Encenſo, taxing, *Cenſus.*

Encentar, to ſet abroach, *Delibare.*
Encentadura, ſetting a broach, *Delibatio.*
Encerar, to waxe, *Incerare.*
Encerrar, to ſhut in, to locke in, *Condere, occludere.*
Encías, gums, *Gingiua.*
Encienſo, incenſe, franckincenſe, *Thus.*
Encima, on the top, vpon, *Supra, ſuper.*
Encimar, to ſet on a top, *Faſtigiũ imponere.*
Enclavar, to faſten, to naile faſt, *Clauo figere.*
Enclavado, faſtned, nailed faſt, *Clauo fixus.*
Enclavijar los dedos, to clinch the hands with the fingers one betweene another, *Digitos pectinatim complicare.*
Encobar, to put in a caue, *In cauernam immittere.*
Encobadura o encorvadura, making crooked, *Incurvatio.*
Encoger, to withdraw, to draw togither, *Recipere ſe, contrahere.*
Encogimiento, withdrawing, drawing togither, *Receptio, contractio.*
Encogido, drawen togither, withdrawen, *Contractus, qui recepit ſe.*
Encojar, to trip, to giue a blowe on the leg, *Supplantare.*
Encolar, to glue, *Conglutinare.*
Encolado, glued, *Conglutinatus.*
Encoladura, gluing, *Conglutinatio.*
Encomendar, to commend, to commit, *Commendare, committere.*
Encomendado, recommended, committed, *Commendatus, commiſſus.*
Encomienda, recommending, commendations, a kinde of dignitie ſo called, *Commendatio, commiſſio.*
Enconar, to putrifie, to feſter, to infect, *Contagione inficere, exulcerare.*
Enconamiento, putrifaction, infection, *Contagio, infectio, putredo.*
Encontinente, preſently, *Statim, mox, ilicò.*
Encontrar, to encounter, to meete with, *Obuiare.*
Encontradizo, meeting, *Obuius.*
Encorar, to skin vp, to couer with skin, to couer with leather, *Cicatrice obducere, cutem obducere, corio ſegere.*

Encordio,

Encordio, a swelling in the head oɀ flank, a botch, *Panus, vkus, bubo.*
Encoraçado, he that hath a paper on his head foɀ any offence, *Mitratus.*
Encorporar, to incoɀpoɀate, *Incorporare.*
Encorporado, incoɀpoɀated, *Incorporatus.*
Encorvada, a woɀt, *Securidaca.*
Encorvado, made crooked, *Curuus.*
Encorvar, to make crooked, *Curuare.*
Encorvadura, crookednes, *Curuitas.*
Encoſtrar, to make cruſtie, *Incruſtare.*
Encoſtradura, making cruſtie, *Incruſtatio.*
Encreſpar, to make curled, *Criſpare, calamiſtrare.*
Encreſpado, curled, *Criſpatus, criſpus.*
Encreſpadura, curling, *Criſpatio.*
Encreſtado, creſted, *Criſtatus.*
Encrudecer, to waxe raw, to waxe cruell, *Crudeſcere, ſæuire.*
Encruelecer, to waxe cruell, *Deſæuire.*
Encruzado, croſſed, *In crucis formam compactus.*
Encruzijada, a croſſe way, *Compitum.*
Encubertado, couered, *Coopertus, celatus.*
Encuberta, a couering, the vtter ſhæte of a letter, *Tegmen, tectio, latebra.*
Encubertamente, couertly, *Secreté.*
Encubrir, to couer, to hide, *Tegere.*
Encubridor, a couerer, *Celator.*
Encubredizo, ſecret, *Secretus, latebroſus.*
Encubrimiento, couering, hiding, *Tectio, celatio.*
Encuadernar libros, to binde bookes, *Conſuere libros.*
Encuadernacion, binding of bookes, *Vmbilicatio.*
Encuadernador, a booke binder, *Vmbilicator librorum.*
Encuentro, incounter, meeting, *Congreſſus, conflictus.*
Encumbrar, to lift vp, *Culmen ponere, cacuminare.*
Encumbrado, lifted vp, *Cacuminatus.*
Endechas, mournings at a buriall, *Funebria.*
Endechaderas, the mournings, *Funus.*
Endemoniado, poſſeſſed with a diuell, *Dæmoniacus.*

Endentecer los niños, to haue teeth, *Dentire.*
Endereçar, to direct, to make ſtraight, *Dirigere.*
Enderedor, round about, *Circum, circa.*
Endívia, Endiue, *Intybus.*
Endolencias, a day when pardons are publiſhed, *Indulgentiarum dies.*
Endulçar, to make ſwæte, *Dulceſcere, dulcorare.*
Endulçadura, making ſwæte, *Dulcoratio.*
Endulgencias, pardons, *Indulgentiæ.*
Endurecerſe, to waxe hard, *Dureſcere.*
Endurecimiento, hardnes, waxing hard, *Duritas, durities.*
Endurecido, hardened, *Durus, obduratus.*
Enéa, an herbe wherewith they make mats, *Panicula.*
Enebro, Juniper, *Iuniperus.*
Enechar, to lay out a childe, *Exponere.*
Enechado, laid out, an oɀphan, *Expoſitus.*
Eneldo, Dill, *Anethum.*
Enemigo, an enemie, *Inimicus, hoſtis.*
Enemiſtad, enimitie, *Inimicitia, hoſtilitas.*
Enemiſtar, to beare enmitie, *Inimicare.*
Enemigable, hatefull, *Hoſtilis.*
Enemigablemente, like an enimie, *Hoſtiliter, inimiciter.*
Enemigar, to make enimies, *Inimicare.*
Enero, Januarie, *Ianuarius.*
Enerizar, to waxe ſtiffe, to waxe rough, *Horrere, horreſcere.*
Enerizado, ſtiffe, rough, *Horridus, aſper.*
Enerizamiento, ſtanding vp of the haire, briſtling of the haire, *Horror, echinatus, horripilium.*
Enertarſe, to waxe rough, *Rigere.*
Eneſſar, to couer with moɀter, *Gypſare.*
Enfadar, to grieue, to offend, to tire, to be lothſome, *Faſtidire, diſplicere, fatigare.*
Enfadado, wearied, tired, offended, *Faſtidioſus, fatigatus.*
Enfadoſo, tedious, weariſome, lothſome, *Faſtidioſus.*
Enfamado, famous, *Famigeratus.*
Enfermar, to be ſicke, *Aegrotare.*
Enfermo, ſicke, grieued, *Aegrotus, infirmus, æger.*

E N   E N

Enfermedad, **weakenes, sicknes, griefe,** *Infirmitas, morbus, ægritudo.*
Enfermeria, **an hospitall or spittle,** *Valetudinarium.*
Enflaquecer, **to be weake, to be leane,** *Languere, flaccescere, macrescere.*
Enflaquecido, **weakened,** *Languens.*
Enforrar, **to fur, to line,** *Duplicare.*
Enforrado, **furred, lined,** *Duplicatus.*
Enfotar, **to incourage, to set on,** *Animare.*
Enfotado, **incouraged, set on,** *Animatus.*
Enfrascarse, **to sticke fast, to be intangled,** *Hærere, impediri, intricari.*
Enfrenar, **to bridle, to restraine,** *Frænare, infrænare.*
En frente, **ouer against, afrunt,** *Ex aduerso, è regione.*
Enfriar, **to make cold,** *Frigefacere.*
Enfriadera, **a cooling place,** *Frigidarium.*
Enfriado, **cooled,** *Frigefactus.*
Enfundar, **to swathe, to swaddle,** *Fasciare, fascijs inuoluere.*
Enfurecer, **to be mad, to be furious,** *Furere.*
Enfurecido, **furious, raging,** *Furens.*
Engaço, **a rake,** *Rastrum.*
Engañar, **to deceiue,** *Decipere, fallere, imponere.*
Engañador, **a deceiuer,** *Impostor, fraudulentus, deceptor.*
Engaño, **deceit,** *Fraus, deceptio.*
Engañoso, **deceitfull,** *Fraudulentus, deceptor.*
Engañosamente, **deceitfully,** *Fallaciter, fraudulenter.*
Engarrafar, **to graple,** *Iuncare.*
Engaſtar, **to set a stone in a ring, to set peeces in a bourd or table,** *Cælare.*
Engaſtador, **he that setteth stones,** *Cælator.*
Engaſtado, **set in,** *Cælatus.*
Engaſte, **the setting in,** *Cælatura.*
Engendrar, **to beget,** *Gignere, generare.*
Engendrado, **begotten,** *Generatus, Ingenitus.*
Engeño, **an engine,** *Machina.*
Engeñero, **an engine maker,** *Machinarius.*
Engolfar, **to launch into the deepe,** *In altum nauigare.*
Engordar, **to make fat, to make groſſe,** *Pinguefacere, saginare.*

Engordado, **fatted, groſſe,** *Pinguefactus, saginatus.*
Engorra, **stay, delay,** *Mora.*
Engorrar, **to ſtay, to delay,** *Cunctari.*
Engorrando, **by delaies,** *Cunctanter.*
Engorroſo, **troubleſome to carry,** *Molestus.*
Engrandecer, **to make great, to magnifie, to aggrauate, to extoll,** *Magnificare, exaggerare.*
Engrandecido, **extolled, made great, magnified,** *Magnificatus.*
Engrandecimiento, **extolling, magnifying, making great,** *Magnificatio.*
Engroſſar, **to make fat,** *Saginare.*
Engrudo, **glue,** *Gluten.*
Engrudar, **to glue,** *Glutinare.*
Engrudamiento, **gluing,** *Glutinatio.*
Engrudoſo, **gluie,** *Glutinoſus.*
Engrumecer, **to clot, to quar like cold blood,** *Grumeſcere.*
Engullir, **to swallow vp,** *Deglutire.*
Engurria, **a pleight, or wrinkle,** *Ruga.*
Engurriado, **pleighted, wrinckled,** *Rugoſus.*
Engurriamiento, **pleighting,** *Rugoſitas.*
Enhadar, *vide* Enfadar.
Enhaſtiar, **to loth,** *Faſtidire.*
Enhaſtio, **lothſomnes,** *Faſtidium.*
Enheſtar, **hieſto, to lift vp,** *Erigere.*
Enheſtamiento, **lifting vp,** *Erectio.*
Enhechizar, **to bewitch,** *Faſcinare.*
Enhechizado, **bewitched,** *Faſcinatus.*
Enhetrar, **to intangle,** *Intricare.*
Enhetrado, **intangled,** *Intricatus.*
Enhetramiento, **tangling,** *Intricatio.*
Enhieſto, **lifted vp,** *Eleuatus, erectus.*
Enhilar, **to thred,** *Ad filum dirigere, filo inſerere.*
Enhorcar, **to hang,** *Cruci affigere.*
Enhorcado, **hanged,** *Cruci affixus.*
Enlazar, **to intangle, to catch, to ſnare, to tie,** *Illaqueare, nectere.*
Enlazamiento, **intangling, ſnaring,** *Illaqueatio, connectio.*
Enlazadura, **tying, intangling,** *Nexus, connectio.*

Enlevar,

Enlevar, to lift vp, *Attollere, erigere.*
Enlevamiento, amaſednes, *Stupor, vertigo.*
Enlizar la tela, to make a ſeluage, *Licia addere.*
Enlodar, to durt, *Luto illinere vel conspergere.*
Enlodado, durtie, *Lutoſus.*
Enlodadura, durting, fouling with durt, *Lutamentum.*
Enloſar, to paue, *Pauimentare.*
Enloquecerſe, to become fooliſh, to be frantike, *Ineptire, deſipere, ſurere.*
Enloquecer, to make frantike, to make fooliſh, *Dementare.*
Enluzar, to waſh a wall with lime, *Candicare, dealbare.* (*latus.*
Enlutado, clad in a mourning weede, *Pullutado,*
Enmagrecerſe, *vide* Emmagrecerſe.
Enmagrecido, leane, ſlender, *Macer.*
Ennegrecerſe, to waxe blacke, *Nigreſcere.*
Ennivelado, ruled out, *Delineatus, ad normam directus.*
Ennoblecer, to make noble, *Nobilitare.*
Enñudecer la yerva, to grow in knots, *Geniculare.*
Enodio, the fawne of a ſtag, *Hinnulus.*
Enojarſe, to be angrie, to be offended, *Iraſci, ſuccenſere.*
Enojado, angrie, offended, *Iratus, infenſus, iracundus.*
Enojo, anger, diſpleaſure, trouble, *Ira, iracundia, moleſtia.*
Enojoſo, troubleſome, offenſiue, *Moleſtus, odioſus.*
Enojadizo, angrie, waiward, waſpiſh, *Iracundus, acerbus.*
Enojadamente, angrily, *Iracundè.*
Enojoſamente, noyſomely, offenſiuely, *Moleſtè, odioſè.*
Enrrámar, to couer with bowes, *Ramis ſegere.*
Enrranciarſe, to be ruſtie, *Ranceſcere.*
Enrredar, to take in a net, *Irretire.*
Enrrexar, to ſet vp a lettiſe, *Clatrare.*
Enrrexado, lettiſed, *Clatratus.*
Enrriquecer, to make rich, *Diteſcere, ditare.*
Enrriquecido, inriched, *Locupletatus.*
Enrrizar, to ruffle the haire, *Comam vibrare.*

Enrriſcarſe, to get vp to a mountaine, to indanger, *Ardua montis petere, adire periculum.*
Enrriſcado, ſteepe vp, dangerous, *Acclivis, arduus, periculoſus.*
Enrriſcamiento, ſteepenes, danger, *Præcipitium, periculum.*
Enrriſtrar, to ſet the launce in the reſt, *Haſtam intendere.*
Enrronquecer, to be hoarſe, *Rauceſcere.*
Enrronquecimiento, hoarſenes, *Raucedo.*
Enrroſcar, to lie in round circles as a ſnake, *In orbes ſe colligere.*
Enrroſcadura, lying or winding round, *Sinuatio.*
Enrroxar, to make red, *Rutilare.*
Enrruviarſe, to make yellow, *Flaveſcere.*
Enſayar, to aſſay, to trie, to make proofe, to put on a caſſocke, *Tentare, experiri, periclitari, ſagum induere.*
Enſayo, proofe, triall, aſſay, *Tentatio, periculum, experientia.* (*altare.*
Enſalçar, to extoll, to lift vp, *Erigere, exaltare.*
Enſalçamiento, extolling, *Eleuatio.*
Enſalada, a ſallet of herbs, *Acetarium.*
Enſalmar, to inchant, *Incantare.*
Enſalmo, a charme, *Incantatio, carmen.*
Enſalmador, an inchanter, a charmer, *Incantator.*
Enſalmo de beſtia, a cure or medicine for beaſts, a charme to cure beaſts, *Præſtigium, exorciſmus, carmen.*
Enſanchar, to inlarge, to amplifie, *Amplificare.*
Enſanchamiento, inlarging, amplifying, *Amplificatio.* (*entare.*
Enſangrentar, to imbrue with blood, *Cruentare.*
Enſangrentado, bluddy, *Cruentus.*
Enſangrentamiento, bluddines, *Cruentatio.*
Enſañarſe, to be angry, to be offended, *Iraſci, indignari.*
Enſartar, to put on a ſtring, as beades or pearles, *Filo inſerere.*
Enſangoſtar, to ſtreighten, *In anguſtiam cogere.*
Enſenſios, *vide* Encenſios.
Enſenar, to put into the boſome, *In ſinu condere.*

L 2 Enſeñar,

Enseñar, to teach, *Docere.*
Enseñança, teaching, *Doctrina, eruditio, educatio.*
Enseñado, taught, *Doctus, eruditus.*
Esseñorear, to rule, *Dominari.*
Eseñamiento, teaching, *Educatio, eruditio.*
Ensevar, to grease, *Senare.*
Ensevado, greased, *Senatus.*
Ensilar, to put in a garner, *In granario condere.*
Ensillar, to saddle, *Sternere, insternere.*
Ensillado, saddled, *Stratus, ephippiatus.*
Ensobervecerse, to waxe proude, *Superbire.*
Ensordar, to make deafe, *Surdescere.*
Ensordamiento, the making deafe, *Surditas.*
Ensordedera, red plum, or cats taile, *Panicula.*
Ensuziar, to make foule, to defile, *Sordere, Sordescere, fœdare.*
Ensuziamiento, the making foule, *Fœdatio.*
Entablar, to borde, to plancke, to pant as the flesh of beasts new killed, *Contabulare, palpitare.*
Entablamiento, bourding, *Contabulatio.*
Entallable, that may be graued, *Exculptibile.*
Entallar, to graue, to carue, *Exculpere.*
Entallador, a caruer, a grauer, *Exculptor.*
Entalladura, grauing, caruing, *Exculptura.*
Entallecer la yerua, to grow to a stalke, *Caulescere.*
Entapiar, to stop vp, to close vp, *Obturare.*
Entena, the maine yard of a ship, *Antenna.*
Entenado, a sonne in law, the wiues sonne, *Priuignus.*
Entender, to vnderstand, *Intelligere.*
Entendimiento, vnderstanding, *Intellectus.* (*nisus.*
Enteramente, wholy, entirely, *Integrè, penitus.*
Enterizo, whole, sound, *Integer.*
Entero, whole, sound, *Integer.*
Enterar, to renew, *Integrare.*
Enteramiento, renewing, *Redintegratio.*
Entereza, soundnes, *Integritas, Incolumitas.*
Enternecerse, to be tender, *Tenerescere.*
Enterrar, tierro, to bury, *Sepelire.*

Enterramiento, buriall, *Sepulchrum, funus sepultura.*
Enterrador, he that burieth, *Funerator.*
Enterrado, buried, *Sepultus.*
Entesar, tieso, to bend, to stretch, *Tendere.*
Entesamiento, bending, stretching, *Intensio.*
Entibiarse, to be lukewarme, *Tepere.*
Entibiadera, a warming panne, or pot to keepe any thing lukewarme in, *Tepidarium.*
Entierros, burials, *Funera.*
Entonado, a braging fellow, a ietting fellow, tuned, *Iactabundus, consonus.*
Entonar, to tune, *Consonare.*
Entonces, then, *Tunc, tum.*
Entormecer, *vide* Atormecer.
Entontecer, to become a foole, *Desipere.*
Entorno, round about, *Circum circa.*
Entorpecerse, to be astonied, to be dull, *Torpere.*
Entorpecimiento, dulnes, astonishment, *Torpor.*
Entortar, tuerto de un ojo, to be squint eied, to put out an eie, to make crooked, *Eluscare, Obliquare.*
Entortadura, the putting out of an eie, squintednes, crokednes, *Eluscatio, obliquatio.*
Entrampar, to entangle, *Implicare.*
Entrambos, both, *Ambo.*
Entrañable, harty, *Internus.*
Entrañas, the entrailes, *Viscera.*
Entrañablemente, hartely, *Penitus.*
Entrapar, *vide* Entrampar.
Entrapado paño, cloth died in graine, *Pannus cocco infectus.*
Entrada, an entrie, *Aditus, introitus.*
Entrapajado, bound about the head, *Capite obuoluto.*
Entrar, to enter, *Intrare, introire.*
Entre, betweene, *Inter.*
Entre tanto, meane while, *Interim.*
Entrecoger, to take vp by the way, *Intercipere.*
Entrecortar, to cut off, *Intersecare.* (*dere.*
Entregar, to deliuer, to yeeld, *Tradere, dedere.*
Entrega, deliuery, *Traditio, restitutio.*

Entredezir,

Entredezir, to forbid, *Interdicere*.
Entredicho, forbidding, *Interdictum*.
Entredia, by day, *Interdiu*.
Entremes de la tarafca, a hobby horſe or giant in a maie game, *Manducus*.
Entremeter, to entermedle, *Interponere, infinuare*. (*fitio*.
Entremetimiento, entermedling, *Interpoſitio*.
Entrehuelgo, intermiſſion, *Intermiſſio*.
Entreoyr, to ouer heare, *Inaudire*.
Entreponer, to put betweene, *Interponere*.
Entrepoſtura, putting betweene, *Interpoſitio*.
Entrepueſto, put betweene, *Interpoſitus*.
Entrepunçar, to pricke, to pounce, *Interpungere*.
Entrepunçadura, pricking, pouncing, *Interpunctio*.
Entreſacar, to draw out, to take vp, *Elicere, intercipere*.
Entreſacadura, taking vp, *Interceptio*.
Entre ſe, betweene themſelues, *Interſe*.
Entreſijo de animal, the midriffe, *Meſenterion*.
Entreſuelo, a loft, a ſollar, *Solarium*.
Entretenimiento, entertainment, *Acceptio*.
Entrevalo, the meane ſpace, *Interuallum*.
Entrevenir, to come between, to chaunce, *Interuenire*.
Entrevenimiento, chaunce, hap, *Interuentus, caſus*.
Entreverado, wrought with rods, *Interuirgatus*. (*gere*.
Entreuntar, to annoint betweene, *Interungere*.
Entretexer, to weaue, to worke in, *Intertexere*.
Entretexedura, weauing, wreathing, *Intertextus*.
Entricar, to entangle, *Intricare*.
Entricado, entangled, intricate, *Intricatus, perplexus*.
Entricamiento, entangling, *Intricatio*.
Entricadamente, intricately, *Intricatè, perplexè*.
Entriſtecerſe, to be ſad, *Contriſtari*.
Entriſtecimiento, ſadneſſe, *Triſtitia, contriſtatio*.

Entupecer, to ſtuffe, *Refercire*.
Enturviar, to trouble, to make thick, *Turbare*.
En vano, in vaine, *Fruſtra*.
Envararſe, to be ſtiffe, *Erigere, rigeſcere*.
Envarado, ſtiffe, *Rigidus*.
Envaramiento, ſtiffeneſſe of the bodie, *Tetanus, rigor*.
Envaſar, to put into a veſſell, *In vaſculum infundere*.
Envegerſe, to waxe old, *Seneſcere*.
Envegecido, old, growen old, *Senex, veterator*.
Envelesado, ſlumbering, *Dormitans, ſtupens*.
Envergoncarçe, to be aſhamed, *Pudere*.
Envergonçado, aſhamed, *Pudefactus, verecundus*.
Envergonçamiento, ſhamefaſtneſ, *Verecundia*.
Envernar vierno, to winter, *Hyemare*.
Envernero, a wintering place, *Hiberna, orum*.
Enverniego, perteining to winter, *Hyemalis*.
Enves, the inſide, *Superficies inuerſa*.
En vez, ſomtimes, *Aliquando*.
Enveſſar, to turne in and out, *Inuertere*.
Enveſtir, to aſſaile, to breake in among the enimies, *Inferre ſe in medium, adoriri*.
Enviciar, to grow rancke, *Luxuriari*.
Envilecerſe, to waxe vile, *Vileſcere*.
Enxabonar, to ſoape, *Sapone eluere*.
Enxalmar, *vide* Enſalmar.
Enxalvegar, to white waſhe a houſe, *Creta incruſtare, Dealbare*.
Enxaguar, to waſhe, to water, *Adaquare, aqua conſpergere*.
Enxambre, a ſwarme of bees, *Examen apũ*.
Enxambrar, to ſwarme, *Agmine facto auolare*.
Enxeir de eſcudete, to inoculate, *Inoculare*.
Enxerir, xiro, to graffe, *Inſerere*.
Enxeridor, a graffer, *Inſertor*.
Enxerido, graffed, *Inſertus*.
Enxerto, graffed, *Inſertus, inſitus*.
Enxertar, to graffe, *Inſerere*.

Enxergado,

Enxergado, he that weareth sackecloth, *Cilicio indutus.*
Enxúgar, to dzy, *Exiccare.*
Enxullo de tela, the weauers beame, *Iugum.*
Enxúndia, fat, sticke, sewet, *Adeps, axungia.*
Enxuto, drie, *Siccatus.*
Enzías, the gums, *Gingiua.*
Enzina, an oke, *Ilex, quercus.*
Enzinal, an oke groue, *Ilicetum, quercetum.*

E P

Epigráma, an epigrame, *Epigramma.*
Epístola, a letter, an epistle, *Epistola.*
Epilepsía, the falling sicknes, *Morbus caducus.*
Epitaphio, an epitaph, *Epitaphium.*
Equinocial, the Equinoctiall, *Equinoctialis.*

E R

Era, a yarde, a flooze, a garden bed, an accompt of yeeres by the empire, *Area, monarchia.*
Eral, a steere of a yeere old, *Vitulus vnius anni.*
Erbolario, an herbarie, *Herbarium.*
Erbolecer, to grow vp, *Herbescere.*
Eredad, enheritance, heritage, *Hæreditas.*
Eredar, to enherite, *Hæreditare.*
Eredero, an heire, *Hæres.*
Erencia, heritage, *Hæreditas.*
Erége, an heritike, *Hæreticus.*
Eregía, heresie, *Hæresis.*
Ereticar, to become an heretike, *Hæreticum esse.*
Erético, an heretike, *Hæreticus.*
Erguir, to raise, *Lusitanicum est, Excitare.*
Erguirse, to arise, *Surgere.*
Erguido, raised vp, *Excitatus.*
Erizo, an hedgehog, the huske of a chestnut, also a fish called a Ruffe, *Erinaceus, echinus.*
Erizado, rough, bristly, *Asper, hirtus.*
Ermano, a brother, *Frater germanus.*
Ermana, a sister, *soror.*
Ermandad, brotherhood, *Fraternitas.*

Ermanable, brotherly, *Fraternus.*
Ermar, yermo, to make wast, to spoile, *Vastare, populari.*
Ermadura, wasting, desolating, *Populatio, vastatio.*
Ermador, a waster, *Depopulator.*
Ermíta, an ermitage, *Eremita.*
Ermitaño, an ermite, *Eremita.*
Eroyco, heroicall, *Heroicus.*
Errada, an error, *Error.*
Errado, lost, wandering, *Perditus, erraus.*
Erradizo, a stragler, a wanderer, *Errabundus.*
Errador, a wanderer, *Errator.*
Errar, to erre, to misse, to wander, *Errare.*
Ervaçal, a place for herbes, *Herbidus locus.*
Ervera, the throate boll, *Ingluuies, gula.*
Ervecer, to grow to an herbe, *Herbescere.*
Ervage, herbage, *Pabulum.*
Ervero, he that gathereth grasse, or herbage, *Pabulator.*
Ervato, maidenweede, hogfenell, *Peucedanum.*

E S

Esca, tinder, *Fomes.*
Escabéche, pickle for fishe, *Condimentum, salsugo.*
Escabroso, froward, wilfull, rough, *Peruersus, asper scaber.*
Escabiosa, the herbe scabious, *Scabiosa.*
Escabélo, a fourme, *Scabellum.*
Escabullirse, to slip away, *Elabi, euadere.*
Escabullimiento, slipping away, *Elapsio, euasio.*
Escála, a ladder, *Scala.*
Escalar, to scale with laders, &c. *Scalas, conscendere.*
Escalador, a scaler, a pilferer, *Scalarum conscensor, furunculus.*
Escalentar, liento, to warme, *Calfacere.*
Escalentador, a warming panne, *Calfactorium.*
Escalentamiento, warming, *Calfactio.*
Escaléra, a staire, *Gradus.*
Escalón de escalera, a step of a staire, *Gradus.*
Escalona, a scallion, *Ascalonia.*

Escáma,

Escáma, a scale of a fishe, a plate of brasse or yron, *Squama, lamina.*
Escamoso, scalie, *Squamosus.*
Escamar, to scale fish, *Disquamare.*
Escambroso, *vide* Escabroso.
Escamadura, scaling of fish, *Disquamatio.*
Escamochos, fragments, *Fragmenta.*
Escamondar, to shaue, to make cleane, *Mundare.*
Escamonea, scamonie, *Scamonium.*
Escambrones, a kinde of white bramble, *Ramnus.*
Escampar, to escape, *Euadere.*
Escanciar, to fill drinke, to skincke, *Miscere pocula.*
Escanciano, a skinker, *Pincerna.*
Escandia, a kinde of corne, *Ador.*
Escandalizar, to scandalize, to offende, *Scandalizare.*
Escandalo, a scandale, an offence, *Scandalum.*
Escaño, a benche, *Scamnum.*
Escapar, to escape, *Euadere, elabi.*
Escantar, *vide* Encantir.
Escáque, the chesse, *Scacchius lusus.*
Escaramuça, a skirmish, *Pugna tumultuaria.*
Escaramuçar, to skirmish, *Tumultuario milite rem gerere, lenibus pugnis lacessere.*
Escaramujo, wilde eglantine, *Cynosbatos.*
Escaramugos, a kind of shell worm breeding on rockes, and on the sides of ships, being sharpe towarde the top, *Conch.æ genus in nauigijs crescens.*
Escaravajo, a beetle, a bob in a cowturd, *Scarabeus.*
Escarcelon, a pouch, *Pera, bursa.*
Escardar, to rake, to weed corn, *Sarrire.*
Escardadura, raking, weeding, *Sarritio.*
Escardador, a raker, *Sarritor.*
Escardillo, a rake, a weedhooke, *Sarculum.*
Escarmentar, to affraie, to warne, *Terrere, monere.*
Escarmentado, affrayed, warned, *Territus, admonitus.*
Escarlatin, scarlet, *Coccus.*
Escarnecer, to scoffe, to mocke, *Subsannare.*

Escarnio, escarnecimiento, scoffing, mocking, *Derisio.*
Escarnidor de aqua, an howre glasse, *Clepsydra.*
Escarnecedor, a mocker, *Derisor.*
Escarnecido, mocked, derided, *Derisus.*
Escardas, cychory, *Cychorea.*
Escarpin, a socke, *Vdoonis.*
Escarvagear, to scrible, *Discribere.*
Escarvar, to scrape, *Scalpere.*
Escarvadura, scraping, *Scalptura.*
Escarvador, a scraper, *Scalptor.*
Escarvadientes, a toothpike, *Dentiscalpium.*
Escarvaorejas, an earepike, *Auriscalpium.*
Escasso, couetous, a niggard, short in weight, *Curtus, parcus, auarus. (ritia.*
Escasseza, couetousnesse, *Parsimonia, auaritia.*
Escassamente, couetously, *Parcè, auarè.*
Escatinar, *vide* çaherir.
Escavar arboles, to ridde the earth from trees, *Ablaqueare.*
Escavado arbol, a tree ridded at the root, *Ablaqueatus.*
Escava de arboles, *Ablaqueatio.*
Esclarecer, to be famous, to be cleere, *Clarescere, lucescere.*
Esclarecido, famous, cleere, renowmed, *Clarus, Illustris.*
Esclarecimiento, renowme, *Claritas.*
Esclavina, a cloake, *Palliolum.*
Esclavo, a slaue, *Seruus, mancipium.*
Escluyr, to shut out, *Excludere.*
Escluydo, shut out, *Exclusus.*
Escoba, a brush, a broome, *Scopa.*
Escobajo de uvas, the hulles of grapes, *Putamina.*
Escobilla, drosse, *Scobs.*
Escofia, a coife, *Vitta.*
Escoda para dolar piedras, a masons toole to square stones, *Excussorium.*
Escodar, dolar piedras, to square stones, *Excudere.*
Escofieta, a little coife, *Capillare.*
Escofion, a coife, *Capillare.*
Escofina, a shauing knife, *Scobina.*
Escoger, to choose, *Eligere.*
Escogimiento, choise, *Electio.*
Escogido, chosen, *Electus.*

Escolta,

Escolta, scouts, *Excubiæ*.
Escolar, a scholar, *Scholaris, Scholasticus*.
Escolastico, a schoolemaister, *Scholæ præfectus*.
Escolarse, to slide away, *Elabi*.
Escomearse, to let the vrin passe without being able to stay it, *Vrinam non posse retinere*.
Escombrar, to make cleane, *Purgare*.
Esconder, to hide, *Abscondere, occultare*.
Escondidamente, secretly, *Occulté, clanculum*.
Escondido, hidden, secret, *Occultus*.
Escondidijo, a lurking corner, *Latebra*.
Escondrijo, a lurking corner, *Latibulum*.
Escondimiento, hiding, *Occultatio*.
Escopetina, spittle, *Sputum*.
Escopidura, spittle, *Saliua*.
Escopleár, to scrape, *Scalpere*.
Escoplo, a scraping toole, a plaine for a carpenter, *Scalprum ferreum*.
Escopir, to spit, *Conspuere*.
Escória, drosse, *Scoria*.
Escorche en la pintura, the first draught, *Catagraphe*.
Escorpion, a scorpion, *Scorpio*.
Escotar, to pay the shot, *Symbolum dare*.
Escote, the shot at a reckoning, *Symbolum*.
Escotadura, paying the shot, *Symboli solutio*.
Escozer, to sæthe, *Coquere, elixare*.
Escozimiento, sæthing, *Coctio, elixatio*.
Escrevir, escrivo, to write, *Scribere*.
Escriño, a deske, *Scrinium*.
Escripto, written, *Scriptus*.
Escrivano, a scriuener, *Scriba, notarius*.
Escrivanía, a scriueners trade, a pen and inckhorne, *Notariatus, & Atramentarium*.
Escritório, a deske, *Scrinium*.
Escritúra, writing, *Scriptio, scriptura*.
Escritor, a writer, *Scriptor*.
Escuchar, to hearken, to watch in the night, *Auscultare, excubare*.
Escuchador, a watchman, *Excubitor*.
Escuchas, the night watch, *Excubiæ*.
Escudar, to arme with a target, *Scuto armare*.
Escudado, a targetier, *Scutatus*.
Escudo, a target, *Scutum*.

Escudero, an esquire, a seruingman, *Scutarius, famulus*.
Escudete, *vide* Enxérir.
Escudete, a water lillie, *Nenuphar*.
Escudilla, a dish, *Catinus*.
Escudriñar, to search, *Scrutari*.
Escudriñador, a searcher, *Scrutator*.
Escuela, a schoole, *Schola*.
Escuerço, a toad, *Bufo*.
Esculpir, to graue, to carue, *Exculpere*.
Esculpidor, a grauer, a caruer, *Exculptor*.
Esculpidura, grauing, caruing, *Sculptura*.
Esculpido, graued, carued, *Exculptus*.
Esculror, a grauer, a caruer, *Exculptor*.
Escultura, grauing, caruing, *Sculptura*.
Escupir, *vide* Escopir.
Escupidor, a spitter, *Sputator*.
Escuro, darke, *Obscurus*.
Escurecer, to darken, *Obscurare*.
Escurecido, darkened, *Obscuratus*.
Escurecimiento, darkening, *Obscuratio*.
Escuredad, darkenesse, *Obscuritas*.
Escuribáda, a sudden assault, *Inuasio subita*.
Escurriduras, the dropping of a cup, broken drinke, *Reliquiæ*.
Escurrir, to runne out, *Excurrere*.
Escusar, to excuse, *Excusare*.
Escusacion, an excuse, *Excusatio, immunitas*.
Escusable, excusable, *Excusabilis*.
Escusadora cosa, excusing, *Excusatorius*.
Escusado, excused, *Excusatus, immunis*.
Escusa, an excuse, *Causa*.
Esecutar, to execute, *Exequi*.
Esecucion, execution, *Executio*.
Esecutor, he that executeth, *Executor*.
Esento, exempt, free, *Immunis, exemptus*.
Esencion, exemption, freedome, *Immunitas*. (
Esequias, a funerall, *Exequiæ*.
Esphera, the sphere, *Sphæra*.
Esforçadamente, valiantly, strongly, *Strenuè, fortiter*.
Esforçado, valiant, stout, strong, *Strenuus fortis*.
Esforçar, fuerço, to inforce, to incourage, *Impellere, animare*.
Esforçarse, to take courage, to aduenture boldly, *Animum recipere, audere, confidenter aggredi*.

Esfuerço, courage, stoutnesse, valour, strength, *Animi vis, vigor, virtus, fortitudo.*
Esgremir, grimo, to fence, to flourish the weapon, *Figladiari, vibrare.*
Esgrima, fence play, *Gladiatio.*
Esgrimidor, a fencer, *Gladiator, lanista.*
Esgrimadura, flourishing of a weapon, *Vibratio.*
Eslabon, a steele to strike fire, the swiuell of a chaine, *Ferrum excussorium, annulus catenæ, chalybs.*
Esmalte, enamell, *Encaustice.*
Esmaltado, enamelled, *Encausticus.*
Esmaltar, to enamell, *Encaustare.*
Esmeralda, an emrold, *Smaragdus.*
Esmerejon, a marlion, *Haliætus.*
Esmerado, neat, fine, *Politus.*
Esmerarse, to be fine, to be neat, *Polire se.*
Esmeril, an emrold, *Smyris, smaragdus.*
Esmerilaça, a kinde of artillery called bases, *Tormenti bellici genus.* (um.
Espacio, space, time, leasure, *Spacium, otium.*
Espacioso, large, broad, slow, *Spatiosus, latus, tardus.* (late.
Espáciarse, to walke, *Ambulare, deambulare.*
Espada, a sword, *Ensis, gladius.*
Espada negra, a foile, *Gladius obtusus.*
Espadero, a cutler, *Gladiarius faber.*
Espadado, girt with a sword, *Ensifer, gladio cinctus.*
Espadaña, cats taile, flags, *Acorus, gladiolus.*
Espadarte, a sword fish, *Gladius piscis.*
Espadar lino, to card flaxe, *Carminare.*
Espalda a shoulder, *Humerus, scapula.*
Espaldar, to shoulder, to thrust, *Scapulis impellere.*
Espaldudo, broad shouldered, *Scapulosus.*
Espantable, fearefull, *Terribilis, terrificus.*
Espantarse, to be affraid, to be astonied, to wonder, *Terreri, deterreri, admirari, consternari.*
Espanto, feare, terrour, wondering, *Metus, terror, consternatio, admiratio.*
Espantado, affraid, terrified, wondering, *Territus, consternatus, admirans.*
Espantajo, fright, feare, *Terriculamentum.*

Espantoso, fearefull, terrible, *Terribilis.*
Espantadizo, fearefulll, *Pauidus.*
Espantosamente, fearefully, *Terrificè.*
Espanzirse el papel, to sprinckle or spot *Suffundi.*
Espanzimiento, sprinckling or spotting, *Suffusio.*
Esparrago, sperage, *Asparagus.*
Esparraguera, the stalke of sperage, *idem.*
Esparto, wicker, a kinde of tree whereof they make frailes, *Spartum.*
Espartero, a basket maker, *Spartarius.*
Esparteña, a shoo made of a kinde of wicker, *Solea spartea.*
Esparzidamente, scatteringly, *Sparsim.*
Esparzir, to sprinckle, to scatter, *Spargere.*
Esparzido, sprinckled, scattered, *Sparsus.*
Esparzimiento, sprinckling, scattering, *Aspersio.*
Espécia, spice, *Aromata.*
Especieria, spicerie, *Aromata.*
Especial, especiall, *Specialis.*
Especialmente, especially, *Præsertim.*
Espécie, a kinde, *Species.*
Especiero, a grocer, *Aromatapola.*
Espectaculo, a spectacle, *Spectaculum.*
Especular, to espie, to contemplate, *Speculari, contemplari.*
Especulacion, speculation, *Speculatio, contemplatio.*
Especulativo, contemplatiue, *Speculatiuus.*
Espedir, ido, to deliuer, to dispatch, *Expedire.*
Espedimiento, deliuery, expedition, a dispatch, *Expeditio.*
Espejar, to looke in a glasse, *Speculum intueri.*
Espejo, a looking glasse, *Speculum.*
Espejuelos, spectacles, *Conspicilla.*
Espelta, beere corne, *Spelta, zea.*
Espelunca, a caue, *Spelunca.*
Espeluzarse, to be frighted that the haire standeth vpright, to set vp the bristles, *Horrere.*
Espeluzado, brislly, frighted that the haire standeth vpright, *Horridus, horrens.*

M   Espeluza-

Eſpeluzamiento, ſtanding of the haire vpright, *Horripilium.*
Eſpeluzos, the haire ſtanding vp, *Horripilium.*
Eſperar, to hope, to looke for, to ſtay, *Sperare, expectare, manere.*
Eſpera, a ſphere, *Sphæra.*
Eſperança, hope, *Spes, expectatio.*
Eſperica, round as a ſphere, *Sphæricus.*
Eſperezarſe, to ſtretch out the body, *Exporrigere membra.*
Eſperezo, the ſtretching out, *Exporrectio membrorum.*
Eſperiencia, experience, *Experientia.*
Eſperimentar, to trie, to proue, *Experiri.*
Eſperimento, an experiment, *Experimentum.*
Eſperimentado, tried, *Expertus, peritus.*
Eſpeſſar, to make thicke, *Spiſſare, denſare.*
Eſpeſſado, thickened, *Spiſſatus, denſatus.*
Eſpeſſo, thicke, often, *Spiſſus, frequens, creber.*
Eſpeſſamente, often times, thicke, *Crebrò.*
Eſpeſſura, thickneſſe, *Denſitas.*
Eſpetar, to ſpit meat, *Veru affigere.*
Eſpia, a ſpie, *Explorator.*
Eſpiar, to eſpie, *Explorare.*
Eſpica nardi, ſpikenard, *Nardus.*
Eſpiga, an eare of corne, *Spica, ariſta.*
Eſpigar, to grow to an eare, to gather eares, *Spicas colligere, ſpicare.*
Eſpigon, an eare of corne, *Spicum.*
Eſpigon de cabeça de ajos, a cloue of garlike, *Spicum.*
Eſpina, a thorne, a fiſh bone, *Spina.*
Eſpina blanca, a kind of white thiſtle, *Spina alba.*
Eſpinal, a thorne buſh, *Spinetum.*
Eſpinar, to pricke, *Pungere.*
Eſpinaca, ſpinage, *Spinanca.*
Eſpinilla, the ſhin bone, *Tibia.*
Eſpinazo de animal, the ridge bone, *Spina.*
Eſpinoſo, thornie, *Spinoſus.*
Eſpino majuelo, a hawthorne, *Oxyacantha.*
Eſpino, a bulleſſe tree, *Spinus, prunellus.*
Eſpirar, to breathe, *Spirare.*
Eſpiradero, a breathing place, *Spiraculum.*
Eſpiritu, the breath, the ſpirit, *Spiritus.*

Eſpiritual, ſpirituall, *Spiritualis.*
Eſpiritualmente, ſpiritually, *Spiritualiter.*
Eſpital, an hoſpitall, *Noſocomium, hoſpitale.*
Eſpliega, a kinde of ſweete herbe, ſpike, *Nardi genus.*
Eſpolada, a ſtroke with a ſpur, *Calcarium ictus.*
Eſpolear, to ſpur, *Calcari fodere.*
Eſpolon, a cocks ſpur, *Calcar.*
Eſponja, a ſpunge, a pumiſe, *Spongia, pumex*
Eſponjadura, puiniſing, *Pumicatio.*
Eſponjoſo, ſpungie, *Spongioſus.*
Eſponjar, to ſpunge, to pumiſe, *Spongiare, pumicare.*
Eſportica, eſportilla, a little basket, *Sportula.*
Eſpoſo, a ſpouſe, *Sponſus.*
Eſpoſas, fetters, manacles, *Manica.*
Eſpremir, imo, to expreſſe, to preſſe out, *Exprimere.*
Eſpuela, a ſpur, *Calcar.*
Eſpuerta, a basket, *Sporta, fiſcus.*
Eſpulgar, to plucke out fleas or lice, *Pulices excerpere.*
Eſpuma, fome, froth, ſcum, *Spuma.*
Eſpumoſo, fomie, frothy, *Spumoſus.*
Eſpumar, to fome, to ſcum, *Diſpumare.*
Eſpura, cleare water, *Aqua limpida.*
Eſquadra, ſquare, a ſquire for a carpenter, *Norma.*
Eſquadra y eſquadron, a ſquadron, *Cohors.*
Eſquero, a bag to carrie baite for fiſh, a purſe, *Eſcarium, burſa.*
Eſquife, a skiffe, a ſmall boate, *Cymba, ſcapha.*
Eſquilencia, the ſquinancie, *Synanche.*
Eſquilmar, to milke, *Mulgere.*
Eſquilmo, the frute, the profit of any cattle, *Fatus, fatura.*
Eſquileta, eſquilon, a ſmall bell, *Tintinnabulum.*
Eſquilo, a ſquirrell, *Sciurus.*
Eſquina, a corner, *Angulus.*
Eſquinado, cornered, cleanſed, *Angulatus, purgatus.*
Eſquinar paja, to cleanſe chaffe by caſting it againſt the winde, to winnow, *Purgare, expaleare.*

Eſquinencia,

Esquinancia, esquilencia, a squincie, *Synanche*.
Esquivamente, disdainfully, proudlye, stately, *Superbè, fastidiosè*.
Esquivar, to shun, to auoid, to eschew, to be stately, *Vitare, fastidire*.
Esquivo, auoiding, eschewing, stately, coy, *Euitans, fastuosus*.
Esquividad, esquiveza, shunning, statelines, coyishnes, *Superbia, fastidium, fastus*.
Essa, she, *Illa*.
Esse, he, *Ille*.
Esso, that, it, *Illud*.
Essencia, being, essence, *Essentia*.
Essento, free, exempt, *Liber, exemptus*.
Establo, a stable, a stall, *Stabulum*.
Establerizo, a horsekeeper, a stall keeper, *Stabularius*.
Estable, stable, firme, *Stabilis, firmus*.
Establemente, stably, firmly, *Stabiliter, firmiter*.
Establecer, to establish, *Stabilire*.
Establecido, established, *Stabilitus*.
Establecimiento, establishing, confirming, *Constitutio, confstabilitio*.
Estáca, a stake, a stocke to graffe on, a pale, *Palus, racerra*.
Estacada, a place full of stocks to graffe on, *Nouelletio*.
Estacado, the lists to fight in, *Pergula, palæstra*.
Estadal, a fathome, a furlong, *Statura, stadium*.
Estado, estate, degree, condition, stature, *Status, conditio*.
Estafar, to steale, to rob, to cosen, *Compilare, imponere*.
Estallar, to burst, to breake in sunder, *Crepare*.
Estallido, a cracke, *Crepitus*.
Estambre, the web, *Stamen*.
Estamenea, linsiwoolsie, *Textum stamineum*.
Estampar, to print, to stampe, *Imprimere*.
Estampado, stamped, printed, *Impressus*.
Estancar, to stop, to stay, to stand still, *Sistere, stare, cessare*.
Estancarse el agua, to stande as a poole, *Stagnare*.
Estança, a standing, a place, *Statio, mansio*.

Estandarte, a standart, *Vexillum*.
Estaño, tinne, *Stannum*.
Estañar, to solder with tinne, *Stannare*.
Estanque, a poole, a pond, *Stagnum, piscina*.
Estantales, props, *Fulcra, fulcimenta*.
Estante, standing, *Stans*.
Estar, estoy, estúue, to be, to stand, *Esse, sum, fui, stare*.
Estar sobre si, to be warie, to looke to himselfe, *Esse apud se*.
Estátua, a statue, an image, *Statua*.
Estatuário, an image maker, *Statuarius*.
Estatura, stature, *Statura*.
Estatuto, a statute, *Statutum, plebiscitum*.
Este, esta, esto, he, she, this, *Iste, ista, istud*.
Estender, to stretch out, to bend out, to inlarge, *Extendere, propagare*.
Estendido, inlarged, stretched out, *Extensus*.
Estendimiento, stretching out, inlarging *Extensio*.
Estenso, large, long, *Prolixus*.
Estentino, a gut, *Intestinum*.
Estera, a mat, *Stragulum sparteum, storea*.
Estercolar, to dung, *Stercorare*.
Estercolado, dunged, *Stercoratus*.
Estercolamiento, dunging, *Stercoratio*.
Estero, a lake, a poole, *Aestuarium, stagnum*.
Esterquero, a dunghill, *Sterquilinium*.
Esteril, barren, *Sterilis*.
Esterilidad, barrennes, *Sterilitas*.
Esterlin colorado, scarlet, *Coccum*.
Esteva, the plow handle, *Stiua*.
Estevado, crookelegged, *Varus*.
Estiercol, a dunghill, *Sterquilinium*.
Estilar, to still water, *Distillare*.
Estilo, a stile in enditing, *Stilus*.
Estimar, to esteeme, to prize, *Aestimare*.
Estima, estimation, ualue, *Existimatio, aestimatio*.
Estimacion, *vide* Estima.
Estimado, esteemed, prized, *Aestimatus*.
Estimador, an esteemer, a prizer, *Aestimator*.
Estio, the sommer, *Aestas*.
Estinco, a small kind of fish, smelt, *Smincus*.
Estirar, to set vpright, to draw by close, *Erigere, stringere*.

Estirado,

Eſtirado, vpright, drawen hard, ſtroaked vp as a boote or hoſe, *Strictus, compoſitus.*
Eſtival, pertaining to ſommer, *Aeſtiuus.*
Eſtocada, a thruſt with a weapon, *Punctum.*
Eſtocadas dar, to ſtab, to thruſt, *Punctim cædere.*
Eſtola, a ſtoale, *Stola.*
Eſtomago, the ſtomacke, anger, wrath, *Stomachus.*
Eſtomagarſe, to ſtomacke, to be angrie, *Stomachari.*
Eſtomagado, angrie, *Stomachoſus.*
Eſtopa, towe, *Stuppa.*
Eſtopeño, belonging to towe, *Stuppeus.*
Eſtoque, a poynado, a thruſt, a ſtab, *Sica, punctum.*
Eſtoque yerva, corne gladen or corn flag, *Gladiolus.*
Eſtoraque, ſtorax, *Storax.*
Eſtornija de carro, the trigger of a cart, *Sufflamen.*
Eſtornino, a ſtare, *Sturnus.*
Eſtornudar, to neeze, *Sternutare.*
Eſtornudo, neezing, *Sternutatio.*
Eſtorvar, to ſtop, to let, to ſtay, to trouble, *Obſtare, obſiſtere, impedire.*
Eſtorvo, let, ſtop, trouble, *Obſtaculum, impedimentum.*
Eſtraçar, to teare, *Lacerare.*
Eſtraço, tearing, *Laceratio.*
Eſtrado, a bed, a pallet, *Stratum.*
Eſtragar, to ſpoile, to mar, to waſte, *Corrumpere.*
Eſtragado, marred, waſted, ſpoiled, *Corruptus.*
Eſtragamiento, eſtrago, ſpoile, ſlaughter, *Corruptio, ſtrages.*
Eſtrago, a ſlaughter, *Strages.*
Eſtrangero, a ſtranger, *Aduena, externus.*
Eſtrañar, to eſtrange, *Alienare.*
Eſtraño, ſtrange, rare, *Alienus, externus, rarus.*
Eſtrañeza, ſtrangenes, *Peregrinitas.*
Eſtrangúria, the ſtrangurian, *Stranguria.*
Eſtregar, ſtriego, to curry, to wipe cleane a horſe, *Strigilare.*
Eſtregadero, a horſecombe, *Strigilis.*

Eſtréchar, to ſtraighten, *Anguſtare, arctare.*
Eſtrechamente, ſtraightly, *Arctè.*
Eſtrecho, ſtraight, *Anguſtus.*
Eſtrechura, ſtraightnes, *Coarctatio.*
Eſtrecho, a ſtrait of the ſea or lande, *Fretum, iſthmus.*
Eſtrella, a ſtar, *Stella.*
Eſtrellar, to ſet with ſtars, *Stellare.*
Eſtrellada, ſtarwurt or ſharwurt, *Aſter atticus.*
Eſtrellado, ſet with ſtars, *Stellatus.*
Eſtrellero, an aſtronomer, *Aſtronomus.*
Eſtremado, extreame, paſſing, exceeding, *Extremus.*
Eſtremo, extremitie, *Extremitas.*
Eſtremecer, to tremble, to quake, *Tremere.*
Eſtrena, handſell, a preſent, *Strena.*
Eſtrenar, to take handſell, *Strenas accipere.*
Eſtreñir, ſtriño, to reſtraine, *Stringere, reſtringere.*
Eſtreñido, reſtrained, *Strictus, reſtrictus.*
Eſtribar, to ſtraine, to endeuor, *Niti.*
Eſtribo, a ſtirup, a prop for a houſe, *Stapeda, fulcrum.*
Eſtribadura, endeuoring, *Nixus.*
Eſtribadora coſa, endeuoring, *Nitibundus.*
Eſtropeçar, pieço, to ſtumble, *Ceſpitare, offendere.*
Eſtropieço, ſtumbling, *Ceſpitatio.*
Eſtropear, to racke with cords, *Funibus diſtendere.*
Eſtruendo, a noiſe, a great crack, *Strepitus.*
Eſtrujar o apretar, to ſtreine, *Premere.*
Eſtuche, a caſe of tooles, a boxe of tooles, *Theca.*
Eſtúdiar, to ſtudie, *Studere.*
Eſtudio, ſtudie, *Studium, diligentia.*
Eſtudiante, a ſtudent, *Studioſus.*
Eſtudioſamente, ſtudiouſly, *Studiosè.*
Eſtodioſo, ſtudious, *Studioſus.*
Eſtufa, a ſtoue or a hothouſe, *Hypocauſtum.*

E T

Eternamente, eternally, *Aeternè.*
Eternidad, eternitie, *Aeternitas.*
Eternizar, to eternize, *Aeternum facere.*
Eterno, eternall, *Aeternus.*
Ethico, he that is ſicke of the conſumption, *Hecticus.*

Evacuar,

E V

Evacuar, to emptie, to make void, *Exinanire*.
Evangelio, the Gospell, *Euangelium*.
Evano, Ebenus, sugarchest, *Hebenus*.
Euforbio, a certaine gum of a tree found first by king Iuba, *Euphorbium*.
Eufrásia, Eiebright, *Eufragia*.

E X

Exambre, a hiue of bees, a swarme of bees, *Examen*.
Examen, examination, *Examen*.
Examinar, to examine, *Examinare*.
Examinacion, examination, *Examinatio*.
Examinador, an examiner, *Examinator*.
Exceder, to exceed, *Excedere*.
Excelente, excellent, *Excellent*.
Excelencia, *vide* Ecelencia.
Exe, an axletree, *Axis*.
Exea, a spie, a scout, *Speculator*.
Exemplar, an example, *Exemplar*.
Exemplo, an example, *Exemplum*.
Exemplificar, to exemplifie, *Exemplificare*.
Exercicio, exercise, occupation, trade, *Exercitium, exercitatio*.
Exercitar, to exercise, *Exercere*.
Exercitador, an exerciser, *Exercitor*.
Exercitadora cosa, that may be exercised, *Exercitatorius*.
Exercito, an armie, *Exercitus*.
Eximir, to exempt, *Eximere*.
Exortar, to exhort, *Hortari*.
Exortacion, exhortation, *Exhortatio*.
Exortador, an exhorter, *Exhortator*.
Ezquerdear de camino, to go out of the way, *Deuiare*.

F A

Fabrica, a frame, a worke, *Fabrica*.
Fabricador, a framer, a worker, Fabricator. (*cari*.
Fabricar, to frame, to worke, *Fabricare*.
Fabricado, framed, wrought, *Fabricatus*.
Fabricacion, working, *Fabricatio*.
Fabricadamente, cunningly, *Affabrè*.
Fabrificado, framed, *Fabrefactus*.
Fabrificar, to frame, *Fabreficare*.
Fabula, a fable, *Fabula*.
Fabuloso, fabulous, *Fabulosus*.
Fabulosamente, falsely, *Fabulose*.
Fácil, easie, *Facilis*.
Facilidad, easines, facilitie, *Facilitas*.
Facilitar, to make easie, *Facilitare*.
Facilmente, easilie, *Faciliter*.
Faciones, fashions, maners, *Mores*.
Facultad, facultie, abilitie, *Facultas*.
Faisa, a kerchefe, a wastebande, *Fascia*.
Faisar, to wrap, *Fasciare*.
Faysan, a phesant, *Phasianus*.
Falda, the lap of a coate, the skirtes, the quarters of a coate, *Fimbria, sinus*.
Faldamentos, skirts of a ierkin, *Sinus*.
Faldetes, *vide* Falda.
Faldriquera, a pocket, *Pera*.
Falsado, counterfetted, *Adulterinus*.
Falsar, to falsifie, *Adulterare*.
Falsário, he that falsifieth, *Falsarius*.
Falsedad, falshood, *Fallacia*.
Falsamente, falsely, *Falso*.
Falso, false, *Falsus*.
Falta, want, a fault, *Culpa, defectus*.
Faltar, to want, to offende, *Deesse, deficere*.
Fallar, *vide* Faltar.
Falla, *vide* Falta.
Fama, fame, report, *Rumor, fama*.
Famoso, famous, *Celebris, famosus*.
Famosamente, famouslly, *Famosè*.
Familia, a family, *Familia*.
Familiar, familier, *Familiaris*.
Familiaridad, familiaritie, *Familiaritas*.
Familiarmente, familiarly, *Familiariter*.
Fanal, the lanterne in the admirall ship, *Lucerna nauis pretoriæ*.
Fanfa, a play, an enterlude, *vide* Farça.
Fanfarron, a bragger, a brauer, *Iactabundus, gloriosus*.
Fanfarronería, bragging, boasting, *Gloriatio, iactatio*. (*maginari.*
Fantasear, to conceiue in the fantasie, *Imaginari*.
Fantasía, fantasie, *Phantasia*.
Fantasma, a walking spirit, *Phantasma*.
Fantástico, fantastike, *Phantasticus*.

Faraute,

F E

Faraute, an interpreter, *Interpres.*
Farças, playes, enterludes, *Comedia.*
Fardo, fardel, a packe, a fardle, *Fasciculum, sarcina.*
Farro, brenne, *Furfur.*
Faron, a watch towre, *Pharus.*
Fasol, fenegreke, *Fænum græcum.*
Fastidiar, to loath, *Fastidire.*
Fastidiado, loathed, *Fastiditus.*
Fastidio, lothsomnesse, *Fastidium.*
Fastidioso, loathing, disdainefull, *Fastidiosus.*
Fasto, fausto, pride, *Fastus.*
Fatal, fatall, *Fatalis.*
Fatiga, wearines, greefe of minde, *Lassitudo, angor.*
Fatigado, wearied, *Lassus.*
Fatigar, to wearie, *Delassare.*
Fatigoso, wearisome, *Delassatorius.*
Fator, a factor, *Factor, exercitor.*
Fatoría, factorship, *Procuratio.*
Favorecer, to fauor, *Fauere.*
Favor, fauor, *Fauor.*
Favorecedor, a fauorer, *Fautor.*
Favorecido, fauored, *Probatus acceptus.*
Favorable, fauorable, *Fauorabilis.*
Favorablemente, fauorably, *Fauorabiliter.*
Faxa, a wasteband, *Fascia.*
Faxar, to binde, to swathe, *Fasciare.*
Faxína, boughes and stakes to make a rampier, *Materies.*

F E

Fe, faith, *Fides.*
Fealdad, filthines, *Fœditas.*
Febrero, Februarie, *Februarius.*
Feeza, filthines, *Fœditas.*
Feble, feeble, *Debilis.*
Feblemente, feebly, weakely, *Debiliter.*
Febledad, weakenes, feeblenes, *Debilitas.*
Felicidad, felicitie, *Fælicitas.*
Feligrez, a parishioner, *Paræcus.*
Felpa, vnshorne veluet, flush, *Sericum intonsum.*
Fenecer, to finish, *Finire.*
Fenecimiento, finishing, *Finis, terminatio.*
Feno, haye, *Fænum.*
Feo, foule, *Fædus.*

F I

Feria, a holiday, a faire, a market, *Feriæ, nundinæ.*
Feriar, to buy and sell, to keepe holiday, *Feriari, nundinari.*
Ferocidad, fiercenes, *Ferocia.*
Feroz, fierce, *Ferox.*
Fertil, fertill, *Fertilis.*
Fertilidad, fertilitie, *Fertilitas.*
Festival, festiual, *Festus.*
Festejar, to feast, to entertaine, *Conuiuari, conuiuio excipere.*
Feudo, fee, *Feodum, feudum.*
Feudatário, a feodarie, *Feodatarius.*

F I

Fiador, a suertie, *Vas, dis, Fideiussor.*
Fiar, to trust, to become suertie, *Vadari, fideiubere.*
Fiança, credite, putting in suerties, bayling, *Sponsio, fideiussio.*
Ficion, a fiction, *Fictio.*
Fiebre, a feuer, *Febris.*
Fiel, faithfull, *Fidelis.* (*men.*
Fiel de pesos, the triall of waight, *Examen.*
Fielmente, faithfully, *Fideliter.*
Fieldad, fidelitie, *Fidelitas.*
Fieltro, a felt, *pannus intextus.*
Fiera, a wilde beast, *Fera.*
Fiereza, wildnes, sauadgenes, fiercenes, *Feritas.*
Fiero, fierce, *Ferus.*
Fiesta, a feast, *Feriæ.*
Figura, a figure, a shape, *Figura.*
Figurado, figured, *Figuratus.*
Figurar, to figure, *Figurare.*
Figurativo, figuratiue, *Figuratus.*
Figuradamente, figuratiuely, *Figuratè.*
Figurilla, a little picture, *Figura parua.*
Filipendola, filipendula, *Filipendula.*
Filete, a lace, a bone lace, *Tænia.*
Filosofia, Philosophie, *Philosophia.*
Filosofo, a philosopher, *Philosophus.*
Filosofar, to play the philosopher, *Philosophari.*
Filo, the edge of a knife, thread, *Acies, filum.*
Fin, an ende, *Finis.*
Final, finall, *Finalis.*

Finalmente,

Finalmente, finally, *Tandem, demum.*
Finar, to ende, to die, *Finire, terminare, mori.*
Finado, ended, dead, *Finitus, mortuus.*
Finamiento, the dieng, the deceasing, death, *Defunctio, mors.*
Fingir, jo, to faine, *Fingere.*
Fingido, fained, *Fictus.*
Fingimiento, fainting, *Fictio.*
Fingidor, a fainer, *Fictor.*
Fingidamente, fainedly, *Ficté.*
Fino, fine, cunning, *Perfectus, astutus.*
Finiquito, an acquittance, *Apocha.*
Firma, a firme of the hand, *Signatio.*
Firmar, to firme, to confirm, to establish, *Firmare.*
Firme, firme, stedfast, *Firmus.*
Firmemente, firmely, stedfastly, *Firmiter.*
Firmeza, firmenes, strength, stablenesse, *Firmitas.*
Fiscal, a basket, perteining to the excheqver, *Fiscalis, fiscus.*
Fisco, the exchequer, *Fiscus.*
Fisico, a physician, *Medicus.*
Fistigo, *vide* Alhocigo.
Fistola, a fistula, *Fistula.*
Fixar, to fasten, *Figere.*
Fixado, fastened, *Fixus.*
Fixamente, faste, surely, *Firmiter.*
Fixo, faste, *Fixus.*

F L

Flaco, leane, weake, *Macer, exilis, debilis.*
Flamenco, a fleming, a kinde of birde like a shoueler, *Belga.*
Flaqueza, weakenes, leanenes, sickenes, *Macies, debilitas.*
Flarco, a bottle, *Vter.*
Flauta, a pipe of reede, a flute, *Fistula.*
Flautador, a piper, a fluter, *Fistulator.*
Flecha, an arrow, *Sagitta.*
Flechar, to shoote, *Sagittare.* (*nere.*
Fletar, to pay passage money, *Naulum soluere.*
Flete, passage money, *Portorium, naulum.*
Flocadura, flocks, *Flocci.*
Flor, a flower, *Flos.*
Florecer, to florish, *Florere.*
Florido, florishing, *Floridus.*
Floresta, a forest, *Nemus, saltus.*
Florestero, a forester, *Viridarius, saltuarius.*
Floretada, a fillip, *Talitrum.*
Florin, a flozen, *Monetæ genus.*
Flota de naves, a fleete, a nauie, *Classis.*
Floxedad, weakenesse, sloth, negligence, idlenes, *Debilitas, ignauia, negligentia, pigritia.*
Floxo, weake, slowe, negligent, idle, *Debilis, piger, negligens, desidiosus, ignauus.*
Floxamente, weakely, idelly, slowly, negligently, *Debiliter, otiosé, pigré, ignauiter.*
Fleuco, flockes, smal frenges, *Floccus, laciniæ.*
Fluxo, a flixe, *Fluxus.*

F O

Fofo, softe in feeling, *Turgidus, mollis.*
Fogon, a hearth, *Focus.*
Fogoso, fierie, *Ignitus.*
Follajes, mantelling in armes, florishing, *Mangonizatio.*
Follon, a lewde person, *Nequam.*
Fondoso, deepe, *Profundus.*
Fontanal, a place of sprigs, a place of fountaines, *Scatebra.*
Fontezuela, a little fountaine, *Fonticulus.*
Forodado, *vide* Horodado.
Forastero, a stranger, *Aduena.* (*rus.*
Foraño quasi çahereña, fierce, wilde, *Ferus.*
Forçado, forced, *Necessarium, coactum.*
Forçar, fuerço, to force, to rauish, *Vim afferre, cogere, stuprare.*
Forçador, a forcer, a rauisher, *Violentus, sturpator.*
Forçoso, violent, forcible, *Violentus.*
Forçosamente, violently, forciblie, *Violenter, inuisé.*
Forcejar, to endeuour to the vttermost, *Tentare, vires experiri, conari gnauiter.*
Forera, currant money, also a kinde of taxe, *Census.*
Forja, a forge, *Fabrica.*
Forjar, to forge, *Fabricare.*
Forjado, forged, *Fabricatus.*
Formaje, cheese, *Caseus.*
Forma, a forme, a fashion, *Forma.*
Formado, formed, framed, fashioned, *Formatus.*

Formal,

F R   F R

Formal, formall, *Formalis*.
Formar, to forme, to frame, to fashion, *Formare*.
Formulario, a præsident booke of paper, *Formularium*.
Formalmente, formally, *Formaliter*.
Fornecer, to furnish, *Munire, instruere*.
Fornecimiento, furniture, *Munitio, instructio*.
Fornicar, to follow whores, *Fornicari*.
Fornicacion, whoredome, fornication, *Fornicatio*.
Forraje, forrage, *Pabulum*.
Fortaleza, strength, a fortresse, a bulwarke, *Fortitudo, Locus aut arx munita*.
Fortalecer, to build a rampire, to fortifie, *Munire*.
Fortalecimiento, fortifieng, *Munitio*.
Fortificar, to fortifie, *Munire*.
Fortificador, a fortifier, *Munitor*.
Fortificamiento, fortifieng, *Munitio*.
Fortuna, fortune, *Fortuna*.
Foso, softe, swelling, *Turgidus, mollis*.
Fossa, fosso, a ditch, *Fossa*.

F R

Fraçada, a couerlet, *Stragulum*.
Fragada, a fregot, *Nauigij genus*.
Fragoso, rough, stonie, *Asper, confragosus*.
Fraguar, to harden, to dry, or waxe firme, *Obdurescere*.
Fragua, a forge, the smith coale, *Fabrica, pruna, carbo*.
Frayla, a nun, *Monacha*.
Frayle, a frier, *Frater*.
Fraylezillo, ave, an oupe. *Sitta*.
Francamente, franckely, liberally, *Munificè*.
Franco, francke, free, liberall, *Liberalis*.
Francolin, a godwit, *Attagen*.
Franjas, frenges, *Lacinia*.
Franqueza, liberalitie, *Liberalitas*.
Franquear, to giue libertie, *Liberare*.
Frasco, *vide* Flarco.
Fraternidad, brotherhood, *Fraternitas*.
Freça, a strawberie, *Fragum*.
Freçada, *vide* Frazada.
Frecha, *vide* Flecha.

Frechar, *vide* Flechar.
Frechadura, drawing the bowe, shooting, *Sagittatio*.
Frechero, an archer, fletcher, *Sagittarius*.
Fregar, friego, to rub, *Fricare*.
Fregado, rubbed, *Fricatus*.
Fregadero, a rubber, *Strigilis*.
Fregadura, rubbing, *Fricatio*.
Fregadientes, a rubber for the teeth, *Dentifricium*.
Freyle, a brother of an order of knighthoode, *Frater*.
Freyr, frio, to frie, *Frigere*.
Freydura, frying, *Frictio*.
Frenesi, the frensie, *Phrenesis*.
Freneticar, to be franticke, *Insanire, furere*.
Frenetico, franticke, *phreneticus*.
Frenar, to bridle, *Frænare*.
Freno, a bridle, *Frænum*.
Frenillo de la lengua, the stringe of the toong, *Fibra lingua*.
Frente, the browe, the forehead, *Frons*.
Frequente, often, *Frequens*.
Frequentadamente, oftenly, *Frequenter*.
Frequentar, to frequent, *Frequentare*.
Fresar, to bruse, to rub one thing with another, *Fricare, confricare*.
Fresada de ceuada, barly water, ptisane, *Ptisanum*. (*cens, algidus*.
Fresco, fresh, newe, somewhat colde, *Recens, algidus*.
Frescor, frescura, freshnes, coldnes, pleasantnes of the aire, *Algor, Frigus*.
Fresquezito, somewhat fresh weather, somewhat colde, *Subalgidus*.
Frezno, an ashe, *Fraxinus*.
Fretar nave, to hire a ship, to fraight, *Conducere nauem*.
Frete, the fraight, passage mony, *Naulum, onus*.
Frialdad, coldnes, *Frigiditas*.
Friamente, coldly, *Frigidè*.
Frio, cold, *Frigidus*.
Friollego, somewhat colde, *Gelidè*.
Friera de pies, a kibe, a chilblaine, *Pernio*.
Frisar, to rub, to cotten, to freese clothe, *Fricare*.
Frisóles, a kinde of pulse, small whyte pease, kidney beanes, *Phaseoli, Smilax*.

Frito,

Frito, fried, *Frixus.*
Frontal, a forehead cloth, *Frontale.*
Frontera, the frontiers, *Confinium.*
Frontero, ouer againſt, afront, *E regione.*
Frontiſpicio, the firſt face, the firſt ſhewe, *Superficies.*
Frotar, to rub, *Fricare.*
Fruſlera, a ieſt, a mockery, *Scomma.*
Fruta, frute, *Fructus.*
Fruta de ſarten, a fritter, *Bellaria fricta.*
Frutal, a tree bearing fruite, *Pomifera arbor.*
Frutuoſo, fruitefull, *Fructuoſus.*
Frutifero, fruitefull, *Fructifer.*
Frutificar, to fructifie, to giue fruite, *Fructificare.*

F u

Fuego, fire, *Ignis.*
Fuelle, bellowes, *Follis.*
Fuelleſuelo, ſmall bellowes, *Folliculus.*
Fuente, a fountaine, an ewre, *Fons, malluuium.*
Fuera, without, beſides, except, moreouer, *Foris, præter, excepto.*
Fuerça, force, violence, ſtrength, valour, *Vis, robur, violentia.*
Fuerte, ſtrong, valiant, *Fortis.*
Fuero, the lawe, the cuſtome, the court of lawe, *Ius, mos, conſuetudo, forum.*
Fugitivo, fugitiue, *Fugitiuus.*
Fullero, a coſener, a pilferer, *Deceptor, impoſtor, compilator.*
Fulano, ſuch an one, *Quidam.*
Fumoſidad, fumoſitie, *Fumoſitas.*
Funda de almohado o colchon, a pillowbeere, *Faſcia puluinaria.*
Fundar, to lay a foundation, *Fundare.*
Fundador, a founder, *Fundator.*
Fundamento, the foundation, *Fundamentum.*
Funda de meſa, the treſſels, *Fulcrum.*
Fundicion, caſting of mettell, *Conflatio, liquefactio.*
Fundir, to caſt mettall, *Conflare.*
Furia, fury, *Furia.*
Furioſamente, furiouſly, *Furioſè.*
Furioſo, furious, *Furioſus.*

Furor, rage, madneſs, *Furor.*
Furriel, a harbinger, *Manſionarius.*
Fuſlera, braſſe, *Aes fuſile.*
Fuſtan, fuſtian, *Pannus goſſapinus.*
Fuſta, a foiſt, *Epibatum, nauigij genus.*
Fuſte de cilla, the ſaddle tree, *Lignum cellularium.*
Fuzia, truſt, *Fiducia.*

G A

Gaçafatones, fooliſh talke, rauing talke, *Deliria.*
Gaçapo, gaçapito, a rabbet, *Laurex.*
Gafeti, agrimonie, *Eupatorium.*
Gafas, benders of a croſſebowe, *Vertibulum arcuarium.*
Gacelo, a wilde goate, *Capra ſylueſtris.*
Gafo, a lazare, a leaper, *Leproſus.*
Gafedad, lepzoſie, *Lepra.*
Gayta, a pipe, a bagpipe, *Viriculus.*
Gaytero, a plaier on the bagpipe, *Vtricularius.*
Gajo, a cluſter of grapes, *Botrus.*
Gajes, wages, *Salarium, ſtipendium.*
Gala, brauerie, *Elegantia, lautitia veſtium.*
Galan, a gallant, braue, *Elegans, lautus.*
Galanemente, brauely, gallantly, *Eleganter.*
Galardon, a reward, *Merces.*
Galardonar, to reward, *Remunerare.*
Galardonado, rewarded, *Remuneratus.*
Galardonador, a rewarder, *Remunerator.*
Galapágo, a ſnaile, *Teſtudo.*
Galbano, a gum called galbanum, *Galbanum.*
Galbanado, gummed with galbanum, *Galbaneus.*
Galea, y galera, a gally, *Biremis.*
Galeaça, a galliaſſe, *Quadriremis.*
Galeóta, a little gally, *Biremis.*
Galeote, a rower, *Remex.*
Galeon, a galeon, *Nauis grandior.*
Galgana, a kinde of pulſe, *Cicera.*
Galgo, a french dog, *Canis Gallicus.*
Gallardetes, ſtreamers in ſhips, *Vexilla.*
Gallardamente, gallantly, *Eleganter.*

N Gallardo,

Gallardo, gallant, *Elegans*.
Gallego, southsouthwest, *Caurus*.
Galleta, a kind of vessell for wine, *Trulla*.
Gallillo o campanillo, the uuula, *Nuca*.
Gallina, a hen, *Gallina*.
Gallina ciega, a woodcocke, *Gallinago*.
Gallina ponedera, o adriana, a laying hen, *Gallina oua ponens*.
Gallinero, a poulterer, a roust, *Gallinarius, pertica*.
Gallinaça, hen doong, *Fumus gallinaceus*.
Gallochas çapatos de paño, a kinde of sock of cloth, *Soccus*.
Gallocresta, herbe Clarie, *Gallitricum*.
Gallo, a cocke, *Gallus*.
Gallipávo, a turkie cocke, *Gallus Indicus*.
Gallofo, a begger, *Mendicus*.
Gallopear, to gallop, *Citato equo vadere*.
Gama, a deare, *Dama*.
Gamon, daffadill, *Asphodelus*.
Gamonital, a bed of daffadils, *Locus asphodelis plenus*.
Gamonito, white daffadill, *Anthericos*.
Gamonilla, the flower of daffadill, *Flos asphodeli*.
Gana, will, desire, lust, *Libido, libentia*.
Ganado, a flocke, *Pecus, armentum, grex*.
Ganadero, a heardsman, *Pecuarius, armentarius*.
Ganancia, gaine, *Lucrum, quæstus*.
Gananciosso, gainefull, *Quæstuosus*.
Ganapan, a porter, *Baiulus*.
Ganar, to gaine, *Lucrari*.
Ganado, gotten, *Lucratus*.
Gancho, a sheeps crooke, knops in a greble staffe, braunches in a stags horne, *Pedum, spina, rami*.
Ganchoso, knobbie, branched, *Ramosus*.
Gango, a barnacle, one that speaketh through the nose, *Chenolopex*.
Ganso, a gander, *Anser masculus*.
Ganzua, a false keye, a pickelocke, *Clauis adulterina*.
Gañan, a plowman, *Arator*.
Gañir, to snarle, to grin, *Gannire*.
Gañido, the snarling of a dogge, *Gannitus*.
Gañon, the throat, *Guttur, rumen, ingluuies*.

Garañon, a stallion horse, *Equus admissarius*.
Garavato, a hooke, *Vncus, creagra, harpago*.
Garbo, the bulke of any thing, the form, the shape, *Figura, species, forma*.
Garça, a hearon, *Ardeola*.
Garcetas, antlyers, *Amynteres*.
Garçon, a wooer, an amorous fellowe, *Procus*.
Garçonear, to court women, to wooe, *Procari*.
Garço de ojo, grey eied, *Glaucus*.
Garço, agaricke, *Agaricum*.
Garho, a hooke, *Vncus*.
Garfiar, to hooke, *Vnco arripere*.
Gargagear gargarizar, to washe the throte, *Excreare*.
Gargajo, spittle and fleame, *Excreatum*.
Garganta, a throte, *Guttur*.
Garganta del pie, the instep, *Astragalus*.
Gargantilla, a carkanet, *Collare*.
Garganton, a glutton, *Helluo*.
Garguero, the throte, *Guttur*.
Gargantez, gluttony, *Ingluuies*.
Gargavero, the throte boale, *Guttur*.
Gargola, lyne seed, *Lini semen*.
Garita, a little tower on a wall, a watching tower, *Pharus*.
Garlito, a swele, *Nassa*.
Garra, a pawe, *Vnguu*.
Garráfa, a glasse to drinke in, a small bioll, *Vitriolum, ampulla*.
Garrapáta, a tike in a sheepe, *Ricinus*.
Garrido, fine, feate, nice, *Elegans*.
Garridamente, finely, *Eleganter*.
Garrideza, finenes, deintines, *Elegantia*.
Garrocha, a pricke, a goade, a short dart made of a cane, *Stimulus, hasta*.
Garrote, a cudgell to winde a cord, as Carriers do to packe with, *Fustis quo funem torquent in ligandis sarcinis*.
Garrote dar, to strangle, *Guttur frangere*.
Garrova, a kind of frute or pulse, *Siliqua*.
Garrovo, the tree *Siliqua*.
Garruvia, *vide* Garrovo.
Garvanço, a pease, *Pisum*.
Garvines, night cappes of silke, *Pilei nocturni*.

Gasajo,

Gafajo, mirth, curtefie, *Alacritas, hilaritas, humanitas.*
Gaſtar, to ſpend, *Conſumere.*
Gaſtador, a ſpender, *Conſumptor.*
Gaſtado, ſpent, *Conſumptus.*
Gaſto, coſt, expences, charges, *Sumptus, impenſa.*
Gato, a cat, *Catus, felis.*
Gatear, to crepe, *Repere.*
Gatopaus, a munkie, *Cercopethecus.*
Gatillo, a chit, *Catulus.*
Gato cerval, *Lupus cernarius.*
Gavanço, dog brier, *Cynosbatos.*
Gavia de nave, the top of a ſhip, *Carcheſiū.*
Gavilla, a ſtacke of corne, a houſe of corne, a bauen, *Faſciculus.*
Gavilon, a ſparhauke, a drie flower, *Accipiter, pappus.*
Gaviota, a ſea gull, a ſea cob, *Gauia.*
Gaznate, the throte boll, *Guttur.*
Gaznar, to chatter as a bird that ſingeth not perfectly, *Garrire.*

G E

Gelofia, iealouſie, alſo a window lid, *Zelotypia.*
Gemido, groning, *Gemitus.*
Gemir, gimo, to grone, *Gemere.*
Genciana, gentian, *Gentiana.*
Generacion, generation, linage, *Generatio.*
General, generall, *Generalis.*
Generalidad, generalitie, *Generalitas.*
Generalmente, generally, *Generaliter.*
Genero, kinde, ſtocke, linage, *Genus.*
Generoſidad, generoſitie, gentilitie, *Generoſitas.*
Generoſamente, generouſly, gentlemanlike, *Generose.*
Gengibre, ginger, *Gingiber.*
Gente, a nation, *Gens.*
Gentiana, felwourt, gentian, *Gentiana.*
Gentil, proper of perſonage, handſome, fine, *Scitus, bellus.*
Gentileza, propernes, fineneſ, beautie, *Elegantia, pulchritudo, venuſtas.*
Gentilmente, properly, finely, *Bellè, ſcitè.*
Geografia, geographie, *Geographia.*
Geometria, geometrie, *Geometria.*

Geometra, a geometer, *Geometra.*
Gerarchia, hierarchie, *Hierarchia.*
Geriplega, hiera picra, a drug, *Hiera picra.*
Geſto, the countenance, the geſture, *Geſtus.*
Gifero, a butcher, *Lanius.*
Gigante, a giant, *Gigas.*
Ginete, a ginnet, a light horſeman, *Equus & eques leuis armaturæ.*
Girifalte, a iarfalcon, *Gyrifalco.*
Girafa animal, *Camelopardalis.*
Girofe, a gilloflower, *Gariophyllum.*
Gironados, of many colours, *Multicolor.*
Giron de veſtidura, a gard of a garment, *Fimbria, ſegmentum.*

G L

Gleva, armadura de piernas, greaues, *Tibialia.*
Gloria, glorie, *Gloria.*
Gloriarſe, to brag, to boaſt, *Gloriari.*
Glorificar, to glorifie, *Glorificare.*
Glorificacion, glorifying, *Glorificatio.*
Glorioſo, glorious, *Glorioſus.*
Glorioſamente, glorriouſly, *Gloriosè.*
Gloſa, a gloſe, an expoſition, *Gloſa, expoſitio.*
Gloſador, an expounder, *Expoſitor, commentator.*
Gloſar, to expound, *Commentari.*
Glotonia, gluttonie, *Ingluuies.*
Glotonear, to play the glutton, *Glutire, ligurire.*
Gloton, a glutton, *Hellus.*

G O

Gobio, a gudgeon, *Gobius.*
Gofo, rude in ſpeech, *Rudis.*
Goja, a basket, *Corbis.*
Gola, a gorget of iron, *Ferreum pectorale.*
Golfo, a gulfe, *Gurges.*
Golfin, a dolphin, *Delphinus.*
Goldre, a quiuer, a bowcaſe, *Pharetra, theca arcuaria.*
Golondrina, a ſwallow, *Hirundo.*
Goloſo, gluttonous, *Guloſus.*
Goloſear, to play the glutton, *Ligurire.*
Goloſina, gluttonie, *Ingluuies, gula.*
Gollorias, broths, potages, *Cupedia.*

Golpear,

G O

Golpear, to ſtrike, *Ferire, percutere.*
Golpe, a blow, a ſtroke, *Ictus.*
Golpeado, ſtroken, beaten, *Ictus, a, percuſſus, a.*
Goma, gum, a clue of thred, *Gummi, glomus*
Gomitadura, vomiting, *Nauſea.*
Gomitar, to vomit, *Vomere.*
Gomito, vomit, *Vomitus.*
Gomoſo, gummie, *Gummoſus.*
Gondrola, a kind of ſmall barke, *Nauigij genus.*
Gordo, groſſe, fat, *Pinguis, craſſus.*
Gordura, groſſenes, fatnes, *Pinguedo, Craſſities.*
Gordolobo, longwurt or torchherbe, *Verbaſcum.*
Gorgojo, a ſweuell, *Gurgulio.*
Gorgear aues, to ſing, to chatter, to cry out, *Garrire, vociferari.*
Gorgeador, a prater, a babler, a crier out, *Garritor, vociferator.*
Gorgeamiento, prating, babling, crying out, *Vociferatio.*
Gorguera, a gorget, *Collare.*
Gorjal de malla, a gorget of maile, *Pectorale ferreum.*
Gorguzes, the head of a kind of dart, *Spiculum.*
Gormar, *vide* Gomitar.
Gorrion, a ſparrow, *Paſſer.*
Gorra, a hat, *Galerus.*
Gorrioncillo, a yoong ſparrowe, *Paſſerculus.*
Gorvion, *Euphorbium.*
Goſque, a whelpe, *Catulus.*
Gota, a drop, the gout, *Gutta, podagra.*
Gota coral, the falling euill, *Morbus caducus.*
Gotera, a gutter, *Canalis.*
Gotoſo, goutie, *Podagroſus.*
Gotear, to drop, *Inſtillare.*
Goteado, ſpotted with drops, dropped on, *Guttatus.*
Gotilla, a ſmall drop, *Guttula.*
Governar, vierno, to gouerne, to rule, *Gubernare.*
Governador, a gouernor, a ruler, *Gubernator.*

G R

Governalle, the rudder, the helme of a ſhip, *Clauus, gubernaculum.*
Governacion, gouernment, *Gubernatio.*
Governo, gouernment, *Moderatio, gubernatio.*
Gozar, to enioy, to obtaine, *Frui.*
Gozarſe, to be glad, *Gaudere.*
Gozo, ioy, mirth, *Gaudium.*
Gozoſo, ioyfull, *Gaudens, hilaris.*
Gozque, *vide* Goſque.

G R

Gracia, grace, fauor, comlines, beautie, pleaſantnes, thanks, *Gratia, decor, lepos, gratiæ.*
Gracioſo, gratious, pleaſant, comely, thankfull, *Lepidus, decorus, gratus.*
Gracioſamente, pleaſantly, thankfully, graciouſly, *Lepidè, gratè, decorè.*
Grado, a ſtep, a degree, *Gradus.*
Graduar, to prefer to a degree, *Prouehere ad dignitatem.*
Graduado, preferred to a degree, *Prouectus ad dignitatem.*
Gragéa, carawaies, *Confecta ſaccaro.*
Graja o grajo, a chogh, *Gracculus*
Grama, graſſe, *Gramen.*
Gramatico, a grammarian, *Grammaticus.*
Gramática, grammar, *Grammatica.*
Gramoſo, graſſie, *Gramineus.*
Grana, graine to die cloth, *Coccum.*
Grana de parayſo, graines of paradiſe, *Cardamomum.*
Granada, a pomegranate, *Malum punicum.*
Granado, a pomegranate tree, *Malus punica.*
Granado, that hath many graines, *Granorum plenus.*
Granar, to kerne as corne doth, *In grana dureſcere.*
Granças de trigo, the beards of wheate, chaffe, *Acus, eris.*
Granças echar, to put out beards as corne doth, *Acerare.*
Grançones, orts, beards of corne, *Reliquiæ, acus eris.*
Grancer, ço, to haile, *Grandinare.*
Grançoſa, full of beards or of chaffe, *Acerosus.*

Grande,

	Grossura, **grosenes**, *Pinguedo,crassitudo.*
opere.	Grossedad, *Idem.*
tudo, magnifi-	Grossamente, **groselie**, *Crasse.*
	Grosseria, **grosenes** of conceite, **doltish-**
,	nes, *Hebetudo.*
t, to win, to	Grossero, a **groshead**, a **dulhead**, *Hebes.*
are, congerere,	Grua, a crane, *Grus.*
	Gruesso, fat, *Pinguis, opimus.*
reaping vp,	Grulla, a crane, *Grus.*
atio,lucrum.	Grumete, a **grumet** of a **ship**, a **shipboy**,
edium.	*Mesonauta.*
naceum.	Grumo, a **cabbage**, *Brassica.*
mchramis, aci-	Gruñir, to **grunt**, *Grunnire.*
(*nus.*	Gruñidor, a **grunter**, *Grunnitor.*
	Gruñido, the **grunting**, *Grunnitus.*
e in a grape,	Grupera, a **crupper**, *Caudale, postilena.*
	Grupada, a **blow**, *Ictus.* (*uerna.*
inguedo, sagi-	Gruta, a **vault**, a **caue vnder ground**, *Ca-*

Gu

s,saginatus.	
tri.	Guadañador, a **mower** of **haie**, *Fæniseca.*
tificatio.	Guadana, a **sieth**, *Falx.* (*uestris.*
is, molestus.	Guadapero, a **wilde peare tree**, *Pyrus syl-*
Grauitas, mo-	Guadañones, **manacles**, *Manicæ.*
	Guadamecies, **hangings of gilt leather,**
sully, Graui-	*Tapetum coriaceum pictum & deauratum.*
	Guay, alas, **wo**, *Hei, heu.*
:langere.	Guayas, **lamenting**, *Eiulatus.*
:langor.	Guayar, to lament, *Lamentari.*
la.	Gualdo, **pellow**, *Flauus.*
	Guante, a **gloue**, *Chirotheca.*
	Guantero, a **glouer**, *Chirothecarius.*
Bracchæ nau-	Guarda, a **guard**, **custodie**, **keeping**, *Custo-*
	dia, custos.
	Guardado, **guarded**, **kept**, *Custoditus.*
ibialia.	Guardador, a **keeper**, *Custoditor.*
	Guardar, to **guard**, to **looke vnto**, to **keep,**
se, chops in	to **spare**, *Custodire, seruare, parcere.*
	Guardia, a **guard**, *Custodia.*
	Guadrimaña, a **deceit**, a **peece of cosenage,**
grashopper,	*Fallacia, impostura.*
	Guardian, a **warder**, a **gardein that keep-**
	eth, *Custos.*
g vp of the	Guarida, **refuge**, a **retiring place**, *Refugiu.*
	Guarismo, **arithmetike**, *Arithmetica.*
	Guarnecer, to **furnish**, to **fortifie**, to
	freight, to **garnish**, *Instruere, munire, or-*
	nare.

Guarnecido,

G V

Guarnecido, furnished, fortified, freighted, garnished, *Instructus, munitus, ornatus.*

Guarnicion, a garrison, embroderie, garding of a garment, stitching of a garment, hilts of a sword, *Munitio, ornatus, capulus ensis.*

Guarnicimiento, furniture, the furnishing, *Ornatus, ornamentum.*

Guarnicionero, he that maketh furniture an embroderer, *Phrygio, instructor.*

Guedeja de cabellos, a tuffe of haire, *Cincinnus.*

Guedejudo, y guedejoso, he that hath long tuftes of haire, that hath long lockes of haire, *Cincinnatus.*

Guero huevo, an addle egge, *Ouum urinum, ouum putidum.*

Guerra, warre, *Bellum, prælium, militia.*

Guerrear, to make warre, *Belligerare, militare.*

Guerreador, a maker of warre, a warriour, *Bellator.*

Guerrero, a soldier, a warrier, *Miles, bellator.*

Guia, a guide, *Dux.*

Guiador, a guider, *Ductor.*

Guiar, to guide, *Ducere.*

Guiado, led, guided, *Ductus.*

Guija, *vide* Aguija.

Guijarra, a stone, *Saxum.*

Guijuela, a small pible stone, *Glarea.*

Guinda, a sower cherry, *Cerasum acre.*

Guindo, a sower cherrie tree, *Cerasus acris.*

Guiñar, to twinckle the eie, to wincke, *Conniuere, innuere.*

Guirnalda, a garland, *Corona.*

Guisado, sod, dressed, *Coctus.* (dire.

Guisar, to seeth, to dresse meat, *Coquere, condire.*

Guisa, a guise, a fashion, *Mos.*

Guitarra, a rebecke, a gitterne, *Fidicula.*

Gula, gluttony, *Gula.*

Gúmena de nao, a cable, *Rudens.*

Gurupera, a crupper, *Postilena.*

Gusano, a worme, *Vermis.*

Gusanienta cosa, full of wormes, *Vermiculosus.*

Gusanillo, a small worme, *Vermiculus.*

Gusanear, to be full of wormc, *Verminare.*

H A

Gustar, to taste, to like, *Gustare, probare, arridere.*

Gusto, taste, good liking, *Gustus.*

H A

Habla, speech, *Sermo.*

Hablar, to speake, *Loqui.*

Hablador, a speaker, *Vaniloquus, verbosus, loquax.*

Hablar baxo, to speake soft, *Submissa voce loqui.*

Hablar de espacio, to speake leisurely, *Prolixè loqui.*

Hablillas, fables, *Fabulæ.*

Habubilla, a iay, *Graculus.*

Haca y hacanea, a nag, a gelding, a hackney, *Mannus.*

Haça, a plot of ground, *Ager, aruum.*

Hace, a fagot, a bundle, *Fascis.*

Hacecillo, a bauen, a small bundle, *Fasciculus.*

Hacina de leña, a wood pile, *Strues lignorum*

Hacha, an axe, an hatchet, a battell axe, a torch, a linke to burne, *Securis, lychnus.*

Hachuela, a little hatchet, *Securicula.*

Hado, destinie, *Fatum.*

Hadar, to tell destinies, *Fata canere.*

Hadador, he that telleth destinies, *Fatidicus.*

Hadado, fatall, *Fatalis.*

Haya, a bœch, *Fagus.*

Hayal, a bœch groue, *Faginetum.*

Halagar, to cherish, to cocker, to make much of, to flatter, *Blandire, lenire, mulcere, fouere.*

Halagodora cosa, flattering, *Pellex, blandus*

Halago, flatterie, faire speech, faire countenance, *Blanditiæ, illecebræ.*

Halagueño, flattering, *Blandus, blandiloquus*

Halagueñamente, flatteringly, *Blandè.*

Halcon, a falcon gentle, *Falco.*

Halconero, a falconer, *Accipetrarius.*

Haldas, clothes, skirts of the clothes, *Sinus, lacinia.*

Haldudo, he that hath long clothes, *Sinuosus.*

Hallar, to finde, *Reperire.*

Hallado,

Hallado, **found**, *Repertus.*
Hallazgo, **reward for finding any thing**, *Inuentoris merces.*
Hallulla, **pellets to cram pullen**, *Globuli faginandis gallinis.*
Hamacas, **hanging beds**, *Lecti pensiles.*
Hamago, **bees meate**, *Cibus apum.*
Hamapola, **wilde poppie**, *Papauer sylueſtre.*
Hambre, **hunger**, *Fames.*
Hambriento, **hungrie**, *Famelicus.*
Hambrear, **to be hungrie**, *Esurire.*
Handrejo, **a rag**, *Pannus lacer.*
Hanega, **a meaſure containing a buſhell and halfe**, *Seſquimodius, modius.*
Haragan, **a ſlothfull man, a lazie fellow**, *Deſes, piger, iners.*
Haragania, **ſloth, lazines**, *Pigritia, deſidia.*
Harda, **a ſquirrel**, *Sciurus.*
Hardalear, **to be thin**, *Rareſcere.*
Harija, **mill duſt**, *Pollen.*
Harina, **meale**, *Farina.*
Harinillas, **a kind of play at the dice**, *Luſus quidam alearum.* (*farinaria.*
Harinal, **a binne to keepe meale in**, *Arca*
Harma, **wilde rue**, *Ruta ſylueſtris.*
Harnero, **a ſicue to ſift**, *Cribrum.*
Harona beſtia, **a reſtie iade**, *Ignauus equus.*
Haronía, **reſtines**, *Ignauia.*
Haronéar, **to be reſtie**, *Ignauum eſſe.*
Harrear, **to driue beaſts**, *Agere, agitare.*
Harre, **the voice of a harrier or driuer of beaſts**, *Eia.*
Harriero, **a driuer of beaſts, a harrier**, *Agitator, agaſo.*
Harpa, **a harpe**, *Cythara.*
Harpador, **a harper**, *Cytharædus.*
Harpia, **an harpie**, *Harpyia.*
Harpada cara, **the face croſſed, the face wounded**, *Facies cicatricum plena.*
Harpar, **to croſſe the face**, *Faciem vulnerare.*
Hartar, **to fill, to ſatiſfie**, *Satiare.*
Harto, **filled, ſatiſfied, ynough**, *Satiatus, ſa-*
Harto mas, **much more**, *Multò plus.* (*tis.*
Harto menos, **much leſſe**, *Multò minus.*
Hartura, **ynough, fulnes**, *Satietas.*
Haſta, **vntill, vp to**, *Vſque, tenus.*
Haſta aqui, **hitherto**, *Hucuſque.*
Haſta agora, **till now**, *Vſque nunc.*

Haſta alla, **thitherto**, *Illuc vſque.*
Haſta que, **vntill that**, *Vſque dum.*
Haſtio, **aver haſtio, loathing, to loath**, *Faſtidium, ſaties, faſtidire.*
Haſtioſo, **loathſome**, *Faſtidioſus.*
Hataca, **a pot ſtick**, *Rudicula.*
Hato, **a heard, a ſtocke, a droue**, *Grex, armentum peculium.*
Hava, **beanes**, *Faba.*
Havar, **a field of beanes**, *Fabale.*
Havas de perro, **dog beanes**, *Cynocrambe.*
Hava de beſtias en la boca, **the lampas**, Havarraz, *vide* Avarraz. (*Rana.*
Haz, **the face, an armie**, *Facies, acies.*
Hazahar, *vide* Azahar.
Hazaleja, **a napkin**, *Mantile.*
Hazaña, **an exploit, a deed**, *Facinus.*
Hazañoſo, **doughtie, he that doth ſome great deed, or valiant exploit**, *Facineroſus, magnificus.*
Haze, *vide* Hace.
Hazer, **hago, hize, hare, to do**, *Facere, agere.*
Hazedor, **a doer**, *Factor, actor.*
Hazer dentera, **to ſet the teeth on edge**, *Dentibus ſtuporem inducere.*
Hazer frio, **to be cold weather**, *Frigeſcere.*
Hazer agua, **to raine**, *Pluere.*
Hazer claro, **to be cleere**, *Serenare.*
Házia, **towards**, *Verſus.*
Házia atras, **backward**, *Retrorſum.*
Házia do, **which way, whither**, *Quorſum.*
Hazienda, **wealth, riches, goods**, *Bona, facultas, diuitiæ, res familiaris.*
Hazimiento, **working, doing**, *Opus, actio.*
Hazino o meſquino, **a poore wretch**, *Miſer.*

H E

He aqui, **behold**, *Ecce.*
Hebra, **a ſtring of a roote**, *Fibra.*
Hebrero, **Februarie**, *Februarius.*
Helo, **behold**, *Eccum.*
Hechizero, **a witch**, *Veneficus.*
Hechizos, **witcheries, witchcraft**, *Veneficium.*
Hech izeria, *vide* Hechizos.
Hechizar, **to bewitch**, *Faſcinare.*
Hechizo o hecho, **any thing to be done**, *Factitius.*

Hecho,

H E

Hecho,a dœd,an act,done,*Factum.*
Hechura, the fashion,the making,*Factio, forma, effectio.*
Heder,hiedo,to stinke,*Fœtere.*
Hediondo,stinking,*Fœtidus.*
Hedor,stinch,*Fœtor.*
Helecho,fearne,*Filix.*
Helgadura de dientes, the parting of the teeth, *Discrimina dentium.*
Helgado,*idem.*
Hembra,a woman,the female, *fœmina.*
Hembra de corchete,a maile, *Macula.*
Hemencia,behemencie,*Vehementia.*
Hemencioso,behement,*Vehemens.* (*stare.*
Hemenciar,to be behement, *Efflagitare, in-*
Henchir y hinchir, to fill,to swell, *Implere, tumescere.* (*tumor.*
Henchimiento, filling,swelling, *Impletio,*
Hender hiendo,to cleaue,*Findere.*
Hendedura,a cleft,*Fissura, rima.*
Hendimiento,cleauing,*Discuneatio, fissura.*
Hendido,cleft,*Bifidus.*
Hendible,that may be cleft,*Fissilis.*
Heno,haie,*Fanum.*
Hera,*vide* Era.
Hermano,*vide* Ermano.
Hermosamente,fairely, *Pulchrè,decenter.*
Hermoso, faire, beautifull, *Formosus,pulcher.*
Hermoséar,to make faire, *Decorare,ornare.*
Hermosura,bewty, *Pulchritudo,forma.*
Herida,a blowe,a stripe,*Ictus.*
Herido,stroken, *Percussus,ictus.*
Herir,hiero,to strike,*Ferire,percutere.*
Heridor,a striker, *Percussor.*
Herir de punta,to thrust with a weapon *Confodere.*
Herrada,a paile, a bucket,*Situla.*
Herrado,shod with iron,*Ferratus.*
Herrador, a smith that shoeth horses, *Calceator.*
Herradura,a horse shooe,*Solea ferrea.*
· Herramiento, the shoing of a horse,iron works, *Soleatio,ferramenta.*
Herramental, iron stuffe, *Ferramentarium.*
Herrar,to shoe with iron, to mark with a hot iron, *Solea re,ferro inurere.*
Herren,prouender,*Farrago,Ocymum.*

H I

Herrero,a smith,*Faber ferrarius.*
Herreruelo,a cloake,*Pallium.*
Herrambre,ruste,drosse of iron, *Ferrugo.*
Herver hiervo,to be hot, to boile,to seeth *Fernere.*
Hervera,the throate bole,*Gula.*
Hervor,heate,*Feruor.*
Heruiente,hot,feruent, *Feruidus.*
Hevilleta,a little button,*Fibula.*
Hevilla,a button,a claspe,*Fibula.*
Hevillar,to button,to claspe,*Fibulare.*
Hez,dregs,*Fœx.*
Heziento,full of dregs,*Fæculentus.*

H I

Hiçar,to hoyse,*Tollere in altum.*
Hidalgo,a gentleman, *Generosus,ingenuus, patricius.*
Hidalguía,gentility, *Generositas.*
Hidiondo,*vide* Hediondo.
Hiel,gall,*Fel.*
Hiel de tierra,centorie, *Centaurium minus.*
Hienda,dunge,durte,*Stercus, canum.*
Hieltro,a felt,*Pannus intextus.*
Hienes,the temples of the head, *Tempora.*
Hierro,iron, *Ferrum.*
Higa,higas dar,the middle finger, to bore the nose, *Digitus medius, verpum offendere.*
Hígado,the liuer,*Iecur.*
Higadillo,a little liuer,*Iecur parvum.*
Higo,a fig,a disease in the head, a kinde of pyles,*Ficus,sycosis,marisca.*
Higuera,a fig tree,*Ficus.*
Higueral,an orchard of figs,*Ficetum.*
Higuera de infierno, palma christi, *Ricinus.*
Higuera loca,sycamore,*Sycamorus.*
Hija,a daughter,*Filia.*
Hijo,a son,a colt,*Filius,pullus.*
Hijadas,the small guts, *Ilia.*
Hijares,*idem.*
Hijastro,a son in lawe,*Filiaster.*
Hijastra,a daughter in lawe, *Filiastra.*
Hilada,a rowe, a ranke,*Ordo,series.*
Hilar,to spin,*Nere.*
Hilazas, thredes,dregs in vrine, *Lineamenta,fila,strumbus.*

Hilo,

Hilo, thred, the edge, a rowe, a ranke, *Filum, series.*
Hiladera, a spinster, *Filacista.*
Hincar, to fasten, to sticke fast, *Figere, hærere.*
Hincar de rodillas, to bowe the knees, to kneele, *Genu flectere.*
Hincado, fastened, *Fixus.*
Hinchar, to swell, to puffe vp, *Turgere, tumescere.*
Hinchado, swollen, filled vp, *Tumidus, refertus.*
Hinchamiento, swelling, *Tumor.*
Hinchazon, a swelling, *Struma, tuber.*
Hinchazoncillo, a little swelling, *Tuberculus.*
Hinchir, *vide* Henchir.
Hinestra, a windowe, *Fenestra.*
Hiñir, to kneade dowe, *Subigere massam.*
Hinojo, fennell, the knees, *Fæniculum, genu.*
Hinojo marino, sampire, *Crithmum.*
Hippa, the hicke vp, the peske, *Singultus, hifta.*
Hipar de estomago, the peske, the hick vp, *Redundantia stomachi.*
Hirviente, *vide* Herviente.
Hiscal, a corde, a rope, *Funis.*
História, an history, *Historia.*
Hito, a marke, a white to shoote at, *Meta,*
Mirar en hito, to looke earnestly vppon, *Intueri, obtueri.*

H O

Hobacho, a greasie iade, by metaphor, a beauy idle fellowe, *Equus pinguis, & ignauus, deses.*
Hoce, a hooke, a sickle, *Falx.*
Hocicar, to rote as a pigge, to busse, or beake, *Rostro fodere, dissuauiari.*
Hocico, a snout, *Rostrum.*
Hocino, a reape hooke, *Falcula.*
Hogaça, a loafe of breade, *Massa panis.*
Hogar, the hearth, the chimney, *Focus.*
Hoguera, a great fire, *Pyra, rogus.*
Hoguero, a pile of wood, *Strues lignorum.*
Hoyo, a ditch, *Fossa, scrobs.*
Hoyuelo, a little ditch, *Scrobiculus.*
Hoja, a leafe, the blade of a sword, a plate, *Folium, gladius, lamina.*
Hojalde, a tarte, *Placenta.*
Hojoso, full of leaues, *Frondosus.*
Hojecer los arboles, to haue leaues, *Frondescere.*
Hojuela, a pan cake, *Laganum.*
Holgar huelgo, to rest, to bee quiet, to bee glad, *Quiescere, gaudere.*
Holgura, rest, ioy, *Quies, gaudium.*
Holgança, rest, quietnes, *Quies, otium.*
Holgaçanes, idle companions, *Otiosi, desides.*
Hollar huello, to tread on, *Calcare.*
Holladura, the treading on, *Calcatio.*
Hollado, troaden on, *Calcatus.*
Hollejo, the skin, the huske, the peele or shale, *Valuulus, siliqua, anguis exuuia, putamen.*
Hollin, soote, smut, *Fuligo.*
Holliniento, sootie, *Fugilinosus.*
Hollores, the swellings, *Olores.*
Homarrache, a bisarde, a maske, *Persona.*
Hombrezillos, hops, *Lupulus salictarius.*
Hombre, *vide* Ombre.
Honda, a sling, *Funda.*
Hondero, a slinger, *Funditor.*
Hondo, deepe, *Profundus.*
Hondon, the depth, the bottome, *Profunditas.*
Hondura, deepenes, *Profunditas.*
Honesto, *vide* Onesto.
Hongo, a mushrome, *Fungus.*
Hongoso, full of mushromes, *Fungosus.*
Honsario, hossario, a place for dead mens bones, *ossarium.*
Honrra, *vide* Onrra, honor, *Honor.*
Hontanales, places of springs, *Fontanalia.*
Hora, an hower, *Hora.*
Horadado, bored through, *Perforatus.*
Horadar, to bore through, *Perforare.*
Horado, a hole, *Foramen.*
Horca, a gallowes, a gibbet, a forke, *Furca, crux, patibulum.*
Horcaso, a forke, *Furca.*
Horquilla, a pickforke, *Furcilla.*
Horma de çapatero, a laste for a shoomaker, *Forma.*

O   Hormiga,

H O

Hormiga, an ant, *Formica.*
Hormiguero, an ant heape, *Formicarium, myrmicetum.*
Hormiguear, to tickle in the feete, to haue the feete a sleepe, *Formicare.*
Hormigon de pared, the plaistering, or morter, *Crusta calcaria.*
Hornaza, a fornace, *Fornax, caminus.*
Hornazo, an egge pie, *Artouum.*
Hornaguera tierra, burning ground, *Carbunculus.*
Hornaguear, to burne brakes on the ground, *Carbunculari.*
Horno, an ouen, *Furnus, clibanus.*
Hornero, a furner, *Furnarius.*
Horneria, the furners worke, *Furnaria.*
Hornear, to set in bread, *Furnariam exercere.*
Hornezino, a bastard, *Spurius.*
Hornija, bauen to heate ouens, *Furnaria ligna.*
Hornillo, a little ouen, *Fornacula.*
Horro, a slaue freed, a free man, *Libertus, liber.*
Hortiga, a nettle, *Vrtica.*
Hortigar, to stinge with a nettle, *Vrtica vrere.*
Hortiga muerta, archangell, *Vrtica iners.*
Hortiguilla muerta, Mercurie, *Mercurialis.*
Hosco, browne, dun, *Fuscus.*
Hossario, *vide* Honsario.
Hostigar, to pricke forwards, to driue forwards, *Incitare, instigare.*
Hostigamiento, driuing forwardes, *Instigatio.*
Hoto, en hoto, by the egging, by the setting on, *Animatio.*

H u

Huebra, a worke, an acre of grounde, *Opera, Iugerü.*
Hueco, hollow, *Cauus.*
Huego, fire, *Ignis.*
Huelgo, breath, *Halitus.*
Huero, adle, *Vrinum ouum.*

H V

Huérfano, an orphane, *Orbus.*
Huerto, a garden, an orchard, *Hortus.*
Huesped, an oste, *Hospes.*
Huesso, a bone, *Os, ossis.*
Hueste, an hoste of men, an armie, *Exercitus.*
Hueuo, an egge, *Ouum.*
Huyda, flight, running away, *Fuga.*
Huyr, to flie, to run away, *Fugere.*
Huydo, fled, *Fugax.*
Huydor, he that flieth, *Fugax.*
Huydizo, a runnagate, *Fugitinus.*
Humano, *vide* Vmano.
Humear, to smoake, *Fumare.*
Humero, a tunnell for the smoake, *Fumarium.*
Humedecer, *vide* Vmedecer.
Humilde, *vide* Vmilde.
Humo, smoake, *Fumus.*
Humoso, smoakie, *Fumosus.*
Hundir, to cast mettall, to sincke, *Fundere conflare, sidere.*
Hundiblo, that may be caste, *Fusilis.*
Hundido, caste, molten, *Conflatus, fusus.*
Hundicion, casting, melting, *Conflatio, fusio.*
Hundidor, a melter, or caster of mettall, *Fusor.*
Hundimiento, sincking, *Subsessio.*
Hura de cabeça, dandro, *Furfures.*
Hurgar, to plucke, *Vellere.*
Hurganero de horno, a furner, a malkin, *Rutabulum, Peniculus.*
Huron, a firret, *Viuerra.*
Hurraca, a pie, *Pica.*
Hurtar, to steale, *Furari.*
Hurtado, stollen, *Furatus.*
Hurto, theft, *Furtum.*
Hurtador, a stealer, *Furator.*
Hurtadamente, by theft, theeuishly, secretly, *Furtiuè.*
Hurtible, that may be stollen, *Furtiuum.*
Hurtiblemente, by stealth, *Fursim.*
Huso, a spindle, *Fusus.*
Husada, o, maçorca, flaxe on the distaffe, *Pensum.*
Huzillo, a presse for syder, *Torcular.*

jacinto,

J A

IAcinto, a iacint ſtone, a iacint flower, *Hyacinthus.*
jaezes de cavallo, the trappings of a horſe, *Phalerae.*
jalde, yellow, *Flauus.*
jamon, a gambone, *Perna.*
jamas, for euer, neuer, *In perpetuum, perpetuò, nunquam.*
jaola, *vide* jaula.
jaqueta, a kinde of iacket made cloſe before, and open by the ſides, *Tunicula.*
jardin, a garden, *Hortsi,orum.*
jardinero, a gardiner, *Hortorum curator.*
jardineria, gardening, *Hortorum curatio.*
jarro, a pot, *Vrceus.*
jarrillo, an herbe called wake Robin, a little pot, *Arus, aaron, vrceolus.*
jaſpe, a iaſper ſtone, *Hiaſpis,*
jaſpeado, trimmed with iaſpar, *Hiaſpide ornatus.*
jaſſar, to ſcarifie, *Scarificare.*
jaſſadura, ſcarifying, *Scarificatio.*
jaſſador, a ſcarifier, *Sacrificator.*
javali, a wilde boare, *Aper.*
jaula, a cage, *Cauea.*
jazmin, a kinde of white flower very ſweete, much like the muſke roſe, *Alba viola.*

J O

joya, a iewell, houſholde ſtuffe, *Supellex monile.*
joyel, a tablet, *Emblema, gemma, monile.*
joyero, a ieweller, *Gemmarius.*
joyo, cockle, *Lollium.*
joyo ſylveſtre, wilde darnell, wall barly, *Phaenix.*
jornada, a iourney, *Iter diei.*
jornal, a daies wages, *Merces.*
jornalero, a day laborer, *Mercenarius.*
jorro, llevar la nave a jorro, to tow a ſhip, *Remulcare.*
jota, a iot, *Iota.*

J V

jubileo, the iubilie, *Iubileus.*
jubilado, freed from trauell, *Emeritus.*
jubilar, to be free, *Emereri.*
jubon, a dublet, *Thorax, diplois.*
jubetero, a dublet maker, *Thoracarius ſartor*
juderia, the Jewiſh religion, *Iudaiſmus.*
judio, a Jew, *Iudaeus.*
judia, *vide* Friſoles.
judiego, pertaining to a Jew, *Iudaicus.*
judihuelo, a Jew, elſo a ſmall kind of white peaſe, *Iudaeus, Phaſeolus,* vide Friſoles.
judicial, iudiciall, *Iudicialis.*
judicatura, iudgement, *Iudicium.*
juego, play, *Iocus, luſus, ludus.*
juego de paſſa paſſa, iugling, *Praeſtigiae.*
juego de cañas, running on horſebacke with canes, *Equeſtris pugnae leuis armaturae ſimulachrum.*
juevez, thurſday, *Dies Iouii.*
juez, a iudge, *Index.*
jugar, juego, to play, *Ludere.*
jugador, a plaier, *Luſor.*
juglar, a iugler, *Ioculator.*
juyzio, iudgement, *Iudicium.*
jujuba, *vide* Açofeyfa.
julepe, a kind of potion, *Potio.*
júlio, Julie, *Iulius menſis.*
juncal, a place where bulruſhes growe, *Iuncetum.*
junco, a bull ruſh, *Iuncus.*
juncia, galingale, *Cyperus.*
juncoſo, full of ruſhes, *Iuncoſus.*
júnio, June, *Iunius.* (*gatus.*
juntado, ioined, aſſembled, *Iunctus, congregatus.*
junta, an aſſemblie, a counſell, *Congregatio, concilium.*
juntar, to ioine, to aſſemble, to ſet togither, *Iungere.*
juntamente, iointly, togither, *Iunctim, ſimul, vnd.*
junto, ioined, *Iunctus.*
junto, neare, *Propè.*
juntura, the ioining, *Iunctio.*
jura, an oth, *Iſiurandum.* (*rus.*
jurado, ſworne, a conſtable, *Iuratus, epho-* juraderia,

juraderia, a conſtableſhip, *Ephoria.*
juramento, an oth, *Iuramentum.*
jurar, to ſweare, *Iurare.*
juridicion, iuriſdiction, *Iurisdictio.*
jusbarba, knæ holme, *Ruſcus.*
juſta, a iuſting on horſebacke, *Aequalis haſtis certatio.*
juſtar, to iuſt, *Aequalis haſtis certare.*
juſto, iuſt, right, vpright, *Iuſtus, rectus.*
juſtamente, iuſtly, *Iuſtè.*
juſticia, iuſtice, law, *Iuſtitia, ius, Aequitas.*
juſticiar, to do iuſtice, to execute the law, *Iudicium ferre, iudicium exequi.*
juſticiero, a ſeuere iudge, *Iudex ſeuerus.*
juvenil, youthfull, *Iuuenilis.*
juzgar, to iudge, to eſteeme, *Iudicare, aeſtimare.*
juzgado, iudged, *Iudicatus.*

I D

Ida, the going, the departing, *Profectio.*
Idea, an example, a conceiued figure, *Idea, figura.*
Idiota, an idiot, a lay man, *Idiota.*
Idolatria, idolatrie, *Idololatria.*
Idolatrar, to worſhip idols, *Idola colere.*
Idolo, an idoll, *Idolum.*
Idolatra, an idolater, *Idololatra.*
Idropeſia, the dropſie, *Hydrops.*
Idropico, ſicke of the dropſie, *Hydropicus.*

I G

Igleſia, a church, *Eccleſia.*
Ignorante, ignorant, *Ignorans.*
Ignorancia, ignorance, *Ignorantia.*
Ignominia, reproch, ſhame, *Ignominia.*
Igual, equall, *Aequalis.*
Igualmente, equally, *Aequaliter, equè.*
Igualdad, equalitie, *Aequalitas.*
Igualar, to match, to make equal, *Aequare.*

I J

Ijada, the ſmall ribs, the collike, the belly peece of a fiſh, *Colica paſſio, ilia, abdomen.*
Ijares, the ſmall guts, *Ilia.*

I L

Ilicito, vnlawfull, *Illicitus.*
Ilicitamente, vnlawfully, *Illicitè.*

Iluminar, to illuminate, to lighten, to limne, *Illuſtrare, miniculari, depingere.*
Iluminador de libros, a limner, *Miniculator.*
Iluſtre, famous, excellent, honorable, *Illuſtris.*

I M

Imágen, an image, *Imago.*
Imaginar, to imagine, *Imaginari.*
Imaginacion, imagination, *Imaginatio.*
Imaginado, imagined, *Imaginatus.*
Imaginativo, imagining, *Cogitabundus.*
Iman, a loade ſtone, *Magnes.*
Imitar, to imitate, *Imitari.*
Imitacion, imitation, *Imitatio.*
Imitador, an imitator, *Imitator.*
Imoderado, immoderate, *Immoderatus.*
Imortal, immortall, *Immortalis.*
Imortalmente, immortally, *Immortaliter.*
Imortalidad, immortalitie, *Immortalitas.*
Imovible, vnmoueable, *Immobilis.*
Impaciencia, impacience, *Impatientia.*
Impaciente, impacient, *Impatiens.*
Impacientemente, impaciently, *Impatienter.*
Impaſſible, that cannot ſuffer, *Impatibilis.*
Impedir pido, to let, to hinder, *Impedire.*
Impedimiento, let, hindrance, *Impedimentum.*
Impelir, to thruſt forwards, *Impellere.*
Imperfeto, vnperfect, *Imperfectus.*
Imperial, imperiall, *Imperialis.*
Imperiales o çahones, a kinde of breeches of linnen, *Braccharum genus.*
Império, the empire, *Imperium.*
Impetrar, to obtaine, *Impetrare.*
Impetracion, obtaining, *Impetratio.*
Impetu, force, violence, *Impetus.*
Impetuoſo, violent, *Violentus.*
Implacable, implacable, *Implacabilis.*
Imponer, to lay vpon, *Imponere.*
Importar, to bring in, to import, *Importare.*
Importáncia, importance, *Momentum.*
Importunidad, impoſtunity, *Importunitas.*
Importuno, impoſtune, *Importunus.*
Importunamente, importunately, *Importunè.*
Importunar, to be importunate, *Flagitare.*
Impoſſible,

Impoſſible, vnpoſſible, *Impoſſibilis.*
Impoſſibilidad, impoſſibility, *Impoſſibilitas.*
Impoſicion, laying on, *Impoſitio.*
Impoténcia, weaknes, impotencie, *Impotentia.*
Impotente, weake, impotent, *Impotens.*
Impremir, to imprint, *Imprimere.*
Impreſſion, imprinting, *Impreſſio.*
Impreſſo, imprinted, *Impreſſus.*
Impreſſor, a printor, *Impreſſor.*
Imprudentemente, vnwiſely, *Imprudenter.*
Imprudente, vnwiſe, *Imprudens.*
Imputar, to impute, *Imputare.*

I N

Inabilitar, to make vnapt, *Inhabilem facere.*
Inabil, vnable, vnapt, *Inhabilis, ineptus.*
Inabilidad, vnablenes, vnaptnes, diſabilitie, *Inhabilitas, ineptitudo.*
Inabilmente, vnaptly, *Inhabiliter.*
Inadvertencia, retchleſnes, carcleſnes, *Securitas.*
Inadvertido, inconſiderate, *Securus, improuidus.*
Inclinar, to incline, to bow, *Inclinare.*
Inclinacion, inclination, bowing, *Inclinatio.*
Inclinado, bent, inclined, *Inclinatus.*
Inconſiderado, inconſiderate, *Inconſideratus.*
Inconſiderancia, raſhnes, vnaduiſednes, *Inconſiderantia.*
Inconſtante, inconſtant, *Inconſtans.*
Inconſtantemente, inconſtantly, *Inconſtanter.*
Inconſtancia, inconſtancie, *Inconſtantia.*
Incontinente, incontinent, *Incontinens.*
Incontinencia, incontinencie, *Incontinentia.*
Inconveniente, inconuenient, *Incouenicns.*
Inconveniencia, inconuenience, *Inconuenientia.*
Inceſto, inceſt, *Inceſtus.*
Incierto, vncertaine, *Incertus.*
Incitar, to incite, to ſtir vp, *Incitare.*
Incitado, ſtirred vp, incited, *Incitatus.*
Incitador, he that ſtirreth vp, he that prouoketh, *Incitator.*
Incitamiento, ſtirring vp, *Incitatio.*

Increyble, vncredible, *Incredibilis.*
Incredulo, increduluous, he that will not beleeue, *Incredulus.*
Increpado, rebuked, *Increpatus.*
Indiferente, indifferent, *Indifferens.*
Indigeſto, vndigeſted, *Indigeſtus.*
Indigeſtion, want of digeſtion, *Indigeſtio.*
Indignacion, indignation, wrath, *Indignatio.*
Indignidad, indignitie, vnworthines, *Indignitas.*
Indigno, vnworthie, *Indignus.*
Indiſpueſto, ſickly, il at eaſe, *Valetudinarius.*
Indiſpoſicion, ſickines, *Valetudo.*
Indiviſible, that cannot be diuided, *Indiuiſibilis.*
Induſtria, induſtrie, diligence, endeuour, *Diligentia, induſtria.*
Induſtrioſo, diligent, induſtrious, *Induſtrius.*
Indulgencia, pardon, *Indulgentia, venia.*
Induzir, duzgo, to induce, to perſwade, *Inducere, ſuadere.*
Induzimiento, inducing, perſwaſion, *Inductio, ſuaſio.*
Induzidor, a perſwader, *Inductor, ſuaſor.*
Ineſtimable, vneſtimable, *Ineſtimabilis.*
Ineuitable, ineuitable, *Ineuitabilis.*
Inexpugnable, impregnable, *Inexpugnabilis.*
Infamar, to defame, *Defamare.*
Infámia, Infamie, *Infamia.*
Infame, Infamous, *Infamis.*
Infamado, defamed, *Infamis, ignominioſus.*
Infançon, an infant, *Infantulus.*
Infantería, the band of footmen, *Peditatus.*
Inferior, inferior, lower, *Inferior.*
Infernal, infernall, *Infernus.*
Inficionado, infected, *Infectus.*
Inficionar, to infect, *Inficere.*
Infiel, vnfaithfull, an infidell, *Infidelis.*
Infieldad, infidelitie, *Infidelitas.*
Infierno, hell, *Infernum, orcus.*
Infinidad, infinitenes, *Immenſitas.*
Infinito, infinite, infinitely, *Infinitus, immenſus, infinité.*
Infinitamente, infinitely, *Infinité.*

Inflamado,

Inflamado, **inflamed**, *Inflammatus*.
Inflamacion, **an inflamation**, *Inflammatio*.
Inflamar, **to inflame**, *Inflammare*.
Informacion, **information**, *Informatio*.
Informar, **to informe**, *Informare*.
Infortunado, **unfortunate**, *Infælix*.
Infundir, **to powre in**, *Infundere*.
Infundido, **powred in**, *Infusus*.
Ingenio, **witte**, *Ingenium*.
Ingenioso, **wittie**, *Ingeniosus*.
Ingeniosa mente, **wittily**, *Ingeniosè*.
Ingle, ingre, **the thigh, the flancke**, *Inguen*.
Inhiesto, **lifted vp**, *Sublatus*.
Inhumano, **vngentle, inhumane**, *Inhumanus*.
Inhumanidad, **crueltie, inhumanitie**, *Inhumanitas*.
Injúria, **wrong, iniurie**, *Iniuria, contumelia*.
Injuriar, **to doe wrong, to reuile**, *Conuitiari, iniuriam inferre*.
Injuriadora, cosa, **wrongfull**, *Iniurius*.
Injuriado, **wronged, reproched**, *Malè habitus*.
Injuriador, **he that wrongeth, he that reuileth**, *Iniurius*.
Injuriosamente, **iniuriously**, *Per iniuriam*.
Injurioso, **iniurious**, *Iniurius, contumeliosus*.
Injusticia, **iniustice**, *Iniustitia*. (*sus*.
Injustamente, **vniustly**, *Iniustè*.
Injusto, **vniust**, *Iniustus*.
Inobediente, **disobedient**, *Inobediens*.
Inobediencia, **disobedience**, *Inobedientia, refragatio*.
Inocencia, **innocencie**, *Innocentia*.
Inocente, **innocent**, *Innocens*.
Inocentemente, **innocently**, *Innocenter*.
Inojo, **the knee**, *Genu*.
Inojales, **canions**, *Genualia*.
Inogil, **the garters**, *Vincula*.
Inorme, **enormious, heynous**, *Enormis*.
Inovar, **to innouate**, *Innouare*.
Inovacion, **innouating**, *Innouatio*.
Inquietadora cosa, **vnquiet**, *Inquietus*.
Inquieto, **vnquiet**, *Inquietus*.
Inquietar, **to disquiet**, *Inquietare*.
Inquietud, **disquietnes**, *Inquietudo, molestia*.
Inquiridor, **a searcher, an enquirer**, *Inquisitor*.

Inquirir, quiero, **to enquire, to search**, *Inquirere*.
Inquisicion, **inquisition, search**, *Inquisitio*.
Inquisidor, **an inquisitor**, *Inquisitor*.
Insaciable, **vnsatiable**, *Insatiabilis*.
Insaciabilmente, **vnsatiablie**, *Insatiabiliter*.
Insigne, **notable**, *Insignis*.
Insignias, **ensignes, armes**, *Insignia, insignia gentilitia*.
Insonoro, **vntunable**, *Dissonus*.
Instable, **vnstable**, *Instabilis*.
Instabilidad, **vstabilitie, vnstablenes**, *Instabilitas*.
Instancia, **instance, earnestnes**, *Instantia*.
Instante, **an instant**, *Instans*.
Instar, **to be earnest**, *Instare*.
Instinto natural, **naturall inclination**, *Instinctus*.
Instituir, tuyo, **to appoint, to instruct**, *Instituere*.
Institucion, **instruction**, *Institutio*.
Instrumento, **an instrument**, *Instrumentum*.
Insuffrible, **intolerable**, *Intollerabilis*.
Intencion, **intent**, *Propositum*.
Interior, **the inner**, *Interior*.
Intercessor, **an intercessor**, *Intercessor*.
Interpretar, **to interprete**, *Interpretari*.
Interpretacion, **interpretation**, *Interpretatio*.
Interprete, **an interpretor**, *Interpres*.
Interromper, **to interrupte**, *Interrumpere*.
Intervalo, **a space**, *Interuallum*.
Intestino, **the gut**, *Intestinum*.
Intimar, **to intimate, to signifie**, *Intimare*.
Intitular, **to intitle**, *Intitulare*.
Intrectable, **vntractable**, *Intrectabilis, morosus*.
Intricar, **to entangle**, *Intricare*.
Intricado, **intricate**, *Intricatus, implicitus*.
Intrínseco, **inward**, *Intrinsecus*.
Introducion, **introduction**, *Introductio*.
Introduzir, duzgo, **to bring in**, *Inferre, introducere*.
Introduzido, **brought in**, *Introductus*.
Inumerable, **innumerable**, *Innumerabilis*.
Invencion, **inuention**, *Inuentio*.
Inventar, **to inuent**, *Inuenire*.
Inventario,

Inventario, an inuentorie, *Inuentarium.*
Inventor, an inuentor, *Inuentor.*
Invernal, perteining to winter, *Hibernus.*
Invernar, to winter, *Hybernare.*
Invierno, winter, *Hyems.*
Invisible, inuisible, *Inuisibilis.*

I P
Ipocresia, hypocrisie, *Hypocrisis.*
Ipocrita, an hypocrite, *Hypocrita.*

I R
Ira, anger, *Ira.*
Irado, angrie, *Iratus.*
Irregular, without rule, irregular, *Irregularis.*
Irregularidad, the being without rule, *Irregularitas.*
Irregularmente, irregularly, without rule, *Irregulariter.*
Irreparable, that cannot be repaired, *Irreparabilis.*

I S
Isla, an ile, *Insula.*
Isopo, hysope, *Hysopus.*
Istoria, an historie, *Historia.*
Istoriador, an historian, *Historicus.*
Istorial, perteining to an historie, *Historicus.*

I T
Item, also, *Item, præteres.*
Itericia, the iaundise, *Ictericia.*
Iterico, sicke of the iaundise, *Ictericus.*

Y
Y. and, *Et.*
Ya, alreadie, so, now, *Sic, iam.*
Yazer, to lie, *Iacere.*
Yazija, condition, estate, qualitie, lying, *Status, conditio, cubitus.*
Yantar, to breakefast, *Ientare.*

Y E
Yedra, iuie, *Hedera.*
Yegua, a mare, *Equa.*
Yeguada, a race of mares, *Equaria.*

Yeguarizo, he that keepeth mares, *Equarius.*
Yelo, froste, *Gelu, glacies.*
Yelar, to freese, to congeale, *Congelare.*
Yelmo, an helmet, *Galea.*
Yema, the yelke of an egge, *Vitellus.*
Yema de vid, the knot of a vine branch, *Gemma.*
Yermo, a desert, *Solitudo, eremus.*
Yerno, a sonne in law, *Gener.*
Yero, a kinde of tare, *Erui species.*
Yerro, an error, *Error.*
Yerto, rough, bristled, *Hirtus.*
Yerva, an herbe, grasse, poison, *Herba, gramen, venenum.*
Yerva estrella, buckhorne planteyne, or harteshorne, *Coronopus.*
Yerva de ballestero, næsingwoorte, beare= foote, *Helleborus.*
Yerva de tunez, maidenweed, *Pucedanum.*
Yerva de santa Maria, tansie, *Athanasia.*
Yerva de san Iuan, S. Johns woort, *Hypericon.*
Yerva almisclera, muske herbe, *Herba muscata.*
Yerva arretica, herbe Iuie, *Chamæpytis.*
Yerva buena, mynts, *Mentha.*
Yuerva mora, broome rape, *Orobancha.*
Yerva xabonera, sopewoort, *Saponaria.*
Yerva puntera, sempertuiuum, *Aizous.*
Yerva piñuela, orpine, liblong, *Crassula.*
Yerva gatera, cats mint, *Calamintha.*
Yerva de golondrina, celandine, *Chelidonia.* (tonum.
Yerva lombriguera, southernwood, *Abro*
Yerva lanaria, dyers weed, *Herba lutea.*
Yerva cana, groundswell, *Senecio.*
Yervato, hart stronge, *Peucedanum.*
Yervo, betches, tares, *Eruum.*
Yesca, tinder, baite, *Esca.*
Yesso, morter, also that which they laye on parchement to make writing ta= bles, *Gypsum.*
Yesgo, walwoort, *Ebulus.*

Y O Y R
Yo, I, *Ego.*
Yr, voy, ius, sue, to go, *Ire, eo, is.*

Yra,

Y V
Yva, grounde pine, herbe Iuie, *Chamæpytis.*
Yugo, a yoake, *Iugum.*
Yugada, an acre, *Iugeris.*
Yunque, an anuile, *Incus.*
Yunta, a yoake of oxen, *Iugum.*

Y Z
Yzquierdo, the left, *Sinister, leuus.*
Yzquierda mano, the left hand, *Siniſtra.*

L A
L A, the, *Articulus fæmininus, hæc, illa.*
Labios, lips, *Labia.*
Labor, labour, *Labor.*
Laborcica, a finall worke, *Opuſculum.*
Labrar, to worke, to till, *Laborare, colere terram.*
Labrador, a laborer, a tiller of the ground *Laborator, colonus.*
Labrança, tillage, *Agricultura.*
Labrandera, a laundreſſe, *Lotrix.*
Lacayo, a footeman, *Pedes, à pedibus.*
Lacargama, wilde bugloſſe, *Anchuſæ.*
Lacio, weake, *Languidus.*
Lacha, a kinde of fiſh, *Piſciculi genus.*
Lacre, merchants waxe, *Cera emporetica.*
Ladear, to ſhake the head, to wagge the head, *Nutare.*
Ladera, the ſide of a hill, *Cliuus.*
Ladillas, neetes in the eye liddes, *Palpebrarum lens.*
Ladino, latyne, cleare, *Latinus, clarus.*
Lado, a ſide, *Latus.*
Ladrar, to barke, *Latrare.*
Ladrído, the barking of a dog, *Latratus.*
Ladrillar, to paue with brickes, *Latere pauimentare.*
Ladrillar, a place where brickes are made, *Laterum furnus.*
Ladrillado, brickworke, *Latericium.*
Ladrillo, brick. *Later.*
Ladrilejo, ſmall brickes, *Laterculus.*
Ladron, a theefe, *Latro.*
Ladroncillo, a yong theefe, a petty theefe, *Latrunculus.*
Ladronía, theeuing, ſtealing, *Latrocinium.*
Ladronicio, theft, *Latrocinium.*
Lagañas, filth in the eyes, matter in the eyes, *Lippitudo, epiphora.*
Lagar do piſan uvas, a great fatte to tread grapes in, *Lacus.*
Lagar de viga, a preſſe, *Torcular, prælum.*
Lagareta do piſan uvas, a ſmall tubbe, *Lacuſculum.*
Lagarto, an Efte, a Lizarde, *Lacertus.*
Lagartija, an Efte, a Lizard, *Lacerta, ſeps.*
Lago, a lake, *Lacus.*
Lagoſta, a Locuſt, a great Graſhopper, a kinde of fiſh, *Locuſta.*
Lagoſtines, a kinde of fiſh, *Piſciculi genus.*
Lágrima, a teare, *Lachryma.*
Lagrimar, to weepe, *Lachrymari.*
Lagrimal del ojo, the corner of the ey, *Oculi hircus.*
Lagrimoſo, weeping, ful of teares, *Lachrymoſus.*
Laguna, o lagunajo, a lake, *Lacuna, palus.*
Lamia, a plate, butt, myre, *Lamina, Cænum, Lutum.*
Lamedal, a puddle, *Lutoſum, voluttabrum.*
Lamedor, he that licketh, *Linctor.*
Lamedura, licking, *Linctus.*
Lamer, to licke, *Lingere.*
Lamentable, lamentable, *Lamentabilis.*
Lamentacion, lamentation, *Lamentatio.*
Lamentar, to lament, *Lamentari.*
Lamina, a plate of mettall, a leafe of mettall, *Lamina.*
Lampara, a lampe, *Lampas.*
Lamparones, the kings euill, *Scrophula.*
Lampazo, a burre, *Perſonata.*
Lampiño, ſmoothe, *Depilis, glaber.*
Lampréa, a Lamprey, *Murena.*
Lana, wooll, *Lana.*
Lança, a launce, a dart, *Haſta, ſpiculum, pilũ.*
Lançada, a blowe with a launce, *Lanceæ ictus.*
Lançadera de texidor, a weauers ſhuttle, *Radius Liciatorius.*
Lançar, to throwe out, to ſtrike out, to ſtrike with a launce, *Lancinare, emittere.*
Lançarotes, a kinde of gumme to cloaſe woundes, *Sarcocolla.*
Lance, a blowe, a ſtripe, a caſte, *Ictus, iactus.*
Lancero,

Lancero,a **Lancier**,*Lancearius*.
Lanceta,a small dart, a Surgeons knife to let blood, *Lanceola, scalpellus*.
Lancuela,a small launce,*Lanceola*.
Lançon,a launcing knife,*Cultellus*.
Landre,kernels in the necke or thigh, the blaines, botches, the pestilence, *Glandula,vlcus,pestis*.
Landrezilla,blaynes,*Glandula*.
Lanero, a wooll man, *Qui lanam mercatur*.
Langosta,a great Grashopper,*Locusta*.
Lanterna,a lanterne, *Laterna*.
Lanudo,wooliie,*Lanatus*.
Lañar,to bewayle,to lament,*Lamentari*.
Laña,bewayling, lamentation, *Lamentatio*.
Lapa,the hollownes under a banke side, or the purging of wine, *Flos vini, ripa subruta*.
Lapidario,a lapidarie,*Gemmarius*.
Lardo,larde,*Lardum*.
Largamente,largely,*Largiter*.
Largar,to set at large, to set at libertie, *Liberare,emittere,dimittere*.
Largo,long,large, liberal, *Longus,largus,liberalis*.
Largueza,franknes,*Liberalitas*.
Largura,length,longitude, *Prolixitas*.
Lasaña,a pancake, *Laganum*.
Lastar,to be beaten, to be punished,*luere*.
Lastimar,to hurt,to wound,to grieue,*ledere,dolere*.
Lástima,greefe,hurt,*Læsio,dolor*.
Lastre,ballast for ships,*Saburra*.
Lastrar,to ballast a shippe,*Saburrare*.
Látigo,a leather strap,*Corrigia*.
Latin,latine,*Latinus*.
Latinidad,the perfection of the latine,*Latinitas*.
Latir,to pant,to breathe, *Anhelare, Palpitare*.
Laton.latton,*Aurichalcum*.
Laud,a lute,*Testudo*.
Laudano, the gum labdanum, used in pomanders,*Ladanum*.
Laurel,a bay,*Laurus*.
Lauredal,a place where bayes grow,*Lauretum*.

Launas,plates to make corslets, *Lamina*.
Laureola,laurieli,*Daphnoides*.
Lavar,to wash, *Lauare*.
Lavador,a washer, *Lotor*.
Lavandera,a laundres,*Lotrix*.
Lavadero,a washing place,*Lauacrum*.
Lavadura,the washing,*Lotio*.
Lavanco,a drake,a mallard,*Anas mas*.
Lavajo,lavajal, a puddle,*Volutabrum*.
Lavazas,filthy washed off,*Proluuies*.
Lazada,a snare,a riddle, a laced button, *Gryphus,laqueus, pedica,fibula*.
Lazo, a knot, a ginne, a trap, *Nodus,laqueus*.
Lazéria,miserie,*Miseria,angustia,calamitas*.
Lazerado,miserable,*Miser,calamitosus*.
Lazillo,a little snare, a little trap, *Laqueolus,pedicula*.

L E

Leal,loyall,*Fidus*.
Lealtad,loyaltie,*Fides,fidelitas*.
Lealmente,loyally,*Fideliter*.
Lebrada,hare broath, *Iusculum leporinum*.
Lebrastilla,a leueret,*Lepusculus*.
Lebrel,a greyhound,*Canis leporarius*.
Lebrillo,a pot of earth, a bason of earth, *Labellum,catinus*.
Lebrillejo,a little bason of earth, *Catinus paruus*.
Lebruno,perteyning to a hare,*Leporinus*.
Lecion,a lesson,*Lectio*.
Lechal,perteyning to milke,*Lacteus*.
Lechera piedra, a pretious stone called Galactite.
Leche de gallina, white field onion, *Ornithagalon*.
Leche,milke,*Lac*.
Lechetrezna,spurge herbe,*Tithymalus*.
Lechiga, a beere for dead bodies, *Pheretrum*.
Lechin azeytuna,a kind of long oliue,*Radius*.
Lecho,a bed,*Lectus*.
Lechon,a sucking pig,*Porcellus lactans*.
Lechúga,lettuse,*Lactuca*.
Lechuguino,small lettise,*Lactucula*.
Lechuza,an Owle,*Bubo*.

L O   L O

Lironcillo, a little field mouſe, *Nitela.*
Liſiar, to hurt, *Lædere, Elidere.*
Liſiado, hurt, *Læſus, illiſus.*
Liſion, hurting, *Læſio.*
Liſo, ſmooth, *Lænis, glaber.*
Liſonja, flatterie, *Adulatio.*
Liſongeado, flattered, *Adulatus.*
Liſongear, to flatter, *Adulari.*
Liſongero, a flatterer, *Adulator.*
Liſta, the liſte of a garment, alſo a role of names, alſo ready, prompt, *Fimbria, catalogus nominum, paratus promptus.*
Liſtada, ſtriped with many coulours, *Variegatus.*
Liſtones, garters, liſtes, *Subligacula, fimbriæ.*
Liſura, ſmoothnes, *Leuor.*
Litéra, a horſelitter, *Lectica.*
Litigar, to chide, to braule, *Litigare.*
Litigador, a brawler, *Litigator.*
Litigioſo, full of ſtrife, litigious, *Litigioſus, contentioſus.*
Livianamente, lightly, *Leuiter.*
Liviandad, livianeza, lightnes, *Leuitas.*
Livianos, the lights of a beaſt, *Pulmo, onis.*
Liviano, light, light headed, *Leuis.*
Lixa, a great mullet fiſh, *Mullus.*
Lixo, *vide* Cieno.
Lizo, the web, *Licium.*

L O

Lo, it, that, *Illud, articulus neutrius generis.*
Loable, laudable, *Laudabilis.*
Loablemente, laudablie, *Laudabiliter.*
Loar, to praiſe, *Laudare.*
Loba, a ridge, a kinde of caſſocke, a ſhee wolfe, *Porca, tunicula genus, lupa.*
Labanillo en el cuerpo, a kinde of ſwelling, *Tuberculum.*
Lobado en el cuerpo, bunches in the fleſh the faſhion in an horſe, *Tuber, ſtruma.*
Lobadado, ſwollen with bunches, *Strumoſus.*
Lobo, a wolfe, *Lupus.*
Lobo marino, a ſea calfe, *Phoca.*
Lobezno, lobillo, a wolfes whelpe, *Catulus lupinus.*
Lobito, a little wolfe, *idem.*

Lobera, a caſſocke furred with wolfes *Tunica.*
Lobrego, darke, ſad, mornefull, *Obſcurus, lugubris.*
Lobuno, perteining to a wolfe, *Lupinus.*
Locamente, fooliſhly, madly, *Stulté, furioſé.*
Loco, a foole, a frantike man, *Stultus, inſanus, vecors.*
Locura, follie, madnes, *Stultitia, furor, vecordia.*
Loça, veſſels of earth, *Vas fictile.*
Loçano, wanton, braue, gallant, frollick, *Laſciuus, elegans.*
Loçania, brauerie, gallantnes, *Elegantia, Laſciuia.*
Lodo, durt, *Lutum.*
Lodoſo, durtie, *Lutoſus, lutulentus.*
Logico, a Logician, *Logicus.*
Lógica, Logicke, *Logica.*
Lograr, to win, to gaine, *Lucrari, ſaneraari.*
Logrado, mal logrado, vnfortunate, *Inſælix.*
Logrero, an vſurer, *Fœnerator.*
Logro, vſurie, *Fœnus.*
Lomas, ridges of hils, *Cacumina montium.*
Lombarda, a gun, *Tormentum.*
Lombardero, a gunner, *Tormentarius.*
Lombriz, an eaſle, an earth worme, *Lumbricus.*
Lombriguera, ſouthernwoode, *Abrotonum.*
Lomo, the loines, the backe, a ridge, *Lumbus, porca.*
Lomo de libro, the boſſe of a booke, *Vmbo.*
Longaniza, a pudding, *Farcimen.*
Longura, length, *Longitudo.*
Lonja de tocino, a lunch of bacon, *Fruſtum lardi.*
Lonja de mercaderes, a rowe of merchants, *Emporium.*
Lonja de caſa, a gallerie, *Ambulacrum.*
Loor, praiſe, *Laus.*
Loquear, to be fooliſh, *Furere, ineptire.*
Loriga, a breaſtplate, a maile, a habergion, *Lorica.*
Lorigado, armed with a habergion, *Loricatus.*

Loro,

Loro, dun, *Fuscus*.
Los, they, *Illi*.
Losa, a trap for birds, a pauement, *Decipula, pauimentum*.
Losar, to paue, *Pauimentare*.
Losado, paued, *Pauimentatum*.

L u

Luciernago, a glowe worme, *Nitedula*.
Lucha, wrestling, *Lucta*.
Luchador, a wrestler, *Luctator*.
Luchar, to wrestle, *Luctari*.
Ludir, to rub, *Confricare*.
Luego, by and by, therefore, then, *Statim, Ilico, Ergo*.
Luenez, long, *Longè*.
Luengamente, long, very long, *Longè, diu*.
Luengo, long, *Longus*.
Lugar, a place, opportunitie, *Locus, oportunitas*.
Lumbre, light, the fire, *Lumen, ignis, focus*.
Lumbrera, that giueth light, *Illuminans*.
Lumbroso, lightsome, *Luminosus*.
Lumbral, a threshold, the timber, or stone ouer a dore, *Limen*.
Luminar libros, to limne books, *Miniculari*
Luminador de libros, a lymner, *Miniculator*. (*latio*.
Luminacion de libros, lymning, *Miniculatio*.
Luna, the moone, *Luna*.
Lunático, lunaticke, *Lunaticus*.
Lunar piedra, a stone called *Selenites*.
Lunar, the moonelight, a spot in the body, *Lunæ lumen, næuus*.
Lunes, monday, *Dies lunæ*.
Lustre, the shew, the glasse of any colour, *Splendor*.
Lutado, clad in mourning weeds, *Pullatus*.
Luto, mourning, mourning apparell, *Luctus, veflis pulla*.
Luxuria, lecherie, *Luxuria, salacitas, libido*.
Luxurioso, lecherous, *Libidinosus*.
Luxuriosamente, lecherouslie, *Libidinosè*.
Luxuriar, to be lecherous, *Libidinari, luxuriari*.
Luz, light, *Lux*.
Luziernaga, a glowe worme, *Nitedula*.

Luzero, the morning star, *Lucifer*.
Luzio, shining, *Lucens, lucidus*.
Luziente, shining, *Lucens, lucidus*.
Luzillo, a tombe, *Tumba*.
Luzimiento, the lightening, *Illustratio*.
Luzir, to shine, *Lucere*.

Ll A

Llaga, a wound, *Plaga, vulnus*.
Llagar, to wound, *Vulnerare*.
Llagado, wounded, *Vulneratus*.
Llagoso, full of wounds, *Plagosus*.
Llama, a flame of fire, *Flamma*.
Llamar, to call, to knocke at a gate, *Vocare, pulsare*.
Llamador, a caller, *Vocator*.
Llamado, called, *Vocatus*.
Llamamiento, calling, *Vocatio*.
Llanamente, plainly, *Planè*.
Llano, plaine, *Planus*.
Llanura, plainnes, a plaine, *Planities*.
Llanta, a plant, *Planta*.
Llanten, planten, *Plantago*.
Llanto, mourning, lamentation, *Planctus*.
Llantear, to bewaile, *Plangere*.
Llares o ollares, pot-hangers, *Ollares catellave, a key, Clauis*. (*næ*.
Llauerizo, a key bearer, *Clauiger*.

Ll E

Llegada, an assemblie, *Concilium*.
Llegado, assembled, gotten togither, come neare to, *Congregatus, congestus, qui appropinquauit*.
Llegar, to gather togither, to come neare, *Congregare, appropinquare*.
Lleno, full, *Plenus*.
Llevar, to bring, to beare, to carrie, to draw, to lift, to take away, *Trahere, portare, elenare, auferre*.
Llevador, a bearer, a lifter, *Portator, bainlus, sublenator*.

Ll O

Llorar, to weepe, to waile, *Plorare, flere*.
Lloro, weeping, *Fletus*.
Llorosamente, mournfully, weepingly, *Flebiliter*.

Lloroso,

lloroſo, **mournfull**, *Flebilis*.
llover, **lluevo, to raine**, *Pluere*.
llovediza agua, **raine water**, *Aqua pluuia*.
lloviznar, **to drizle, to be ſhowry**, *Pluitare*.

Ll u

Llúvia, **raine**, *Pluuia*.
lluvioſo, **rainie**, *Pluuius, pluuioſus*.

M A

Macarrones, **freſh cheeſe & creame**
   Caſeus recens cum flore lactis.
Maça, **a hammer, a beetle, a mace**, *Malleus, claua*.
Maçapan, **a marchpane**, *Panis dulciarius*.
Maçacote, **the ſtuffe whereof glaſſe is made**, *Armonitrum*.
Macero, **a mace bearer**, *Clauiger*.
Maciço, **ſound, ſolide**, *Solidus*.
Macias, **the poet Macer**, *Macer*.
Macicez, **ſoundneſ**, *Soliditas*.
Maciçar, **to make ſound**, *Solidare*.
Maço, **a hammer, a beetle**, *Malleus, fiſtuca*.
Maçonéar, **to driue downe with a hammer or beetle**, *Fiſtucare*.
Maçonería o maçonadura, **beating in, ramming in**, *Fiſtucatio*.
Maçorca, **flaxe on the diſtaffe**, *Penſum*.
Macho, **the male**, *Maſculus*.
Machorra, **barren**, *Sterilis*.
Machucar, **to ſtampe or beate**, *Contundere*.
Machucado, **ſtamped**, *Contuſus*.
Machucadura, **ſtamping**, *Contuſio*.
Madera, **timber**, *Tignus, materia*.
Madero, **wood**, *Lignum*.
Maderar, **to timber**, *Contignare*.
Maderado, **timbered**, *Materiatus, cōtignatus*.
Madero, **a beame**, *Aſſer*.
Maderamiento, **timbering**, *Contignatio*.
Madexa, **a ſkeine of thred**, *Forago*.
Madraſta, **a mother in law, a ſtepmother**, *Nouerca*.
Madre, **a mother**, *Mater, vterus*.
Madre de rio, **the chanell**, *Alueus*.
Madreſelva, **woodbine**, *Periclymine*.
Madriguera de conejo, **a conie hole**, *Cuniculus*.

Madrina, **a godmother**, *Mater ſpiritualis, ſuſceptrix*.
Madriz, **a wombe**, *Matrix*.
Madroño, **a kind of wild orenge**, *Arbutus*.
Madrugar, **to riſe early**, *Diluculo ſurgere*.
Madrugada, **the morning**, *Antelucanum tempus*.
Maduro, **mellow**, *Maturus, mollis*.
Maduradamente, **ripely**, *Maturè*.
Madureza, **ripeneſ**, *Maturitas*.
Madurarſe, **to be ripe**, *Maturari*.
Maeſtre, **a maſter**, *Magiſter*.
Maeſtre eſcuela, **a ſchoolemaſter**, *Ludimagiſter*.
Maeſtría, **maſterſhip, cunning**, *Magiſterium*.
Maeſtrazgo, **maſterſhip**, *Magiſtratus*.
Maeſtre ſala, **a gentleman vſher**, *Structor*.
Mageſtad, **maieſtie**, *Maieſtas*.
Magnificamente, **worſhipfully, liberally**, *Magnificè*.
Magnifico, **worſhipfull, bountifull**, *Magnificus*.
Magnificentia, **magnificence, bountifulneſ**, *Magnificentia*.
Magnanimo, **valiant, coragious**, *Magnanimus*.
Magnanimidad, **corage, valour**, *Magnanimitas*.
Magnanimamente, **valiantly, coragiouſly**, *Magnanimiter*.
Magrecerſe, **to be leane**, *Macreſcere*.
Magreza, **leanneſ**, *Macies*.
Magro, **leane**, *Macer*.
Maguera, **although**, *Quamuis, etſi, licèt*.
Magullar, **to bruſe, to beate blacke and blew**, *Contundere, ſuggillare*.
Magullado, **bruſed, beaten blacke and blew**, *Contuſus, ſuggillatus*.
Magulladura, **bruſing, beating black and blew**, *Suggillatio*.
Maherir, hiero, **to preſſe ſoldiers**, *Deligere, conſcribere*.   (*lectus*.
Maherimiento, **preſſing of ſoldiers**, *Delayo*, Maie, *Maius*.
Mayor, **greater, the elder**, *Maior*.
Mayormente, **eſpecially**, *Præſertim, præcipuè*.

                       Mayordomia,

Mayordomia, a ſtewardſhip, *Oeconomia.*
Mayordomo, a ſteward, *Oeconomus.*
Mayoral, the chiefe, the chiefe herdſman, *Princeps, magiſter pecoris.*
Mayorana, *vide* Amoradux.
Mayorazgo, the elderſhip, the elder brother, the heire, *Primogenius, primogenitura.*
Maytinero, that ſaieth mattens, *Precator matutinus.*
Maytines, mattens, *Preces matutinæ.*
Mayvete, a ſtrawberrie, *Fragum.*
Majar, to beate with a peſtill or hammer, to powne, *Tundere, contundere, conterere, malleare.*
Majador, he that beateth with a peſtill or hammer, *Malleator, contuſor.*
Majadura, hammering, ſtamping, powning, *Malleatio, contuſio.*
Majadero, a peſtill, a dolt, a peſtill head, a beetle head, *Peſtillum, iners, excors, ſtipes.*
Majada, a lodging, a folde for ſheepe, a ſheepehouſe, *Manſio, magalia.*
Majuelo, a little peſtill, *Peſtillum.*
Majuelas, hawthorne berries, *Baccæ oxyacanthæ.*
Majorana, mayorana, *vide* Amoradux.
Majuelo, vines new planted, *Nouellæ vites*
Mal, hazer mal a cavallo, il, naught, a diſeaſe, to manage a horſe, *Malus, nequam, morbus, equum ſubigere.*
Malamente, naughtily, *Malè, nequiter.*
Malagueta, graines of paradiſe, *Cardamomum.*
Malaventurado, unfortunate, *Infortunatus*
Malavez, very little, *Pauciter.*
Mal eſtar, to be ſicke, to be diſpleaſed, *Aegrotare, infenſum eſſe.*
Malático, ſicke, *Aegrotus.*
Malato, *idem.*
Maldad, naughtineſ, wickedneſ, *Malitia, improbitas, malignitas.* (*nequam.*
Maldadoſo, wicked, naughtie, *Malitioſus.*
Maldadoſamente, naughtily, leudly, *Malignè, improbè.*
Maldezir, to ſpeake il, to curſe, *Maledicere.*
Maldicion, euil ſpeaking, curſing, a curſe, *Maledictio.*

Maldiziente, ſpeaking euill, curſing, *Maledicus.*
Maldizimiento, ſpeaking ill, curſing, *Maledictio.*
Maldizidor, a curſer, an euil ſpeaker, *Maledicus.*
Maldicho, ill ſpoken, accurſed, *Maledictus, execrabilis.*
Maldito, curſed, *Maledictus, execratus.*
Maléar, to bring forth before the time, *Abortiri, malè parere.*
Maleficio, an ill deed, an offence, *Maleficium.*
Malefico, an offender, an euill doer, *Maleficus.*
Malenconico, melancholike, *Melancholicus.*
Melenconia, melancholie, *Melancholia.*
Maleta, a budget, *Mantica.*
Maleza, a brier buſh, *Rubetum.*
Malhecho, an euill act, *Malefactum.*
Malhechor, an euill doer, *Malefactor.*
Malicia, malice, *Malitia.*
Malicioſamente, maliciouſly, *Malitiosè.*
Malicioſo, malicious, *Malitioſus.*
Malignidad, naughtineſ, *Malignitas.*
Maligno, wicked, naught, *Malignus.*
Mal mirado, inconſiderate, *Inconſideratus.*
Malo, euill, *Malus.*
Mal querer, to wiſh ill to, *Malè cupere.*
Malqueriente, an euill willer, *Maleuolus.*
Malquiſto, ill beloued, *Diſplicens.*
Malquerencia, euill will, *Maleuolentia.*
Malſin, a promoter, an accuſer, *Sycophanta*
Malva, mallowes, *Malua.*
Malvar, a place where mallowes growe, *Maluarium.*
Malva viſco, marſh mallowes, *Althæa.*
Malvaviſco ſalvage, cut mallowes, *Alcæa.*
Malvadamente, naughtily, *Nequiter.*
Malvado, naught, *Nequam.*
Malvaſia, malmſey, *Vinum malnaticum.*
Malla, a maile, *Lorica.*
Malla de la red, the meſh of a net, *Macula.*
Mallero, a maile maker, *Loricarius.*
Mama, mamme, *Mamma.*
Mamar, to ſucke, *Sugere.*
Mamanton o mamon, a ſucker, *Lactens.*
Mampeſada, the night mare, *Incubus.*

Mana,

Mana, **manna**, *Manna.*
Manada, **a flocke**, *Grex.*
Manar, **to flowe**, *Manare.*
Manancial, **flowing**, *Perennis.*
Manadero, **a streame**, *Flumen.*
Mancar, **to want, to maime**, *Carere, truncare.*
Mançana, **an apple**, *Malum.*
Mançano, **an apple tree**, *Malus.*
Mançanal, **an orchard**, *Pomarium.*
Mançanilla bastarda, **maudlin**, *Balsamita minor.*
Mançanilla, **camomill**, *Chamæmela.*
Mançanilla loca, **oxe eie**, *Buphthalmum.*
Mancebo, **a youth, a yong man**, *Iuuenis.*
Mancebia, **youth, the stewes**, *Iuuenta, lupanar.*
Manceba, **a wench, a strumpet**, *Adolescentula, scortum.*
Mancha, **a spot**, *Macula.*
Manchado, **spotted**, *Maculatus.*
Manchar, **to spot**, *Maculare.*
Manco, **maimed**, *Mancus.*
Manda de testamento, **a legacie**, *Legatum.*
Mandado, **bequeathed, commanded**, *Legatus, iussus, mandatus.*
Mandar, **to bequeath, to command**, *Legare, iubere, mandare.*
Mandamiento, **a commandement**, *Mandatum, iussus, præceptum.*
Mandador, **a commander**, *Mandator, iussor.*
Mandatario, **he to whom any thing is bequeathed**, *Legatarius.*
Mandadero, **he that is commanded**, *Mandatarius.*
Mandilete, **a bawd, an applesquire**, *Leno.*
Mandillon, *idem.*
Mandon, **he that commandeth much, an imperious fellow**, *Imperiosus.*
Mando, **commandement**, *Mandatum, imperium, iussio.*
Manear bestias, **to fetter**, *Compedes addere.*
Mandragora y mandragula, **mandrakes**, *Mandragora.*
Mandron, **a kind of instrument, a blowe with the backe of the hand**, *Auersæ manus ictus.*
Manera, **the maner, the guise, the fashi-**

on, **the sleue of a garment**, *Mos, modus, vsus, manica vestis.*
Manga, **a sleue**, *Manica.*
Mangado, **long sleued**, *Manicatus.*
Manguillo o guante, **a gloue, a gauntlet**, *Chirotheca, manica ferrea.*
Mango de cuchillo, **the haft of a knife**, *Manubrium.*
Mangorreo cuchillo, **a knife hafted**, *Manubriatus cultellus.*
Mangonada, **a bob on the nose**, *Nasictus.*
Maniaco, **vnapt, filthie**, *Fœdus, turpis.*
Manido, carne manida, **tender flesh, flesh made tender with hanging by the wals**, *Caro tenera.*
Manida, **a lodging**, *Mansio.*
Manifiesto, **manifest**, *Manifestus.*
Manifestamente, **manifestly**, *Manifestè.*
Manifestacion, **making manifest**, *Manifestatio.*
Manifestar, **to make manifest**, *Manifestare.*
Manilla y manija, **a bracelet**, *Armilla.*
Maniroto, **prodigall**, *Prodigus.*
Manjar, **meate, foode**, *Cibus, esca, obsonium.*
Manjar blanco, **meate made of starch, sugar, and the brests and wings of hens and capons**, *Cupediarum genus.*
Maña, **skil, cunning, deceit**, *Ars, dolus, technæ.*
Mañana, **the morning**, *Cras, manè.* (na.
Mañanear, *vide* Madrugar.
Mañear, **to deuise subtilties**, *Dolos nectere.*
Mañero, mañoso, **subtil, cunning**, *Astutus.*
Mañera, **a barren woman**, *Sterilis.*
Mano, **the hand**, *Manus.*
Mano de papel, **a quire of paper**, *Codex.*
Manojo, **a handfull**, *Manipulus.*
Manopla, **a gauntlet**, *Manus ferrea.*
Manpesada, y manpesadilla, **the night mare**, *Incubus.*
Mansamente, **gently**, *Mansuetè.*
Mansedumbre, **gentlenes**, *Mansuetudo.*
Manso, **gentle, tame**, *Mansuetus, cicur.*
Manta, **a cloke, a mantle**, *Pallium.*
Manta de pared, **hangings**, *Aulæum.*
Manta de guerra, **a defence against darts**, *Testudo.*
Manteca, **butter**, *Butyrum.*
Manteles, **table clothes**, *Mappa.*

Mantener,

M A

Mantener,tengo, to maintaine, to feede, *Alere,nutrire.*
Mantenimiento, maintenance, foode, *Victus,cibus.*
Mantelero, a towell maker, *Mapparius.*
Manteo y manto, a mantle, a cloake, *Pallium.*
Mantequillas, *vide Natas.*
Manual, pertaining to the hand, *Manualis*
Manzera, the plow taile, *Stiua.*
Manzilla, a spot, pitie, mercie, *Macula, miseratio.*
Manzilla aver, to pitie, *Misereri.*
Manzillado, full of spots, *Maculatus.*
Manzillar, to spot, to pitie, *Maculare, miseri-*
Maqui, a kind of ginger, *Machir.* (*reri.*
Mar, the sea, *Mare.*
Maraña, intangling, *Intricatio.*
Marañado, intangled, *Intricatus,implicitus.*
Marañador, an intangler, *Intricator.*
Marañar, to intangle, *Implicare,inuoluere.*
Maravedi, the 34 part of a riall of plate, *Monetæ genus.*
Maravilla, a maruel, a woonder, *Miraculū.*
Maravillarse, to woonder at, to maruell, *Mirari.*
Maravillado, woondering, astonied, *Admirans.*
Maravilloso, maruellous, *Mirus.*
Maravillosamente, maruellously, *Mirè.*
Marca, a marke, *Signum.*
Marcar, to marke, to signe, to seale, to graue or stamp, *Signare, signare nummum*
Marcado, palabras marcadas, marked, words woorth the noting, *Signatus, verba animaduertenda.*
Marco de plata, the value of 65 rials, *Monetæ Hispanicæ reales 65.*
Março, March, *Martius mensis.*
Marçal, of March, *Martialis.*
Marchitar, to wither, *Marcescere.*
Marchitable, that may wither, *Marcescibilis.*
Marchito, withered, *Marcidus.*
Marchitura, the withering, *Marcor.*
Marear, to vomite at sea, to be sea sicke, *Vomere.*
Maréta, a rough tide, *Aestus.*

M A

Maréa, the swell winde, *Zephyrus.*
Marfil, Iuorie, *Ebur.*
Margen, the margent of a booke, *Margo.*
Margarita, a pearle, *Margarita, vnio.*
Margomar, to feather, *Plumare.*
Marhojo, mosse, *Muscus.*
Marhojador, he that scrapeth off mosse, *Qui muscum abradit.*
Maridable, mariageable, *Nubilis.*
Marído, a husband, *Maritus.*
Maridar o casar, to marry, *Maritare.*
Marino, of the sea, *Marinus.*
Marinero, a mariner, *Nauta.*
Maripóso, a butter flie, *Papilio.*
Marisma, the sea coast, *Ora maritima.*
Marisco, of the sea, *Marinus.*
Mariscal, a marshall, *Metator.*
Maritimo, neere the sea, *Maritimus.*
Marlota, a kind of garment of the moors, *Tunicula punica.*
Marmol, Marble, *Marmor.*
Marmolejo, a small piller of marble, *Columella marmorea.*
Marmoleño, of marble, *Marmoreus.*
Marmota, a munky, a marinoset, *Cercopethecus.*
Marómas, cables, *Rudentes.*
Marques, a Marquesse, *Marchio.*
Marquesa, a ladie Marquesse, *Marchiona.*
Marquesado, a Marquessate, *Marchionatus.* (*citis.*
Marquesita, a stone of brasse color, *Chalmarra, a paring shouell, *Marræ.*
Marra, want, *Defectus.*
Marrar, to want, to erre, to misse, *Deficere, Errare.*
Marrano, a hog of a yeere old, *Porcus vnius anni.*
Marroqui, a kind of red lether to make buskins, *Corium rubrum cothurnis conficiendis.*
Marrubio, horehound, *Marrubium.*
Marsopa, a kind of whale fish, *Physeter.*
Marta, a marterne, *Martes.*
Martes, twesday, *Dies Martis.*
Martello, box tree, *Buxus.*
Martillar, to hammer, *Malleare.*
Martillado, hammered, *Malleatus.*

Q Martilladas,

M A

Martilladas, blowes with a hammer, *Ictus malleoli.*
Martillo, a hammer, *Malleolus.*
Martilogio, a kalender, *Martyrologium.*
Martillejo, a small hammer, *Malleolus.*
Martir, a martyr, *Martyr.*
Martirio, martirdome, *Martyrium.*
Mas, more, but, moreouer, *Plus magis, sed, tamen.*
Mascar, to chew, to eate, to gnaw or bite, *Mandere, manducare.*
Mascado, chewed, *Manducatus.*
Máscara, a maske, a visard, *Persona, larua.*
Mascarado, masked, *Personatus, laruatus.*
Massa, a masse, dowe, *Massa.*
Massar to heape vp, *Cumulare.*
Mastegar, to chewe, *Manducare.*
Mastel, a mast of a ship, *Malus, arbor.*
Mastin, a mastiue dog, *Molossus.*
Mastrando, wilde mints, *Menthastrum.*
Mastratos, wilde sage, *Polemonia.*
Mastuerço, water cresses, *Nasturtium.*
Mata, a bush, a shrub, *Frutex, virgultum.*
Matalahuga, anise, *Anisum.*
Matar, to kill, to murder, to destroy, to combate, to swying, to put out a candle, *Interficere, pugnare, mactare, vrere, extinguere.*
Matador, a killer, a murderer, *Interfector.*
Matadura, killing, *Interfectio.*
Matalotage, victuals for the sea, *Victus nauticus.*
Matança, slaughter, *Cades, strages.*
Materia, matter, also filth, rottennesse, *Materia, sanies, pus.*
Material, materiall, stuffe, *Materialis.*
Matiz, the shadow of a picture, *Vmbra.*
Matizado, painted, *Depictus.*
Matizar, to shadow in painting, *Illustrare, depingere.*
Matorrizales, bushes, *Vepreta.*
Matraca, a flout, *Scomma.*
Matracas dar, to laugh at, to mocke, to scoffe, *Irridere, ludere.*
Matricaria, feuer fewe, *Parthenium.*
Matricular, to matriculate, *In matriculam redigere.*
Matricula, a roll of names, *Catalogus.*

M E

Matrimonio, matrimonie, *Matrimonium.*
Matrimonial, pertaining to matrimonie, *Matrimonialis.*
Matrona, a matrone, *Matrona.*
Matronal cosa, belonging to a matrone, *Matronalis.*
Mazmorra, a dungeon, a prison, *Ergastulum.*
Mazmorilla de Baldreses, a leather whip, *Scutica coriacea.*

M E

Mear, to pisse, *Mingere.*
Meado, be pissed, *Mictus.*
Meados, vrine, *Vrina.*
Meaja, the little white in the yelke of an egge, also a pound, *In vitello oui subalbidum quiddam, mna.*
Mecánico, mechanicall, *Mechanicus.*
Mecer, to mingle, *Miscere.*
Mecedor, a mingler, *Qui miscet.*
Mecedura, mingling, *Mistio.*
Mecer el ojo, to twinckle with the eie, *Nuere.*
Mecedera, a stick to mixe with, *Rutabulū.*
Mecha de candil, the wœke of a candle, also match, *Lychnus, Ignarius fomes.*
Mechero, the nose of a candlestick, *Myxa.*
Medalla, mettell, old money, *Metallum, moneta antiqua.*
Médanos, a kinde of fruite of the Indies, *Pomi Indici genus.*
Medianamente, meanelie, *Mediocriter.*
Mediano, meane, *Mediocris.*
Medianero, a mediator, *Mediator.*
Mediania, mediocritie, *Mediocritas.*
Medianería, mediation, *Mediatio.*
Medias calças, netherstockes, *Tibialia.*
Medicamento, a medicine, *Medicamentum.*
Medicina, physicke, a medicine, *Medizina.*
Medicinal, medicinall, *Medicinalis.*
Medicinable, that may be vsed in medicine, *Medicinalis.*
Medicinar, to cure, *Curare, medevi.*
Medico, a Physition, *Medicus.*
Medida, measure, *Mensura.*
Medido, measured, *Mensus.*
Medidor, a measurer, *Metator, mensor.*

Medir,

Medir, mido, to meaſure, *Metiri, menſurare.*
Medio, a meane, the middle, the halfe, *Medius, modus.*
Medio dia, noone, *Meridies.*
Medrar, to thriue, *Proficere.*
Medra, thrift, *Profectus.*
Medroſo, fearefull, *Mericuloſus.*
Meitad, the halfe, *Dimidium.*
Mejor, better, *Melior.*
Mejorar, to mende, to growe better, *Meliorescere, conualeſcere.*
Mejoramiento, mending, *Conualeſcentia.*
Mejoria, mending, *idem.*
Mejorana, *vide* Majorana.
Melanconia, melancholie, *Melancholia.*
Melancónico, melancholicke, *Melancholicus.*
Melcocho, ſuger pils, breade made with honie, *Melcoctum.*
Melcochero, he that maketh ſugar pils, *Piſtor dulciarius.*
Meléna, a horſe collar, *Tomex.*
Melezina, a medicine, *Medicina.*
Mella, cutting, *Curtatio, ſciſſio.*
Melladura, *Idem.*
Mellar, to cut, *Scindere.*
Mellado, toothleſſe, *Edentulus.*
Mellizo, twins, *Gemini.*
Melliza, a kinde of pudding, *Farciminis genus.*
Mello de paja, a heape of chaffe, *Stramenti congeries.*
Melindre, louing lookes, and countenances, *Blanditiæ, vultus & nutus ad amorem conciliandum compoſiti.*
Meliloto, melilote, *Melilotos.*
Melodia, melodie, *Harmonia.*
Melocoton, a peach, *Perſicum.*
Melon, a melon, a badger, *Pepo, melis, caſtor.*
Melonar, a bed of melons, *Cucumerarium.*
Meloxa, water that honie is ſod in, *Mellis proluuies.*
Membrana, parchment, the ſkin ouer the braine, *Pergamena.*
Membrar, to recite, to remember, *Memorare.*
Membrillo, a quince, or quince tree, *Malus cydonia, & malum cydonium.*

Menbrudo, large lymmed, *Toroſus.*
Memoria, memorie, *Memoria.*
Memorial, a memoriall, *Memorial.*
Mencion, mention, *Mentio.*
Mendigar, to beg, *Mendicare.*
Medigo, a begger, *Mendicus.*
Mendiguez, beggery, *Mendicitas.*
Mendrugo, a caſt of bread, *Panis emendicatus.*
Mencar, to wag, to weeld, *Motitare, mouere*
Meneſter, want, penury, neede, *Penuria, opus, egeſtas.*
Meneſtril, a minſtrell, *Muſicus.*
Meneſteroſo, needie, *Egenus.*
Mengua, want, pouertie, diſcredite, penurie, *Egeſtas, inopia.*
Menguado, in want, empouerished, diminiſhed, poore, *Inops, diminutus.*
Menguar, to diminiſh, to empouerish, *Minuere.*
Menguante de luna, the wane, *Luna decreſcens.*
Menguante de la mar, the ebbe, *Maris receſſus.*
Meñique dedo, the little finger, *Digitus minimus.*
Menjuy, a kind of ſwoete odour, *Odoris genus.*
Menor, leſſe, vnder age, *Minor, pupillus.*
Menoria, nonage, *Pubertas.*
Menorar, to make leſſe, *Minorare.*
Menoſcabo, loſſe, contempt, *Diſpendium, contemptus.*
Menoſcabado, deſpiſed, diſcredited, *Contemptus, ſpretus.*
Menoſpréciar, to deſpiſe, to make light of, *Spernere.*
Menoſprecio, deſpiſing, making light, *Contemptus.*
Menoſpreciando, deſpiſingly, *Contempsim.*
Menſage, a meſſage, *Nuncium.*
Menſagero, a meſſenger, *Nuncius.*
Mentar, to mention, *Memorare.*
Mente, a minde, *Mens.*
Mentir, miento, to lie, *Mentiri.*
Mentira, a lie, *Mendacium.*
Mentiroſo, lying, *Mendax.*
Mentiroſamente, lyingly, *Mendaciter.*
Menudamente, by little & little, *Minutim.*
Menudo,

M E   M E

Menudo, little, *Minutus, paruus.*
Menudencias small matters, *Minutiæ.*
Menudo, a menudo, often, *Sæpè.*
Meollo, braines, marrowe, the pith of bread, the kernell of a nut, *Cerebrum, medulla, nucleus.*
Mercar, to buie, *Mercari.*
Mercadear, to play the merchant, *Mercaturam exercere.*
Mercadería, merchandise, *Mercatura, merx.*
Mercancia, trafficke, *Commercium, mercimonium.*
Mercader, a merchant, *Mercator.*
Mercado, a market, *Mercatus.*
Merced, curtesie, worship, pleasure, *Beneficium, gratum, humanitas.*
Mercedero, a maulkin, *Peniculum.*
Merceria, mercerie, *Merx.*
Merchante, a merchant, *Mercator.*
Mercurial, Mercurie, *Mercurialis.*
Merda, a turde, *Merda.*
Merdoso, beraied, *Merdosus.*
Merecer, to deserue, *Mereri.*
Merecedor, a deserued, *Meritus.*
Merecimiento, desert, *Meritum.*
Merendar, to take the noonemeat, *Meridiari.*
Merienda, a noonemeate, *Merenda, prandiŭ.*
Merma, want in measure, losse in measure, *Intertrimentum.*
Mermelada, mermelade, *Cidoniatum.*
Merina, sheepe driuen from the winter pastures to the sommer pastures, or the wooll of those sheepe, *Oues ad æstiua abacta, & earum lana.*
Mesaraicas venas, vains that go frõ the stomacke to the liuer, *Mesentericæ venæ.*
Mes, a month, *Mensis.*
Mesar cabellos, to teare the heare, *Comas laniare, depilare.*
Mesadura, tearing of the heare, *Depilatio.*
Mesa, a table, *Mensa.*
Mesillo, a poore wretch, *Miser, misellus.*
Mesmo, the same, *Idem.*
Mesnada, a lodging, an hoste of men, *Exercitus, vide* Aposento.
Meson, an inne, an alehouse, *Caupona, taberna.*

Mesonero, an innekeeper, *Caupo.*
Mesto, mingled, *Mistus.*
Mestengo y mostrenco, a straier, *Ouis errans, palans.*
Mesto, a kinde of tree that beareth maste, *Arbos glandifera.*
Mestruo, a womans flowers, *Menstruum.*
Mesturar, to mingle, *Miscere.*
Messana vela, the mizine saile, *Velum medium.*
Messar, *vide* Mesar.
Messoria, a bucket, *Situla, mergus.*
Mesura, modesty, grauity, curtesie, *Modestia, vrbanitas, ciuilitas.*
Mesuradamente, courteously, modestlie, *Modestè, ciuiliter.*
Mesurado, curteous, graue, *Modestus, grauis*
Mesurarse, to put on a graue countenãce, *Temperare vultum, ad modestiam componere.*
Metad, the halfe, *Dimidium.*
Metal, metall, *Metallum.*
Metalado, metteled, *Metallicus.*
Meter, to put, *Ponere, indere.*
Metro, meter, *Metrum.* (mala.
Mexillas, the iawes, the cheekes, *Maxilla,*
Mescladura, the mingling, *Mixtura.*
Mezana, *vide* Messana.
Mezclar, to mingle, *Miscere.*
Mezclado, mingled, *Mistus.*
Mezcladura, mingling, *Commixtio.*
Mezcla, *idem.*
Mezquinidad, wretchednes, miserablenes, couetousnes, *Miseria, auaritia.*
Mezquino, wretched, poore, miserable, *Miser.*
Mezquinamente, wretchedly, *Miserè.*
Mezquita, the Turcks temple, *Aedicula Mahumetæ.*

M I

Mi, mia, mio, mine, *Meus, mea, meum.*
Miar, to cric as a cat, *Felire.*
Miça, the terme to call a cat, as we saie pusse, *Vox catum vocantis.*
Miedo, feare, *Metus.*
Miel, honie, *Mel.*
Mielgas, spanish trefoyle, *Herba medica.*

Mielga

Mielga para arraſtrar paja, a rake, Raſtrum.
Miembro, a member, Membrum.
Mientras, in the meane time, Interim.
Miera, oyle of iuniper, Oleum iuniperinum.
Miercoles, wedneſday, Dies Mercurij.
Mierda, vide Merda.
Mierla, a blacke thruſh, Merula.
Mierra, a rake, Raſtrum.
Mieſſe, harueſt, Meſſis.
Miezgado, vide Mayvete.
Miga, a crum, Mica.
Migaja, a crum, a little peece, Mica.
Mijo, millet, Milium.
Mil, a thouſand, Mille.
Mil vezes, a thouſand times, Millies.
Milagro, a miracle, Miraculum, prodigium.
Milagroſamente, miraculouſly, Mirabiliter, prodigiosè.
Milagroſo, miraculouſe, Prodigiosus, mirabilis.
Milano, a kyte, Miluius.
Milhoja, y mil en rama, yarrowe, Millefolium.
Milicia, warfare, Militia.
Milla, a mile, Milliarium.
Melladeres, millions, Millia multa.
Millar, a thouſand thouſande, Mille millia.
Millon, a million, Millies mille millies.
Mimar, to flatter, Adulari.
Mimbre, willowes, oſiers, rods, Vimina.
Mina, a myne, Cuniculus.
Minado, myned, Cuniculatus.
Minador, a myner, Cuniculorum foſſor.
Minando, vnderminingly, Cuniculatim.
Minar, to myne, Cuniculos agere.
Mineral, pertaining to a mine, Metallicus.
Minero, a mine, a vaine of mettall, Vena, metallum.
Minuta, a memoriall, Memoriale, commentarius.
Miniſtro, a miniſter, Miniſter.
Mio, mine, Meum.
Mirabolano, mirabolanes, Mirabolani.
Mirar, to ſee, to behold, to regard, Aspicere.
Miradero, a watch tower, a loop hole, Specula.

Mirada, the looking on, Conſpectus.
Mira, the looking on, Aspectus, us.
Mirado, looked on, beholde, reſpected, Conſpectus, contemplatus.
Mirla, vide Mierla.
Mirra, myrrhe, Myrrha.
Mirtho, a mirtle, Myrtus.
Miruédanos, ſtrawberries, Fraga.
Miſerable, miſerable, wretched, Miſer.
Miſerablemente, miſerably, wretchedly, Miſerè.
Miſeria, miſerie, Miſeria.
Miſericordia, mercie, Miſericordia.
Miſericordioſo, mercifull, Miſericors.
Miſericordioſamente, mercifully, Miſericorditer.
Miſmo, the ſame, Idem.
Miſſa, the maſſe, Miſſa papiſtica.
Miſſal, perteyning to the maſſe, Miſſalis.
Miſterio, a myſterie, Myſterium.
Mitad, vide Metad.
Mitigar, to mitigate, Mitigare.
Mitra, a miter, Mitra.
Mitridatico, mithridate, Antidotum.

M O

Moco, ſneuel, ſnot, Mucus.
Mocoſo, ſnotty, Mucoſus.
Moça, a young maid, a wench, a ſeruant, Puella, famula.
Mocedad, youth, Puerilitas, adoleſcentia.
Mocetona, a big wench, Puella grandior.
Moço, a boy, a ſeruant, Puer, famulus.
Moço de eſpuelas, a lackey, A pedibus.
Moçuela, a little girle, Puellula.
Moçuelo, a lad, Puellus.
Mochar, to mayme, to cut off the hornes, Mutilare.
Mochila, a wallet, a ſcrip, Mantica.
Mocha, without hornes, notted, Mutilus cornibus.
Mochuelo, a kind of Owle, Aſio.
Modelo, a pattern, Modus, typus.
Moderatamente, moderately, Moderate.
Moderacion, moderation, Moderatio.
Moderar, to moderate, Moderari.
Moderado, moderate, Moderatus.
Moderno, of this time, of this age, Modernus.

Modeſta-

Modestamente, modestly, *Modestè*.
Modéstia, modestie, *Modestia*.
Modesto, modest, *Modestus*.
Modo, the meanes, measure, the manner, *Modus*
Modorra, the drowsie ill, *Stupor mentis*.
Modorro, sick of the letargie, a foole, *Stupidus*.
Modorra, the second watch, *Vigilia secunda*
Moderrilla, the third watch, *Vigilia tertia*.
Modorrear, to be foolish, *Stupere, desipere*.
Mofar, to mocke, *Subsannare*.
Mofo, mockerie, *Subsannatio, scomma*.
Mofadura, mocking, *Subsannatio*.
Mofador, a mocker, *Subsannator*.
Mohatrar, to borow of one to pay to another, *Versura soluere*.
Moharrache, vide Homarrache.
Mohéda, a wood, *Nemus, oris*.
Mohino, offended, displeased, mouse dunne, a colte of a shee asse, and a horse, *Infensus, fuscus, burdo*.
Moho, mosse, mouldines, *Mucor, muscus*.
Mohoso, mossie, mouldie, *Mucosus, muscosus*
Mojar, to wette, *Madescere, madefacere*.
Mojado, wette, *Madidus*.
Mojadura, wetting, *Mador*.
Mojon, a bound, a bound stone, *Limes*.
Mojonar, to bound, *Limitare*.
Molde, a mould, *Typus*.
Moler, uelo, to grinde, *Molere*.
Moledor, a grinder, a miller, *Molitor*.
Molidura de colores, grinding of colours *Tritura*.
Molestamente, troublesomely, *Molestè*.
Molestar, to trouble, *Molestiam exhibere*.
Molestia, trouble, græfe, disquietnes, *Molestia*.
Molesto, troublesome, *Molestus*.
Molestador, a troubler, *Molestus*.
Molido, ground with a mill, &c. *Molitus*.
Molienda, a gryste, *Frumentum mola conterendum*.
Molinero, a Miller, *Molendinarius*.
Molino, a mill, *Molendinum*.
Molleja, the tender parte in any birde, which in a goose we call the soule, *Præcordia*.

Mollentar, to make soft, *Mollire*.
Mollera de cabeça, the crown of the head *Vertex*.
Mollete, soft bread, *Panis mollis*.
Mollir, to make softe, to make a bed, *mollire, sternere lectum*.
Mollido, made soft, *Mollitus*.
Mollidura, making soft, making of a bed, *Mollitudo, substratio lecti*.
Mollidor, a stirrer, a troubler, *Excitator*.
Mollinas, soft showers, Scottish mistes,
Mollidura, softnes, *Mollicies*. (*Nebulæ*.
Momia, mummy, *Mummia*.
Momento, a moment, *Momentum*.
Momo, a uice in a play, a iester, *Momus*.
Mona, an ape, *Simia*.
Monacordio, an Instrument with one string, *Monachordum*.
Monarchia, a monarchie, *Monarchia*.
Monazillo, a litle ape, a little monke, a litle priest, *Simiolus, monachellus sacrificulus*.
Mondar, to make cleane, *Mundare*.
Mondaduras, cleansings, parings, *Purgamenta, præsegmina*.
Monda dientes, a tooth pike, *Dentiscalpium*
Monda orejas, an eare pike, *Auriscalpium*.
Moneda, money, *Moneta, nummus*.
Monedero, a copner, *Monetarius*.
Monesterio, a monastery, *Monasterium*.
Monge, a monke, *Monachus*.
Mongia, monkery, *Monachatus*.
Mongil, a monks garmēt, *Vestis monachalis*.
Monipodio, conspiracie, *Conspiratio*.
Monja, a nunne, *Monacha*.
Mono, an ape, *Simius*.
Montar, to amount, *In summam excrescere*.
Montaña, a mosītain, a wood, *Mons, saltus*.
Montañes, perteyning to a mountayne, *Montanus*.
Montanero, a mountaineman, *Saltuarius*.
Monte, a hil, a mount, a wood, *Mons, nemus*.
Montero, a hunter, also a hatte made of *Mcloath, Venator, galerus*.
Monteria, hunting, *Venatio*.
Montear, to hunt, *Venari*.
onteso, of the mountayne, of the wood, *Montanus*.
Montesillo, a little hill, *Colliculus*.
Montesino,

Montesino, of the wood, *Syluestris*.
Monton, a heape, *Aceruus, agger*.
Montoso, hillie, *Montuosus*.
Monumento, a monument, *Monumentum*.
Mora, a mulberie, *Morum*.
Moral, a mulberie tree, *Morus*.
Morada, a dwelling, *habitatio, domus*.
Morar, to dwell, *Habitare*.
Morador, a dweller, *Habitator, incola*.
Morado color, iron colour, *Ferrugo*.
Morbo caduco, the falling euill, *Morbus caducus*.
Morcella, a sparke of fire, *Scintilla, fauilla*.
Morcielago, a batte, *Vespertilio*.
Morcilla, a pudding, *Botulus*.
Mordaza, a bitte of a bridle, *Luparum, lupus*.
Morder, to bite, *Mordere*.
Mordella, *vide* Mardaza.
Mordedor, a byter, *Mordax*.
Mordedura, byting, *Morsus*.
Mordido, bitten, *Admorsus*.
Morella, nightshade, *Morella solanum*.
Morillo, browne, *Subfuscus*.
Morena, a Lamprey, *Murœna*.
Morezillos, the sinewes, *Musculi*.
Morir, muero, to die, *Mori*.
Mormollo, a murmuring, *Murmur*.
Mortaja, a shroude, a buriall, *Feralis amictus, funus*.
Mortajar, to shroud, to burie, *Lino inuoluere, funerare*.
Mortajador, he that shroudeth, hee that maketh graues, *Libitinarius*.
Mortal, mortall, deadly, *Mortalis*.
Mortalidad, mortalitie, *Mortalitas*.
Mortandad, *vide* Mortalidad.
Mortero, a morter, *Mortarium*.
Morteruela, greene sauce, *Moretum*.
Mortezino, carion, *Morticinium, cadauer*.
Mortuorio, a buriall, *Exequiæ*.
Morro, baxó el morro, he determined, *Decreuit*.
Mosca, a flie, *Musca*.
Moscarda, a horse flie, *Oestrus*.
Moscadero, a fan to make winde, a flap for flies, *Flabellum, muscarium*.
Moscada, a nutmeg, *Miristica nux*.

Moscador, a plume of feathers, *Pluma, vmbraculum*.
Moscatel, a muske grape, *Vua muscata*.
Moscon, a great flie, *Musca grandior*.
Mosillones, muscles, *Mitulus*.
Mosquear, to driue away flies, *Muscas abigere*.
Mosqueador, he that driueth away flies, *Muscarum abactor*.
Mosquito, a gnat, *Culex*.
Mosquetero, a musketier, *Sclopetarius*.
Mosquilla, a little gnat, *Culiculus*.
Mostaza, mustard, *Sinapis*.
Mostajo, a tree like laurell, *Mustax*.
Mosto, sweete wine, *Mustum*.
Mostrar, muestro, to shew, *Monstrare*.
Mostrador, a shewer, *Monstrator*.
Mostrenco, a straier, *Ouis aberrans*.
Mota, a hoze, a moat, a heap, *Atomus, moles*.
Mote y motete, a saying, a quip, a nip, *Dicterium, scomma*.
Motejar, to quippe, to taunt, *Subsannare, taxare*.
Motejado, quipped, nipped, taunted, *Subsannatus, taxatus*.
Motejador, a quipper, *Subsannator, taxator*.
Motilado, shorne neare, polled near, notted, *Detonsus*.
Motin, a mutinie, *Seditio*.
Motivo, a motiue, a purpose, *Causa mouens*.
Mover, muevo, to moue, to stir, to remoue, *Mouere*.
Mover la muger, to be deliuered before the time, *Malè parere, abortiri*.
Movedura, bringing forth before the time, *Partus immaturus, abortus*.
Movediza, birth vntimely borne, *Abortiuus*.
Movible, moueable, *Mobilis*.
Movedizo, mouing, wauering, *Motitans, mobilis*.
Movedor, a mouer, *Motor*.
Movedura, motion, a mouing, *Mobilitas*.
Movido, moued, *Commotus*.
Movimiento, motion, mouing, stirring, *Motio*.
Moxama, a kinde of salted fish, *Piscis sale conditus*.
Moxicones, bobs on the nose, *Nasi ictus*.

Muceta

M V

Muceta de obispo, a bishops pall or habit, *Epitogium,epomis*.
Muchacha,a wench,*Ancilla,puella*.
Muchacho,a boy,*Puer*.
Mucho,much,*Multus*.
Muchedumbre,a multitude,*Multitudo*.
Muchas vezes,many times,*Sæpè*.
Mudable,changeable,*Mutabilis*.
Mudablemente,changeably,*Mutabiliter*.
Mudado,changed,*Mutatus*.
Mudança,change,*Mutatio*.
Mudamiento,change,*Mutatio*.
Mudar,to change,*Mutare*.
Mudas,painting for womens faces, *Fucus*.
Mudecer,to be dumbe,*Obmutescere*.
Mudo,dumbe,*Mutus*.
Mueble,moueable,*Mobilis*.
Muela, the chocke toth, a hill, a heape, a mill, *Dens molaris,collis, tumulus,mola,moles*.
Muelle,softe,a heape,*Mollis,moles*.
Muellemente,softly,*Molliter*.
Muerdago,mistle,*Viscus quercinus*.
Muermo,the glaunders in a horse, *Morbus veterinæ*.
Muermoso,sicke of the glaunders, *Morbo veterina laborans*.
Muestra,a shewe,*Species, ostentatio*.
Muerte,death, *Mors*.
Muerto,dead,*Mortuus*.
Muger,a woman,*Mulier*.
Mugercilla, a little woman, a poore sillie woman,*Muliercula*.
Mugeril,perteining to a woman, *Muliebris*.
Mugerilmente, womanishly,*Muliebriter*.
Mugeril hombre, an effeminate person, *Mulierosus*.
Mugre,grease,sweate,*Sudor, pinguetudo*.
Mugron, the branch of a vine newe set, *Propago*.
Muy,muy doto,very,very learned, *Valde, admodum doctus,perquam*.
Mula,a mule,*Mula*.
Muladar,a dunghill, *Sterquilinium*.

Mular,perteining to a mule, *Mulonicus*.
Mulatero,a muleter, *Mulio,onis*.
Muleta roma,a colt of an asse and a horse Hinna.
Mullidor,*vide* Mollidor.
Multar,to amerce,*Mulctare*.
Multa,an amercement,*Mulcta*.
Multiplicar,to multiply,*Multiplicare*.
Multiplicacion, multiplying, *Multiplicatio*.
Multiplicado,multiplied,increased,*Multiplicatus*.
Muncho,much,*Multus*.
Mundano,of the world, *Mundanus*.
Mundo,the world,*Mundus*.
Municion,munition,*Munitio*.
Muñeca de niños, a puppet,a babie, *Pupus*.
Muñeca,the wrest,a braselet, *Carpos, brachiale*.
Muñidor, a sturrer, a warner, *Excitator, Monitor*.
Mura, a corde in a ship called the sheade, *Funis quidam nauticus*.
Mur,a mouse,*Mus*.
Muralla,the wall,*Murus*.
Murecillo de braço, the sinewes of the arme,*Musculi, vide* Morezillos.
Murcielago,a bat,*Vespertilio*.
Murgaña,a rat,*Sorex*.
Murmurar,to murmur, *Obmurmurare*.
Murmuracion, murmuring, *Obmurmuratio*.
Murmurador,a murmurer, *Obmurmurator*.
Murmullo de gente, a muttering,a murmuring,*Murmur*.
Muro,a wall,*Murus*.
Murta,priuet,*Myrtus*.
Muruges,pimpernell,*Anagallis*.
Musgaño, a ficlde mouse called a shrewe, *Araneus*.
Musgo,mosse on trees,*Muscus*.
Musaico,antique workes,*Museacum opus*.
Musica,musicke,*Musica*.
Musico,of musicke,*Musicus*.
Muslo,the thigh, *Femur*. (lia.
Muslos de calças,canions of hose,*Femoralia*.
Mustio,withered,*Marcidus*.

Nabo,

N A

N A

Nabo, turneps, *Rapum.*
Nacar, mother of pearle, *Margarita callum.*
Nacer, to be borne, to spring vp, *Nasci, oriri.*
Nacido, borne, sprung vp, *Natus, ortus.*
Nacida, a bile, a blister, *Vlcus, bubo.*
Nacimiento, birth, or birth day, *Ortus, natiuitas, natalis dies.*
Nacion, a nation, *Natio.*
Naçora, *vide* Nata.
Nada, nothing, *Nihil.*
Nadar, to swim, *Natare.*
Nadador, a swimmer, *Natator.*
Nadadero, a swimming place, *Natatorium*
Nadadura, swimming, *Natatio.*
Nadie, no man, no body, *Nemo.*
Naypes, cards to play with, *Chartæ pictæ.*
Nalga, the buttocks, *Nates, clunis, piga.*
Nalgada, a blowe on the buttockes, *Ictus clunium.*
Nalguear, to beate the buttocks, *Pulsare nates.*
Nalgada de tocino, a gamon of bacon, *Perna porci.*
Nao, a ship, *Nauis.*
Naranja, an orenge, *Malum citreum.*
Naranjal, an orcharde of orenges, *Hortus citreorum.*
Naranjo, an orenge tree, *Malus citrea.*
Nardo, spykenard, *Nardus.*
Nariz, the nose, the nostrell, *Naris.*
Narigudo, long nosed, *Nasutus.*
Narrar, to tell, to recount, *Narrare.*
Narra, a tale, *Narratio.*
Narria, a rake, *Traha.*
Nassa, a weele to take fish, *Nassa.*
Narciso, daffadill, *Narcissus, asphodelus.*
Natas, creame, *Pingue vel flos lactis.*
Natiuidad, natiuitie, *Natiuitas.*
Natura, nature, *Natura.*
Natural, naturall, the disposition, *Naturalis, ingenium.*
Naturalmente, naturally, *Naturaliter.*
Naturaleza, a mās natiue cuntry, *Patria.*

N E

Natural de tal lugar, such a cuntrieman, *Natiuus.*
Nava, campo llano, a plaine fielde, *Planities.*
Navaja, a rasor, a boares tuske, *Nouacula, fulmen.*
Naval, perteining to a ship, *Naualis.*
Nauchel, a master of a ship, *Nauclerus.*
Nave, a ship, a cenfor, *Nauis, acerra.*
Navegar, to saile, *Nauigare.*
Navegacion, nauigation, sailing, *Nauigatio.*
Navegante, he that saileth, *Nauigans.*
Navigable, nauigable, *Nauigabilis.*
Navera, a cenfor, *Acerra.*
Navizilla de encensios, a cenfour for incense, *Acerrula.*
Navio, a ship, *Nauis.*
Navidad, christmasse, *Natiuitas christi.*

N E

Nebeda, nepes, *Nepeta.*
Neblina, a miste, *Nebula.*
Nebli, a hauke, *Accipiter.*
Necear, to play the foole, *Desipere, ineptire.*
Necedad, follie, foolishnesse, *Stultitia, ignorantia.*
Necessario, necessary, conuenient, needful, *Necessarius, conueniens.*
Necessariamente, needefully, necessarilie, *Necessario.*
Necessaria, a priuie, a close stoole, *Latrina.*
Necessidad, necessitie, *Necessitas.*
Necessitado, that is in necessitie, *Qui opus habet, indigus.*
Neciamente, foolishly, *Stulté, ignoranter.*
Necio, a foole, *Stultus, insciuus.*
Negar, niego, to denie, *Negare.*
Negacion, deniall, *Negatio.*
Negador, a denier, *Negator.*
Negujon de dientes, the worme in the teeth, *Vermis dentium.*
Negligencia, negligence, *Negligentia.*
Negligente, negligent, *Negligens.*
Negligentemente, negligently, *Negligenter.*
Negociar, to deale in busines, to trafficke, *Negotiari.*

R Negociado

Negociado, buſie, dealing, *Negotioſus.*
Negociador, a dealer, a doer, *Negotiator, inſtitor.*
Negócio, buſines, *Negotium.*
Negociacion, dealing, negotiation, *Negotiatio.*
Negocial, perteining to buſines, *Negotialis.*
Negrillo, a little blacke moore, a negro, *Niger, Aethiops.*
Negreguear, to waxe blacke, *Nigreſcere.*
Negregura, blackneſ, *Nigror.*
Negromancia, nigromancie, *Necromantia.*
Negromantico, a nigromancer; *Necromanticus.*
Negror, blackneſ, *Nigredo.*
Nigreta, a kinde of ducke, *Boſca.*
Neguilla, *vide* Axeuz.
Nema, a quire of paper, *Manus ſiue codex.*
Nenufar, a water Lillie, *Nymphæa, nenuphar.*
Nervio, a ſinewe, *Nervus.*
Nervoſo, full of ſinewes, *Nervoſus.*
Nerviar, to worke with ſinewes, *Neruare.*
Nervoſidad, ſinewie, *Nervoſitas.*
Nervudo, that hath great ſinewes, *Toroſus.*
Nevar, nievo, to ſnow, *Ningere.*
Nevado, full of ſnowe, *Ningidus.*

N I

Ni, nether, *Nec.*
Nidal o nido, a neſt, *Nidus.*
Niebla, a miſte, *Nebula.*
Nieſpra, a medlet, *Meſpilum.*
Nieſpro, a medler tree, *Meſpilus.*
Nieto, nieta, a nephew, a nece, *nepos, napsis.*
Niervo, *vide* Nervio.
Nieve, ſnow, *Nix.*
Nimfa, a nymphe, *Nympha.*
Ninguno, no man, none, *Nullus, nemo.*
Niño, a childe, an infant, *Infans.*
Niñez, infancie, childhood, *Infantia.*
Niñerias, childiſh toies, *Puerilia.*
Niñero, one that loueth children, *Infantiarius.*
Niñear, to play the childe, *Pueriliter ſe gerere.*

Niñetas de los ojos, the apples of the eies *Pupilla.*
Niñilla de los ojos, *idem.*
Niſpero, *vide* Nieſpro.
Nivel, a carpenters ruler, *Norma.*
Nivelar, to rule out, to leuell out, *Norma ſignare.*
Nivelador, that maketh leuell, *Qui norma vtitur.*

N O

No, no, *Non.*
No nada, nothing, *Nihil.*
No ſolo, not onely, *Non ſolum.*
Noble, noble, *Nobilis.*
Nobleza, nobilitie, *Nobilitas.*
Noblecer, to make noble, *Nobilitare.*
Noche, night, *Nox.*
Nocherniega, of the night, *Nocturnus.*
Nocturno, *vide* Noturno.
Nogada ſalſa, a gallimaufry of nuts, *Moretum ex nucibus.*
Nogal, a nut tree, *Nux.*
Nolito, paſſage mony, *Naulum.*
Nombradia, naming, name, *Nomenclatura.*
Nombrar, to name, *Nominare.*
Nombre, a name, fame, report, *Nomen, fama.*
Nono, the ninth, *Nonus.*
Nones, odds, *Impar.*
Noſotros, wee, *Nos.*
Norte, the north, *Boreas, ſeptentrio.*
Nota, a note, *Nota.*
Notable, notable, *Notabilis.*
Notablemenie, notably, *Notabiliter.*
Notado, noted, *Notatus.*
Notacion, noting, *Notatio.*
Notar, to note, *Notare.*
Notario, a notarie, *Notarius.*
Notezilla, a little note, *Annotatiuncula.*
Noticia, knowledge, notice, *Notitia.*
Notificar, to notifie, *Notificare.*
Notificacion, notifying, *Notificatio.*
Notório, knowen, notorious, *Notus, euidens.*
Noturno, of the night, *Nocturnus.*
Novecientos, nine hundred, *Nongenti.*
Novedad, newnes, ſtrangenes, *Nouitas.*
Noventa,

Noventa, ninetie, *Nonaginta.*
Novela, a tale, a ſtoꝛie, *Hiſtoria, fabula.*
Noveleɼo, a teller of tales, *Fabulator.*
Novenas, of nine daies, *Nonendialis.*
Noveno, the ninth, *Nonus.*
Nuvia, a newe married wife, *Noua nupta.*
Noviembre, Ɲoucmber, *Nouember.*
Novicio, a nouice, *Tyro.*
Novilla, a heifer, *Iuuenca.*
Novillo, a ſtœre, *Iniuencus.*
Novio, a new married man, *Nouus maritus.*

N V

ñublado, clowdie, *Nubilus.*
ñublarſe, to be ouercaſt with clowdes, *Nubilum eſſe.*
ñubloſo, clowdie, *Nubilus.*
ñublo en el trigo, blaſting, *Rubigo.*
Nuca de la cabeça, the pole oꝛ the nape of the head, *Occiput.*
ñudo, a knot, *Nodus.*
Nuera, a daughter in lawe, *Nurus.*
Nueſtro, ours, *Noſter.*
Nueva, newes, *Noua.*
Nuévo, newe, yong, *Nonus.*
Nuevamente, newely, lately, *Nouiter, nuper.*
Nueve, nine, *Nonem.*
Nuez, a nut, *Nux.*
Nueza negra, blacke Bꝛionie, *Brionia.*
Numero, number, *Numerus.*
Numeroſo, in great number, *Numeroſus.*
Nunca, neuer, *Nunquam.*
Nuſco, with vs, *Nobiſcum.*
Nutria, an otter, *Luira.*
ñuve, a clowde, *Nubes.*
ñuvada, a ſtoꝛme, *Nymbus.*
ñuve de ojo, the white of the eie, *Albugo.*

O B

O oꝛ, ether, would God, *Vel, aut, vtinam, heus.*
Obedecer, to obey, *Obedire.*
Obediente, obedient, *Obediens.*
Obediencia, obedience, *Obedientia.*
Obedientemente, obediently, *Obedienter.*

Obejarugo, *vide* Abejuruco.
Obelo, a chapter, *Capitulum.*
Obeliſco, a tombe of a great king, *Sepulchrum regium.*
Obiſpo, a biſhop, *Epiſcopus.*
Obiſpado, a biſhopꝛicke, *Epiſcopatus.*
Obiſpal, perteining to a biſhop, *Epiſcopalis.*
Obiſpillo de ave, the rumpe of a bird, *Vropygium.*
Obiſpillo de puerco, the mawe of a pigge, *Ventriculus porci.*
Oblada, an offering, *Libum.*
Obléa, an offering, a rounde offering cake, *Laganum, libum.*
Obligar, to binde, *Obligare.*
Obligado, bound, *Obligatus.*
Obligacion, a bond, obligation, *Obligatis.*
Obra, a woꝛke, *Opus.*
Obrado, wꝛought, *Operatus.*
Obrar, to woꝛke, *Operari.*
Obrero, a woꝛkeman, *Operarius.*
Obſequias, funerals, *Exequiæ.*

O C

Ocaſion, occaſion, cauſe, *Occaſio, cauſa.*
Ocaſionado, occaſioned, cauſed, excuſed, *Cauſatus.*
Ocidental, weſterly, *Occidentalis.*
Ocidente, the weſt, *Occidens.*
Ocioſamente, idlely, leaſurely, *Otioſè.*
Ocio, idlenes, leaſure, *Otium, quies.*
Ocioſidad, idlenes, *Otium, ocioſitas.*
Ochavas, the eights, *Octauæ.*
Ochavario, *idem.*
Ochavero, a deuider into eight parts, *Partitor in octo partes.*
Ochavo, a peece of coin woꝛth two marauedꝭ, *Monetæ genus.*
Ochenta, fourescore, eightie, *Octoginta.*
Ocho, eight, *Octo.*
Ocho cientos, eight hundꝛed, *Octingenti.*
Ocupar, to occupie, to take, *Occupare.*
Ocupacion, occupacion, taking, *Occupatio.*
Ocupado, taken, buſie, *Occupatus.*
Ocurrir, to chaunce, to happen, *Occurrere.*

R 2   Odio,

O D

Odio, hatred, *Odium.*
Odioso, odious, hatefull, *Odiosus.*
Odre, a water budget, a bottle, *Vter, tris.*
Odrería, a bottle makers shop, *Vtearia.*
Odrezillo, a small budget, a little bottle, *Vtriculus.*
Odrina, odre de buey, a budget of an oxe hide, *Cullens.*

O F

Offender, fiendo. to offende, *Offendere, laedere.*
Offensa, an offence, *Offensa.*
Offerta, an offer, *Promissio.*
Offension, offence, *Offensio.*
Official, a crafts man, *Artifex.*
Officio, an office, a trade, *Officium, munus.*
Offrecer, to offer, *Offerre.*
Offrecido, offered, *Oblatus.*
Off. ecimiento, offering, an offer, *Oblatio.*
Offrenda, an offering, a sacrifice, *Libum.*
Offuscar, to make dim, to make dull, *Obfuscare.*

O G

Ogaño, this yeere, *Hornus, hoc anno.*
Ogibundo, gaping, *Oscitans.*

O Y

Oy, to day, *Hodiè.*
Oydo, the hearing, the eares, *Auditus, auris.*
Oydor, a hearer, *Auditor.*
Oyr, oygo, to heare, *Audire.*

O j

Ojear, to twincke, to cast an eie, *Innuere.*
Ojeras hundidas, the eies suncke, *Oculorum recessus.*
Ojo de buey, oxe eie, *Buphthalmus.*
Ojo, an eie, switching with the eie, the meshe of a net, a needles eie, *Oculus, fascinum, macula.*

O L

Ola, a swaue, *vnda, Fluctus.*
Oleado, oyled, *Oleo permixtus.*

O M

Oler, huelo, to smell, *Olere, odorari.*
Oledora cosa, that smelleth, *Odorus.*
Oledor, a smeller, *Olfactor.*
Olfato, the sence of smelling, *Olfactus.*
Oliva, an oliue, an oliue tree, *Oliua.*
Olivar, a garden of oliues, *Oliuetum.*
Olia, oyle, *Oleum.*
Olla, a pot, *Olla.*
Ollero, a potter, *Ollarius.*
Olleta, a pipkin, *Ollula.*
Olmo, an elme, *Vlmus.*
Olmedo, a groue of elmes, *Vlmarium.*
Olor, a smell, a stench, *Odor, olor.*
Oloroso, of a strong smell, *Odorus.*
Olvidar, to forget, *Obliuisci.*
Olvidado, forgotten, *Oblitus.*
Olvidadizo, forgetfull, *Obliuiosus.*
Olvido, olvidança, obliuion, forgetfulnes, *Obliuio.*

O M

Ombligo de Venus, penie wort, *Vmbilicus veneris.*
Ombligo, the nauell, *Vmbilicus.*
Ombre, a man, *Homo.*
Ombrezillo, a little man, a poore silly man *Homuncio.*
Ombrezillos, *vide* Hombrezillos.
Ombro, a shoulder, *Humerus.*
Omenaje, swaging lawe, the toppe of a tower, *Fides publica, culmen.*
Omecida, a manqueller, *Homicida.*
Omecidio, manslaughter, *Homicidium.*
Omillado, *vide* Vmillado.
Omizillo, manslaughter, parricide, *Homicidium, parricidium.*
Omiziano, a manqueller, a parricide, *Homicida, parricida.*

O N

Onça, an ounce, the beast called an ounce *Vncia, panthera.*
Onda, a swaue, *Vnda.*
Ondear, to swaue, to flowe, *Vndare.*
Ondoso, full of swaues, *Vndosus.*
Onestidad, honesty, *Honestas.*
Onesto, honest, *Honestas.*
Onestamente, honestly, *Honestè.*

Onestad,

Oneſtad, vide Oneſtidad.
Oneſtar, to adorne, to beautifie, Honeſtare.
Onor, honor, Honor.
Onorable, honorable, Honorabilis.
Onrra, honor, Honor.
Onrradamente, honorablie, Venerabiliter, honeſtè.
Onrrado, honorable, Venerabilis.
Onrrar, to honor, Venerari.
Onrroſo, honorable, Obſeruandus.
Onrroſamente, honorablie, Venerabiliter.
Onze, eleuen, Vndecim.
Onzeno, the eleuenth, Vndecimus.

O P

Operacion, operation, working, Operatio.
Opinion, opinion, Opinio.
Opinable, that may be thought, Opinabilis
Opinático, opinionatiue, ſelfe willed, Opiniofus.
Opio, iuice of poppie, Opium.
Opilado, ſtopped, Obſtructus.
Oponer, to ſet againſt, Opponere.
Opoſicion, ſetting againſt, Oppoſitio.
Oportunamente, fitly, conueniently, Opportunè.
Oportuno, fit, in good time, Opportunus.
Oportunidad, oppoztunitie, Opportunitas.
Opremir, to oppreſſe, Opprimere.
Opremido, oppreſſed, Oppreſſus.
Opueſto, ſet againſt, Oppoſitus.
Oquedad, hollownes, Concauitas.

O R

Ora, whether, now, Virùm, iam.
Ora, an hower, Hora.
Oracion, a prayer, an oration, Oratio.
Oraculo, an oracle, Oraculum.
Orador, an orator, Orator.
Orar, to pray, Orare.
Oratoria, rhetorike, Rhetorica.
Orça, a pitcher, Vrceus.
Orçuelo del ojo, a pin in the eie, Leuconia.
Orçuclo, a trap for beaſts, Decipula.
Orden, order, Ordo.
Ordenar, to order, to ordaine, to appoint, Initiare, ordinare.

Ordenado, ordered, ordained, Ordinatus, initiatus.
Ordenamiento, ordering, Ordinatio, initiatio.
Ordenadamente, orderly, ordinarily, Ordinatè.
Ordenança, an ordinance, Conſtitutio.
Ordeñar, to milke, Mulgere.
Ordeñada azeytuna, an oliue berry preſſed, Olea compreſſa.
Ordiate, barly water, ptiſan, Ptiſana.
Ordir tela, to ſpin, Ordiri, texere.
Ordiembre, the web, Stamen.
Ordidura, the ſpinning, Orſus.
Orear, to aire, to bleach, Ad auras exponere.
Orégano, organie, Origanum.
Oreja de raton, mouſe eare, Auricula muris.
Oreja, an eare, Auris.
Orejas de abad, a pancake, Laganum.
Orejudo, long eared, Auritus.
Orejar, to wag the eares, Aures excutere.
Orfandad, the wanting of the parents, Orbitas.
Organo, an inſtrument, organs, Organum.
Organiſta, a plaier on the organs, Organiſtes.
Orgullo, wrath, Iracundia.
Orgulloſamente, wrathfully, Iracundè.
Orgulloſo, wrathfull, Iracundus.
Oriente, the eaſt, Oriens.
Oriental, eaſterly, Orientalis.
Origen, the beginning, the birth, Origo.
Original, the original, Originalis, exemplum.
Orilla, the ſhore, the ſkirt, Ora, ora veſtis, fimbria.
Orina, vrine, Vrina.
Orin, ruſt, Rubigo.
Orinal, an vrinall, Matula.
Orinar, to piſſe, Mingere.
Oriniento, ruſtie, Rubiginoſus.
Orizonte, the orizon, Orizon.
Orla, a ſkirt, a border, Ora, limbus.
Orlador, a borderer, Limborarius.
Orlar, to make a border, Oram vel limbum ornare.
Ornamento, an ornament, Ornamentum.
Ornar, to deck, to trim, to adorne, Ornare.
Oro, gold, Aurum.

Orones,

O S

Orones, bankes of earth, *Tumulus, agger.*
Oroguañin, ambar, copper, *Electrum.*
Oropel, leather gilt, painters gold, *Aurata pellis, bractea.*
Oropendola, a kinde of bird, *Galbula.*
Oropimiento, orpiment, *Auripigmentum.*
Orosuz, lickorise, *Glycyrrhiza.*
Oruga, rocket, also a canker wormne or caterpiller, *Eruca, eruca vermis.*
Orrible, horrible, *Horribilis.*
Orriblemente, horribly, *Horribiliter.*
Orror, horror, feare, *Horror.*
Orruras, dregs, *Fæces.*
Orujo, *vide* Borujo.
Ortaliza, herbs, *Olus, eris.*
Ortelano, a gardiner, *Olitor.*
Orza, *vide* Orça.

O S

Osadamente, boldly, *Audacter.*
Osadía, boldnes, *Audacia.*
Osado, bold, *Audax.*
Osar, to be bold, to dare, *Audere.*
Oscuro, darke, *Obscurus.*
Oscurecer, escurecer, to make darke, *Obscurare.*
Osdiembal, *vide* Ordiembre.
O si, would God, O if, *O si.*
Ospedable, that both lodge, or that may lodge, *Hospitalis.*
Ospedablemente, curteously, like a good house keeper, *Hospitaliter.*
Ospedador, that keepeth hospitalitie, *Hospitalis.*
Ospedamiento, y hospedería, a lodging, *Hospitium.*
Ospedar, to ost, to lodge, *Hospitari.*
Ospedaje, lodging, *Hospitium.*
Ospital, an hospitall, *Hospitale, ptochodochium.*
Ospitalero, the master of an hospitall, *Orphanotrophus.*
Osso, a beare, *Vrsus.*
Ossario, a place to cast bones in, *Ossarium.*
Ossero, *Idem.*
Ostia, an oister, *Ostrum.*

Ossudo, gr
 ossa.
Ostay, a co
 spirit to t
 nauticus.
Ostia, an o
 ost, an oi
Ostiario, an
Ostiero, *Iden*
Ostigado, v
Ostinar, to t
Ostinado, o
Ostinadame
Ostra, an oi

Oteár, to loo
Otero, a hi
 looke the
Oroño, hart
Otoñada, h
Otoñar, to
Otorgar, to
Otorgamier
Otro, anoth
Otravez, ag
Otrotanto,
Ortos tanto
Otubre, Oc

Ova, reeke,
 alga, lens p
Ovar las av
 nere.
Oveja, a she
Ovejero, a s
Ovejuela, a
Ovejuno, p
Overa, a he
Ovillo, a clu

Oxala, woi
Oxear, to d
Oxco, dritti
Oxizacre, o
 mel.

P A

Pacer, to feed, *Pascere.*
Pacedura, feeding, *Pastio.*
Pacido, fed, *Pastus.*
Paciencia, patience, *Patientia.*
Paciente, patient, *Patiens.*
Pacientemente, patiently, *Patienter.*
Pacificar, to pacifie, *Pacificare.*
Pacificado, pacified, *Pacificatus.*
Pacificador, a pacifier, *Pacificator.*
Pacificacion, pacifying, *Pacificatio.*
Pacificamente, peaceably, quietly, *Pacatè.*
Pacifico, peaceable, a peacemaker, *Pacificus.*
Pacto, concierto, bargaine, *Pactum.*
Padecer, to suffer, *Pati.*
Padecimiento, sufferance, *Passio.*
Padilla, a hearth, *Caminus.*
Padrasto, a stepfather, pilling of the skin about the nailes, *Vitricus, reduuia.*
Padre, a father, *Pater.*
Padrino, a godfather, he that bringeth a champion into the field, *Susceptor.*
Padron, a patterne, a register, *Typus, matricula.*
Paga, paiment, *Stips, solutio.*
Pagador, a paimaster, *Solutor.*
Pagado, paied, *Solutus.*
Pagar, to pay, to be punished, *Soluere, luere.*
Pagano, a pagan, *Paganus.*
Page, a page, a footeman, *Minister a pedibus, amanuensis.*
Pagezillo, a jackey, a footeboy, *Puerulus.*
Pagiza casa, a small thatched cotage, *Tugurium.*
Pago de viñas o viñedo, a vineyard, *Vinetum.*
Payla, a paile, *Situla, mulctra.*
Paja, chaffe, strawe, litter, *Palea, stipula, stramentum.*
Pajar, a place to keepe chaffe or strawe, *Palearium.*
Pajuela, small straw, short straw, *Palea.*
Pala, a spade, a shouell, a peele, *Pala, infundibulum.*

Pala de grandes dientes, a rowe of great teeth, *Brochitas.*
Palabra, a word, *Verbum.*
Palabrero, a talker, *Verbosus.*
Palabrilla, a little word, a short word, *Verbulum.*
Palacio, a pallace, *Palatium.*
Paladar, the roofe of the mouth, *Palatum.*
Palafren, a palfrey, *Equus, mannus.*
Paladear, to gaspe for breath, *Anhelare.*
Palanca, a leuer, a coultstaffe, *Palanga.*
Palanciano, a courtier, *Aulicus.*
Palanguin, a porter, *Baiulus.*
Palanguero, a maker of leuers, *Palangarius.*
Palazo, a blow with a cudgel, *Fustis ictus.*
Palenque, lists to fight in, *Pergula, palestra.*
Paleta, a trap sticke, *Bacillum luforium.*
Palillo, a little sticke, *Bacillum.*
Pálio, a goale at running, a canopie to beare ouer a prince, *Meta, canopæum.*
Palizada, a bulwarke, *Vallum.*
Palma, palme tree, the palme of the hand, *Palma.*
Palmar, a groue of palme trees, *Palmetum.*
Palmada, a blowe with the hand, *Palma ictus, colaphus.*
Palmatoria, o cañaheja, ferula, *Ferula.*
Palma de remo, the broade ende of an oare, *Tonsa.*
Palmo, a handbreadth, *Palmus.*
Palmito, leaues of the wilde date, *Folia palmæ syluestris.*
Palo, timber, wood, a sticke, a cudgell, the pillory, *Lignum, palus, pasibulum.*
Palomilla, o palomina, fumitorie, *Fumus terra.*
Palomar, a douehouse, *Columbarium.*
Palomriega, a little poore pigeon, *Columba misella.*
Palomina, a yong doue, *Pullus columbinus.*
Palpar, to grope, *Palpare.*
Palpitar, to pant, to crie like a kid, *Anhelare, palpitare, mutire.*
Pampano, a vine branch, *Pampinus.*
Pampanoso, full of vine branches, *Pampinosus.*

Pan,

Pan,corne, bread, wheate, *Panis,triticum.*
Pan porcino, sowe bread, *Cyclaminus.*
Pan y queso, shepheards purse, *Bursa pastoris.*
Pan cenceño, vnleauened bread, *Panis azymus.*
Panadero, a baker, *Pistor.*
Panaderia, Bakers trade, *Pistoria ars, panificium.*
Panal, a hony-combe, *Fauus.*
Panarizo de la vña, a felon that breedeth betweene the nayle and the flesh, *Paronychium.*
Pança, the paunch, *Venter.*
Pançudo, gorbellied, *Ventricosus.*
Pandero, a taber, *Tympanum.*
Panderetero, a tabourer, *Tympanistes.*
Pandilla, a packe made in playing at the cardes, *Sarcina.*
Pando, weake, bowing, *Debilis, pandus.*
Panera, a binne, a basket for bread, a loft, or garner for corne, *Granarium, arca panaria.*
Panezillo, a little loafe, *Pastellus.*
Paniaguados, houshold folkes, *Familia.*
Panojo, pannycke seede, *Pannicula.*
Panfarrona, *vide* Fanfarrona.
Paniza, pannick, *Pannicum.*
Pañales, childrens clouts, *Crepundia.*
Pañezuelo, a napkin, *Mantile.*
Paño, cloath, *Pannus.*
Pañoso, ragged, *Pannosus.*
Pantano, a bogge, a marsh, *Palus.*
Pantera, a Panther, *Panther.*
Pantorilla de la pierna, the calfe of the leg. *Sura.*
Pantufles, pantofles, *Soleæ, crepidæ.*
Papa, the pope, *Papa.*
Papal, belonging to the pope, *Papalis.*
Papadgo, the popedome, *Papatus.*
Papada de buey, the dewelap, *Palear.*
Papada de puerco, the kernel, or buttons vnder a hogs iawe, *Glandula.*
Papagayo, a Parrat, *Psittacus.*
Papahigo, the sayle of the fore mast, *Mendicium.*
Papar, to gorge vp, to fill the gorge, *Effercire.*

Papa, pappe, *Pappa.*
Papa arriba, the gorge vpward, *Resupinus.*
Papel, paper, *Papyrus.*
Papera, the swelling in the cheekes, *Angina.*
Papelon, a paper to put comfites in, *Charta dulciaria.*
Paperote, a fillip, *Talitrum.*
Papon, a kinde of melone, a great large throat, *Melopepo, Guttur.*
Papo, a throat, the gorge, *Guttur, ingluuies.*
Papado, wide throated, *Gutturosus.*
Papudo, *idem.*
Par, a paire, a couple, a yoake, *Par.*
Para, to, for, *Ad, pro, propter.*
Para con, toward, *Erga.*
Parafo, a paragrafe, *Paragraphum.*
Parayso, paradise, *Paradisus.*
Paraje, ouer against, *E regione.*
Paramentos, curteyns, hanging, trappings, *Cortina, tapetium, ornatus, ephippium, peristromata.*
Paramentar, to hang with tapistrie, *Aulea suspendere.*
Paramentado, hanged, trapped, *Aulais septus, Ephippiatus.*
Páramo, a desert, or a downe, or a plaine countrey not inhabited, *Desertum.*
Parar, to stay, to rest, to ende, *Quiescere, sistere, consistere.*
Parar mientes, to marke, to looke to, *Animaduertere.*
Parado, stayed, *Consistens.*
Paradillas, stayes, *Moræ.*
Para siempre, for euer, *In æternum.*
Parcial, partiall, *Partialis.*
Parcionero, a partner, a parttaker, *Particeps.*
Pardal, a Sparrow, *Passer.*
Pardo, pardillo, grey, *Glaucus.*
Pardo animal, a Leopard, *Leopardus.*
Parecer, to be like to appeare, to seem, *Videri, apparere.*
Pared, a wall, *Paries.*
Pareado, coupled, equall, *Æquatus.*
Paredon, a wall, *Paries.*
Parejo, euen, *Parilitas.*
Parejamente, equally, *Æqualiter.*

Parejas,

Parejas,bever a parejas, to drink hand to hand, *Aequatis vicibus bibere.*
Parejura,equalitie, *Aequalitas.*
Parentela,kinred, *Propinquitas,affinitas.*
Parentesco, *idem.*
Pares,the second vine, euen, *Secundæ,par.*
Pargamino,parchment, *Membrana.*
Párias,pledge,hostage, *Vades.*
Parida,a woman deliuered of child, *Puerpera.*
Pariente,a kinsman, *Consanguineus,affinis.*
Parietaria yerva, Pellitorie, *Parietaria.*
Parir,to bring forth, *Parere.*
Paricion,bringing forth, *Partus.*
Parlar,to speake, *Loqui.*
Parla,prating, speech, pratling, *Loquacitas.*
Parlamento, speech, parlie, *Sermo, colloquium.*
Parlero,a talker, *Loquax.*
Párpado del ojo,the eye lidde, *Cilium.*
Parpadear,to twinkle the eies, *Conniuere.*
Parra,a vine, *Vitis.*
Parróchia,a parish, *Parœcia.*
Parrochiano,a parishioner, *Parœcus.*
Parrilla,greediron es, *Craticula.*
Parte,a parte, *Pars.*
Partera,a midwife, *Obstetrix.*
Partería,a midwiues skill, *Obstetricatus,*
Participar,to take part of,to participate, *Participare.*
Participe,a partaker, *Particeps.*
Particular,particular, *Particularis.*
Particularmente, particularly, *Particulariter.*
Partida, a departure, a condition, *Decessus,conditio.*
Partido, departed, deuided, gone, *Discedens,partitus,absens.*
Partidamente,by parts, *Diuisim.*
Partimiento, parting, diuision, *Partitio,diuisio.*
Partidor,a deuider, *Partitor,diuisor.*
Partir,to deuide,to seuer,to depart, to go away, *Diuidere,partire,abscedere,discedere.*
Parto,a birth, *Partus.*
Pascua, Easter,any feast, *Pascha,festus dies.*
Pascual,belonging to Easter, *Paschalis.*

Pasmarse,to fall in a sowne, *Deficere,obstupescere.*
Pasmo,sowning,falling in a sowne, *Defectio,stupor,examinatio.*
Pasmado,sowning, *Deficiens.*
Pasquines,libels, *Libelli infamatorij.*
Passa,a raison, *Vua passa.*
Passa,juego de passa,iugling, *Præstigiæ.*
Passar,to passe, *Transire,traijcere.*
Passage,passage, *Vectura.*
Passagero,a passenger, *Vector.*
Passada,a pace, *Passus.*
Passado,passed ouer, *Traiectus.*
Passadizo,a passenger that passeth, *Traijcens,vector.*
Passadera,a passage, *Traiectio.*
Passador,a quarrel of a crossebow, *Spiculum catapultarium.*
Passamiento de muerte, the poynte of death, *Articulus mortis.*
Passamano de oro,a broad gold lace, *Institia.*
Passatiempo,pastime, *Lusus.*
Passear,to walke, *Ambulare,deambulare.*
Passéo,a walke,a walking place, *Ambulacrum.*
Passeador, *idem.*
Passeadero, *idem.*
Passion,passion, græfe, *Passio,dolor.*
Passo,a steppe, *Passus.*
Passo,softly, *Pedetensim,gradatim.*
Pasta,paste, *Massa.*
Pastel,a pastie, woad, *Artocrea,glastum.*
Pasto,pasture, *Pascua.*
Pastor,a shepheard, *Pastor.*
Pastora,a woman shepheard, *Pecuaria fœmina.*
Pastoril,belonging to a shepheard, *Pastorius.*
Pastorcillo,a little shepheard, *Pastor culus.*
Pata,a duck, *Anas.*
Pata de Leon, Lions pawe, *Leontopetalon.*
Pata,a hoofe, the sole of the foote, *Planta, vngula.*
Patada,a step, *Pedum strepitus.*
Patache,a pinnesse, *Celopparo.*
Patear,to bargaine,to make a noise with the feet,to treade, *Pangere pepegi,calcare.*

Patens,

Patena,a diſh,*Patina.*
Patente,open,*Patens.*
Paternal,fatherly,*Paternus.*
Patilla,a little foote,a little gooſe, *Pes paruus,anſerculus.*
Patin o patio, a ſquare court,*Area,atrium.*
Patico,a goſeling,*Pullus anſerinus.*
Patihendido,clouen footed,*Pes bifidus.*
Pato,a gooſe,*Anſer.*
Pato o partido,a bargayne,*Pactum.*
Patrañas, a noble acte, an olde ſtory, *Facinus.*
Patituerto,clubfooted,*Loripes.*
Patria,a countrey,*Patria.*
Patriarcha, a patriarcke,*Patriarcha.*
Patrimonio,patrimonie,*Patrimonium.*
Patrimonial, belonging to the patrimonie,*Patrimonialis.*
Patron, a patrone, a defender, the owner of a ſhip,*Patronus,magiſter nauis.*
Pauellon, a pauilion, a canopie, *Papilio, tentorium, conopæum.*
Paues,a buckler,a targat,*Clypeus,ſcutum.*
Paueſada, a battel of targatiers, *Phalanx.*
Paueſa, the ſnoebe of a candle,*Fungus.*
Pauilo,the ſnuffe of a candle,*Lychnus.*
Pauimiento,a pauement,*Pauimentum.*
Pauiota,a gull,*Gauia.*
Pauo,paua y pauon,a peacocke,*Pauo.*
Pauonado, ſanguined as a ſword hilt, *Politus.*
Pauonear,to ſanguine,to berniſh, *Polire, vernice illinere.*
Pauor,feare,*Pauor.*
Pauoroſamente,fearfully,*Timidè.*
Pauoroſo,fearfull,*Timidus.*
Pauſa,reſt,ſtay,a pauſe,*Quies,pauſa.*
Pauſar,to pauſe,to reſt,*Quieſcere.*
Paxaro, a bird,*Auis.*
Paxarero,a birder,*Auceps.*
Paxarillo,a little bird,*Auicula.*
Paxaritos, toies of paſte made for children,*Auicula è pane confecta.*
Paz,peace,*Pax.*

P E

Peal,a ſwollen ſocke,*Vdo.*
Peage, toll at a paſſage, *Vectorium,naulum.*

Pebre,pepper,*Piper.*
Pebrado,peppered,*Pipere conditus.*
Peca, a ſpecke,a ſpot in the face,*Macula, næuus.*
Pecado,ſinne,*Peccatum.*
Pecador,a ſinner,*Peccator.*
Pecar,to ſin,*Peccare.*
Pecoſo,full of ſpots,*Maculoſus.*
Pece,fiſhe,*Piſcis.*
Pecilgar,to pinche,*Vellicare.*
Pecilgo,a pinche,*Vellicatus.*
Pecina,a fiſh poole,*Piſcina.*
Peçon,a nipple, a ſmall ſtalk,a ſtem, *Papilla,caulis.*
Pecha,tribute,payment, *Cenſus,tributum.*
Pechero,he that paieth tribute, *Tributarius.*
Pecho,the breaſt,*Pectus.* (us.
Pechuga,the breaſt of a bird, *Pectuſculum auis.*
Pechuguera,the whole bulke of the breſt *Pectus.*
Pechugar, to leane on the breaſt, *Incumbere pectori.*
Pedaço,a peece,*Pars,portio, fruſtum.*
Pedaçuelo,a little peece, *Portiuncula.*
Pedernal,a flint,*Silex.*
Pedeſtal,the baſe of a piller,*Baſis.*
Pedigueño, wanton, frowarde, *Laſciuus petulans.*
Pedimiento, requeſt,demaund,*Petitio.*
Pedir,pido,to aſke,to require,to demand, *Petere.*
Pedo,a fart,*Crepitus ventris.*
Pedorro, pedocio, that farteth ofte, *Qui multùm pedit.*
Pedrada,a blowe with a ſtone, *Saxi ictus.*
Pedregal,a ſtonie place, *Saxetum.*
Pedregoſo,full of ſtones,*Lapidoſus, Calculoſus.*
Pedrera,a quarrie,*Lapidicina.*
Pedrero,a maſon,a ieweller, *Latomus,gemmarius.*
Pedrezita,a little ſtone,*Calculus.*
Pedriſco,haile,*Grando.*
Peer,to fart,*Pedere.*
Pega, *vide* Picaça.
Pegar,to pitch, or ſtick,to cleaue,to cling to ſoulder, to kerne as frute doth, to infect,

infect, *Picare, adhærere, ferruminare, conglutinare, inficere.*
Pegadura, the foldzing, the cleauing to, the gluing, *Conglutinatio, viscositas.*
Pegajoso, sticking, cleauing, gluie, *Viscosus, adhærens.*
Pegamiento, *idem.*
Pegajoso mal, an infectious disease, *Contagiosus morbus.*
Pegones para vello, round bals to pull off the heare, *Globuli quibus pilos euellunt.*
Pegujal, stocke, goods, *Peculium.*
Peynado cerro, a plaine steepe hill without trees or bushes, *Collis pexus.*
Peynar, to combe, to carde, *Pectere, carpere.*
Peyne, muy sobre peyne, a comb, briefely, *Pecten, Succincte.*
Pelado, pilled, *Depilis, glaber.*
Pelar, to pill, to make balde, to make bare, *Depilare, deglabrare.*
Pelador, he that pilleth, *Depilator.*
Peladura, pilling, *Depilatio.*
Pelambre, the pilling of the chin or berd, the pillings of hides, *Depilatio. (rium.*
Pelambrera, a tanners lime pit, *Depilatorium.*
Pélea, fight, battell, *Pugna, prælium.*
Peleador, a fighter, *Pugnax, belligerator.*
Pelechar el ave, to moote, *Deplumescere.*
Pelicano, a pellicane, *Pelecanus.*
Peligrar, to be in perill, *Periclitari.*
Peligrosamente, dangerously, perilously, *Periculose.*
Peligroso, dangerous, *Periculosus.*
Pelillo, a little heare, *Villus.*
Pelitre, wilde pellitorie, *Pyrethrum. (sus.*
Pelo arriba, against the heare, *Pilus aduersus*
Pelo abaxo, down the haire, *Pilus secundus*
Pelon, a pield fellow, a poore wretch, *Depilis, miser.*
Peloso, hairie, *Pilosus.*
Pelo, heare, *Pilus.*
Pelota, a pellet, a ball, *Pila, globus tormentarius. (lus.*
Pella, a ball, a pellet, a bullet, *Pila, globulus*
Pellejo, the skin or hide, *Pellis.*
Pellejero, a skinner, *Coriarius, Pellio. (tia.*
Pellejeria, a skinners trade, *Pellionis scien-*

Pellico, a leather ferkin, a quip, a taunt, *Vestis pellicea, dicterium.*
Peltre, pewter, *Stannum.*
Pelliscar, to pinch, *Vellicare.*
Peltrechos, *vide* Pertrechos.
Pena, punishment, *Pæna, mulcta.*
Penal, penall, *Pænalis.*
Penar, to punish, to be punished, *Multare, punire, & pænas pendere.*
Penacho, the crest of the helmet, *Crista.*
Penca, the stalke of lettise or colewortz, *Caulis. (bes.*
Pendejo, heare about the priuities, *Pubes*
Pendencia, a sute in lawe, a quarrell, *Lis.*
Pendola, peñola, a pen, *Penna, pluma.*
Pendon, a signe of a tauerne, a streamer, *Signum, vexillum.*
Pendiente, hanging, *Pendens.*
Penétrar, to pierce, *Penetrare.*
Penitencia, repentance, *Pænitentia.*
Penitencial, *vide* Penitente.
Penitente, penitent, *Pænitens.*
Penoso, painefull, grieuous, *Molestus.*
Pensar, to thinke, to meditate, to dresse cattell, *Putare, meditari, curare.*
Pensamiento, thought, esteeming, *Cogitatio, Existimatio.*
Pensativo, pensiue, thoughtfull, *Cogitabundus.*
Pension, a pension, *Pensio. (dus.*
Peña y peñasco, a rocke, *Rupes.*
Peñascola, an iland, *Peninsula.*
Peon, a footeman, a pawne at chesse, a pioner, or laborer, *Fossor, pedes, operarius.*
Peonadura, working of pioners, *Opera fossaria.*
Peonada, a daies worke, *Opera diurna.*
Peonça, a top, *Trochus, turbo.*
Peonia, piony, *Pæonia.*
Peor, woorse, *Peior, deterior.*
Peoria, the decaying, *Detrimentum.*
Pepino, a cucumber, *Cucumis.*
Peormente, woorse, *Peius.*
Pepita, a kirnel of fruit, the pip in a hen, *Nucleus, Pituita.*
Pepitoria, the gibiets of a goose, or anie bird, *Acrocolia, profecta.*
Pequeñico, very little, *Paruulus.*
Pequeño, little, *Paruus.*

S 2 Pera,

Pera,a peare, *Pyrum.*
Peral,a peare tree, *Pyrus.*
Perayle,perayre,a fuller, *Fullo.*
Percha,a perch to measure, the prop of a vine,*Pertica,cantherius.*
Perder,to leese, *Perdere.*
Perdicion,losse, perdition, *Perditio.*
Pérdida,losse, *Amissio perditio,iactura.*
Perdido,lost, *Amissus,perditus.*
Perdidoso,he that hath lost, *Qui perdidit.*
Perdidoloso, a traitor, a trecherons fel=low,*Perduellis,insidiator.*
Perdigar, to lay patridges on coales, to broyle partridges, *Perdices amburere.*
Perdigon,a yoong partridge, *Pullus perdicis.* (*perdicarius.*
Perdiguero perro, a lande spaniell, *Canis*
Perdiz,a partridge,*Perdix.*
Perdon,pardon,*Venia,indulgentia.*
Perdonança,pardoning,*Indulgentia.*
Perdonar, to pardon,*Indulgere,ignoscere.*
Perdurable,lasting,perdurable, *Aeternus.*
Perdurablemente,continually, *Aeterne.*
Perecer,to perish,to die,*Perire,mori.*
Perecimiento,perishing, *Interitus,mors.*
Perecido, perished,dead, *Mortuus, perditus.*
Peregrinar,to trauell into strange countries, to go on pilgrimage, *Peregrinari.*
Peregrinacion, traueiling into strange countries, *Peregrinatio.*
Peregrino,a stranger, a pilgrim, strange excellent, *Rarus,peregrinus, aduena,excellens.*
Perenal,continuall,*Perennis.*
Perenalmente,continually, *Perenniter.*
Perexil, persely,*Petroselinum.*
Pereza,sloth,*Pigritia.*
Perezoso,slothfull,*Piger.*
Perozosamente,slothfully,*Tigre.*
Perfetamente,perfecty,*Perfecte.*
Perfeto,perfect,*Perfectus.*
Perficion,perfection,*Perfectio.* (*tum.*
Perfil,the drawing of a picture, *Lineamen-*
Perfiladura,*idem.*
Perfilar,to draw a picture,*Delineare.*
Perfumar,to perfume,*Suffire.*

Perfumado,perfumed,*Suffitus.*
Perfumes,perfumes,*Thymiama.*
Pergamino,parchment,*Membrana.*
Perjurar,to forsweare,*Peierare.*
Perjuro,periured,*Peieratus,periurus.*
Periudicar,to preiudicate,*Praeiudicare.*
Periuyzio,preiudice,*Praeiudicium.*
Perla,a pearle,*Vnio.*
Perlado,a prelate, *Antifles.*
Pérlatico,sicke of the palsie, *Paralyticus.*
Perlesia,the palsie,*Paralysis.*
Permanecer,to remain,to continue,*Permanere.*
Permission,sufferance,*Termissio.*
Permiter,to suffer,*Permittere.*
Permutar,to change,*Permutare.*
Permutacion,change,*Permutatio.*
Pero,a peare, *Pyrum.*
Peral,a peare tree,*Pyrus.*
Pero,but,*Sed,iamen,at.*
Pernil de tocino, a gamon of bacon,*Perna.*
Perpétuar,to continue,to make perpetu=all,*Perpetuare.*
Perpetuidad, continuance, perpetuitie, *Perpetuitas.*
Perpétuo,perpetuall,*Perpetuus.*
Perpiaños, the whole stones that go through a wall,*Lapis frontarius.*
Perque,a libell,*Libellus infamatorius.*
Perra,a bitch,*Canis.*
Perrazo,a curre dog,*Gregarius canis.*
Perrito perrillo, a whelpe, a little dog,a puppie,*Catellus,catulus.*
Perro,a dog,*Canis.*
Perruno,belonging to a dogge,*Caninus.*
Persecucion,persecution,*Persecutio.*
Perseguir,figuo,to persecute,*Persequi.*
Perseguimiento,persecuting,*Persecutio.*
Perseguido,persecuted,*Persecutus.*
Perseverar,to perseuer, *Perseuerare.*
Perseveracion,perseuering,*Perseueratio.*
Perseverancia,perseuering,continuance, *Perseuerantia.*
Pérsego,a peach, *Malum persicum.*
Persiles, the laying on of coulours in painting,*Circumlitiones.*
Persona,a person,*Persona.*

Personal,

P E

Perſonal, perteining to a perſon, *Perſonalis.*
Perſonalmente, perſonally, *Perſonaliter.*
Perſuadir, to perſwade, *Perſuadere.*
Perſuaſion, perſwaſion, *Perſuaſio.*
Pertinácia, ſtubburnes, *Pertinacia.*
Pertenencia, perteining, *Pertinentia.*
Pertenecer, to pertaine, *Pertinere.*
Perteneciente, perteining, *Pertinens.*
Pertiga de carreta, the toong of a plowe, *Temo.*
Pertiga, a perch to meaſure with, *Pertica.*
Pertiguero de ygleſia, the verger, *Sceptrifer.*
Pertinaz, ſtubburne, *Pertinax.*
Pertrechos, furniture, prouiſion, *Munitio.*
Perturbar, to trouble, *Perturbare.*
Perturbado, troubled, *Perturbatus.*
Perturbacion, trouble, *Perturbatio.*
Peruétano, a wilde peare, *Pyrus ſylueſtris.*
Peſadamente, heauily, ſorrowfully, *Grauiter, grauatè, ægrè.*
Peſar, to weigh, to be ſorrowfull, to bee diſpleaſed, to repent, *Pendere, dolere, pænitere, diſplicere.*
Peſadó, weightie, heauy, ſorrowful, *Grauis, ponderoſus.*
Peſador, he that weigheth, *Ponderator.*
Peſadumbre, griefe, diſpleaſure, weight, *Grauitas, dolor, ponderoſitas.*
Peſar, ſorrow, griefe, repentance, *Dolor, ægritudo, panitentia.*
Peſcador, a fiſher, *Piſcator.*
Peſcado, fiſh, *Piſcis.*
Peſcar, to fiſh, *Piſcari.*
Peſca, fiſhing, *Piſcatio.*
Peſcadero, a fiſhmonger, *Cetarius.*
Peſcadería, the fiſhmarket, *Cetaria.*
Peſcudar, to ſearch, to fift out a matter, to aſke, *Scrutari, percunctari.*
Peſcuda, a queſtion, a demande, *Scrutatio, percunctatio.*
Peſcoçon, a blow in the necke, *Colaphus.*
Peſcoçado, *idem.*
Peſcueço, the necke, *Collum, ceruix.*
Peſebre, a manger, *Præſepe.*
Peſebrera, *idem.*

P I

Peſo, weight, *Trutina, pondus.*
Peſquiſar, *vide* Peſcudar.
Peſquiſa, ſearching, examining, *Inquiſitio, quæſtio.*
Peſquiſidor, a ſearcher, an examiner, *Inquiſitor.*
Peſquería y peſquera, a fiſhing place, *Piſcatio.*
Peſtañas, the heare of the eie lids, *Palpebra, cilium.*
Peſtilencia, the peſtilence, *Peſtis.*
Peſtilencial, peſtilent, *Peſtifer.*
Peſtillo, the bar of a doore, *Peſſulum.*
Peſtorejo de puerco, a pigs cheeke, *Sinciput porcinum.*
Peſuña, the faſhion in a horſe, *Struma.*
Petaca, a baſket, a hamper, *Corbis.*
Petafio, an Epitaph, *Epitaphium.*
Petril, a rayle to leane the breaſt on, *Pectorale.*
Peticion, a petition, *Petitio.*
Pex, the glue of a kinde of fiſhe, *Ichthiocolla.*
Pez, pitch, *Pix.*
Pezpita, a wagtaile, *Motacilla.*

P I

Piar, to peepe as a chicken, *Pipire.*
Piadoſo, pitifull, *Clemens, miſericors.*
Piadoſamente, pitifullie, *Miſericorditer.*
Piara, a flocke, a heard, *Grex, armentum.*
Piedad, pittie, mercy, *Clementia, miſericordia.*
Pica, a pike, *Lancea.*
Picaça, a pie, *Pica.*
Picar, to picke, to bite as fiſh at a hooke, to pecke, *Veſci.*
Picadillo, a kinde of broth, *Iuſculi genus.*
Picado, a pricke, a pecke, *Morſus, punctura.*
Picaño, a lewd fellow, a baſe fellow, *Nequam, ſordidus, obſcurus, ignobilis.*
Picaviento, a contrarie wynde, *Ventus aduerſus.*
Picaro, a baſe fellowe, a poore laborer, or porter, *ignobilis, operarius, baiulus.*
Piçarras, peble ſtones, *Calculus.*

Pico

Pico de cigueña, **stocks bil**, *Geranium*.
Pico, the beake of a birde, an pton pike, a woodwall, *Rostrum, picus*.
Picina, a fish poole, *Piscina*.
Picota, a pillorie, *Palus*.
Picóte, a kinde of sackcloth, *Saccus*.
Pie, a foote, *Pes*.
Pie de anada, duckes foote, *Chenopus*.
Pie de liebre, hares foote, *Lagopus*.
Pieça, a peece, *Pars, portio*.
Piedad, pitie, mercie, *Pietas, misericordia*.
Piedra, a stone, *Petra, lapis, saxum*.
Piel o pelleja, a skin, *Pellis*.
Pielago, the sea, *Pelagus*.
Pienso de bestia, prouender, *Pabulum, ocymum*.
Pierna, a leg, *Sura, tibia, crus*.
Piesgo, the nose of a bottle, *Lura, orificium, gula*.
Pifaro, a fife, a flute, *Aulos, fistula*.
Piguelas, pihuelas, haukes iesses, *Lemniscus*.
Pila, a funt, a pot of water, *Baptisterium, Crater*.
Pilar, a piller, *Columna*.
Pilaje, pillage, *Spolia, exuuiæ*.
Píldora, a pill to purge, *Pillula*.
Pilica, a little pot, *Ollula*.
Pilon, a morter, a trough, *Pila, mortarium*.
Pilota, a pilot, *Gubernator nauis*.
Pimienta, pepper, *Piper*.
Pimpollo, a succor that groweth out of the bodies of trees, *Stolo*.
Pimpinela, pimpernell, *Anagallis*.
Pinar y pinal, a grout of pines, *Pinetum*.
Pinjantes, spangles, *Bracteolæ*.
Pinjado, one that hath lost all his monie, *Perditus*.
Pinillo oloroso, wild dill, *Meu vel Meum*.
Pinillo, herbe iue, *Chamæpytu*.
Pino, a pine tree, *Pinus*.
Pinariego, belonging to the pine, *Pinaceus*.
Piña, the vtter shell of a pine nut, *Putamen pineum*.
Piñon, the kernell of a pine nut, *Nucleus pineus*.
Pinsado, a kinde of pine, *Sapinus*.

Pinta, a spot, *Macula, næuus*.
Pintar, to paint, *Pingere*.
Pintor, a painter, *Pictor*.
Pintura, painting, *Pictura*.
Pintado, painted, *Pictus*.
Pinzel, a pensill, *Penicillum, stilus*.
Piogera, a place where lice breed, *Locus pediculosus*.
Piojo, a louse, *Pediculus*.
Piojento, piojoso, lousie, *Pediculosus*.
Pipa, a vessell called a pipe, *Dolium*.
Pisar, to tread on, to paue, *Calcare, pauimentare*.
Pisada, a step, *Vestigium*.
Pison, a beetle to paue with, *Vectis ligneus*.
Pitar, to pay ready monie, *Pretium repræsentare*.
Pitañoso, bleare eied, tender eied, *Lippus*.
Pito, a woodwall, *Iynx, picus*.
Pivetes, a kind of perfume, *Suffitus genus*.
Pixa, a pissel, a yard of a beast, *Virga, penis*.
Pixita de niños, a childes pricke, *Pipina*.

P L

Plaça, a streete, a market place, *Platea, forum, macellum*.
Placartes, patents, *Diplomata*.
Placero, common, publike, *Publicus*.
Placeramente, publikely, commonly, *Palàm, publicè*.
Playa, a wharfe, a plaine place by the sea side to land on, *Portus*.
Plana, an instrument called a plaine, a leafe of paper, *Læuigatorium, folium, pagina*.
Planeta, a planet, *Planeta*.
Planta de pie, the sole of the foote, *Planta*.
Planta, a plant, *Planta*.
Plantar, to plant, *Plantare*.
Plasmador, a creator, *Creator*.
Plasta, *vide* Pasta.
Plata, filuer, monie, *Argentum, pecunia*.
Platero, a siluer smith, *Argentarius*.
Platano, a plaine tree, *Platanus*.
Platear, to couer with siluer, *Deargentare*.
Plateado, plated with siluer, *Deargentatus*.
Platel, a dish, a platter, *Patina, catinus*.
Platica, speech, talke, *Sermo*.

Plato,

Plato, a platter, a bason, *Catinus, malluuium.*
Plazer, pleasure, mirth, to please, *Voluptas, placere.*
Plazentéro, pleasant, *Iucundus.*
Plazo, summons, citing, *Citatio, comperendinatio.*
Plebeyo, common, vulgar, *Publicus, vulgaris.*
Plegar, pliego, to fold, *Plicare, complicare.*
Plegadura, folds, folding, *Plicatura.*
Plegado, folded, *Plicatus.*
Plegaria, prayer, *Preces.*
Pleyto, law, suite in lawe, *Lis.*
Pleyto omenage, an oth, *Fides publicè data, sacramentum.*
Pleytear, to go to law, *Litigare, ius persequi.*
Pleyteante, he that hath a suite in lawe, *Litigator.*
Pleyteador, a pleader, *Litigator, actor, causidicus.*
Pleytesia, a sute in law, waging of lawe, *Causa, iuramentum.*
Pleytista, a sollicitor, *Leguleius.*
Pliega, a pleate in a garment, *Ruga.*
Pliego de papel, a sheete of paper, *Plaga.*
Plomada, a plummet, *Plumbata.*
Plomado, leaded, *Plumbeus.*
Plomar, to set a leaden seale to a pardon, *Adplumbare.*
Plomo, lead, *Plumbum.*
Pluma, a feather, a pen, *Pluma.*

P O

Poblacion, peopling, *Colonia.*
Poblador, he that peopleth a countrie, an inhabiter, *Qui coloniam deducit, colonus.*
Poblar, to people, to inhabite, *Coloniam deducere.*
Poblazo, the multitude, *Populus, plebs, vulgus.*
Pobre, poore, *Pauper.*
Pobrezillo, a poore wretch, *Pauperculus.*
Pobreza, pouertie, *Paupertas.*
Pocilga, an hogs stie, *Hara.*
Pocas vezes, seldome, *Rarò.*
Poco, little, *Parum, paulùm.*
Poco a poco, by little and little, *Paulatim.*

Poco mas o menos, thereabouts, *Circiter.*
Podar vides, to prune vines, *Amputare, putare.*
Podador, a pruner, *Putator.*
Podado, pruned, *Putatus.*
Podadera hoce, a pruning hooke, *Falx putatoria.*
Podaçon, pruning time, *Putatio.*
Podenco, a dog called a bloodhounde, *Sagax, indagarius.*
Poder, power, abilitie, wealth, *Potestas, diuitiae, potentia.*
Poder, puedo, púde, podré, to be able, *Posse.*
Poderío, power, *Potentia.*
Podorosamente, mightily, *Potenter.*
Podoroso, mightie, powerfull, able, *Potens.*
Podrecer, to rot, *Putrescere.*
Podre, rottennes, filthe, corruption, *Tabes, pus.*
Podrecimiento, rotting, ranckling, *Suppuratio, putredo.*
Podricion, rotting, *Tabes, suppuratio.*
Podrimiento, *vide* Podricion.
Podriqueria, *vide* Podricion.
Podrido, rotten, *Putidus.*
Podrir, to rot, *Putrescere.*
Poesia, poetrie, *Ars poetica.*
Poeta, a poet, *Poeta.*
Poyo, a bench, *Podium, scamnum.*
Poyal, a bench cloth, *Stragulum podiale.*
Polea, a pully, penniriall, *Vertebra, pulegium.*
Poleada, pap, *Pappa.*
Polaymas, hose without feete, hand ruffs *Tibialia abscissis pedibus, sinus manuales.*
Póliça, the charter partie in a shippe, *Syngraphum.*
Policia, policie, finenes, *Politia, elegantia.*
Polidamente, finely, neately, *Politè, eleganter.*
Polidero, a polishing tole, *Politorium.*
Polideza, comelynesse, finenesse, *Politura, elegantia.*
Polido, neate, cleane, *Politus, nitidus.*
Polir, to polish, *Polire.*
Polipodio, polipodie, *Polipodium.*

Polilla,

Polilla,a moth,*Tinea.*
Polo,the pole,*Polus.*
Polvito,small duſt, *Puluiſculus.*
Polvo,duſt,*Puluis.*
Polvora, powder, gunpowder, duſt,*Puluis.*
Polvorear,to beat to duſt,*Puluerare.*
Polvoroſo, duſtie, *Puluerulentus.*
Polvoramiento,duſting,raiſing of duſte, *Puluerate.*
Pollo, a chicke,a colt,*Pullus.*
Pollazon,bringing vp of chickins, *Pullatio.*
Pollero,a poulterer, alſo a place to keepe poultrie,*Pullarius.*
Pollino,an aſſe colt,*Pullus aſininus.*
Poma,a pomander, *Olfactorium,paſtillus.*
Pompa,pompe,*Pompa.*
Pompoſo,pompous,*Pompoſus.*
Ponçoña,poyſon,*Venenum.*
Ponçoñoſo,venemous,poiſoned,*Venenoſus.*
Ponçoñar,to poiſon, *Veneno inficere.*
Ponderar, to ponder, to waie, *Perpendere.*
Ponedera gallina,a laying hen,*Gallina oua ponens.*
Poner, pongo, puſe, to put,to lay,to ſet, *Ponere,parere,occidere tanquam ſol,plantare.*
Poner fin,to make an end, *Finem imponere.*
Poner en depoſito o terceria, to ſequeſter *Sequeſtrare.*
Poner en cobro,to ſet ſafe,*Reponere.*
Pontificado,the eſtate of a biſhop, *Pontificatus.*
Pontifical,pontificall, *Pontificalis.*
Poniente,the weſt, *Occidens.*
Pontifice,a biſhop,*Pontifex.*
Ponton,a bridge,*Pons.*
Popa,the ſterne of a ſhip,*Puppis.*
Popular,popular,common, *Publicus,popularis.*
Populoſo,populous,*Populoſus.*
Poquedad, baſenes of mind, ſmalnes of abilitie, a little, *Puſillanimitas, debilitas, paucitas.*
Poquito,very little,*Parum.*
Por,by,for,*Per,pro.*

Poraventura,peradventure, what? *Foriè num,numquid.*
Pordonde,which way, *Qua?*
Pordemas,in vaine,*Superfluus.*
Porende,therefore,*Ideo.*
Por eſſo,por eſto, for this cauſe,therfore, *Propterea.*
Porfia,contention, *Contentio,pertinacia.*
Porfiar,to contend,to perſeuer, *Contendere,perſeuerare.*
Porfiando,a vie,*Certatim.*
Porfido,red marble,*Porphyrites.*
Porhijar, to adopt,*Adoptare.*
Poridad,a ſecret,*Secretum,arcanum.*
Pórque,wherefore, *Quapropter,ideò.*
Porqué,why, *Quare?*
Porquero,a pigheard,*Suarius.*
Porquería,ſwiniſhnes,*Mores ſpurci.*
Porquerones,ſergeants men,catchpoles *Lictor,apparitor.*
Porra,a club,*Claua.*
Porrada,a blow with a club,*Ictus clauæ.*
Porretas,leeke blades,*Porrina.*
Porrilla,a little club,*Claua parua.*
Porta cartas,a deſke,*Scrinium.*
Portada,a wicket,*Forula,portula.*
Portadgo,tribute,toll,*Portorium.*
Portadguero,a toll gatherer,*Publicanus.*
Portal,a porch,*Porticus.*
Portañola,a port hole,*Porta.*
Portanario inteſtino, the gut that paſſeth from the ſtomacke to the belly,*Pylorus.*
Porte de cartas, hire for cariage of letters, *Merces pro vectura.*
Portero,a porter,*Ianitor.*
Portezuela,a little gate,a wicket,*Portula.*
Portillo de muro, the battlements, *Minæ murorum.*
Poſada, a lodging, an inne, *Hoſpitium, taberna.*
Poſadero,a ſeate,a ſtoole,*Sedes,ſedile.*
Poſar,to ſit,to reſt,*Sedere,quieſcere.*
Poſpelo, againſt the haire,*Pilus aduerſus.*
Poſponer,to ſet behind, *Poſtponere.*
Poſſeer,to poſſeſſe,*Poſſidere.*
Poſſeſſion,poſſeſſion,*Poſſeſſio.*
Poſſedor,a poſſeſſor,*Poſſeſſor.*
Poſſible,poſſible,*Poſſibilis.*

Poſſiblemente,

Possiblemente, possibly, *Possibiliter.*
Possibilidad, possibilitie, *Possibilitas.*
Posta, a post, a watchman, *Cursor, præcursor.*
Poste, a post, a piller, *Postis, sublicium, columna.* (*Furor.*
Postema, an impostume, a rage, *Apostema.*
Postigo, a posterne gate, *Posticus.*
Postilla, a push, a wheale, *Pustula.*
Postilloso, full of pushes, ful of wheales, *Pustulosus.*
Postillon, a postillon, a guide for a post, *Dux præcursoris.*
Postizo, counterfetted, *Suppositius.*
Postrero, postrimero, the latter, the last, the former, *Postremus.*
Postremeria, the latter daies of a man, *Finis, terminus.*
Postura, laying downe, laying a wager, *Positura.*
Potáge, potage, *Ius.*
Potencia, power, *Potentia.*
Potente, mightie, *Potens.*
Potestad, power, *Potestas.*
Potra, burstines, *Hernia, ramex.*
Potroso, burst, *Herniosus, ramicosus.*
Potranca, a mare colt of three yeeres old, *Equa trima.*
Potrico, a hog colt, *Pullus equinus.*
Potro, a colt, a pisse pot, *Pullus, matula fictilis.*
Pozero, a well maker, *Puteárius.*
Pozo, a well, *Puteus.*

P R

Prado, a meadow, *Pratum.*
Pradezuelo, dim. a prado, a little meadow.
Pradillo, dim. a prado, a little meadow.
Pratica, practise, talke, *Praxis, sermo.*
Praticar, to practise, to talke, *Factitare, loqui.*
Preambulo, a preamble, *Proæmium.*
Preceder, to go before, *Præcedere.*
Preciar, to esteeme, to account of, to vaunt, *Existimare, iactare.*
Precio, price, *Pretium.*
Precioso, pretious, *Pretiosus.*
Predicar, to preach, *Prædicare.*

Predicador, a preacher, *Prædicator.*
Predicacion, preaching, *Prædicatio.*
Predipatorio, a pulpit, *Pulpitum.*
Prefacion, a preface, *Præfatio.*
Preferir, fiero, to prefer, *Præferre.*
Pregarias, praiers, *Preces.*
Pregonero, a crier, *Præco.*
Pregonar, to crie, to proclaime, *Præconio declarare.*
Pregon, a proclamation, *Præconium.*
Pregunta, a question, a demand, *Quæstio, percontatio.*
Preguntar, to aske, *Percontari, quærere.*
Preheminencia, preheminence, *Præeminentia.*
Prelacia, prelacie, *Antistitium.*
Prelado, perlado, a prelate, *Antistes.*
Premiar, to force, to compell, to reward, *Cogere, retribuere.*
Premia, force, compulsion, *Vis, coactio.*
Premiador, a rewarder, *Retributor.*
Prematica, a law, a statute, *Lex, senatusconsultum.*
Premilla, the first fault pardoned, *Prima culpa condonata.*
Premio, a reward, *Præmium.*
Premir, to presse, *Premere.*
Prenda, a gage, a pledge, *Pignus.*
Prendar, to pledge, to take a pledge, *Oppignorare, pignus capere.*
Prender, to take, *Accipere.* (*hensio.*
Prendimiento, taking, *Prehensio, comprehensio.*
Prender la planta, to take roote, *Radices agere.*
Preñada, with childe, great with yong, *Grauida.*
Preñez, being with childe, *Fætura.*
Prensa, a presse, *Prælum.*
Preparar, to prepare, *Præparare.*
Prefado, a presse, *Prælum.*
Presa, a pray, a bootie, a handle, a flud-hatch, *Præda, ansa, septum, catarracta.*
Presea, a iewell, *Gemma.*
Presencia, presence, *Præsentia.*
Presente, present, a present, a gift, *Præsens, donum, munus.*
Presentar, to present, to giue, to represent, *Donare, offerre, exhibere.*
T   Presentacion,

Presentacion, giuing, presenting, *Oblatio.*
Presentado, presented, giuen, *Oblatus, donatus.*
Presidencia, presidencie, gouernment, *Præsidis munus.*
Presidente, a president, a gouernor, *Preses.*
Presilla pelada, vallence for a bed, *Margo.*
Preso, taken, fastened, *Prehensus, fixus.*
Prestar, to lend, to suffice, *Mutuare, sufficere.*
Prestador, a lender, *Mutuator.*
Prestido, lent, *Mutuatus, mutuus.*
Prestado, *Idem.*
Prestado tomar, to borrow, *Mutuum accipere.*
Prestadiza cosa, any thing lent, *Mutuatitius.*
Prestamo, loane, *Mutuum.*
Prestamente, quickly, *Citò, statim.*
Presteza, quicknes, *Celeritas.*
Presto, ready, quickly, *Promptus, statim.*
Presumir, to presume, *Insolescere, arrogare.*
Presuncion, presumption, *Arrogantia, insolentia.*
Presuntuosamente, presumptuously, *Arroganter.*
Presuntuoso, presumptuous, *Arrogans, insolens.*
Pretal, a poytrell, *Pectorale.*
Pretil, *vide* Petril.
Pretina, a girdle, *Cingulum.*
Pretor, a pretor, a mayor, *Prætor.*
Pretender, to pretend, *Prætendere.*
Pretensor, a pretender, he that purposeth *Prætensor.*
Prevalecer, to preuale, *Valere.*
Prevaricar, to offend, to breake the lawe, to take monie of both parties, *Prævaricari.*
Prevaricador, an offender, an ambidexter, *Prævaricator.*
Prevenir, to preuent, *Prævenire.*
Previlegio, a priuilege, *Priuilegium.*
Previlegiado, priuileged, *Priuilegiatus.*
Previlegiar, to priuilege, *Priuilegium concedere.*
Prez, price, *Pretium.*
Priessa, haste, speed, *Celeritas, expeditio.*
Priessa dar, to make haste, *Festinare.*
Prieto, blacke, browne, *Niger.*
Primavera, the spring time, *Ver.*
Prima, the miniken in an instrument, *Nete.*
Primo, the best, the chiefest, a cosen german, *Primus, princeps, frater patruelis.*
Primeramente, first, *Primò.*
Primero, the first, the chiefest, *Primus.*
Primeriza, a woman in childe bed of hir first childe, *Primipara.*
Primicias, the first fruits, *Primitiæ.*
Primor, the excellencie of any thing, *Bonitas, excellentia.*
Primogenito, the first begotten, *Primogenitus.*
Princesa, a princesse, *Princeps.*
Principado, a principalitie, *Principatus.*
Principal, principall, *Præcipuus.*
Principalmente, principally, *Præcipuè.*
Principe, a prince, *Princeps.*
Principiar, to begin, *Incipere.*
Principio, a beginning, *Principium.*
Pringue de torrezno, barrowes grease, *Abdomen, axungia.*
Pringar, *vide* Empringar.
Prior, a prior, *Prior.*
Priorado, a priorie, *Prioratus.*
Prisco, *vide* Aprisco.
Prision, prison, the taking, *Carcer, captus.*
Prisionero, a prisoner, *Captiuus.*
Privada, a priuie, a draught, a iakes, *Latrina.*
Privado, a familiar, a friend, a princes minion, *Familiaris, priuatus.*
Privar, to depriue, to take away, to be familiar, *Priuare, familiarem esse.*
Privado, depriued, *Orbus.*
Privadero, a iakes farmer, *Latrinæ purgator.*
Privacion, priuation, depriuing, *Priuatio.*
Pro, buen pro os haga, much good do it you, *Profit.*
Proa, the foreship, *Prora.*
Procurar, to procure, to looke to, *Curare, procurare.*
Procurador, a proctor, a procurer, an atturnie, *Procurator.*

Procuradora,

Procuradora cosa, that which procureth, *Procuratorius.*
Procuracion, procuring, looking to a cause, *Procuratio.*
Proceder, to proceede, to go forwarde, *Procedere.*
Procession, going forward, procession, *Processus, letania.*
Processo, processe, *Processus.*
Prodigalidad, prodigalitie, *Prodigalitas.*
Prodigo, prodigall, *Prodigus.*
Produzir, duzgo, to bring forth, *Producere.*
Profacio en la missa, the preamble to the masse, *Præfatio.*
Profaçar, to bid much good do it, *Bene precari vescentibus.*
Profanar, to profane, *Profanare.*
Proferir, to vtter, to speake out, *Proferre, eloqui.*
Profession, profession, *Professio.*
Professo, professed, *Professus.*
Profecia, prophesie, *Prophetia.*
Profeta, a prophet, *Propheta.*
Profetizar, to prophesie, *Prædicere.*
Profundamente, profoundly, *Profunditer.*
Profundidad, profoundnes, *Profunditas.*
Profundo, deepe, profound, *Profundus.*
Prohejar, to beare against the winde, *In ventum eniti.*
Prohémio, a proeme, *Proæmium.*
Prohibir, to forbid, *Prohibere.*
Prohibido, forbidden, *Prohibitus.*
Prolixidad, length, tediousnes, *Prolixitas.*
Prolixamente, long, *Prolixè.*
Prolixo, long, *Prolixus.*
Prologo, a prologue, *Prologus.*
Prolongar, luengo, to prolong, *Protrahere.*
Promessa, a promise, *Promissum.*
Prometimiento, a promise, *Promissio.*
Prometer, mito, to promise, *Promittere.*
Prometedor, a promiser, *Promissor.*
Prometido, promised, *Promissus.*
Promulgar, to publish *Publicare.*
Prompto, ready, *Promptus.*
Promptitud, readines, *Promptitudo.*
Pronosticar, to prognosticate, *Diuinare.*

Pronostico, prognosticating, *Diuinatio.*
Pronunciar, to pronounce, *Pronunciare.*
Pronunciacion, pronunciation, *Pronuntiatio.*
Proponer, to propose, to purpose, *Proponere.*
Proponimiento, purpose, *Propositum, destinatio.*
Proposito, purpose, *Propositum.*
Proporcion, proportion, *Proportio.*
Proposicion, proposition, *Propositio.*
Propiamente, properly, *Propriè.*
Propriedad, propriety, *Proprietas.*
Proprietario, he that hath the propertie, *Proprietarius.*
Propio, proper, *Proprius.*
Propuesta, purpose, *Propositum.*
Prosa, prose, *Prosa, sermo solutus.*
Prosperamente, prosperously, *Prosperè.*
Prospero, prosperous, *Prosper, fælix.*
Prosperidad, prosperitie, *Fælicitas, prosperitas.*
Protesto, a protestation, *Protestatio.*
Protonotario, a prenotarie, *Protonotarius.*
Provable, probable, *Probabilis.*
Provablemente, probablie, *Probabiliter.*
Provança, proofe, *Probatio.*
Provar, pruevo, to proue, to taste, to trie, to assaie, to allow, *Periculum facere, experiri, probare, gustare.* (*stator.*
Provador, a prouuer, a taster, *Probator, gustator.*
Provado, tried, tasted, proued, assayed, *Probatus, gustatus.*
Provecho, profit, *Commodum, vtilitas.*
Provechosamente, profitablie, *Vtiliter.*
Provechoso, profitable, *Vtilis.*
Provechar, to profit, *Proficere, conducere.*
Proveer, to prouide, to take heed, to foresee, *Prouidere.*
Proveido, forescene, *Prouisus.*
Proveidamente, prouidently, *Prouidè.*
Proveimiento, foresight, *Prouidentia.*
Provena o mugron de vid, a braunch of a vine, *Propago.*
Proverbio, a prouerb, *Prouerbium.*
Providencia, prouidence, *Prouidentia.*
Provincia, a prouince, *Prouincia.*
Provincial, perteining to a prouince, also

a gouernour of a prouince, *Prouincialis præses.*
Prouision, prouision, store, *Prouisio, penus.*
Prouisor, a prouidor, an ouerseer, *Prouisor, curator.*
Prouocar, to prouoke, *Prouocare.*
Prouocacion, prouocation, *Prouocatio.*
Prudencia, wisedome, *Prudentia.*
Prudente, wise, *Prudens.*
Prudentemente, wiselie, *Prudenter.*
Prueua, proofe, triall, taste, *Probatio, periculum, gustus.*

P V

Pua, a stocke to graffe on, a prickle, a thorne, the tooth of a combe, *Talea, surio spina, aculeus, cuspis.*
Puagre, the gout in the feete, *Podagra.*
Publicamente, publikely, *Publicè.*
Publicar, to publish, *Publicare.*
Publicacion, forfeiting, confiscating, *Confiscatio.*
Publicado, published, *Publicatus.*
Publico, publicke, *Publicus.*
Puchas, pulse, a kinde of pap, *Puls, pulsicula.*
Puchero, an earthen pot, a pipkin, *Pulsarium.*
Pueblo, people, *Plebs, populus.*
Puente, a bridge, *Pons.*
Puerca, a sowe, a hog louse, *Sus, millipeda.*
Puerca de husillo, a spindle of a distaffe, *Fusus.*
Puercamente, filthily, *Spurcè.*
Puerco, a swine, *Porcus.*
Puericia, childhood, *Pueritia.*
Puerco espina, a porcupin, *Histrix.*
Puerco montes, *vide* javali.
Puerro, leekes, *Porrum.*
Puerta, a gate, *Porta, ostium.*
Puerto, a port, a hauen, an entraunce betweene hils, *Portus.*
Pues, therfore, nowe, *Ergo, igitur.*
Puesta, a peece, *Tortio.*
Puestoque, although, *Quamuis.*
Puesto, put, placed, a standing, *Positus, statio.*

Puja, setting to sale, *Licitatio.*
Pujamiento, renting of a commoditie, buying by great, *Redemptio.*
Pujar, to rent a subsedie, to cheapen, to bid money, *Licitari, redimere.*
Pujança, puissance, *Potentia.*
Pujavante, a smithes buttris, *Scaber, botrax.*
Pujesigo, the middle finger, *Digitus medius.*
Pulga, a flea, *Pulex.*
Pulgar, the thumbe, *Pollex.*
Pulgada, an inche, *Vncia.*
Pulgaradas, bruising with the thumbe, *Pollicis contusio.*
Pulgoso, full of fleas, *Pulicosus.*
Pulgon, a worme that eateth vines, *Bruchus.*
Pullas, mocks, scofs, brabling, brawling, *Litigatio, dicteria, conuitia.*
Pulmon marino, a froth in the sea that giueth light, *Pulmo marinus.*
Pulmones, the lungs, *Pulmo.*
Pulpa, flesh without bones, *Pulpamentū.*
Pulpejo, the brawn of the hands or arms *Torus.*
Pulpito, a pulpit, *Pulpitum.*
Pulpo, a cuttle, *Polypus.*
Pulso, the pulse, *Pulsus.*
Punçar, to pricke, to pounce, *Pungere, sedicare.*
Punçadura, pricking, pouncing, *Punctura.*
Punçada, a pricke, *Punctum.*
Punçon, a bodkin, a pouncing yron, *Stilus, graphium.*
Punçoncico, a little bodkin, *Dimin. à punçon.*
Punicion, punishment, *Pœna, punitio.*
Punir, to punish, *Punire.*
Punta, the point of a weapon, *Cuspis, aculeus.*
Puntado, pointed, *Aculeatus.*
Puntada, a point, *Punctum.*
Puntar, to point, *Pungere.*
Puntal, a poste to vnderprop a house, *Sublicium.* (us.
Puntero, a marking yron, *Graphium, radi-*
Puntil-

Puntillazo, spurning with the feete, *Tedis ictus.*
Puntapie, *idem.*
Punto, a point, a moment, the size of a shoo a stitch, *Punctum, momentum, sumentum.*
Puñada, a blow with the fist, *Pugni ictus.*
Puño, a fist, *Pugnus.*
Puños, rufes, *Sinus.*
Puñal, a poynado, a dagger, *Pugio.*
Puñalada, a stabbe with a dagger, *Pugionis ictus.*
Puñado, a fist, *Pugnus.*
Pupilo, a pupill, *Pupillus.*
Puramente, purely, *Pure.*
Pureza, puritie, purenes, *Puritas.*
Purga, a purgation, *Purgatio, potio.*
Purgar, to purge, *Purgare, expiare.*
Purgacion, purging, *Purgatio, expiatio.*
Purgativo, that purgeth, *Purgatorius, piacularis.*
Purificar, to purifie, *Purificare.*
Puridad, puritie, *Puritas.*
Puro, pure, *Purus.*
Purpura, purple, *Purpura.*
Pusilanimo, weake harted, base minded, *Pusillanimis.*
Pusilanimidad, weakenes of heart, *Pusillanimitas.*
Puta, a whore, *Scortum, meretrix.*
Putañero, a whoremaster, *Scortator.*
Putanear, to follow whores, *Scortari.*
Putería, the stewes, *Lupanar.*
Puto, a ganymedes, *Cynædus.*
Puxavante, *vide,* Pujavante.
Puxo de vientre, griping in the belly, *Tenasmus, tormen.*

Q V A

Quaderno, fowerth, *Quartus.*
Quadra de casa, a square court *Atrium.*
Quadrar, to make square, to make fit, *Quadrare.*
Quadrada, squared, *Quadratus.*
Quadratura, squaring, *Quadratio.*
Quadrangula, a quadrangle, *Quadrangularis.*

Quadrante, a quadrant, *Vmbilicus, Gnomon.*
Quadrilla, a little companie of footemen, *Cohors.*
Quadril, the hip, *Coxendix.*
Quadro, a square, a squadron of soldiors *Quadratura, cohors.*
Quajado, crudded, congealed, *Coagulatus.*
Quajar, to crud, to congeale, *Coagulare.*
Quajamiento, crudding, congealing, *Coagulatio.*
Qual, which, *Qui, quis.*
Qualquier, whosoeuer, *Quicunque.*
Quando, when, *Quando.*
Quantas vezes, how often, *Quoties.*
Quantidad, quantitie, *Quantitas.*
Quanto, how much, *Quantum.*
Quantos, how many, *Quot.*
Quanto mas, howe much more, *Quanto plus.*
Quarenta, fortie, *Quadraginta.*
Quarto, the fourth, *Quartus.*
Quartel, a squadron of soldiors, a quarter of a campe, *Cornu exercitus.*
Quartago, a nagge, *Cantherius.*
Quarto, a peece of monie woorth fower marauedies, *Moneta genus.*
Quartilla, a three halfe penie peece, *Quarta pars realis.*
Quartal, a quarter, *Quadrantal.*
Quatro, fower, *Quatuor.*
Quatrocientos, fower hundred, *Quadringensi.*

Q V E

Que cosa, what, *Quid.*
Que, which, that, for, *Quod, quia.*
Quebrada de monte, the breach of a hill, a valley, *Faux, vallis.*
Quebrado, broken, *Fractus, ruptus, Herniosus.*
Quebrar, quiebro, to breake, *Frangere, rumpere.*
Quebradura, brenking, *Ruptura.*
Quebrantado, broken, *Ruptus.*
Quebrantador, a breaker, *Ruptor, fractor.*
Quebran-

Quebrantamiento,breaking,*Ruptio,fractio violatio.*
Quebrantar, to breake, *Frangere, violare.*
Quebranta huessos,a kinde of eagle,*Aquilæ genus,ossifragus.*
Quedar,to staie,to rest,to stand still,*Consistere,manere.*
Quedada,staying,resting,*Mansio.*
Quedo,still,quiet,*Quietus.*
Quemado,burned,*Vstus,ambustus.*
Quemadura,burning,*Combustio.*
Quemar, to burne,to blaste, *Vrere,siderare.*
Quema,burning,blasting,*Combustio,sideratio.*
Querella,a complaint,*Querela.*
Querelloso,complaining,*Querulus.*
Querellarse, to complaine,*Queri.*
Querer,quiero, to desire, to endeuour,to will,to loue, *Velle, cupere, optare, niti, amare.*
Querencia,loue,*Amor.*
Ques cosa y cosa,a ridle,*Aenigma.*
Queso,cheese,*Caseus.*
Question,a question,a quarrel,a controuersie, *Quæstio,lis.*
Quexa,a complaint,*Querela.*
Quexarse,to complaine,*Queri.*
Quexigo,a kinde of oke, *Quercus,ornus.*
Quexoso,complaining,*Querulus.*
Quexura, haste,instaunce, earnestnesse, *Festinatio.*

Q V I

Quiça,perhaps,peraduenture,*Forte.*
Quicial, quicio de puerta, hinges of a doore,*Cardo, nis.*
Quienquiera,whosoeuer,*Quicunque.*
Quien,who, he which, *Quis,qui.*
Quietamente,quietly,*Quietè.*
Quietar,to make quiet,*Pacare.*
Quieto,quiet, *Quietus.*
Quilate,the touch of gold, the finenesse, *Gradus auri.*
Quilatar,to touch, to trie gold, to make perfect or excellent, *Gradum explorare, perpolire.*

Quilla,the keele of a ship,*carina.*
Quinientos,fiue hundred,*Quingenti.*
Quiñon,a part,a portion,*Portio,pars.*
Quiñonero,a deuider,a partner,*Partitor, particeps.*
Quintal, an hundred weight, *Pondus centenarium.*
Quinterno, the number of leaues in printing being fiue to a letter, *Quinternio.*
Quinto,the fift,*Quintus.*
Quinze,fifteene, *Quindecim.*
Quitar, to take away, to withdraw, to remoue, to breake off, *Auferre, eripere, amouere.*
Quitado,taken away,*Ablatus,amotus.*
Quitamiento,taking away,*Ablatio.*
Quixada,a iawe,*Maxilla,mandibula.*
Quixar,*Idem.*
Quixones, bastard parsley or wilde cheruile,*Caucalis,scandix.*
Quixore, terces,armor for the thighes, *Femorale.*

R A

Rabaças,water parsley,*Sium.*
Rabadan, a shepheards boy, *Pastoris puer.*
Rabadilla de ave,the scut of a bird, the rumpe,*Vropygium,piga.*
Rabear, to wag the taile, *Caudam motitare.*
Rabel, an instrument called a rebecke, *Fidicula.*
Rabicano, an horse with a gray taile, *Equus cauda cana.*
Rabanos,radish,*Raphanus,radicula.*
Rabo,a taile,*Cauda.*
Rabo de puerco, maidenweede, *Peucedanum.*
Raça de sol,the sun beame,*Radius.*
Raça de paño, the place where cloth is foere or thinne,*Panni raritas.*
Racamenta, the parle of a ships yard,*Aplustre.*
Racion,a porcee,a portion,*Pars,portio.*
Racionero,a steward,*Dispensator.*

Raer

Raer raygo, **to ſhaue, to raſe, to blot,** *Radere, obliterare.*
Raedura, **ſhauing, raſing of wꝛiting,** *Ramentum, raſura.*
Raedera, **a raſer,** *Radula, raſorium.*
Raez, **eaſe,** *Facilis*
Raya, **a fiſh called a ray, a line, a ſtrake,** *Raia, linea, radius.*
Rayado, **lined, marked out, raſed, ſtroked out,** *Delineatus, raſus, ſignatus.*
Rayar, **to marke, to ſtrake out, to make beames as the ſunne,** *Delineare, ſignare, radiare.*
Rayo del ſol, **the ſunne beame,** *Radius.*
Rayo, **the ſpoake of a wheele, a flaſh of lightening,** *Radius, fulmen, coruſcamen.*
Rayola, **a raſer,** *Nouacula.*
Raydo, **raſed, ſhauen,** *Raſus.*
Raygar, **to take roote,** *Radices agere.*
Rayz, **a roote, a round head as of garlike, oinions, &c,** *Radix.*
Raja, **a chip, a lath,** *Aſtula, aſſula.*
Rajar madera, **to cut into laths, to hew out,** *In aſſulas diſſcindere.*
Rajuelas, **little chips,** *Aſſulæ.*
Ralo, **thinne,** *Rarus.*
Ralas vezes, **ſeldome,** *Raró.*
Ralear, **to make thinne,** *Rareſcere.*
Raleza, **ſeldomnes,** *Raritas.*
Raléa, **a race, an heritage of hoꝛſes,** *Genus.*
Ralero, **a ſieue to ſift with,** *Cribrum.*
Rallo, **a ſhauing iron,** *Scalprum, ſcobina.*
Rama, **a bough,** *Ramus.*
Ramada, **an arbour, a tent of boughes,** *Scæna.*
Ramal y ramon, **a bough,** *Ramus.*
Ramera, **a whoꝛe, a ſtrumpet,** *Meretrix.*
Ramo, **a bough,** *Ramus.*
Ramoſo, **full of boughes,** *Ramoſus.*
Rampojos, **the pꝛicks of bꝛiers,** *Tribuli, murex.*
Rampones, **caukes in a hoꝛſe ſhooe,** *Calcaneum ſoleæ equinæ.*
Rana, **a frog,** *Rana.*
Ranacuajo, **a little frog, a todpoole,** *Ranunculus, coagulum rubetæ.*
Rancio, **ruſtie, ranimiſh in ſmell,** *Rancidus.*

Rancioſo, **ruſtie, ful of rammiſhnes,** *Rancidus.*
Rancho, **a ranke, a rowe,** *Ordo, ſeries.*
Rancor, **rancoꝛ, hatred,** *Odium.*
Randa, **a net woꝛke, open woꝛke,** *Rete, reticulum.*
Rapar, **to ſhaue,** *Radere.*
Rapaz, **a ſoldiers boy, a waggiſh boy,** *Cacula.*
Rapacejos, **fringes,** *Laciniæ.*
Rapiña, **rapine,** *Rapina.*
Rapoſa, **a foxe,** *Vulpes.*
Rapoſuno, **pertaining to a foxe,** *Vulpinus.*
Raro, **ſeldome,** *Raró.*
Raſar medida, **to pare a meaſure, to ſtrike a meaſure,** *Hoſtire.*
Raſadura, **the ſtriking of a meaſure,** *Hoſtimentum.*
Raſero, **a ſtrike of a meaſure,** *Hoſtiorium.*
Raſcar, **to ſcrape,** *Scalpere.*
Raſcador, **a ſcraping toole,** *Scalptorium.*
Raſcadura, **ſcraping,** *Scalptura.*
Raſcuño, **a ſcratch,** *Scalptus.*
Raſcuñar, **to ſcratch, to ſcrape,** *Scalpere.*
Raſgar, **to teare,** *Lacerare.*
Raſgados ojos, **faire large eies,** *Buphthalmus.*
Raſgon, **a ſcratch, a ſcrape,** *Scalptura.*
Raſo, **plaine ſhaued, a plaine field, ſatten,** *Planities, ſericum raſum, planus, læuis.*
Raſpa, **a file, alſo an eare of coꝛne,** *Lima, ariſta.*
Raſpar, **to ſhaue, to pare, to fret, to file,** *Radere, limare.*
Raſtilla, **a card foꝛ flaxe,** *Raſtellum.*
Raſtillar, **to carde flaxe oꝛ hempe,** *Carminare.*
Raſtillado, **carded,** *Carminatus.*
Raſtrillo, **a little rake,** *Raſtellum.*
Raſtro, **an harrow, a ſtep, a trace, a ſent, the reſt, a rake,** *Crates, veſtigium, indagatio, oderatio, reliquum, raſtrum.*
Raſtrojo y reſtojo, **ſtubble,** *Stipula.*
Raſuras, **parings, ſhauings, dꝛoſſe, dꝛegs oꝛ lees of wine,** *Ramenta, fæx.*
Raſuras de cuba, **the raſing of the ſkin, which the ſurgeons make in boxing,** *Stigmon.*

Rata,

Rata, a part, a portion, *Rata portio.*
Rata, raton, a moufe, *Mus.*
Ratoncillo, a little moufe, *Mufculus.*
Ratonera, a moufe trap, *Mufcipula.*
Rato, a fpace, *Spacium.*
Ravano, reddifh, *Raphanus.*
Ravano gagifco, blacke helleboze, *Polyrhi-zon.*
Raveço, a wilde goate, *Oryx.*
Raudo, fwift, *Rapidus.*
Raudal, a fwift ftreame, *Profluens.*
Ravia, rage, madnes, *Rabies.*
Raviofo, mad, raging, *Rapidus, rabiofus.*
Raviar, to rage, *Lymphari, furere.*
Raviofamente, ragingly, *Rabidè.*
Razimo, a bunch of grapes, *Racemus, botrus.*
Razonable, reafonable, *Rationalis.*
Razonablemente, reafonably, *Rationabiliter.*
Razonamiento, reafoning, difcourfe, *Ratiocinatio, oratio, concio.*
Razonar, to reafon, *Ratiocinari.*
Razon, reafon, *Ratio.*

R E

Real, roiall, a campe, a riall of plate amounting to vj. pence, *Regalis, caftra, realis.*
Realengo, pertaining to the king, *Regius.*
Realmente, roially, indeed, *Regiè, reuera.*
Reatar, to binde againe, *Religare.*
Reatadura, binding againe, *Religatio.*
Reata, a binding againe, *Religaculum.*
Rebaño, a flocke of fheepe, *Grex.*
Rebañego, of the flocke, *Gregarius.*
Rebañar, to make a flocke, to gather together, *Gregare, congregare, congerere.*
Rebatar, to fnatch, to catch, *Arripere.*
Rebatado, fnatched, catched, *Arreptus.*
Rebato, a tumult, a fudden ftur, *Tumultus, feditio.*
Rebatina, a fcrambling, a muffe, a fudden fkirmifh, *Rapina, raptus, pugna tumultuaria.*
Rebatir, to beate backe, *Repercutere.*
Rebeço, a wilde goate of Barbarie, *Oryx.*
Rebelar, to rebell, *Rebellare.*
Rebellion, rebellion, *Rebellio.*
Rebelde, a rebell, *Rebellis.*

Rebellin, a platforme to lay ordinance on, *Balifarium, agger.*
Rebeldía, rebellion, *Rebellio.*
Rebentar, to breake in funder, to crake, *Crepare, vumpere.*
Rebentaçon, a breach, *Ruptus, crepitus.*
Rebezar, to keepe turne, *Viciffim aliquid agere.*
Rebezero, he that keepeth turne, *Viciffitudinarius.*
Reboçar, to wimple, to go with the face hidden, *Caput inuoluere.*
Rebidar, to renie, *Reduplicare.*
Rebite, a renie, *Reduplicatio.*
Rebivir, to reuiue, *reuiuefcere.*
Rebolar, to flie againe, *Reuolare.*
Rebolcar, to tumble, *Volutare.*
Rebolcadero, a poole to tumble in, *Volutabrum.*
Rebolver, to ouerturne, to rol vp, to turmoile, to difquiet, *Renoluere, inuoluere, mifcere.*
Rebolvedero, any thing turned ouer, *Inuolucrum.*
Rebolvedor, an ouerturner, a turmoiler, a difquieter, *Perturbator.*
Reboltofo, *Idem.*
Rebolton, a woorm that deftroieth vines, *Inuoluolus.*
Rebolvimiento, ouerturning, turmoiling, difquieting, *Perturbatio.*
Reboffar, to run ouer, to ouerflow, *Vndare, inundare.*
Reboffadura, ouerflowing, *Inundatio.*
Rebotar, to make dull, *Obtundere.*
Rebotado vino, dead wine, *Vappa.*
Rebotado, made dull, *Obtufus.*
Rebotadura, dulnes, *Hebetudo, obtufio.*
Rebuelto, cavallo rebuelto, ouerturning, turmoiling, difquietnes, a luftie doing horfe, *Volutatio, perturbatio, equus fternax.*
Rebufca, the leafing of corne, *Spicilegium, racematio.*
Rebuznar, to cric as an affe, *Rudere.*
Recabar y recaudar, to recouer, *Recuperare.*
Recaer, to fall againe, *Recidere.*
Recaydo, fallen againe, *Recidiuus.*

Recalcar,

Recalcar, to stuffe, to stop cliftes, to beate in, *Refercire, stipare, inculcare.*
Recalcadamente, thickly, fully, *Confertim.*
Recamar, to lace, to lay on with lace, *Vermiculare.*
Recamo, lacing wauie, *Vermiculatio.*
Recamado, laced, laied with lace, *Vermiculatus.*
Recamara, a wardrop, a dining chamber, *Vestiarium, conclaue.*
Recatarse, to be warie, to be circumspect, *Circumspicere.*
Recatado, wearie, circumspect, *Circumspectus.*
Recatamiento, warines, *Circumspectio.*
Recaton, the pike of a staffe, *Cuspis.*
Recaudar, to recouer, to procure, *Recuperare, exigere, procurare.*
Recaudador, a recouerer, *Recuperator, exactor.*
Recaudamiento, recouerie, *Recuperatio, exactio.*
Recaudo, a warrant, a letter of attorney, successe, *Rei cautio, successus.*
Reclamar, to call backe, *Reclamare.*
Reclamacion, calling backe, gainsaying, *Reclamatio.*
Reclamo, a call for birds, *Illex.*
Recobrar, to recouer, *Recuperare.*
Recobrador, a recouerer, *Recuperator.*
Recogedor, a gatherer, a taker vp, *Collector, receptor.*
Recoger, to gather vp, to take vp, to retire, to withdraw, *Recolligere, recipere.*
Recogimiento, gathering, withdrawing, *Collectio, receptus.*
Recogido, retired, gathered, withdrawen, *Collectus, receptus, qui se recepit.*
Recomendar, to recommend, *Commendare.*
Recomendacion, recommending, *Commendatio.*
Recomendado, recommended, *Commendatus.*
Recompensar, to recompence, *Compensare.*
Recompensacion, recompence, *Compensatio.*
Reconcentrado, vnited, *Vnitus.* (tio.
Reconciliar, to reconcile, *Reconciliare.*
Reconciliado, reconciled, *Reconciliatus.*

Reconciliador, a reconciler, *Reconciliator.*
Reconciliacion, reconciling, *Reconciliatio.*
Reconocer, to acknowledge, to biew, *Agnoscere, speculari.*
Reconocido, biewing, acknowledging, *Agnoscens, speculans.*
Reconocimiento, ouerlooking, acknowledging, *Agnitio.*
Recontar, to recount, to tell, *Narrare.*
Reconualecer, to recouer the health, *Conualescere.*
Recopilar, to compile, to gather out of bookes, *Compilare.*
Recopilado, gathered togither out of bookes, compiled, *Collectus.*
Recopilador, a compiler, *Collector.*
Recordar, to remember, to call to memorie, *Recordari.*
Recorrer, to run vnto, to run backe, *Recurrere.*
Recoser, to sowe againe, *Resuere.*
Recozer, to seethe againe, *Recoquere.*
Recrear, to recreate, *Recreare.*
Recreacion, recreation, *Recreatio.*
Recrecer, to increase, to grow, *Recrescere.*
Recrecimiento, increase, growing, *Incrementum.*
Recua, a droue of hogs, a heard of oxen, *Armentum, grex.*
Recuajo, frie of fish, *Oua piscium, coagulum piscium, cordulus.*
Recudir, to restore, to pay rent, *Reddere.*
Recudimiento, restoring, paying rent, *Redditio.*
Recuero, a muleter, *Agaso.*
Recuesto, the hanging of an hill, *Cliuus.*
Recuperar, to recouer, *Recuperare.*
Recuperable, recouerable, *Recuperabilis.*
Recuperacion, recouerie, *Recuperatio.*
Recular, to refuse, *Recusare.*
Reçagua, the rereward, *Tergum exercitus.*
Recebimiento, receit, intertainment, *Receptus, exceptio.*
Recebido, receiued, *Acceptus.*
Recebidor, a receiuer, *Acceptor, receptor.*
Recebir, cibo, to receiue, *Recipere.*
Recelarse, to feare, to take heede of, to suspect, *Timere, suspicari.*

V Recelo,

Recelo, feare, warines, suspition, *Metus, cautio, suspicio.*
Receptar, to receiue, *Recipere.*
Receptor, a receiuer, *Receptor.*
Rechaça, driuing backe, *Repulsio.*
Rechaçar, to driue backe, *Repellere.*
Reçongador, a murmurer, *Murmurator.*
Rechinar, to riue, to cracke, to make a shrill noise, *Diffindi, stridere, crepare.*
Red, a grate, a lettise window, a net, a caule, *Crates, transenna, rete, reticulum.*
Redero, a net maker, *Retiarius.*
Redezilla, a little net, *Reticulum.*
Redaño, the caule of a beast, the fat about the intrailes, *Omentum intestinorum.*
Redarguyr, to reproue, *Redarguere, refellere.*
Rededor, round about, *Circumcirca.*
Redemir, dimo, to redeeme, to raunsome, *Redimere.*
Redemido, redeemed, *Redemptus.*
Redemcion, redemption, *Redemptio.*
Redemptor, a redeemer, *Redemptor.*
Redoblar, to double, *Reduplicare.*
Redoble, double, *Duplex.*
Redomado, *vide* Refalçado.
Redoma, a biall of glasse, *Ampulla vitrea.*
Redondear, to make round, *Rotundum facere.*
Redondez, roundnes, *Rotunditas, connexitas.*
Redondo, rounde, *Rotundus, orbicularis, connexus.*
Redrojo, a new bud, *Regerminatio.*
Redropelo, against the haire, *Pilus aduersus.*
Reduzimiento, bringing backe, reducing, *Reductio.*
Reduzido, brought backe, *Reductus.*
Reduzir, duzgo, to reduce, to bring back, *Reducere.*
Refalçado, malicious, *Malitiosus.*
Referir, fiero, to report, *Narrare, referre.*
Refinar, to refine, *Reconcinnare, repolire.*
Resitolero, a gentleman vsher, *Atriensis.*
Reflorecer, to florish againe, *Reflorescere.*
Reforçar, to reinforce, *Vires de inuegro addere.*

Reformar, to reforme, to redresse, *Reformare.*
Reformador, a reformer, *Reformator.*
Reformacion, a reformation, *Reformatio.*
Refran, a prouerbe, *Adagium.*
Refregar, to rub againe, to weare, to fret, *Refricare, terere, atterere.*
Refregadura, fretting, *Attritio.*
Refregamiento, fretting, *Refricatio.*
Refregado, fretted, *Refricatus.*
Refrescar, to renewe, to refresh, *Renouare, Refrigerare.*
Refrenar, to refraine, *Refrenare, coercere.*
Refriega, a skirmish, *Pugna tumultuaria, velitatio.*
Refrigerio, a refreshing, *Refrigerium.*
Refugio, a refuge, *Refugium.*
Refunsuñar, to mumble, to mutter, to murmur, *Murmurare, obmurmurare.*
Regaçar, to tucke vp the clothes, *Suffarcinare, succingere.*
Regaçado, tucked vp, *Suffarcinatus.*
Regaço, the lap, *Gremium.* (*factio.*
Regalamiento, melting, thawing, *Liquefactio.*
Regalar, to cocker, to make much of, to melt, *Liquefacere, indulgere.*
Regalo, gentle blage, deintines, *Humanitas, indulgentia.*
Regaladamente, gentelie, curteouslie, deintlie, *Delicate, indulgenter.*
Regalillo, a womans gloue, a fauor, *Symbolum amatorium.*
Regaliza, lickorise, *Glycyrhiza.*
Regar, riego, to water, *Adaquare.*
Regadio, regadura, watering, *Adaquatio.*
Regadizo, wateric, *Irriguus.*
Regaton, a pedler, a broaker, a pincher in buying, a huckster, *Minutus mercator, inflitor, promercator.*
Regatonear, to sell pedlerie ware, to play the huckster, *Promercari, cauponari.*
Regatonia, pedling, buying of small wares, *Promercatura.* (*gere.*
Regañar, to grinne as a dog, *Frendere, ringere.*
Regañon, a grinning fellowe, also the north winde, *Ringens, boreas.*
Regoldar, gueldo, to belke, *Eructare.*
Regibado, crookebacked, *Gibbosus.*

Regir,

Regir,rijo,**to gouerne**,*Regere*.
Regimiento,**rule,regiment,gouernment** *Regimen,gubernatio*.
Regidor,a **gouernor**, *Rector,gubernator*.
Registro,a **register**, *Registrum*.
Registrar,**to register**,*Registro ascribere*.
Region,a **countrie,a region**,*Regio*.
Regla,a **rule**,*Regula*.
Regolfo,a **whirle poole**,*Refluxus,verter*.
Regorgido,regordido,**swollen,full**,*Tumidus,refertus*.
Regularmente,**by rule**,*Regulariter*.
Regular,**perteining to a rule**,*Regularis*.
Regueldo,**belking**,*Eructatio*.
Regozijo,**ioye**,*Gaudium*. (*habitus*.
Regozijado,**feasted**, *Conuiuio acceptus,laute*
Regozijar,**to reioice,to solace**,*Gaudere,delectare*.
Reguera,**a path betweene beds in a garden**,*Semita*.
Reguizar,**to be stiffe**,*Rigere*.
Rehazer, **to renewe,to rallie**, *Reficere,instaurare*.
Rehazio,**renewed,rallied**,*Refectus,instauratus*.
Rehazimiento,**a renewing**,*Refectio*.
Rehecho,**strongly set in the bodie, bigge limmed**,*Robustus*.
Rehen,**a pledge,an hostage**,*Obses,pignus*.
Rehenchir, **to fill againe**,*Replere*.
Rehollar,**to tread vnder the feete**,*Recalcitrare, pessundare*.
Rehundir, **to drench againe**, *Submergere, remergere*.
Rehusar,**to refuse**,*Recusare*.
Rehusamiento,**refusing**,*Recusatio*.
Rey,a **king**,*Rex*.
Reyna,a **Queene**,*Regina*.
Reynar,**to reigne**,*Regnare*.
Reyno,a **kingdome**, *Regnum*.
Reyr,rio,**to laugh**,*Ridere*.
Reja, a **plough , an yron grate**, *Aratrum vomer,crates*.
Rejalgar,**poison, arsenicke,or ratsbane**, *Venenum,aconitum,arsenicum*.
Rejo de cinta, **the claspe, or buckle of a girdle**,*Fibula*.
Relamer,**to licke againe**,*Relingere*.

Relampago,**lightening**,*Fulgur*.
Relampaguear,**to lighten**,*Fulgurare*.
Relatar,**to relate,to tell an historie**, *Referre,narrare*.
Relacion,**recounting,telling**, *Relatio,narratio*. (*rator*.
Relator,a **recounter,a teller**, *Relator*, *narRelavar,**to washe againe**,*Relauare*.
Relentecer,**to waxe weake, to relent, to yeeld**,*Dedere,lentescere*.
Relexes,**the knobs, the bunches in a table or stone**, *Tubercula in re alioqui plana*.
Relicario,**a relicke boxe**,*Reliquiarium*.
Relieve,**embossed workes**, *Toreumata, vide Relexes*.
Religion,**religion**,*Religio*.
Religiosamente,**religiouslie**,*Religiose*.
Religioso,**religious**,*Religiosus*.
Reliquario,**a relicke boxe**,*Reliquarium*.
Reliquias,**relickes**,*Reliquiæ*.
Relinchar, **to neigh as a horse**,*Hinnire*.
Relinchido,**the neighing of a horse**, *Hinnitus*.
Relox, **a clocke,a diall, an hower glasse**, *Clepsydra,horologium*.
Relumbrar,**to lighten,to shine**, *Lucere*.
Reluzir,**to shine**,*Lucere*.
Rellanado,**any thing plained**,*Planus*.
Relleno,**a pudding**,*Fartum*.
Rellenar,**to fill,to stuffe**,*Refercire*.
Rellenado,**filled**, **stuffed**,*Refertus*.
Remanchado de nariz, **flat nosed**, *Simus*.
Remador,**a rower with oares**,*Remex*.
Remadura,**rowing**,*Remigatio*.
Remar,**to rowe**,*Remigare*.
Remanecer,**to remaine**, *Remanere*.
Remaniente,**remaining**,*Remanens*.
Remanso de rio,**an eddie**,*Refluxus,vertex*.
Rematar,**to sum vp**,*In summam redigere*.
Remate, **the sum of an accompt,the end, the toppe**, *Summa,finis,cacumen*.
Remedar,**to imitate**,*Imitari*.
Remedamiento,**imitating**, *Imitatio*.
Remediar,**to cure,to remedie**, *Mederi, curare*.
Remedio,**remedie**,*Remedium*.
Remembrar,**to remeber,to put in minde**, *Meminisse, recordari*.

Remembrança, remembraunce, *Memoria, commemoratio.*
Remendar, to mende, *Resarcire.*
Remendado, mended, *Resartus.*
Remendon, a botcher, a cobler, *Sartor veteramentarius.*
Remessar, to tear the haire, *Comā discindere.*
Remiendo, a patch, a peece, *Assumentum.*
Remero, a rower, a gally slaue, *Remex igis.*
Remirar, to ouerlooke, to looke on, *Respicere.*
Reminecencia, remembrance, *Commemoratio.*
Remitir, to remit, *Remittere.*
Remitido, remitted, *Remissus.*
Remo, an oare, *Remus.*
Remoçar, to be yong againe, *Repueraf- (cere.*
Remocecer, *idem.*
Remojar, to wet againe, *Macerare, remollire.*
Remojo, wetting, steeping, *Maceratio.*
Remolcar, to towe with a ship bote, *Remulcare.*
Remolino, a whirle winde, a whirlpoole, the turning of the haire, *Vertex, turbo.*
Remolinado, turning round, as a whirlpoole, *Verticosus, in turbinis morem conuolutus. (agi.*
Remolinarse, to be turned round, *Circum-*
Remondar, to make cleane, *Emundare.*
Remontar, to go vp the hill, to run, *Collem subire.*
Remorder, to byte againe, *Mordere.*
Remordimiento, remorse, *Morsus conscientiæ.*
Remostecerse el vino, to waxe mustie, *Mustescere.*
Remover, to remoue, *Remouere.*
Rempuxar, to push forward, *Impellere.*
Rempuxon, a thrust, *Impulsus.*
Remudar, to change, *Mutare.*
Remunerar, to reward, *Remunerare.*
Remuneracion, rewarding, *Remuneratio.*
Ren, o reñon, the raines of the backe, *Ren.*
Renacer, to be borne againe, to spring againe, *Renasci.*
Rendajo, a iay, *anis imitatrix.*

Rendir, rindo, to yeld, *Dedere se.*
Rendido, yelded, giuen vp, *Deditus.*
Renegar, to denie, to forsake the fayth, *Denegare, apostatam esse.*
Reniego, apostasie, *Apostasia.*
Renegado, an apostata, *Apostata.*
Renglada o reñonada, fat about the loins *Seuum iuxta renes.*
Renglon, a line, *Linea.*
Renombre, a surname, *Cognomen.*
Renouacion, renewing, *Renouatio.*
Renouar, to renewe, *Renouare.*
Renovero y renuevo de arbel, the bud of a tree, *Germen.*
Renovero, a vsurere, *Fanerator.*
Renuevo, vsurie, *Fænus.*
Renta, rent, *Redditus, prouentus.*
Rentar, to let to farme, to hire, *Locare, conducere.*
Rentero, he that letteth to farme, he that hireth, *Locator, conductor.*
Renunciacion, renouncing, *Abdicatio.*
Renunciar, to renounce, *Abdicare.*
Renzilla, a braule, a brabble, *Rixa, iurgium.*
Renzilloso, brabling, brawling, *Rixosus.*
Reñir, riño, to chide, *iurgare, litigare.*
Reo, accused, *Reus.*
Reparar, to repaire, to amend, to defend, *Defendere, reficere, inflaurare.*
Reparo, reparation, a bulwark, a defence *Refectio, vallum, defensio.*
Repartir, to deuide, *Partire.*
Repartimiento, deuision, parting, *Partitio.*
Repastar, to feede, *Pascere.*
Repecho, the side of a hill, *Cliuus aduersus.*
Repelo, the pilling of the nailes, *Reduuia.*
Repentino, sudden, *Repentinus.*
Repentimiento, repentance, *Pænitentia.*
Repentirse, to repent, *Pænitere.*
Repetir, pito, to repeate, *Repetere.*
Repicar, to sounde as bels, to iangle, to clatter, *Crepitare.*
Repique, a noise, as the iangling of bels, *Cymbalorum crepitus.*
Replicar, to reply, *Replicare.*
Replicacion,

Replicacion,replying,*Replicatio.*
Repollo de berça, the top of a colewoꝛt, *Cima.*
Reportamiento, ſettling of himſelf, quieting, *Sedatio.*
Reportarſe, to quiet himſelfe, to ſettle himſelfe, *Sedare, quieſcere.*
Reportar, to wꝛite, oꝛ ſet in a booke, *Reponere.*
Reportado, quieted, ſetled, *Sedatus, Quietus.*
Reportorio, a memoꝛiall, *Repertorium.*
Repoſar, to reſt, to repoſe, *Quieſcere.*
Repoſo, reſt, repoſe, *Quies.*
Repoſado, quiet, pacified, *Quietus, Pacatus.*
Repoſtero, a carpet, a couerlet, a ſewer *Stragulum, inſtrator.*
Repueſto, laied vp, *Repoſitus.*
Reprehender, to repꝛoue, *Reprehendere.*
Reprehenſion, repꝛoofe, *Reprehenſio.*
Reprehendido, repꝛoued, *Reprehenſus.*
Repreſada agua, a ſtanding water, *Aqua ſtagnans.*
Repreſar, to ſtop a water courſe, *Siſtere aquam.*
Repreſentar, to repꝛeſent, to play a comedie, *Repreſentare, imitari, exhibere, agere.*
Repreſentacion, repꝛeſenting, *Repreſentatio.*
Repreſentador, a repꝛeſenter, a plaier of comedies, *Actor.*
Repremir, to repꝛeſſe, to keepe downe, *Reprimere.*
Reprochar, to repꝛoch, to repꝛoue, *Exprobrare.*
Reproche, repꝛoch, repꝛoofe, *Conuitium, opprobrium.*
Reprovar, to repꝛoue, to diſallow, *Reprobare.*
Reprovacion, repꝛoofe, repꝛobation, *Improbatio.*
Reprovado, repꝛoued, *Reprobus, improbus.*
Repudiar, to diuoꝛce, *Diuorſum facere, dimittere.*
Repudio, diuoꝛce, *Repudium.*
Repugnar, to ſtriue againſt, *Repugnare.*
Repugnancia, ſtrife, *Lis, contentio.*

Repulga, a hem in cloth, *Limbus, fimbria.*
Reputar, to repute, to account of, *Reputare, æſtimare.*
Reptar, *vide* Repurar.
Reputacion, reputation, *Aeſtimatio, exiſtimatio.* (*procari.*
Requebrar, quiebro, to make loue, *ambire.*
Requebrado, a louer, *Amator, procus.*
Requebrador, a maker of loue, a wooer, *Procus.*
Requerir, quiero, to require, to warne, *Admonere, requirere, poſtulare.*
Requerimiento, requiring, *Poſtulatio, requiſitio.*
Requeſta, a requeſt, *Poſtulatum, requiſitio.*
Requeſtada, requeſted, *Rogatus.*
Requeſtar, to requeſt, *Poſtulare, rogare.*
Requeſon, whey cruds, *Coagulum ſeri.*
Requiebros, loue toies, *Geſtus amatorij.*
Res, a thing, the game in hunting, *Res, pecus.*
Reſabio, an ill taſte, *Malus guſtus.*
Reſabido, a taunting fellow, a pꝛeſumptuous man, *Subſannator, arrogans.*
Resbalar, to ſlip, to ſlide, *Relabi.*
Resbaladero, a ſlipperie place, *Labina, lapſus.*
Resbaloſo, ſlipperie, *Labilis.*
Reſcatar, to redeeme, to raunſome, *Redimere.*
Reſcate, raunſome, *Redemptio.*
Reſcolde, whot imbers, *Fauilla.*
Reſcrevir, to wꝛite againe, *Reſcribere.*
Reſeña, a muſter, *Cenſus.*
Reſerver, to reſerue, *Seruare.*
Resfriarſe, to waxe colde, *Refrigeſcere.*
Resfriado, cold, cooled, *Refrigeratus.*
Reſidir, to be reſident, *Reſidere.*
Reſignar, to reſigne, *Reſignare.*
Reſignacion, reſignation, *Reſignatio.*
Reſina, roſin, *Reſina.*
Reſinoſo, full of roſin, *Reſinoſus.*
Reſiſtir, to reſiſt, *Reſiſtere.*
Reſiſtencia, reſiſtance, *Reſiſtentia.*
Reſolgar, ſuelgo, reſollar, ſuello, to bꝛeath, *Reſpirare.*
Reſolver, ſuelvo, to reſolue, *Reſoluere.*
Reſolucion, reſolution, *Reſolutio.*

Reſonar,

Resonar, to resound, *Resonare.*
Respectar, to respect, to regard, *Respicere.*
Respecto, respect, regard, *Respectus.*
Respectado, respected, regarded, *Veneratus, respiciendus.*
Respigon, the pilling about the nayles, *Redunia.*
Respirar, to breath, *Respirare.*
Respiracion, breathing, *Respiratio.*
Respiradero, a breathing place, *Spiraculum.*
Resplandecer, to shine, *Resplendescere.*
Resplandeciente, shining, *Resplendens.*
Resplandor, brightnes, *Splendor.*
Responder, to answer, *Respondere.*
Repuesta, an answer, *Responsio.*
Resquebrajarse, to chap, to cleaue in two, *Hiare, hiscere.*
Resquebrajadura, a chap, a cliffe, *Rima, hiatus.*
Resquebrajado, cleft, chapped, *Rimosus, hiulcus.*
Resquicios, chaps, clifts, *Rima, fissura.*
Restañar, o restriñir, to stench, to stop, *Sistere, restinguere.*
Restar, to remaine, to arrest, *Restare, sistere.*
Restaurar, to renewe, *Renouare, instaurare.*
Restriñidora cosa, stiptike, binding, *Stipticus.*
Restituir, tuyo, to restore, *Reddere, restituere.*
Restituydo, restored, *Restitutus.*
Restitucion, restitution, *Restitutio.*
Resto, the rest, *Residuum.*
Restribar, to straine, to enforce, *Eniti.*
Restriñir, to restraine, *Restringere, coercere.*
Resvalar, *vide* Resbalar.
Resultar, to resolue, to redounde, *Decernere, redundare.*
Resuellos, breathing, *Respiratio.*
Resumir, to begin againe, *Iterare.*
Resurtir, to rebound, *Resilire.*
Resuscitar, to raise, *Resuscitare.*
Resuscitado, raised, *Resuscitatus.*
Resurrection, resurrection, *Resurrectio.*
Retablo, a painted table, *Tabula picta.*
Retajar, to cut short off, *Rescindere, curtare.*
Retajado, cut off, *Curtatus.*

Retal, the cutting off, *Curtatio.*
Retáma, a kinde of binding shrubbe or broome, *Genista.*
Retardar, to delay, to stay, *Remorari.*
Retener, to hold, *Retinere.*
Retencion, holding, *Retentio.*
Retesar las tetas, to strout out, *Turgescere, distendi.*
Retesamiento, strouting out, *Distensio.*
Retiñir, to sound as a bell, *Tinnire.*
Retinte, the ringing of monie, *Tinnitus.*
Retificar, to make right, *Rectum facere.*
Retirar, to retire, *Recipere se.*
Retoçar, to tickle, *Titillare, lasciuire.*
Retoço, tickling, wantonnes, *Titillatio, lasciuia.*
Retoçon, a wanton, *Lasciuus.*
Retoño, the bud of a tree, *Regerminatio.*
Retoñecer, to bud out, *Regerminare.*
Retorcer, tuerço, to wreathe, to bende backe, *Retorquere.*
Retorcido, wreathed, bent backe, *Retorsus.*
Retorcedura, bending backe, *Retortio.*
Retorcimiento, wreathing, *Retorsio.*
Retorcedura, *Idem.*
Retorica, rhetoricke, *Rhetorica.*
Retor, a rhetorician, *Rhetor.*
Retornar, to returne, *Redire, reciprocare.*
Retornado, returned, *Rediens.*
Retorno, againe, a returne, *Iterum, reditus, reditio.*
Retraer, traygo, truxe, to withdraw, to retire, *Retrahere, recipere se.*
Retraydo, withdrawen, retired, *Quirecepit se.*
Retraymiento, withdrawing, retreate, a closet, *Receptus, conclaue.*
Retratar, to portrait, *Delineare.*
Retrato, the portraiture, *Delineatio.*
Retronar, trueno, to resound, *Resonare.*
Retuerto, bent backe, *Retorsus.*
Revanada, a shred of cloth, a slice of bread *Segmentum panni, frustum panis.*
Revanar, to cut, to shred, *Discindere.*
Revelar, to reueale, *Reuelare.*
Revelacion, reuealing, *Reuelatio.*
Revelado, reuealed, *Reuelatus.*

Revender,

Revender, to sell againe, *Reuendere.*
Revenir, to returne, *Redire.*
Reverberar, to beate backe, *Reuerberare.*
Reverberacion, beating backe, *Reuerberatio.*
Reverencia, reuerence, *Reuerentia.*
Reverenciar, to reuerence, *Reuereri.*
Reverendo, reuerend, *Reuerendus, venerandus.*
Reverdecer, to waxe greene, *Reuirescere.*
Reves, backward, contrarie, *Tranfuerfus, obliquus.*
Revesar, to ouerturne, *Euertere.*
Revesado, traviesso, froward, *Peruerfus.*
Revestir, visto, to cloath againe, *Reueftire.*
Reuma, the rheume, *Rheuma.*
Reutador, an accuser, a challenger, *Accufator, prouocator.*
Revocar, to reuoke, to cal backe, *Reuocare.*
Revolucion, reuolution, *Reuolutio.*
Rexa y rexal, a lettise window, a grate, *Tranfenna, clatrus.*
Rexada, lettised, grated, *Clatratus.*
Rezar, to pray, to recite, to meditate, *Orare, recitare, meditari.*
Rezador, he that praieth, *Orator.*
Rezagado, the last, *Poftremus.*
Rezentar, to make fresh, *Recentare.*
Rezental, fresh, *Recens.*
Reziente, fresh, new, *Recens.*
Rezien, newly, lately, *Recens.*
Rezio, hard, difficult, strong, lusty, *Durus, difficilis, robuftus.*
Reziura, hardnes, difficulty, *Duritas, robur.*
Rezma de papel, a reame of paper, *Quinquagenarium scapus.*
Rezmilla, the top of a mans yard, *Glans, balanus.*
Rezno, a tike, *Ricinus.*

R I

Ria, a riuers mouth, a port, *Portus, oftium.*
Riatillo, a little streame, *Amniculus.*
Ribaço, a high banke, *Ripa.*
Ribera, the banke, the shore, *Littus, ripa.*
Ricamente, richly, *Opulenter.*
Ricazo, wealthie, *Opulentus, locuples.*
Rico, rich, *Diues.*

Riço, a tuffe of feathers, *Crifta.*
Ridiculo, ridiculous, *Ridiculus.*
Riel, a kind of iewell, *Gemma, monile.*
Riendas, the raines of a bridle, *Lora.*
Riezgo, danger, *Periculum.*
Risa, wringing, grinning, fretting, a braule, *Litigatio, pugna, rictus.*
Risar, to grin, to braule, *Iurgare, ringere.*
Risador, he that fretteth, he that chafeth, *Rixofus.*
Rigor, rigour, *Rigor.*
Rigoroso, rigorous, *Rigidus.*
Rigorosamente, rigorously, *Rigidè.*
Rima, rimero, a heape, *Cumulus, agger.*
Rima, a rime, *Rythmus.*
Riña, chiding, a braule, *Lis, rixa.*
Rincon, a corner, *Angulus.*
Riñones, the raines of the backe, *Renes.*
Rio, a riuer, *Riuus.*
Ripia, a lath, a single, *Affula, afferculus, scandula.*
Ripiar pared, to lath, to rob a wall, *Affulis munire.*
Riqueza, riches, *Diuitiæ.*
Risa, laughter, *Rifus.*
Riftra, a rope of oinions, *Reftis ceparum.*
Risueño, a laughing fellow, a ieering fellow, *Ridiculus, ringens.*
Risco, a crag, a rocke, *Rupes.*
Rito, a cuftome, a rite, *Ritus.*
Rixa, fretting, chasing, *Rictus, rixa.*
Rixoso, fretting, chasing, *Rixofus, iracundus.*
Riza, a scattering, a putting to flight, *Profligatio.*

R O

Robar, to rob, *Compilare, diripere.*
Robado, robbed, *Compilatus.*
Robador, a robber, a theefe, *Latro.*
Robo, theft, robberie, *Latrocinium.*
Roble, an oke, *Robur.*
Robledal, an oke groue, *Quercetum.*
Roblezo, strong as an oke, *Robuftus.*
Robusto, strong, *Robuftus.*
Roca, a rocke, *Rupes scopulus.*
Roçar, to plucke vp, *Runcare.*
Roça, ground new grubbed, *Terra aberruncata.*

Roçador,

Roçador, a grubbing toole, *Runcina.*
Roçagante vestido, a long side garment, *Vestis defluens.*
Rocin, a horse, a gelding, *Equus castratus, cantherius.*
Rocío, dew, *Ros oris.*
Rociado, bedewed, *Roscidus.*
Rociar, to bedew, to sprinkle, *Rorare.*
Rodapies, a settle about a bed, *Sessibulum.*
Rodar, to wheele about, to go round, *Rotare.*
Rodaja, a rowell of a spur, a dance called the round, *Stimulus, trochlea, saltatio orbicularis.*
Rodajo, a pullie, *Trochlea.*
Rodovallo, a turbut, *Rhombus.*
Rodear, to go round, to compasse, *Rotare, circuire.*
Rodeado, compassed, *Lustratus.*
Rodela, a buckler, *Pelta, parmula.*
Rodéo, a compasse, a circuit, *Lustratio, circuitus.*
Rodetes, rolls for the head, *Cesticillus.*
Rodezno, a pullie, *Trochlea.*
Rodilla, a knee, a wad to put on the head to carie on, *Genu, cesticillus.*
Rodrigon para vid, the prop of a vine, *Ridica.*
Rodrigar, to prop vp, *Ridicare.*
Roer, roygo, to gnaw, *Rodere.*
Roedura, gnawing, *Corrosio.*
Rofian, a ruffian, a whooremaster, *Scortator, leno.*
Rofianería, bauderie, whoredome, *Lenocinium, scortatio.*
Rofianear, to play the whoremaster, *Machari.*
Rogar, ruego, to aske, to desire, to pray, *Rogare.*
Roydo, gnawed, *Corrosus.*
Roydo de gentes, *vide* Ruydo.
Rojo, abrun headed, *Subrufus.*
Rollete de muger, *vide* Rodete.
Rollizo, round, *Rotundus.*
Rollo, any round thing, a pibble stone, a gallowes, a gibbet, *Rotundus, cochlea, patibulum, crux, calculus.*
Romance, the Castilian toong, *Sermo latinus castellanus.*

Romançar, to turne into Spanish, *In Hispanicum vertere.*
Romadizarse, to take the rheume, *Rheumate grauari.*
Romadizo, the rheume, *Rheuma.*
Romaza, patience, *Rumex.*
Rombon, a stopper, *Obturatorium.*
Romero, rosemary, a pilgrim, *Rosmarinus, peregrinus.*
Romería, a pilgrimage, *Peregrinatio.*
Romo, flat nosed, *Simus.*
Romper, to breake, *Rumpere.*
Rompido, broken, *Ruptus.*
Rompimiento, breaking, *Ruptura.*
Rompidamente, brokenly, *Abruptè.*
Ronca, a partisan, *Bipennis.*
Roncar, to snort, to rout, *Stertere.*
Ronco, snorting, hoarse, *Raucus, sternens.*
Ronquedad, hoarsenes, *Raucedo.*
Ronquera, *Idem.*
Ronquido, hoarsenes, snorting, *Roncus.*
Roncear, to be idle or lazie, *Desidere, inertem esse.*
Roncero, a flatterer, a glosing fellow that by his faire speech goeth about to set debate, *Adulator, sycophanta.*
Ronzería, flatterie, setting at debate, *Adulatio, sycophantia.*
Roncha, the pricke of a nettle, the marke of a stripe, *Vibex.*
Rondo, the circuite of a libertie, *Pomœrium.*
Rondar, to go round about, *Lustrare, circuire.*
Ronda, the round, a watch, *Circuitus, lustratoriæ excubiæ.*
Roña, a scab, *Scabies.*
Roñoso, scabbed, *Scabiosus.*
Ropa, a garment, *Vestis.*
Ropilla, a cassocke, *Tunicula.*
Ropanegero, a broaker, *Institor.*
Ropero, a tailor, *Sutor vestiarius.*
Ropon, a gowne, a rug gowne, *Toga, toga gausapina.*
Roque de axedrez, the rooke at chesse, *Turris scaccaria.*
Roquete, a bishops rochet, *Superpellicium.*
Rosa, a flower, a rose, *Rosa.*

Rosado,

Rosado, rose coloured, *Roseus.*
Rosal, a rosebanke, *Rosarium.*
Rosa montes, Pionie, *Peonia.*
Rosa sylvestre, o gavança, sweet brier, eglantine, *Cynosbatos.*
Rosario, the picture of the crosse, *Rosarium*
Rosca de husillo, reeling of thred, the lying of a snake round togither, *Spira, spirula.*
Rosquete, a pancake, *Lagenum.*
Rosquilla, a clue of thred, *Globulus.*
Rostrituerto, looking awry, *Toruus.*
Rostro, the face, the visage, *Vultus, facies.*
Rotura, breaking, a breach, *Ruptura.*
Rosuz, lickorise, *Glycyrhizum.*
Roxo, yealow, *Rutilus, flauus.*

R V

Rubi, a rubie, *Carbunculus.*
Rubrica, the marke on a booke, *Rubrica.*
Ruciada, a charge of shot, *Impressio.*
Rúcio, rucio rodado, grey, dapple grey, *Cæsius, scintulatus.*
Ruda, rew, *Ruta.*
Rudo, rude, *Rudis, tardus.*
Rudamente, rudely, *Ruditer, crassè.*
Rudeza, rudenes, *Hebetudo.*
Rueca, a distaffe, *Colus.*
Rueda, a wheele, *Rota.*
Ruego, intreatie, request, prayer, *Rogatio.*
Rufian, *vide* Rofian.
Ruga, a wrinkle, *Ruga.*
Rugido, a noise, a crying, *Rugitus.*
Rugimiento de tripas, the crying of the guts, *Rugitus ventris.*
Rugir, to rore, *Rugire.*
Rugoso, full of wrinkles, *Rugosus.*
Ruibarbo y ruipontico, rubarbe, *Raponticum.*
Ruydo, a noise, an affray, *Fremor, strepitus, pugna.*
Ruypontigo, centaurie, *Centaurea maior.*
Ruyponces, wilde rapes, *Rapunculus.*
Ruyn, naught, leud, *Malus, nequàm.*
Ruyseñor, a nightingale, *Luscinia.*
Rumbo, a stopple, *Obstructorium.*
Rumiar, to chew the cud, *Ruminare.*
Rumor, a rumor, a noise, *Rumor.*

Rusticamente, rudely, clownishly, *Rustikè.*
Rustico, rude, clownish, *Rusticus.*
Rustiqueza, rusticidad, rudenes, clownishnes, *Rusticitas.*
Ruvia, madder, *Rubia.*
Ruvio, red, *Rufus, fuluus.*
Ruvion, red wheate, *Triticum subrubeum.*

S A

Sabado, saturday, *Dies sabbati.*
Saber, se, supe, sabre, to knowe, to sauor, *Scire, sapere.*
Sabiamente, wisely, *Sapienter.*
Sabio, wise, skilfull, cunning, *Sapiens, sciens, peritus.*
Sabidora, knowen, knowing, *Conscius, præscius.*
Sabiduría, wisedome, knowledge, *Sapientia, scientia.*
Sabido, knowen, *Cognitus.*
Sabidor, he that knoweth, *Cognitor.*
Sabina, sauine, *Sabina.*
Sabor, sauour, taste, *Sapor.*
Saborear, to make sauorie, *Saporem addere.*
Sabroso, sauorie, *Sapidus.*
Sabuessos, a blood hound, *Plaudus canis.*
Saca, a sacke, *Saccus.*
Sacabuche, a sagbut, *Tuba ductilis.*
Sacaliña, a dart, *Aclis idis.*
Sacar, to draw out, to pull out, to take out, *Eruere, eximere, extrahere, depromere.*
Sacerdote, a priest, *Sacerdos.*
Sacerdocio, priesthood, *Sacerdotium.*
Sacerdotissa, a shee priest, *Sacerdos.*
Sachar o escardar la tierra, to harrow, to rake, *Sarrire.*
Sachador, a harrower, *Sarritor.*
Sachadura, harrowing, *Sarritio.*
Saco, a sacke, the sacking of a towne, *Saccius, direptio.*
Sacomanos, light horsemen, scoutes, *Excubiæ, leuis armaturæ equites.*
Sacramento, the sacrament or an oth, *Sacramentum.*
Sacre, a hauke called a sacre, also a peece of ordinance called a sacre, *Hyerax.*
Sacrificar, to sacrifice, *Sacrificare.*

X   Sacrificio,

S A   S A

Sacrificio, **facrifice**, *Sacrificium.*
Sacrilegio, **facrilege**, *Sacrilegium.*
Sacrilego, **a church robber**, *Sacrilegus.*
Sacriftan, **a fexteine**, *Aedituus.*
Sacriftania, **a fextcines office, or a chappell**, *Aeditui munus, facellum.*
Sacudir, **to shake, to shake off**, *Difcutere, excutere.*
Sacudimiento, **shaking off**, *Excuffio.*
Sacudido, **shaken off**, *Excuffus.*
Sacudidamente, **briefly**, *Breuiter.*
Saeta, **an arrow**, *Sagitta.*
Saetera, **a lope hole for ordinance**, *Cauum balistarium.*
Sagaz, **wife, circumfpect, sharpe witted**, *Sagax.*
Sagacidad, **sharpnes of wit**, *Sagacitas.*
Sagazmente, **wittily**, *Sagaciter.*
Sage, **a diuine, a wife man, a foothfaier**, *Sagax, præfagus.*
Sagittario, **the figne Sagittarius**, *Sagittarius.*
Sagrado, **holy**, *Sacer.*
Sagrario, **a fanctuarie**, *Sanctuarium, afylum, adyta.*
Sahornado de fudor, **filthie with fweate**, *Sudore diffluens.*
Sahornamiento, **filthines of fweate**, *Subluuies.*
Sahorno, *Idem.*
Sahumado, **perfumed**, *Suffitus.*
Sahumador, **a perfuming pan, or a perfumer**, *Suffitorium, fuffitor.*
Sahumar, **to perfume**, *Suffire.*
Sahumerio, **perfume**, *Suffitus.*
Sahumadura, **the perfuming**, *Suffitio.*
Sayal, **a caffocke**, *Sagum.*
Saya, **a womans coate**, *Tunica muliebris.*
Sayalero, **a tailor**, *Sutor vestiarius.*
Sayn, **fat**, *Sagina, adeps.*
Sayncre, **daintie meate, pellets to cram with**, *Saginula.*
Saynar, **to fat, to feed fat**, *Saginare.*
Sayon, **a hangman**, *Carnifex, tortor.*
Sayete, **a caffocke**, *Sagum.*
Sal, **falt**, *Sal.*
Salar, **to falt**, *Salire.*
Salacio, **a faufage**, *Lucanica.*

Salada, **a falat of hearbs**, *Acetaria.*
Salado, **falted, wittie**, *Salitus, falfus, facetus.*
Saladura, **falting**, *Salfura, falitura.*
Salamanquefa, **a falamander**, *Salamandra.*
Sala, **a hall, a banket**, *Aula, epulum.*
Salagarda, **a trap, an ambush**, *Infidiæ.*
Salario, **wages**, *Stipendium.*
Salchicha, **a faufage**, *Lucanica.*
Salero, **a faltfeller**, *Salinum.*
Salida, **a falie, a going out, an efcape**, *Exitus, egreffio, euafio.*
Salir, **to falie, to go foorth, to efcape**, *Erumpere, exire, euadere.*
Salidizo, **the iuttie of an houfe, the bearing out of a wall**, *Proiecta.*
Salinas, **falt pits**, *Salinæ.*
Salinero, **a falt maker**, *Salinator.*
Salitre, **niter**, *Nitrum.*
Salitrofo, **full of niter**, *Nitrofus.*
Salitral, **a place to dig or make niter**, *Nitraria.*
Saliua, **fpittle**, *Saliua.*
Salivofo, **full of fpittle**, *Saliuofus.*
Salmifta, **a pfalmift**, *Pfalmifta.*
Salmo, **a pfalme**, *Pfalmus.*
Salmon, **a falmon**, *Salmo.*
Salmorejo y falmuera, **pickle for fifh, brine**, *Muria, falfugo.*
Salobre, **fower, fauorie**, *Amarus, falfus.*
Salpicaduras, **dashings**, *Confperfiones.*
Salpicar, **to dash with durt**, *Confpergere.*
Salpicado, **dashed with durt**, *Confperfus.*
Salprefa, **brine**, *Muria.*
Salfa, **fauce**, *Condimentum.*
Salfero, **falfereta, a faucer**, *Acetarium.*
Saltar, **to leape**, *Saltare.*
Saltear, **to affaile, to rob**, *Inuadere, latrocinari, compilare.*
Salteador, **a robber, an affailer**, *Inuafor, latro, compilator.*
Salterio, **a pfalter**, *Pfalterium.*
Salto, **a leape, an effault, a robberie, a forreft**, *Saltus, inuafio, latrocinium, nemus.*
Saltero, **a forefter**, *Saltuarius.*
Salud, **health**, *Salus.*
Saludable, **wholfome**, *Salutaris.*
Saludar, **to falute**, *Salutare.*

Saludable

Saludablemente, wholesomly, *Salubriter.*
Saludador, a saluter, a charmer, *Salutator, incantator.*
Salutacion, a salutation, *Salutatio.*
Salva, a taste, a salutation, *Gustus, salutatio.*
Salvadera, a dust boxe, *Puluere feruando pixis.*
Salvador, a sauiour, *Saluator.*
Salvado, bzan, *Furfures.*
Salvage, sauage, wilde, *Syluestris, ferus.*
Salvamente, safely, *Securè.*
Salvamiento, sauing, *Salutatio.*
Salvar, to saue, *Saluum facere.*
Salvo, safe, except, *Saluus, excepto.*
Salvo conducto, safe conduct, *Fides publica.*
Salvia, sage, *Saluia.*
Salze, a willow, *Salix.*
Salvonor, a close stoole, *Latrina, cacabunda.*
Sanable, curable, *Sanabilis, curabilis.*
Sanamente, soundly, *Sanè.*
Sana munda yerva, a gilloflower, *Gariophillata.*
Sanar, to heale, *Sanare.*
Sano, whole, sound, *Sanus.*
Sandia, a kinde of melon, *Melonum genus.*
Sandio, a foole, *Stultus.*
Sandalos, sandals, pantofles, *Sandalium.*
Sanear, to satisfie, to make good, *Satispræstare, satisdare.*
Saneado, satisfied, *Cui satisfactum est.*
Saneamiento, satisfying, *Satisdatio.*
Sangluto, the yeske, *Singultus.*
Sangostar, to streighten, to binde, *In angustias coger*.
Sangrar, to let blood, *Venam incidere.*
Sangrador, a blood letter, *Venæ incisor.*
Sangradera, a toole to let blood, a pipe or trench to let out water, *Scalpellus, Emissarium.*
Sangraza, a bloodie place, *Locus sanguine & tabe diffluens.*
Sangre, blood, *Sanguis.*
Sangriento, bloodie, *Sanguineus.*
Sangria, letting blood, *Venæ incisio.* (*tare.*
Sangrentar, to defile with blood, *Cruentare.*
Sangrelluvia, bleeding, bloodie fixe, *Sanguinis profluuium.*

Sanguaza, blood and matter togither, *Sanies.*
Sanguisuela, a blud sucker, *Hirudo.*
Sanidad, health, *Sanitas.*
Saña, wrath, furie, rage, *Ira, iracundia, odium.*
Sañudo, wrathfull, furious, *Iracundus.*
Santero, an hermite, *Eremita.*
Santidad, holines, *Sanctitas.*
Santificar, to sanctifie, *Sanctificare.*
Santificacion, sanctifiyng, *Sanctificatio.*
Santificador, a sanctifier, *Sanctificator.*
Santiguar, to blesse, *Sanctificare, signare se cruce.*
Santo, holie, *Sanctus.*
San Pablo, saint Paule, *Sanctus Paulus.*
Sapo escuerço, a toade, *Bufo.*
Saquear, to sacke, *Diripere.*
Saqueado, sacked, *Direptus.*
Saqueador, a sacker, *Direptor.*
Saquito, a little sacke, *Sacculus.*
Saquillo, a little bag, *Idem.*
Saráo, a hall to daunce in, *Atrium.*
Sarampion, a tetter, *Impetigo.*
Sargal, serge, *Linostema.*
Sargenta, a kinde of weapon like an halberd, *Teli genus.*
Sargo, a kinde of fish, *Sargus.*
Sardina, a little pilcherd, a sardine, *Halecula.*
Sarmiento, a vine branch, *Sarmentum, palmes, pampinus.*
Sarna, a scab, a sore, *Scabies.*
Sarnoso, scabbie, *Scabiosus.*
Sarta de higos, a rope of figs, *Resticula ficuum.*
Sartal de cuentos, a cast of counters, *Linea calculorum.*
Sarten, a frying pan, *Sartago.*
Sartar, to put on a string, *Filo inserere.*
Sastre, a tailor, *Sutor vestiarius.*
Sassifragia, saxifrage, *Saxifragia.*
Satyra, a satyre, *Satyra.*
Satyrion, satyrion, *Orchis.*
Satisfazer, to satisfie, *Satisfacere.*
Satisfacion, satisfaction, *Satisfactio.*
Savalo, a kinde of fish, *Pisciculi genus.*
Sevañon o fricras, kibes, *Pernio.*

X 2   Saiico,

Saúco, an elder tree, *Sambucus.*
Sauzegatillo, an ofier, *Salix viminalis.*
Sauze, a willowe, *Salix.*
Sauzedal, a willow bed, *Salictum.*
Savanas, sheetes, *Lodices linteæ.*
Saxifragua yerva, saxifrage, *Saxifragia.*
Sazonar, to season, to ripen, *Maturare.*
Sazon, season, *Tempestivitas.*
Sazonado, seasoned, *Tempestivus.*

S C

Scamonea, scamonie, *Scamonium.*
Scota, the sheade, *Funis nauticus.*
Scopetina, spittle, *Sputum.*

S E

Seca, a kernell in the armeholes, drouth, *Glandula sub alis, siccitas.*
Secaces, friendes, followers, *Clientes, amici.*
Secar, to dry vp, *Siccare.*
Seco, dry, *Siccus.*
Secretario, a secretarie, *à Secretis.*
Secretamente, secretly, *Secretò.*
Secreto, secret, *Secretus, arcanus.*
Secrestar, to sequester, *Sequestrare.*
Secresto, sequestration, *Sequestratio.*
Secura, drouth, *Siccitas.*
Secrestracion, *vide* Secresto.
Sed, aver sed, thirst, to be drie, *Sitis, sitire.*
Seda, a haire, a silke thred, *Seta, bombyx.*
Sedal, a fishing line, *Linea piscatoria.*
Sedeña, *Idem.*
Sedadera, the finest of the silke, *Sericum.*
Sedero, a silkeman, *Bombycinus artifex.*
Sediente, thirstie, *Siticulosus.*
Segar siego, to cut, to reape, to mowe, *Secare, metere.*
Segador, a mower, a reaper, *Messor.*
Segazon, haruest, *Messis.*
Seguir, sigo, to follow, *Sequi.*
Seguidor, a follower, *Sequax, assecla.*
Seguimiento, following, *Sectatio, insequutio.*
Segun, according, as, *Secundum, iuxta.*
Segundo, the second, *Secundus.*
Segur, an axe, a battle axe, *Securis, bipennis.*
Segureja, an hatchet, *Securicula.*

Seguramente, surely, securely, *Securè, tutò.*
Seguro, safe, *Securus, tutus.*
Seguron o hache de armas, a battle axe, *Bipennis.*
Seguridad, safetie, *Securitas.*
Segurar, to make safe, *Securum facere.*
Seys, sixe, *Sex.*
Seys cientos, sixe hundred, *Sexcenti.*
Sellar, to seale, *Obsignare, sigillare.*
Sellador, a sealer, *Obsignator, sigillator.*
Sello, a seale, *Sigillum.*
Selladura, sealing, *Obsignatio, sigillatio.*
Semana, a weeke, *Septimana.*
Semanera cosa, weekely, *Hebdomaticus.*
Semanero, one hyred by the weeke, *Septimanarius operator.*
Semblante, like, semblable, shewe, countenance, *Pariter, Vultus, species.*
Sembrar, to sowe seed, or corne, *Seminare, serere.*
Sembrado, sowen, a corne fielde, *Seminatus, aruum.*
Sembrador, a sower, *Seminator.*
Sembradura, sowing, *Seminatio, satio.*
Semejar, to liken, to resemble, *Assimilare.*
Semejança, resemblance, likenesse, *Similitudo.*
Semejante, like, an image, *Similis, instar, simulachrum.*
Semejantemente, likewise, in like maner, *Similiter.*
Sementera, a sowing season, *Satio.*
Sementar miento, to sowe, *Seminare.*
Semental cosa, that which is sowen, *Sementinus.*
Semiente, seede, *Semen.*
Semola. *vide* Acemite.
Sen, senie, *Senia.*
Senado, a senate, *Senatus.*
Senador, a senator, *Senator.*
Senda, a pathe, *Semita.*
Sendilla, a little pathe, *Semita angusta.*
Sendero, a path, *Trames.*
Sendos, euery one, one by one, *Singuli.*
Seno, a crooke, the bosome, *Sinus.*
Sensible, sensible, *Sensibilis.*
Sentar, siento, to sit, *Sedere.*
Sentado, sitting, *Sedens.*

Sentarse

Sentarſe, en cuclillas, to cowre downe, *Coſſim ſedere.*
Sentencia, a ſentence, an opinió, a iudgement, *Sententia, opinio, decretum, iudicium.*
Sentenciar, to iudge, *Sententiam ferre, iudicare.*
Sentenciado, iudged, *Iudicatus.*
Sentina, a ſincke, a pumpe in a ſhip, *Sentina, nautea.*
Sentido, fœling, ſence, *Senſus.*
Sentimiento, ſenſe, fœling, *Senſus.*
Sentir, ſiento, to be grieued, to fœle, to iudge, to perceiue, *Dolere, ægrè ferre, ſentire, cenſere.*
Senzillamente, ſingle, *Simpliciter.*
Senzillo, ſingle, ſimple, plaine, pure, *Simplex.*
Senzillez, ſinglenes, *Simplicitas.*
Señal, a ſigne, an enſign, a marke, a ſhew, an earneſt penny, *ſignum, vexillum, nota, indoles, arrhabo.*
Señalar, to marke, to note, to point at, *Signare, notare, indicare.* (*gius.*
Señalado, excellent, eſpeciall, *Inſignis, egregius.*
Señaladamente, excellentlie, eſpeciallie, *Egregiè, eximiè.*
Seña, a becke, a watchworde, a nodde, a wincke, a token, *Nutus, teſſera, nictus, ſignum.*
Señero, alone, ſolitarie, *Solus, ſolitarius.*
Señeramente, ſolitarilie, *Solitariè.*
Señora, a ladie, a miſtreſſe, *Domina, hera.*
Señor, a maſter, a lorde, *Herus, dominus.*
Señoría, a lordſhip, a title of honor, *Dominatio.*
Señorear, to rule, to gouerne, *Dominari gubernare.*
Señoreado, ruled, gouerned, *Subditus, gubernatus.*
Señoreador, a ruler, *Gubernator.*
Señorio, lordſhip, *Dignitas, dominatus.*
Señoril, lordly, *ad dominatum pertinens.*
Señorilmente, lordlike, *Imperioſè, honorificè.*
Señuelo, a lure, *Illicium.*
Sepulchro, a graue, *Sepulchrum.*
Sepultar, to burie, *Sepelire.*
Sepultura, a buriall, *Sepultura.*

Sepulturero, a digger of graues, *Buſticeta.*
Sequedad, drouth, drines, *Siccitas.*
Sequero, drie by nature, that cannot be watered, *Siccaneus.*
Sequillas, kernels in the necke, *Glandula.*
Ser, ſoy, era, fuy, ſeré, to be, *Eſſe, ſum, fui.*
Serafin, a ſeraphim, *Seraphim.*
Sera, a baſket, *Fiſcina, corbis.* (*penum.*
Serapino, a kinde of gum or roſen, *Sagapino.*
Serena, a mermaid, *Syren.*
Sereno, the euening dewe, the blaſting aire, *Ros veſpertinus, ſideratio.*
Serenar, to make cleere, *Serenare.*
Serenidad, cleerenes, *Serenitas.*
Sereno, cleere, *Serenus, ſudus.*
Sermon, a ſermon, *Concio.*
Sermonear, to preach, *Concionari.*
Seron, *vide Sera.*
Serpa, a branch of a vine, *Sarmentum.*
Serpentino, a ſtone called a ſerpentine, *Draconites lapis.*
Serpiente, a ſerpent, *Serpens, anguis.*
Serpol, wilde time, pellamountaine, *Serpillum.*
Serrano, hillie, *Montanus.*
Serania, a hillie countrie, *Montoſa regio.*
Serva, a fruite called a ſeruice, *Sorbum.*
Serval, a ſeruice tree, *Sorbus.*
Servenda, late ripe, *Serotinus.*
Servicio, ſeruice, *Seruitium.*
Servidor, a ſeruant, a cloſe ſtoole, a trey, *Seruus, cliens, miniſter, ſcaphium, trulla.*
Servidumbre, bondage, *Seruitus.*
Servil, ſeruile, ſlauiſh, *Seruilis.*
Servilla, a clowte, *Pannus linteus.*
Servilleta, a table napkin, *Linteolum, mantile.*
Servir, ſiervo, to ſerue, *Seruire, miniſtrare.*
Seſſar, to ceaſſe, *Ceſſare.*
Seſſenta, threeſcore, *Sexaginta.*
ſeſito, little wit, *Ingeniolum.*
Seſgo, calme, quiet, deepe, *Placidus, quietus, Profundus.*
Seſmo, the ſixte, *Sextus.*
Seſo, braine, wit, ſence, *Cerebrum ſenſus, ingenium.*

Seſudo,

Sesudo, senfible, witty, *Senfatus, ingeniofus.*
Sestear, to passe the heate of the day, *Meridiari.*
Sesteadero y sesteador, a sommer house, *Aestiua orum.*
Seta, a sect, *Secta.*
Setenta, seauentie, *Septuaginta.*
Setecientos, seauen hundred, *Septingenti.*
Setenas, the seauenth, *Septima, septuplum.*
Setenar, to punish by the seauenth, *Septuplo multare.*
Setenal, of seauen yeeres olde, *Septennis.*
Setiembre, September, *September.*
Setimo, the seauenth, *Septimus.*
Seto, a hedge, *Sepis, septum.*
Setro, a scepter, *Sceptrum.*
Seueramente, seuerelie, *Seueriter.*
Seueridad, seueritie, *Seueritas.*
Seuero, seuere, *Seuerus.*
Seuo, tallow, *Seuum.*
Seuoso, full of tallow, *Seuosus.*
Sexo, sexe, *Sexus.*

S I

Si, if, yea, *Si, etiam.*
Siempre, alwaies, *Semper.*
Siempreviua, sengreene, *Aizous.*
Sien, the temples of the head, *Tempus.*
Sierpe, a serpent, *Serpens.*
Sierra, a hill, a mountaine, a sawe, *Collis, mons, serra.*
Siervo, a seruant, *Seruus.*
Sierva, a maid seruant, *Ancilla.*
Siesta, heate of the sommer, *Aestus.*
Siesso, a close stoole, *Sedes, cacabulum.*
Siete, seauen, *Septem.*
Sieteñal, of seauen yeeres old, *Septennis.*
Siete en rama, seauen leaued grasse, *Heptaphyllon.*
Siguiente, following, *Sequens.*
Siglo, an age, *Sæculum.*
Signar, to signe, to seale, *Signare, sigillare.*
Signatura, signing, *Signatio.*
Signo, a signe, *Signum.*
Significar, to signifie, *Significare.*
Significacion, signification, *Significatio.*
Silaba, a sillable, *Syllaba.*

Silencio, silence, *Silentium.*
Silla, a seate, a chaire, a stoole, a saddle, *Sedes, cathedra, sedile, sella.*
Silleta, a little stoole, *Subsellium.*
Sillero, a stoole maker, a sadler, *Sedilis faber, sellarius, stragularius.*
Silo, a garner, *Granarium, annonarium.*
Silvo, hissing, *Sibilus.*
Silvar, to hisse, *Sibilare.*
Silvestre, of the wood, *Syluestris.*
Silva, a wood, *Sylua.*
Simar, a dungeon, a deepe pit, *Ergastulum, barathrum.*
Simiente, seede, *Semen.*
Simonia, symonie, *Symonia.*
Simoniaco, he that vseth symonie, *Symoniacus.*
Simular, to faine, to dissemble, *Simulare.*
Simulador, a fainer, a dissembler, *Simulator.*
Simuladamente, dissemblingly, *Simulate.*
Simple, simple, *Simplex.*
Simpleza, simplicitie, *Simplicitas.*
Simplemente, simply, *Simpliciter.*
Sino, if not, *Nisi.*
Sin, without, *Sine, absque.*
Sincel, a grauing toole, grauen worke, *Calum, cælatura.*
Sincelado, graued, carued, *Cælatus.*
Sincelar, to graue, to carue, *Cælare.*
Sindicado, iudged, *Iudicatus.*
Siniestro, the left, *Sinister.*
Sirga llevar barcos a la sirga, to drawe with a rope, *Trahere.*
Sirguero, a drawer of a boat with a rope, *Tractor.*
Sirguerito, a goldfinch, *Acanthis, carduelis.*
Sirgo, silke twist, *Sericum.*
Siringa, siringe, a spout, *Clistere, sipho.*
Sirviente, a seruant, *Seruus, minister.*
Sisa, an assise, solder for gold, *Census, pondus, decretum, santerna, mensura.*
Sitia, a stoole and a cushion, *Sedile cum puluino.*
Sitio, scituation, seate, siege laid to a towne, *Situs, obsidio.*
Sitiar, to besiege, to seate himselfe, *Obsidere, sedem figere.*

So,

S O

So, vnder, *Sub, infra.*
Sobaco, the arme holes, *Ala.*
Sobacar, Sobarcar, to trusse vp, *Suffarcinare.*
Sobajar, to moulde dow, to grope, *Subigere, palpare.*
Sabaquina, stinche of the armeholes, *Hircus.*
Soberado, a sollar, a loft, *Tabulatum, contignatio.*
Soberadar, to lofte, *Tabulare, contignare.*
Soberamente, soueraignely, from aboue, *Supremè supernè, desuper.*
Soberano, soueraigne, *Supremus.*
Sobervia, pride, *Superbia.*
Soberviamente, prowdely, *Superbè.*
Sobervio, prowde, *Superbus.*
Sobornal, surplus in measure, *Auctuarium.*
Sobornar, to suborne, *Subornare.*
Sobra, surplus, to much, *Nimium, superatio.*
Sobrar, to passe, to surpas, to be to much *Excedere, excellere, superesse.*
Sobrado, excellent, passing, superfluous, a lofte, a parlor, a dining chamber, *Excellens, immodicus, superfluus, coenaculum, tabulatum.*
Sobre, vpon, aboue, *Super, supra.*
Sobre nombre, a surname, *Cognomen.*
Sobrescrivir, to write vpon, *Superscribere.*
Sobrescripto, a superscription, *Superscriptio.*
Sobrepujar, to excell, *Excellere.*
Sobrepelliz, a surplice, *Superpellitium.*
Sobreponer, to put vpon, *Superimponere.*
Sobrestante, standing ouer, *Superstans.*
Sobresalido, impatient, rashe, *Impatiens, temerarius.*
Sobresalto, a sudden passion, *Passio subita.*
Sobreropa, an vppergarment, *Vestis superior.*
Sobreseer, to sit on, to surcease, *Supersedere.*
Sobrevenir, to come vpon, *Superuenire.*
Sobr evista armadura, *vide* Bavera.

Sobrina, a nece, *Neptis ex fratre vel sorore.*
Sobrino, my brothers sonne, *Nepos ex fratre, vel sorore.*
Socarrar, to iest, to mock, to singe, *Subsannare, amburere.*
Socarran, the caues of a house, *Subgrunda.*
Socavar, to digge vnder, *Cauare.*
Socolor, by pretence, vnder colour, *Praetextu.*
Socorrer, to succor, *Succurrere.*
Socorro, succor, *Auxilium.*
Socrosio, a medecine, *Medicina.*
Sofrenar, to refraine, *Refrænare.*
Sofrenado, refrained, *Refrænatus.*
Soga, an halter, *Restis.*
Sojuzgar, to subdue, *Subijcere, subdere.*
Sol, the sun, *Sol.*
Solazar, to solace, *Oblectare.*
Solar, perteining to the sun, a flore, to paue, to make a flore, *Solum, tabulatum, pauimentare.*
Solana, a sunnie place, *Solarium, apricum.*
Solado, flored, *Tabulatus.*
Solano, the easte winde, *Oriens.*
Solamente, onely, *Solummodo.*
Solapar, to hide, to conceale, *Celare.*
Solapado, hidden, concealed, *Celatus.*
Solaz, solace, pleasure, *Solatium.*
Soldan, a Souldan, *Sultanus.*
Soldada, paiment, wages, *Stips, stipendium.*
Soldado, a soldior, *Miles.*
Solda y sonda, a sounding plummet, *Bolis, idis.*
Soldado, souldered, *Ferruminatus, consolidatus.*
Soldar, to soulder, *Ferruminare, consolidare.*
Soldadura, souldering, *Ferruminatio.*
Soledad, lonenesse, solitarines, *Solitudo.*
Soleno, solemne, *Solennis.*
Solenemente, solemnlie, *Solenniter.*
Solenidad, solemnitie, *Solennitas.*
Soler, suelo, to be woont, *Solere.*
Solicitamente, carefully, *Sollicitè.*
Solicitar, to sollicite, *Sollicitare.*
Solicito, carefull, *Sollicitus.*
Solicitud, carefulnes, diligence, *Sollicitudo.*

Soliman,

Soliman, Mercurie fublimate, *Argentum viuum fublimatum.*
Solitario, folitarie, *Solitarius.*
Soliviar, to releeue, *Subleuare.*
Solo, alone, onely, *Solus, folum.*
Sollar, fuello, to blowe, *Spirare, anhelare.*
Sollamar, to feare, to burne off haires, to fcorch, *Amburere.*
Sollo, fturgeon, *Sturio.*
Solloços, fighes, *Singultus.*
Solloçar, to fighe, to fob, *Singultire.*
Soltar, fuelto, to loofe, to fet loofe, *Soluere, dimittere.*
Soltero, a fingle man, *Cælebs.*
Soltador, a loofer, an expounder of dremes or ridles, *Solutor, coniector.*
Soltería, a fingle life, *Cælibatus.*
Soltura, loofing, deliuering, *Solutio, dimiſſio.*
Somas, brown bread, courfe bread, *Panis furfuraceus.*
Sombra, fhadow, *Vmbra.*
Sombrajo, a fhadowie place, *Vmbraculum.*
Sombra hazer, to fhadow, *Obumbrare.*
Sombrerera, butter burre, *Petafites.*
Sombrero, a hat, *Galerus.*
Sombrio, fhadowy, darke, *Vmbrofus, opacus.*
Somero, the higheſt, *Summus.*
Someter, to fubmit, to put vnder, *Submittere.*
Sometido, fubmitted, *Submiſſus.*
Somo, vpon, *Super.*
Somorgujo, ducking, diuing, a diedapper, *Vrinatio, vrinatrix.*
Somorgujar, to ducke, to diue, *Vrinari.*
Somorgujador, a diuer, *Vrinator.*
Son, a founde, *Sonus.*
Sonada, an acte much fpoken of, *Facinus.*
Sonable, that may be founded, *Sonabilis.*
Sonaja, y fonajeras, a kinde of muficall inftrument, *Sonalium.*
Sonar fueno, fonar las narizes, to found, to blowe the nofe, *Sonare, nares emungere.*
Sonda, a founding plummet, *Bolis.*
Sonido, a founde, *Sonitus.*
Sonoro, founding, *Sonorus.*
Soñor, fueño, to dreame, *Somniare.*
Soñoliento, fleepie, *Somnolentus.*

Sopa, a fop, *Offa.*
Sopear, to fop, to put vnder the feete, *Offas intingere, Peſſundare.*
Soplar, to blowe, *Flare, fpirare.*
Soplo, the breath, *Flatus, fpiritus.*
Soplodora, that may be blowen, *Flatilis.*
Soporifero, that bringeth fleepe, *Soporifer.*
Soportar, to fupport, *Sufferre.*
Sordedad, deafenes, *Surditas.*
Sordecer, to be deafe, *Surdefcere.*
Sordo, deafe, *Surdus.*
Sortear, to caft lots, *Sortiri.*
Sorver, fuervo, to fup vp, *Sorbere.*
Sorvible, that may be fupped vp, *Sorbilis.*
Sorva, a feruice fruite, *Sorbum.*
Sorvo, fupping vp, *Sorbitio.*
Sorvito, a fip, *Sorbitiuncula.*
Sorze, a rat, *Sorex.*
Sofedad, vnfauerines, *Infulfitas.*
Soflayo, athwart, a floope, *Ictus tranfuerfus.*
Sofo, vnfauerie, *Infulfus.*
Sofpecha, fufpition, *Sufpicio.*
Sofpechar, to fufpect, *Sufpicari.*
Sofpechofamente, fufpitioufie, *fufpitiosè.*
Sofpechofo, fufpitious, *Sufpitiofus.*
Sofpirar, to figh, *Sufpirare.*
Sofpiro, fighing, *Sufpirium.*
Soffacar, to feduce, to deceiue, to vndermine, *Seducere, imponere, fupplantare.*
Soffegar, fiego, to pacifie, to quiet, *Sedare, Pacare.*
Soffegado, pacified, quiet, *Pacatus, fedatus.*
Soffegadamente, quietly, *Pacatè quietè.*
Soffiego, quietneſſe, *Quies, tranquillitas.*
Softener tengo, to fuftcine, *Suftinere.*
Softenido, fufteined, *Suftentatus.*
Softituyr, tuyo, to fubftitute, *Subftituere.*
Softenimiento, fufteining, *Suftentatio.*
Sota, the knaue at cardes, *Nebulo.*
Soterraño, a vault vnder ground, *Crypta.*
Soterrar, to burie, *Defodere.*
Sotilmente, fubtillie, *Subtiliter.*
Sotileza, fubtiltie, *Subtilitas.*
Sota, a hedge, *Seps.*

Sotoviento,

Sotaviento, the lee side, *Sub vento.*
Sovar, y sovajar, to knead dowe, to beate with the hands, *Subigere.*
Sovadura, y sovajadura, kneading of dow, *Subactio.*
Sovina, a pin for bourds, a swallow taile to ioyne timber, *Subscus.*

S T
Straça, papel de straça, waste paper to binde ware, *Carta emporetica.*

S V
Suave, swœte, *Suauis.*
Suavemente, swœtely, *Suauiter.*
Suavidad, swœteneſſe, *Suauitas.*
Subdito, a subiect, *Subditus.*
Subida, the going vp, *Ascensus.*
Subido, loftie, *Superbus, altus.*
Subir, to goe vp, *Subire, ascendere.*
Subiente, going vp, *Ascendens.*
Subitamente, suddenly, *Subitò.*
Subito, sudden, *Subitus.*
Sublimar, to sublimate, *Sublimare.*
Suceder, to succœde, *Succedere.*
Suceſſor, a succeſſor, *Succeſſor.*
Suceſſiuo, succeſſiue, *Succeſſiuus.*
Suceſſion, succeſſion, *Succeſſio.*
Suceſſo, succeſſe, *Succeſſus.*
Sudar, to sweate, *Sudare.*
Sudario, a handkercheef, *Sudarium.*
Sudadero, a sweating place, *Sudatorium.*
Sudito, a subiect, *Subditus.*
Sudor, sweate, *Sudor.*
Suegro, the wiues father, *Socer.*
Suegra, the wiues mother, *Socrus.*
Suela, the sole of a shoe, *Solea.*
Suelda, comferie, *Consolida.*
Sueldo, pay, wages, *Stipi, stipendium, merces.*
Suelo, a floore, the bottome, *Solum, pauimentum.*
Sueltamente, freely, lightly, nimbly, *Soluté, celeriter.*
Suelto, loose, free, nimble, quicke, luſtie, *Solutus, liber, agilis, celer, alacer, impiger.*
Sueño, ſleepe, a dreame, *Somnus, somnium.*
Sueño ſuber, a kinde of sowning ſleepe, *Corodæus somnus.*

Suero, wheye, *Serum.*
Suerte, echar ſuertes, lot, chaunce, to caſt lots, *Sors, casus, sortiri.*
Suez, base, filthie, naughtie, *Sordidus, fædus, malus.*
Suficiente, sufficient, *Sufficiens.*
Sufre, brimſtone, *Sulfur.*
Sufrimiento, ſufferaunce, *Patientia.*
Sufrido, patient, *Patiens, Aequanimis.*
Sufrible, toilerable, *Tollerabilis.*
Sufrir, to ſuffer, *Pati, tolerare.*
Sugeto, subiect, *Subiectus, subditus.*
Sugecion, ſubiection, *Subiectio.*
Sugetaiſe, to be subiect, *Subijci.*
Sugetar, to make subiect, *Subijcere.*
Sugoso, full of iuyce, *Succidus.*
Sujuſgar, *vide* Sojuſgar.
Suyo, his, *Suus.*
Sulcar, to make furrowes, *Sulcare.*
Sulco, a forrow, *Sulcus.*
Sulfoncte, a match with brimſtone, *Sulphuratum.*
Suma, a summe, *Summa.*
Sumar, to summe vp, *Summare.*
Sumario, the groſſe summe, the effect, *Summarium.*
Sumir, to ouerwhelme, to drench, *Mergere. (ſus.*
Sumido, ouerwhelmed, drenched, *Submerſus.*
Summamente, eſpecially, excellently, *Summé. (lautitiæ.*
Sumptuoſidad, sumptuouſneſſe, *Sumptus.*
Sumptuoso, sumptuous, *Sumptuosus, lautus.*
Sumptuosamente, sumptuously, *Sumptuosé, superbé, lauté.*
Superfluamente, ſuperfluouslie, *Superfluè.*
Superfluidad, ſuperfluitie, *Superfluitas.*
Superfluo, ſuperfluous, *Superfluus.*
Suplimiento, ſupplie, *Supplementum.*
Suplir, to ſupplie, *Supplere.*
Suplicar, to intreate, to beſeech, *Supplicare.*
Suplicacion, intreatie, beſeeching, *Supplicatio.*
Surgir, to ariſe, *Surgere.*
Surzir, to mende, to botch, to stitch vp, *Sarcire.*
Surzidor, a mender, a botcher, *Sartor.*

Surzi-

Surzidera, a woman botcher, *Sarcinatrix.*
Suspender, to suspend, *Suspendere.*
Suspenso, doubtfull, *Dubius, suspensus.*
Suspension, doubt, *Dubitatio.*
Suso, vp and downe, *Sursum, deorsum.*
Sussurrar, to murmur, *Susurrare.*
Sustancia, substance, *Substantia.*
Sustancial, substantiall, *Substantialis.*
Sustentar, to sustaine, to proppe vp, to maintaine, to nourish, *Sustinere, fulcire, tueri, alere.*
Sustentamiento, sustenance, sustaining, holding vp, *Subleuatio, sustentatio.*
Sustengo, sustenance, *Sustentatio, alimentum.*
Sutil, subtill, *Subtilis.* (*ium.*
Suziamente, filthily, *Spurcè, fœdè, sordidè.*
Suziedad, filthines, *Spurcities, fœditas.*
Suzio, filthie, foule, sluttish, durtie, *Sordidus, spurcus, illotus.*

T A

Tabano, a horseflie, a hornet, *Crabro.*
Tabarro, *Idem.*
Tabaquillo, a basket, *Fiscella.*
Tabardillos, the blew spots called Gods marks, *Pestichia.*
Tabernaculo, a tabernacle, *Tabernaculum.*
Tabique, a thinne wall of rods, *Paries craticius.*
Tabla, a planke, a boord, *Tabula, asser.*
Tablado, planked, boorded, *Tabulatus.*
Tablas, tables to play at, *Abacus, alueus.*
Tablaje, boords, *Tabula.*
Tablero de axedrez, a chesse boord, tables to play with, *Tabula scacchariæ.*
Tablilla, writing tables, a scroe, *Tabella, asserculus.*
Tablones, large boords, *Assamenta.*
Taça o taçon, a cup, *Phiala.*
Tacañerias, leudnes, villanie, *Nequitia.*
Tacha, a fault, *Macula, culpa, vitium.*
Tachar, to find fault with, *Culpare, taxare.*
Tachonado, studded, nailed, *Bullatus, clauatus.*
Tachones, studs, a kind of nailes, *Bullæ, claui.*
Tafurea, a horse boate, *Hippagium.*

Tagarote, a kind of hauke, *Falconis genus.*
Tahur, a barretor, a gamester, a dicer, *Vitilitigator, ludio, aleator.*
Tahurazo, a gamester, an vnthrift, *Ludio, aleator, perditus.*
Taja, a score or tally, *Tessera.*
Tajada, a cut of flesh, a slice of bread, *Segmentum, scissura, laminula.*
Tajado, cut, scored, *Sectus, signatus.*
Tajar, to cut, to score, *Secare, in tessera signare.*
Tajante, cutting, scoring, *Secans, in tessera signans.*
Tajo, a yew tree, *Taxus.* (*signans.*
Tajon, a boord to cut flesh on, a dressing boord, *Abacus, repositorium.*
Tajoncillo, a rounde three footed stoole, *Tripus.*
Taheño en la barva, red bearded, *Ænobarbus.*
Taita, dad, a word which children vse, *Pappa.*
Taymado, a close subtill fellow, *Astutus.*
Tal, such, *Talis.* (*versutus.*
Tal qual, such as, *Talis, qualis.*
Talar, to spoile, to forray, *Depopulari.*
Tala, forraying, spoiling, *Depopulatio.*
Talabarte, swoord hangers, *Subcingulum.*
Taladrar, to bore through, *Terebrare.*
Taladro, a borer, a wimble, *Terebrum.*
Talamo, a bed chamber, *Thalamus.*
Talanquera, railes, a gallerie about a beare baiting place, *Pergula, podium.*
Talante, desire, will, *Voluntas, libido.*
Talantoso, wilfull, *Libidinosus.*
Talega, a wallet, *Mantica.*
Taleguilla, a little budget, *Manticula.*
Talegon, a budget, *Saccus, pera.*
Talion, the punishment of equall losse for a wrong done, *Talio.*
Talon, the ankle, *Talus.*
Talla, an earthen pot, a chip, *Olla, assula.*
Tallar, to carue, *Curtare, scindere.*
Talle, the shape, the proportion, the stature, *Species, statura.*
Tallecer la yerva, to grow to a stalke, *Caulescere.*
Tallo, a stalke or stem, *Caulis.*
Talludo, growen to a stalke, *Caulescens.*
Talque,

Talque, clay to make goldsmithes pots, *Tasconium*.
Talvina, water and branne, or froth, or fome, *Aqua & furfur,cremor,siue spuma*.
Tamaño, so big, the bignes, *Tantus,magnitudo*.
Tamariz, **Tamarix**, *Tamarix*.
Tamaraviento, horehound, *Marrubium*.
Tamarindos, an Indian date, *Dactylus ex Indîa*.
Tambien, aswell, *Aequè*.
Tampoco, as little, *Aequè minus*.
Tan, as, as much, *Tam*.
Tam presto, as soone, *Tam citò*.
Tansolamente, onely, *Tantummodo*.
Tantear, to account, to rate, to ceafe, *Taxare*.
Tanto, as much, *Tantus*.
Tantas vezes, so many times, *Toties*.
Tanto mas, so much more, *Tanto magis*.
Tanto menos, so much lesse, *Tanto minus*.
Tanto que, as much as, *Tantum quantum*.
Tanto, a counter, *Calculus*.
Tañer, to play on an instrument, *Canere, pulsare*.
Tañedor, a plaier or sounder of any instrument, *Cantor, musicus*.
Tapar, to stop, *Obturare*.
Tapador, a stopper, *Obturatorium*.
Tapetados, the inside of a cordouan skin turned outwards in shoes or ierkins, *Corium inuersum*.
Tapete, a tarpet, a peece of hangings, *Tapetum*. (*exstruere*.
Tapiar, to make a mud wall, *Lutamentum*
Tapial, boords between which they make mud wals, also a mall to beate downe earth, *Tabulae caementitiae malleus*.
Tapices, arras cloth, *Tapes, periftromata*.
Tapicerias, arras, tapestrie, *Periftromata*.
Tapion, tapiño, a stopper, *Obturatorium*.
Taponcico, a stopple, *Obturatorculum*.
Taragontia, taragon, *Draguntea*.
Tarahe, tamarix, *Tamaris*.
Tarantola, an efte, an euet, *Stellio*.
Tarasca entremes de la tarasca, a giant made of clothes, &c. in a Maygame, *Manducus*.
Tardar, to stay, to be slow, *Morari, cunctari*.
Tardança, stay, tariance, *Mora, cunctatio*.

Tardador, he that staieth, *Cunctator*.
Tarde, late, euening, *Tardè, vesper*.
Tardo, slow, *Tardus*.
Tardio, late, *Tarditas, vespertinus*.
Tardiamente, lately, slowely, *Tardè, segniter*.
Tardon, a slow fellow, *Cessator, cunctabundus*.
Tarea, a taske, *Ostium, pensum*. (*dus*.
Tarja, a peece of monie of 9 marauedies, *Numismatis genus*.
Tarrenas chapas para tañer, a kinde of instrument, *Crotalum*.
Tarro, a paile, *Situla, mulctra*.
Tartamudo, stammering, *Titubans, balbus*.
Tartamudear, to stammer, *Balbutire*.
Tartago, fiue leaued grasse, *Quinquefolium*.
Tarrugo, a swallow taile to ioine timber, a pin of timber, *Impages, clauus, subscus*.
Tascar, to play on the bit, *Mandere*.
Tascos, towe, *Tomentum*.
Tassador, a tasker, a taxer, *Taxator, censor*.
Tassar, to taxe, *Taxare, aestimare*.
Tassacion, taxing, *Taxatio, censura*.
Tassajo, a cut of flesh, *Tegmentum carnis*.
Tassugo, a little kinde of beast, *Animalculi genus*.
Tataraneito, a nephew of the fourth degree, *Trinepos*.
Tavano y tavarro, *vide* Tabarro.
Taverna, a tauerne, *Taberna, caupona*.
Tavernero, a tauerner, *Caupo*.
Tavernear, to keepe a tauerne, *Cauponari*.
Tavernera cosa, belonging to a tauerne, *Tabernarius*.

T E

Tea, a splinter, a torch, *Assula, taeda*.
Teatro, a theater, *Theatrum*.
Tecla, the key of virginals, *Clauis*.
Techar, to couer a house, *Tegere*.
Techo, an house, the roofe of an house, *Tectum*.
Techumbre, *vide* Açotea.
Teja, a linden tree, slate, tile, *Tilia, tegula*.
Tejado o techo, the roofe of an house, *Tectum*.
Tejar, a tile oft, *Tegularia*. (*tium*.
Tejero, a tiler, a tile maker, *Tegularius*.

Tejo,

Tejo, a tile couering, *Tectum tegulare.*
Tejuela, a pœce of a tile, *Tegulæ fragmen.*
Tela, a web, a tilt, the hart string, *Tela, præcordia.*
Telaraña, a cobweb, *Arachnæa.*
Telar, a weauers loome, *Machina textoria, textrinum.*
Telica, a little web, *Tela.*
Tema, wilfulnes, earnestnes, *Peruicacia.*
Tematico, contentious, *Peruicax.*
Temblar, tiemblo, to tremble, *Tremere.*
Temblor, trembling, *Tremor.*
Temblador, a trembler, *Tremens.*
Temedera cosa, fearfull, *Formidabilis.*
Temer, to feare, *Timere.*
Temerario, rash, *Temerarius.*
Temeroso, fearfull, *Timidus.*
Temerosamente, fearfully, *Timidè.*
Temor, feare, *Timor.*
Temor auer, to feare, *Timere.*
Tempano, a couer of corke, a bung, *Obturatorium suberinum, obstructorium.*
Tempero, temper, season, *Temperamentum, temperies.*
Tempestad, tempest, *Tempestas.*
Tempestoso, stormie, *Nimbosus.*
Templar, tiemplo, to temper, to rule, *Temperare.*
Templa, temper, temperature, *Temperies, temperamentum.*
Templança, temperance, temperature. *Temperantia.*
Templado, temperate, seasonable, sober, modest, *Temperans, temperatus sobrius, modo.*
Temple, *vide* Templa. (*destus.*
Templo, a church, a temple, *Templum.*
Temporal, temporall, *Temporalis.*
Temprano, early, soone ripe, in good time, *Matutinus, præcox, opportunus.*
Tenada, a hey loft, *Fænile.*
Tenazas, pincers, *Forceps.* (*pare.*
Tenazar, to plucke with pincers, *Forci-*
Tenazadas, pluckt with pincers, *Forcipi vellicatio.*
Tenazuelas, little pincers, *Volsella.*
Tendejon, a tent, *Tentorium.*
Tendedero, a place for a tent, *Tentorium.*
Tendero, a shop keeper, *Tabernarius.*

Tender tiendo, to bende, to stretch, *Tendere.*
Tenebregoso, darke, *Tenebrosus.*
Tener, tengo, túve, tendré, to hold, to haue, *Tenere, habere.*
Tener el moço, to haue 51 at primero, *Quinquagenarium numerum habere in lusu chartarum.*
Tener en poco, to esteeme little, *Paruifacere*
Tener de yr, to be bound to any place, *Iturire.*
Teniente, he that holdeth, *Tenens.*
Tenencia de fortaleza, the holding of a fort, *Præsidium.*
Tenor, tenor, sound, tune, *Tenor, sonus.*
Tentar tiento, to assay, *Tentare.*
Tentacion, temptation, *Tentatio.*
Tentador, a tempter, *Tentator.*
Teñir, to die colours, *Inficere, tingere.*
Teñido, died, *Tinctus, infectus.*
Teñidura, dying, *Infectio, tinctura.*
Teologo, a diuine, *Theologus.*
Teologia, diuinitie, *Theologia.*
Tercero, the third, a broaker, a mediator, *Tertius, instlitor, leno, mediator.*
Terceria, broakerie, *Instlitura, lenocinium.*
Terciana, a tercian ague, *Febris tertiana.*
Terciar, to plow the ground, to shake a launce, *Tertiare, vibrare.*
Terciados, short arming swords, *Enses breuiusculi.* (*tiatis.*
Terciazon, plowing of the ground, *Tertiopelo, beluet, Sericum gausapinum.*
Tericia, *vide* Itericia.
Terco, a sower fellow, a boi'sterous fellow, *Austerus, robustus.*
Terliz, tissue of three threds of diuers colours, *Trilicis.*
Termentino, turpentine, *Terebinthus.*
Termino, an end, a bound, *Terminus, limes.*
Ternero, veale, *Caro vitulina.*
Terneza, ternura, tendernes, *Teneritas.*
Ternezuelo, somwhat tender, *Tenellus.*
Ternilla, a gristle, *Cartilago.*
Ternilloso, full of gristles, *Cartilaginosus.*
Ternura, tendernes, *Teneritas.*
Terrado, a flat couering of an house, *Tectum planum.*

Terremoto,

Terremoto, an earthquake, *Terræmotus.*
Terrenal, of the earth, *Terrenus.*
Terrero, a but, *Meta.*
Terron, a clod of earth, *Gleba.*
Terroncillo, a little clod, *Glebula.*
Terregoso, cloddie, *Glebosus.*
Terrible, terrible, *Terribilis.*
Territorio, a territorie, *Territorium.*
Terror, terror, feare, *Terror.*
Terruño, a vaine of earth, a laire, *Terrarum vena.*
Tesbique, a wall of rods, *Paries craticius.*
Teso, stiffe, tough, wilfull, headstrong, *Rigidus, tenax, peruicax, effrenis.*
Teson, obstinacie, wilfulnes, contention, *Peruicacia, contentio, contumacia.*
Tesoneria, *Idem.*
Tesorero, a treasurer, *Thesaurarius.*
Tesoro, treasure, *Thesaurus, ærarium.*
Tesorar, to heape vp treasure, *Thesaurum congerere.*
Testar, to make a will, *Testari.*
Testamentario, belonging to the will, *Testamentarius.*
Testamento, a testament, *Testamentum.*
Testador, a testator, *Testator.*
Testificar, to testifie, *Testificari.*
Testigo, a witnes, *Testis.*
Testiguar, to witnes, *Testari.*
Testimonio, witnes, *Testimonium.*
Testo, the text, *Textus.*
Teta, a dug, *Mamilla.*
Tetuda, that hath great dugs, *Mammosa.*
Texbique, *vide* Tesbique.
Texer, to weaue, *Texere.*
Texedor, a weauer, *Textor.*
Texedura, weauing, *Textura.*
Texido, weaued, *Textus, contextus.*
Texendo adverbio, by weauing, *Contextim*
Texillo, a girdle weaued, *Cingulum textum.*
Texo, an ewe tree, *Taxus.*
Texon, a badger, *Meles, castor.*

T I

Thapsia, wilde ferula, *Thapsia.*
Tia, an aunt, *Amita.*
Tibar, oro del tibar, oro apurado, fine gold, *Aurum obryzum.*

Tibiamente, warmely, *Tepidè.*
Tibio, warme, luke warme, *Tepidus.*
Tibieza, warmenes, *Tepiditas.*
Tiempo, time, *Tempus.*
Tienda, a shop, *Fabrica, officina.*
Tienta, a searching instrument, *Specillum.*
Tiento, gesse, assaie, *Coniectura, sensatio.*
Tierra, earth, *Terra.*
Tiernamente, tenderly, *Teneriter.*
Tierno, tender, *Tener.*
Tiesso, stiffe, tough, *Rigidus, lentus, tenax.*
Tiesto, an earthen vessell, a pot shearde, *Testa.* (*ria.*
Tigeras, scissers, snuffers, *Forfices, emunctoria.*
Tigeretas de la vid, the tendrels of a vine *Capreoli.*
Tigeruelas, little scissers, *Forficulæ.*
Tigre, a tigre, *Tigris.*
Tilde, a title, *Titulus.*
Tilla en la nave, hatches of a ship, *Fori.*
Timon, the rudder of a ship, *Clauus, temo.*
Tina, a diers caldron, *Ahenum tinctorium.*
Tino, order, *Ordo.*
Tinada de leña, a woode pile, *Congeries lignorum.*
Tinaja, a barrell, a tub, a steane, *Dolium.*
Tinieblas, darknes, *Tenebræ.*
Tiña de la cabeça, a white scurffe, *porrigo.*
Tiñoso, scuruie, *Porriginosus.*
Tinta, incke, the die of any colour, *Atramentum, tinctura.*
Tinte, a diers caldron, *Ahenum.*
Tintero, an inckehorne, *Cornu atramentarium.*
Tintor, a dier, *Tinctor.*
Tintura, dying, *Tinctura, infectio.*
Tinuelo, a little moth in flaxe, *Tinea.*
Tio, an vncle, *Patruus.*
Tira braguera, a garter, *Subligaculum.*
Tira, a rag of cloth, a peece of cloth, *Segmentum panni.*
Tirania, tyrannie, *Tyrannis.*
Tirano, a tyrant, *Tyrannus.*
Tiranizar, to tyrannize, *Tyrannizare.*
Tirado, taste, drawne, throwne, hurled, *Iactus, tractus, coniectus.*
Tirar, to plucke, to throwe, to hurle, to shoote, *Trahere, iacere, coniicere, emittere.*
Tiricia, *vide* Itericia.

Tiro,

Tiro, a caske, a dart, alſo a ſerpent called a dart, *Iactus, Acontiu.*
Tiſeras, *vide* Tigeras.
Tirones, pluckes, puls, *Vulſus, conuulſus.*
Tiſica, the tyſicke, *Phthiſis.*
Tiſico, ſicke of the tyſicke, *Phthiſicus.*
Titulo, a title, *Titulus.*
Tizne, *vide* Hollin.
Tiznado, ſmeered with ſoote, *Fuliginoſus.*
Tiznar, to ſmoere with ſoote, *Fulgine illi-*
Tizon, a firebrand, *Titio.* (*nere.*

T O

Toaja, a towel, *Mantile.*
Toalla, a towell, *Idem.*
Toca de camino, a cloake, *Penula.*
Toco, tocador, a veyle or kercheefe, *Velamen, rica.*
Tocada, *Idem.*
Tocar, to touch, to perteine, to put on a kercheefe, *Tangere, attincre, velo tegere.*
Tocamiento, touching, *Tactio.*
Tocante, touching, appertaining to, *Tangens, pertinens.*
Tocino, bacon, *Lardum.*
Toda via, neuertheleſſe, notwithſtanding *Attamen.*
Todo, all, *Totus.*
Todo poderoſo, almightie, *Omnipotens.*
Toldo, a curtaine, *Cortina, periſtroma.*
Tolano, the lampaſſe, *Rana.*
Toldado, hunge with clothes, *Auleis ornatus.*
Tolondron, a ſwelling of a blowe, *Vibex, tuber.*
Tollido, *vide* Tullido.
Tollo, a kinde of fiſh, *Piſciculi genus.*
Toma, taking, *Captura.*
Tomar, to take, to win, to get, to coape with, *Capere, luctari.*
Tomamiento, taking, *Captio, captus.*
Tomador, a taker, *Captor, captator.*
Tomar a ſu cargo, to take vpon him, *Suſci-*
Tomillo, time, *Thymus.* (*pere.*
Tomiza, a kinde of ſmall corde made of Sparto, *Funiculi genus.*
Tonel, a tun, *Dolium.*
Tonelero, a tun maker, *Doliarius faber.*

Tontedad, folly, fooliſhneſſe, *Stultitia.*
Tonto, a dolt, a foole, *Stultus.*
Toñino, a porpeiſe, *Turſio, tyrſio.*
Topar, to meete, *Obuiare, occurrere.*
Topacio, a topace ſtone, *Topazius.*
Topetar, to puſh as a ram, *Cornupetere.*
Topo, a mole, *Talpa.*
Toque, a touchſtone, a touch, *Index lapis, Tactus.*
Torcaza, a ring doue, *Palumbus.*
Torçal, a wreath, *Torculum, funis tortilis.*
Torcecuello, a bird called a wryneck, *Torquilla.*
Torcer, tuerço, to wreath, to wreſt, *Torquere.*
Torcido, wreathed, wreaſted, *Tortus.*
Torcida, a tent for a wound, a lincke of a chaine, *Penicillus, annulus.*
Torçon, Toroçon, griping in the bellie, *Tormen.*
Torçonado, he that hath the griping in the belly, *Torminoſus.*
Tordo, a ſtare, a ſtareling, *Sturnus.*
Torçuelo, a musket, a taſſel of any hawk, *Mas cuiuſuis accipitris.*
Tordillo color de cavallo, flea bitten, *Maculoſus, lentiginoſus.* (*nans.*
Torionda, a cowe with calfe, *Vacca pregnans.*
Toril, a ſtall for an oxe, *Stabulum.*
Tormenta, a ſtorm, a tempeſt, *Procella, tempeſtas.*
Tormento, torment, *Tormentum, ſupplicium.*
Tormentar, to torment, *Torquere, cruciare.*
Tornar, to returne, to turne, to reſtore, *Reducere, reddere, conuertere, redire.*
Tornada, a returne, *Reditus.*
Tornadizo, a turne coate, a runnagate, *Transfuga.*
Tornadura de tierra, a kind of meaſure of ground of ten foote, *Decempeda.*
Tarnaboda, an after banket at a mariage, *Repotia.*
Tornaſol, turneſole, changeable ſilke, *Heliotropium, ſericum variè coloratum.*
Tornatiles, turning vp, *Aduncus.*
Tornear, to turne as a turner, *Tornare.*
Torneado, turned, *Tornatus.*
Tornero, a turner, *Tornarius.*

Tornillo,

Tornillo, a little turne, *Tornus.*
Tornillo de fuente, the winch of a well, *Torcular.*
Torno, a turne, a winch for a preſſe, *Torcular, prælum.*
Toro, a bull, a buffle, *Taurus, vrus.*
Torondon, *vide* Tolondron.
Torongil, balme, *Apiaſtrum.*
Toronja, a kinde of lymon, a cydzon, *Malum cytreum.*
Toronjo, a cydzon tree, *Malus cytreus.*
Torpe, filthie, a loute, a varlet, *Turpis, nequam.*
Torpedad, loutiſhneſſe, filthineſſe, doltiſhneſſe, *Fœditas, turpitudo, Stupor.*
Torpigo, a crampfiſh, *Torpedo.*
Torre, a tower, *Turris.*
Torreon, a turret on a wall, *Turris extraria.*
Torreado, full of towers, *Turritus.*
Torrear, to make towers, *Turres condere.*
Torrezno, a peece of bacon, a peece of fleſh *Fruſtum lardi, ſegmen carnis.*
Torrijas, ſlices of bread ſpread with honie, *Fruſta panis melle illita.*
Torta, a cake, a whitepot, *Placenta, artolaganum.*
Tortedad, crookedneſſe, wrines, *Obliquitas,*
Tortella, a certaine kind of herbe, *Cucuba.*
Tortero, he that wreatheth, he that wreſteth, *Contortor.*
Tortilla, a tanſie, *Moretum.*
Tortero de huſo, the whirle of a ſpindle, *Verticulum.*
Tortora, a turtle, *Turtur.*
Tortorilla, a little turtle, *Pullus turturinus.*
Tortuga, *vide* Galapago.
Torvellino, a whirlewinde, *Turbo.*
Torviſco, a kinde of ſhrub whereon Coculus India groweth, *Thymelæa.*
Toſco, rude, vnwrought, groſſe, *Rudis, impolitus, craſſus.*
Toſquedad, rudeneſſe, groſeneſſe, *Ruditas, craſſities.*
Toſſe, the cough, *Tuſſis.*
Toſſer, to cough, *Tuſſire.*
Toſſigoſo, coughing, *Tuſſiens.*
Toſtar, to toſte, *Torrere.*

Toſtado, toſted, *Toſtus, torridus.*
Toſtador, a toſting yron, *Toſterium, artopta.*
Tova, the ruſte of the teeth, alſo a pummiſſe, *Scabrities dentium, pumex.*
Tovaja, *vide* Toalla.
Touillo, the anckle, *Talus, malleolus.*

T R

Trabajo, trauel, pain, griefe, labor, *Aerumna, labor.*
Trabajado, trauailed, pained, greeued, *Aerumnoſus, leſſus.*
Trabajar, to trauell, to labor, to be greeued, *Laborare, aerumna premi.*
Trabajador, a traueiler, *Laborator.*
Trabucar, to caſt downe, to ouerthrowe, *Deijcere, euertere.*
Trabuco, a ſling, a kinde of ordinance, a croſſebowe, *Funda, machina, baliſta.*
Traçar, to marke out, to ſtrike out, *Delineare.*
Traço, the marking out, *Delineatio.*
Traduzir, duzgo, to drawe aſide, to tranſlate, *Traducere.*
Traer, traygo, to draw, to fetch, to cary, to bring, *Trahere, afferre, portare, adducere.*
Trafagar, to borrow of one to paie another, to traffick, *Verſura ſoluere, negotiari.*
Tragar, to deuour, *Glutire, vorare.*
Tragadero, the throate, bole, *Guttur, ingluuies.*
Tragedia, a tragedie, *Tragædia.*
Trage, apparell, faſhion of garments, *Veſtitus, veſtium forma.*
Tragon, a glutton, *Helluo, gluto.*
Tragonia, gluttonie, *Gula, vorago.*
Traguntia, taragon, *Dracunculus hortenſis.*
Trago, ſwallowing, *Hauſtus.*
Traicion, treaſon, *Crimen leſæ maieſtatis.*
Traidor, a traitor, *Proditor.*
Traido, drawen, *Attractus.*
Trailla, a ſlip for a dogge, or a leſhe for a dog, *Lorum, numella.*
Trama, the warpe, a ſubtill deuiſe, *Tela, ſubtegmen, techna, dolus.*
Tramar, to weaue, to worke ſome ſubtill fetch, *Texere, dolos nectere.*
Trampa, a trap, *Decipula.*

Trampear,

Trampear, to delay paiment, *Solutionem differre.*
Trampales, myrie places, *Volutabrum, ablu-ium.*
Tramontana, the north winde, *Boreas.*
Tranca de puerta, a bar, *Repagulum.*
Trançada, a fillet, a haire lace, *Vitta, crinale*
Tranco, andar de tranco, to amble, *Tollutare.*
Trance de armas, a battaile, *Certamen singulare, pugna.*
Tranchete, a shoemakers paring knife, *Cultrum sutorium.*
Tranquilidad, calmenes, quietnes, *Tranquillitas, quies.*
Trapala, a noise, *Strepitus.*
Trapo, cloth, *Pannus.*
Trapero, a draper, *Pannarius institor.*
Traperia, drapery, *Pannaria negotiatio.*
Traquear, to crie as a storcke, *Glotcrare.*
Traquido, the blow of a peece, *Crepitus siue sonitus tormenti bellici.*
Trascordado, forgetting, mistaking, *Obliuiosus, errans.*
Trasdoblar, to treble, *Triplicare.*
Tras, behinde, after, *Post, pone.*
Trasdoblado, threefold, *Triplex.*
Trasdobladura, trebling, *Triplicatio.*
Trasdoble, treble, *Triplum.*
Trasero, the hinder part, the latter, *Tergum, posterius, postremus.*
Trasijado, lanke, thinne bellied, *Vietus, sub-strictus.*
Trasgo de noche, robingoodfellow, *Incubus.*
Trasladar, to copie out, to translate, *Describere, transferre.*
Traslacion, the translation, *Translatio.*
Traslado, copied, *Translatus.*
Traslador, a translator, *Translator.*
Trasluzir, to shine through, *Transparere, perlucere.*
Trasluziente, shining through, *Transparens, pellucidus.*
Trasmañana, the next day after to morrow, *Perendie.*
Trasnochar, to watch, to stay all night, *Lucubrare, peruigilare.*

Traspalar, to cast from one place to another, to pale, *Traijcere, palare.*
Trasparente, appeering through, *Transparens.*
Traspassar, to passe ouer, to ouergoe, *Transgredi, anteuertere.*
Traspie, tripping, *Supplantatio.*
Trasponer, to remoue, *Transponere.*
Trasquilones, notches in the haire, *Crena.*
Trassegar, to straine, to put from one vessell into another, *Colare, transfundere.*
Trassegador, he that straineth, he that powreth from one vessel into another, *Colator, transfusor.*
Trastejar casa, to tile a house, *Imbricare, tegulis tegere.*
Trastejadura de casa, tiling, *Imbricatio.*
Traste, lumber of houshold, *Scruta.*
Trastes de laud, the frets of a lute, *Chordæ transuersæ.* (*nare.*
Trastornar, to ouerthrow, *Euertere, resupinare.*
Trastornadura, ouerthrowing, turning vp and downe, *Euersio.*
Trastornado, throwen ouer, *Euersus.*
Trastrocar, trueco, to remoue, *Transponere.*
Trastrocamiento, remouing, *Transpositio.*
Trasunto, the counterfet, the portraiture, *Icon, effigies.*
Tratar, to handle, to deale with, *Tractare, contrectare.*
Tratamiento, dealing, handling, *Tractatio.*
Tratante, he that dealeth with, *Tractans.*
Trato, traffike, *Negotiatio.*
Trato de cuerda, a kinde of torment, *Fidicula.*
Travar, to binde, to knit, to ioine, to ioine battell, *Nectere, connectere, iungere, dimicare.*
Trava de pared, the ioints of a wall, *Compago.*
Travazon, the ioining of timber worke in wals, *Compages.*
Travado, ioined, knit togither, *Connexus.*
Travas de bestia, shackles for a horse, *Compedes.*
Traveseros, bolsters, *Ceruical.*
Travesar, viesso, to lay athwart, *Opponere, obijcere.*

Travessura,

Traueſſura, frowardneſſe, wantonneſſe, waggiſhnes, *Peruerſitas, peruicacia.*
Trauieſſo, froward, wanton, waggiſh, *Peruerſus, peruicax.*
Traueſia, croſſing of a way, a waggiſh part, *Tramitis obliquitas, peruicacia.*
Traues, a plot on a corner of a wall to plant ordinance, *Baliſtarium.*
Trauilla de gorra, the knot of a hatband, *Offendix.*
Trebol real, ſweete trefoile, *Lotus vrbana.*
Trebol, trefoile, *Trefolium.*
Trebejo, a cheſſe boord, a childes crackle, *Abacus, crepitaculum.*
Trecho, a ſpace, *Spatium, tractus.*
Treſe, ſicke of the lungs, *Phthiſicus.*
Treſedad, conſumption of the lungs, *Phthiſis.*
Tregua, truce, *Induciæ.*
Treynta, thirtie, *Triginta.*
Treyntenario, a trentall, *Tricenarium.*
Treyntena, the thirtieth, *Trigeſimus.*
Tremeſino, three monethes old, *Trimeſtris.*
Trementina, turpentine, *Terebinthina.*
Tremielga, a crampe fiſh, *Torpedo.*
Tremedal, a durtie place, *Abluuum.*
Tremulante, twinkling as a ſtar, *Tremens.*
Trena o trença, a lace, a pointing ribben, *Tænia, offendix.*
Trenca de vid, the prop of a vine, *Suffrago.*
Trepa, the border of a garment or a traile *Fimbria, Segmentum.*
Trepar, to daunce on ropes, to clime, *Saltare, ſcandere.*
Trepa, dauncing on a rope, climing, *Petaurum, ſcanſio.*
Trepador, a dauncer on cords, *Funambulus.*
Trepado, a garment bordered, *Segmentatus*
Tres, three, *Tres.*
Treſquilar, to ſheare, *Tondere.*
Treſquilador, a ſhearer, *Tonſor.*
Treſquilado, ſhorne, *Tonſus.*
Treta, a fenue at defence, *Tactus.*
Treuede, a treuet, *Tripus.*
Treze, thirteene, *Tredecim.*
Trezientos, three hundred, *Trecenti.*
Trezeno, the thirteenth, *Tertius decimus.*

Triaca, treacle, *Theriaca.*
Triangolo, a triangle, *Triangulum.*
Triaquero, he that maketh treacle, *Theriacæ confector.*
Tribulacion, trouble, *Tribulatio.*
Tribunal, a iudgement ſeate, *Tribunal.*
Tributario, tributarie, *Tributarius.*
Tributo, tribute, *Tributum.*
Trica, a certaine cord in a ſhip, *Funis quidam nauticus.*
Trigo, wheate, *Triticum.*
Trigaço, pertaining to wheat, *Ad triticum ſpectans.*
Triguera, *vide* Alpiſte.
Triguero, a ſparrow that lieth in wheate, *Paſſer triticarius.*
Trillo, a ſlaile, *Tribulum.*
Trillar, to threſh corne, *Triturare.*
Trillado, threſhed, *Trituratus.*
Trilla o trillazon, the threſhing, *Trituratio.*
Trinchante, a caruer, *Exartuator.*
Trincheo, a trencher, *Quadra.*
Trinchea, a trench, *Foſſa.*
Trinchete de çapatero, a ſhoomakers knife, *Scalprum.*
Trinquete, the forefaile, *Velum antemnale.*
Tripas, the guts, *Ilia, inteſtina.*
Tripa ciega, the panch, *Aluus.*
Tripon, a gorbelly, *Ventricoſus.*
Triſcar, to ieſt, to gibe, *Subſannare.*
Triſte, eſtar triſte, ſad, ſorrowfull, heauie, to be ſad, *Triſtis, mæſtus, triſtari.*
Triſteza, ſadnes, *Triſtitia.*
Triſtel, a gliſter, *Clyſter.*
Triumfar, to triumph, *Triumphare.*
Triumfo, a triumph, *Triumphus.*
Trobador, a rimer, *Verſificator.*
Trobar, to rime, *Verſificare.*
Troba, a rime, *Verſus, ryshmus.*
Trocar, trueco, to change, *Mutare.*
Trocatinte, changeable ſilke, *Sericum verſicolor.*
Troço, the truncheon, *Talea.*
Trocha, *vide* Trecho.
Trochiſco, a muſke ball, *Paſtillus.*
Trofeo, a trophie, *Trophæum.*
Trompa, a trumpet, an Elephantes trunke, *Tuba, promuſcis.*

Z   Trompeta,

Trompeta, a trumpet, a trumpeter, an elephants trunke, *Tuba, tubicen, buccinator, promuscis.*
Trompeçar pieço, to stumble, *Cespitare, offendere.*
Trompeçadero, a stumbling blocke, *Offendiculum.*
Trompeçadura, stumbling, *Cespitatio.*
Trompetear, to sound a trumpet, *Tuba canere.*
Trompetero, a trumpeter, *Buccinator.*
Trompo, a top, *Trochus.*
Trompillar, to throw downe, to fal down, *Deijcere, prosternere, cadere.*
Tronar, trueno, to thunder, *Tonare.*
Tronco, a stocke, a trunke, *Truncus.*
Troncho, the stalke of a colewurt, *Talea caulis.*
Tronchado, broken, *Truncus.*
Tronchar, to breake, *Truncare.*
Tronera, a loop hole to lay out ordinance, *Cauus machinarius.*
Tronido o trueno, thunder, *Tonitru.*
Tropeçar, tropieço, to stumble, *Cespitare.*
Tropel de gente, a band, a company, *Agmen.*
Tropellar, to ouerthrow, *Prosternere.*
Tropellado, ouerthrowen, *Prostratus.*
Tropieço, stumbling, *Cespitatio.*
Trotar, to trot, *Subsultare.*
Trote, trotting, *Subsultatio.*
Troxe, a garner, *Granarium.*
Trucha, a trout, *Tructa.*
Trueco, change, *Permutatio.*
Trueque, *vide* Trueco.
Trueno, thunder, *Tronitru.*
Truhan, a Iester, *Scurra.*
Truhaneria, iesting, *Scurrilitas.* (ri.
Truhanear, to iest, to play the foole, *Scurra-*
Trujaman, an interpreter, *Interpres.*
Trujamanear, to interpret, *Interpretari.*

T V

Tu, thou, *Tu.*
Tuero, *vide* Tizon.
Tuerto, crooked, awry, one eied, *Obliquus, toruus; tortus, monoculus.*
Tuétano, marrow, *Medulla.*

Tufo, the smel of the stomack after wine,
Tuyo, thine, *Tuus.* (*Halitus.*
Tullido, benummed, taken, *Stupens, torpens.*
Tullir, to benum, *Torpescere, stupescere.*
Tullimiento, benumming, *Stupor, torpor.*
Tumba, a tombe, *Bustum.*
Tumbadera red, a toile, *Indago, rete.*
Tumulo, a tombe, *Tumulus.* (dere.
Tundir, to sheare cloth, to full cloth, *Tun-*
Tundidor, a clothworker, a fuller, *Tunsor.*
Tundidura, fulling, *Ars fullonica.*
Tunica, a coate, *Tunica.*
Tupir, to stop clifs or chinks, *Stipare.*
Tupido, stopped, *Obstructus, obturatus.*
Tura, lasting, *Duratio.*
Turar, to endure, to last, *Durare.*
Turbadamente, troublesomly, *Turbaté.*
Turbado, troubled, *Turbatus.*
Turbar, to trouble, *Turbare.*
Turbio, thicke, troubled, puddly, *Turbidus.*
Turbion, a storme, *Procella.*
Turbit rayz, turbith, *Turpetum.*
Turquesa, a turquesse stone, a mould to cast pellets in, *Thalassites, typus.*
Turquesada color, skie coloured, *Glaucus.*
Turma de tierra, a puffe, *Tuber.*
Turma, goats stone or rams stones, *Testiculi capri vel arietis.*
Turnio, goggle eied, *Strabo.*
Turon, a field mouse, *Nitella.*
Turron, a cheese cake, a sweete cake, *Placenta, copta, crustum.*
Turronero, a cakemaker, *Pistor placentarius*
Turvio, goggle eied, one that looketh awrie, *Strabo.*
Tusar, to poll the haire, *Tondere.*
Tutela, tutorship, *Tutela.*
Tutor, a tutor, *Tutor.*

V vocalis B

Vbre, an vdder, *Vber.*
Vbrera en la boca de niños, a sore in a childs mouth, *Aptha.*
uebra, an acre of ground, a daies worke, *Iugeris, opera diei.*
ueco, *vide* Hueco.
uerfano, *vide* Huerfano.
ufano, contented, *Contentus.*

ultima-

V L
ultimamente, laſtly, *Vltimò, poſtremò.*
ultimo, the laſt, *Vltimus.*
ultrajar, to outrage, to do violence, *Vim facere, violare.*
ultrajado, outraged, wronged, *Violatus.*
ultramarino, beyond ſea, *Vltra mare.*

V M
umano, gentle, *Humanus.*
umanidad, humanitie, *Humanitas.*
umanamente, gentle, *Humaniter.*
umbral, a threſhold of a doore, *Liminare.*
umedecer, to moiſten, *Humefacere.*
umidad, moiſture, *Humiditas.*
umido, moiſt, *Humidus.*
umildad, humilitie, *Humilitas.*
umilde, humble, *Humilis.*
umilmente, humbly, *Humiliter.*
umillar, to humble, *Humiliare.*
umor, humor, moiſture, *Humor.*

V N
un, uno, one, ſomebodie, *Vnus, quidam.*
una vez, once, *Semel.*
uncion, annointing, *Vnctio.*
unguento, oinſment, *Vnguentum.*
ungir, to annoint, *Vngere.*
ungido, annointed, *Vnctus.*
unguentario, an oinſment maker, *Vnguentarius.*
unidad, vnitie, *Vnitas.*
union, vnion, *Vnio.*
unicornio, an vnicorne, *Monoceros.*
unigenito, onely begotten, *Vnigenitus.*
univerſal, vniuerſall, *Vniuerſalis.*
univerſalmente, vniuerſally, *Vniuerſaliter.*
univerſidad, an vniuerſitie, *Vniuerſitas, Academia.*
univerſo, vniuerſal, *Vniuerſus.*
untado, annointed, *Perunctus.*
untar, to anoint, *Vngere.*
untador, an annointer, *Vnctor.*
unto, fat, greaſe, *Adeps, axungia.*
untoſo, greaſie, *Vnctus.*
untura, greaſing, anointing, *Vnctio.*
uña oloroſa, a ſhell fiſh like the clawe of a bird, *Vnguis odorata.*

uña, a nayle of the finger or toe, a clawe, *Vnguis.*
uñero, parting of the fleſh frō the nayles, *Pterigium.*
uñir, to ioyne, to yoke, *Vnire, iungere.*
uñidura, yoaking, ioyning, *Iunctio.*

V R
urdiembre, *vide* Ordiembre.
urdir, *vide* Ordir.
urina, brine, *Vrina.*
urna, a pitcher, a pot, *Vrna.*

V S
uſagre, a tetter, *Impetigo, lichen, mentagra.*
uſança, vſage, *Vſus.*
uſar, to vſe, to enioy, to doe an office, *Vti, frui, fungi.*
uſo, vſe, *Vſus.*
uſo fruto, profite, *Vſus fructus.*
uſo fruruario, he that taketh the profite, *Vſufructuarius.*
uſual, vſuall, *Vtilis, vſuarius, communis.*
uſura, vſurie, *Fænus.*
uſurario, vſurer, *Fænerator.*

V T
utrero, a ſteere, *Bos trimus.*

V V
uva, a grape, *Vua.*
uva paſſa, a rayſon, *Vua paſſa.*

V A
Vaca, a cowe, beefe, *Vaca, caro bubula.*
Vacar, to be voide, *Vacare.*
Vacante, vacant, *Vacans.*
Vacacion, vacation, *Vacatio.*
Vacillar, to ſtagger, *Vacillare.*
Vadear, to wade, *Vadum tranſire.*
Vado, a ſhallow, a forde, *Vadum.*
Vadoſo, full of ſhallowes, *Vadoſus.*
Vagabundo, wandring, *Vagus.*
Vagar, to wander, to be idle, *Vagari.*
Vago, wandring, *Vagus.*
Vaguido, turning of the braynes, ſowning, *Vertigo.*
Vayas, bay beries, *Bacca lauri.*

Vayna, a sheath, a scabberd, *Vagina.*
Vayna de los testiculos, the skinne of the stones, *Scrotum.*
Vaynica, a stitch in ruffes, *Macula.*
Vayna, a cod of fruite, *Siliqua.*
Vayo, baye coloured, *Baius.*
Vayeta, bayes to line garments, *Pannus*
Valer, to be woorth, *Valere.* (*villosus.*
Valenton, a fencer, *Gladiator.*
Valeriana, Valerian, *Phu.*
Valeroso, valiant, *Validus, fortis.*
Valia, a nurse, *Nutrix.* (*gladiator.*
Valiente, valiant, strong, a fencer, *Fortis,*
Valientemente, valiantly, *Fortiter, valide.*
Valor, value, pryce, *Valor, pretium.*
Valladar, y vallado, a bulwarke, a rampier, an enclosure, *Vallum, agger, seps.*
Valle, a vallie, *Vallis.*
Vallena, a whale, *Balena.*
Vallico, cocle, *Lolium.*
Vanamente, vainely, *Vane.*
Vanagloria, vaineglory, *Vana gloria.*
Vanagloriosamente, vaineglorioussly, *Gloriose.*
Vanaglorioso, vaineglorious, *Gloriosus.*
Vanasto, a pannier, a dozser, *Alueolus, corVanca, vanco, vide Banco.* (*bis.*
Vanda, a bande, a bende, *Vinculum.*
Vandera, a banner, a streamer, *Vexillum.*
Vandear, to help, to follow a factió, *Auxiliari, factiosum esse.*
Vandeo, helpe, *Suppetiæ.*
Vanderizo, he that followeth faction, *Factiosus.*
Vandero, *Idem.* (*Factiosus.*
Vando, a faction, *Factio.*
Vanderizamente, factioussly, *Factiose.*
Vandolero, a bander, he that followeth a faction, *Factiosus.*
Vanidad, vanitie, *Vanitas.*
Vañar, *Vide* Bañar.
Vanear en palabrar, to trifle, *Nugari.*
Vano, vayne, *Vanus.*
Vapor, a vapour, *Vapor.*
Vaporoso, vaporous, *Euaporans.*
Vaquero, a cow heard, *Bubulcus.*
Vaquera, a heafer, neates leather, also a gunne stocke, *Iuuenca, corium bubulum, tormenti lignum.*

Vara, a rodde, a sticke, a yarde, a cudgell, *Virga, bacillum, vlna, fustis.*
Vara real, a scepter, *Sceptrum.*
Varal, a poale, *Pertica.*
Varallos de hieno, swathes of heye, or corne mowed, *Series.*
Varar, to drawe ships on lande, to strike with a ship on the ground, *In terram illidere.*
Varanda, a gallerie, *Menianum.*
Varear, to beate of with a rodde, *Virga cædere.*
Varilla, a little sticke, *Bacillum.*
Varilla de cuello, the throate, *Iugulus.*
Variar, to varie, *Variare.*
Variable, variable, *Varius.*
Variedad, varietie, *Varietas.*
Vario, diuerse, *Diuersus, varius.*
Varon, a man, a baron, *Vir, baro.*
Varonia, a baronie, *Baronia.*
Varonil, manly, *Virilis.* (*liter.*
Varonilmente, manly, coragioussly, *Viriliter.*
Vasar, a cubboord to set vessell on, *Abacus.*
Vascas, belking, *Eructatio.*
Vascosidad, belking, filth, *Eructatio, turpiVaso, a vessell, *Vas.* (*tudo.*
Vasillo, a small vessell, *Vasculum.*
Vassallo, a vassall, *Subditus.*
Vassura, dust, rubbish, *Puluis, scobs.*
Vaziar, to emptie, *Enacuare.*
Vaziadizo, a molten image, *Idolum.*
Vaziedad, emptines, *Vacuitas.*
Vazio, emptie, *Vacuus.*
Vaziamente, emptily, *Vacue.*

V E

Vecindad, neighborhood, *Vicinitas.*
Vedado, forbidden, *Prohibitus.*
Vedamiento, forbidding, *Prohibitio.*
Vedar, to forbid, *Vetare, prohibere.*
Vedegambre, beare foote, *Veratrum.*
Veedor, an ouerseer, *Renisor.*
Vedriero, a glasier, *Vitrearius.*
Vedrioso, glassie, brittle, *Fragilis.*
Vega, a plaine field, *Planicies.*
Vegada, a turne, *Vicissitudo.*
Veynte, twentie, *Viginti.*
Veyntenal, of twenty yeares, *Vicennalis.*

Vejedad,

Vejedad de tiempo, auncientnes of time, *Antiquitas.*
Vejazo, an old fellow, *Vetulus.*
Vejez, age, old age, *Senectus.*
Vejezuela, an old wretched woman, *Vetula.*
Vela, a vayle, a saile, a candle, a watch, *Peplum, velum, candela, vigilia, excubia.*
Velada, a watch, *Vigilia, excubia.*
Velar, to watch, to couer with a vayle, *Vigilare, peplo tegere.* (*lator.*
Velador, a watchman, a coueror, *Vigil, ve-*
Velarse, to become a nouice in a house of religion, also to marie, *Initiari sacris, ducere vxorem.*
Veleño, henbane, *Hyosciamus.*
Velesa, the hearbe *Gingidium.*
Veleta, a fan for the wind, the toppe of a fishing rodde, *Flabellum, tragula.*
Velo, a vayle for a nunne, *Vitta, velamen.*
Vellaco, a villeyne, *Turpis, inhonestus.*
Vellaqueria, villenie, knauerie, *Turpitudo, nequitia.*
Velleza, beawtie, *Pulchritudo.*
Velleguin, serients, seruaunts attending on officers, *Apparitor, lictor.*
Vello, the heare, mosse of the beard, *Villus, lanugo.*
Vellocino, o vellon, a fleese, *Vellus eris.*
Velloso, hearie, mossie, rough, woollie, *Villosus, lanuginosus, hirsutus.*
Vellota, an acorne, *Glans.*
Velludo, shagge heared, *Villosus.*
Vena, a baine, *Vena.*
Venable, a iaueline, *Venabulum.*
Venage, the streame, *Profluens.*
Vencer, to ouercome, *Vincere.*
Ventedor, an ouercommer, *Victor.*
Vencejo, a marten, *Cypselus.*
Vincejos, straps to binde with, *Vincula.*
Vencido, ouercome, *Victus.*
Vencimiento, victorie, *Victoria.*
Venda, a bende, *Lemniscus.*
Vender, to sell, *Vendere.*
Vendabal, the south wind, *Auster.*
Vendar, to binde, *Vincire.*
Vendado, bounde, *Vinctus.*
Vendedor, a seller, *Venditor.*

Vendido, solde, *Venditus.*
Vendimiar, to make wine, *Vindemiare.*
Vendimiador, a wine maker, *Vindemiator.*
Vendimia, wine haruest, *Vindemia.*
Venera, scalloppe shels, signes worne to to shew that a man hath bene on pilgrimage, *Insignia peregrinantium.*
Venero, a baine of mettall, *Vena.*
Venedizo, a straunger, vide Aduenedizo.
Veneno, poison, *Venenum.*
Venerable, worshipfull, *Venerabilis.*
Veneracion, worship, reuerēce, *Veneratio.*
Venerar, to worship, *Venerari.*
Venenoso, poysonfull, *Venenosus.*
Vengado, reuenged, *Vltus.*
Vengador, a reuenger, *Vltor, vindicator.*
Vengadora cosa, wreakefull, *Vindicatorius.*
Vengança, reuenge, *Vindicta, vltio.*
Vengar, to reuenge, *Vindicare.*
Vengativo, reuengefull, *Vindicatorius.*
Venenos de las mano, pinswels in the handes, *Pustulæ.*
Venida, a comming, *Aduentus.*
Venir, vengo, vine, verné, to come, to fit as apparell, *Venire, conuenire.*
Venidero, to come, that shall come, *Venturus.*
Ventero, a tauerner, *Caupo.* (*rus.*
Venta, a tauerne, sale, *Taberna, venditio.*
Ventar, to sell by retayle, *Distrahere.*
Ventaja, vantage, *Primæ.*
Ventalle, a fanne, *Flabellum.*
Ventana, a window, *Fenestra.*
Ventana enrrexada, a lattise window, *Fenestra, clatrata, transenna.*
Ventanilla, a litle window, *Fenestra parua.*
Ventosa, a gourde, *Cucurbita.*
Ventoso, windie, vaine, *Ventosus.*
Ventisquero, a whirle winde, a blast of winde, *Turbo, flatus.*
Ventor, a bloudhound, *Canis sagax.*
Ventrudo, gorebellied, *Ventriculosus.*
Ventura, aduenture, lucke, *Euentus, casus.*
Venturera cosa, chauncing, *Fortuitus.*
Venturoso, fortunate, *Felix.*
Venturosamente, fortunately, *Faliciter.*
Ver, to see, *Videre.*
Verano, the spring, the summer, *Ver, æstas.*
Veraniego, of the summer, *Æstiuus.*

Veras,

Veras, earneſt, Serio.
Verbena, beruepne, Verbena.
Verdad, truth, Veritas.
Verdadero, true, Verus.
Verdaderamente, trulie, Verè.
Verde, græne, Viridis.
Verdeſcura, a ſad græne, Subuiridis.
Verdeguear, verdecer, to waxe græne, Vireſcere.
Verdura, græneneſſe, freſhnes, Viriditas.
Verdolaga, purſlane, Portulaca.
Verdon, a canarie bird, Auis viridis ex inſula Canaria.
Verdugo, a hangman, Carnifex.
Vereda, a path, Semita.
Verengena, a kinde of fruite common in Spaine, but here vnknowne, Malum inſanum.
Verga, a rod, Virga.
Vergajo de toro, a buls piſſle, Taurea.
Vergantin, a brigantine, Nauigij genus.
Verguenças, the priuities, Pudenda.
Verguença, ſhame, ſhamefaſtnes, Verecundia, pudor.
Vergonçoſo, ſhamefull, Verecundus, pudendus.
Vergonçoſamente, ſhamefullp, Verecundè, turpiter.
Vergel, a groue, an arbor, Viretum.
Veril, the ſtone berill, Berillus.
Verja, a lettiſe for a windowe, the pron grate of a windowe, Crates, tranſenna.
Verruga, a warte, Veruca, vide Berruca.
Verſo, a verſe, Verſus.
Veſtidura, a garment, Veſtis.
Veſtido, clothed, Indutus veſte.
Veſtidos, apparell, Veſtimenta.
Veſtir, viſto, to apparell, Veſtire.
Veta, a vaine of mettell, Vena.
Vexigade perro, winter cherries, Solanum halicacabum.
Vez, a turne, Vicem, vice.
Vezino, a neighbor, a citizen, Vicinus, ciuis.
Vezindad, neighborhod, Vicinitas.

V I

Via, a way, Via.
Viage, a voyage, Iter.
Vianda, vittaile, Victus.

Viandante, a wayfairing man, Viator.
Vicario, a vicar, Vicarius.
Vicio, vice, Vitium.
Vicioſo, vicious, fruitful, rancke, Vitioſus, luxurians.
Victoria, victorie, Victoria.
Victorioſo, victorious, Victorioſus.
Vid, a vine, Vitis.
Vida, life, Vita.
Vidrio, glaſſe, Vitrum.
Vidrial, vitriall, Calcanthum.
Vidriero, a glaſier, Vitriarius.
Vidriado, glaſed, Vitriatus.
Vidueño, a kinde of vine, Vitis genus.
Viejo, old, Senex.
Vieldo, a fanne, Ventilabrum.
Viento, the winde, Ventus.
Vientre, a belly, Venter.
Viernes, friday, Dies Veneris.
Viga, a pile, a poſt, a beame, Tignus, trabes.
Vigilancia, vigilancie, Vigilantia.
Vigilia, watch, Vigilia.
Vigor, force, Vigor.
Vigornia de albeytar, an anuile, Incus.
Vigoroſo, forcible, Robuſtus, fortis.
Vihuela, a bandore, Barbiton.
Vil, vile, Vilis.
Vileza, vilenes, Vilitas.
Vilecer, to be vyle, Vileſcere.
Villa, a towne, Villa, pagus.
Villano, a towneſman, a countrieman, a clowne, Paganus, ruſticus, illiberalis.
Villancico, a ſonet, Cantiuncula.
Villania, villanp, lewdenes, clowniſhnes, Nequitia, ruſticitas.
Villete, a little bill, a little letter, Libellulus, carmen amatorium.
Vimbre, a band, a ſtrap, an oſier, Vimen, lorum, ſalix.
Vimbrera, willowe, oſier, Salix.
Vinagre, vineger, Acetum.
Vinagrero, a vineger bottle, Acetarium.
Vinar barvecho, to breake vp ground, Offringere.
Vinatero, a wine ſeller, Vinarius, vinitor.
Vinculo, a bande, Vinculum.
Viniebla, hounds tong, Cynogloſſa.
Vino, wine, Vinum.

Viña,

Viña, a bineyard, *Vitis, vinea.*
Viñadero, he that keepeth a bineyard, *Vinitor.*
Viñeds, a bineyard, *Vinetum.*
Violable, biolable, *Violabilis.*
Violar, to biolate, to breake, *Violare.*
Violado, biolated, broken, *Violatus.*
Violencia, biolence, *Vis.*
Violen o, biolent, *Violentus.*
Violeta, a biolet, *Viola.*
Violado, of biolets, *Violaceus.*
Vira, a turning pin, a shaft, *Verticulū, subscus, Sagitta.*
Virar, to turne, *Vertere.*
Virey, a biceroy, *Prorex.*
Virgen, a birgin, *Virgo.*
Virgo de donzella, *Pellicula tenuis quæ compressa virgine, tum primum rumpitur, Eugium*
Virginal, of a birgin, *Virgineus.*
Virginidad, birginitie, *Virginitas.*
Virote, a bolt, a shaft, *Sagitta, catapultarium.*
Virtud, bertue, force, balor, *Virtus.*
Virtuoso, bertuous, *Studiosus, virtute præditus.*
Vertuosamente, bertuously, *Studiosè.*
Viruelas, the pocks, *Varæ.*
Visabuelo, a great grandfather, *Abauus.*
Visage, the briage, *Vultus.*
Visagra, the hinges of a table, or of a portall, *Vertebra.*
Visco, birdlime, *Viscum.*
Viscra, a biserd, *Persona, Larua.*
Vislumbre, the twilight, *Crepusculum.*
Visible, bisib:, *Visibilis.*
Vision, a bision, *Visio.*
Visnagra, wilde carrots, *Daucus.*
Visojo, squint eied, *Strabo.*
Visnieto, the sons sons son, *Binepos.*
Visoño, a yoong soldior, *Tyro.*
Visiesto, a leape yeere, *Bissextilis.*
Vista, sight, beholding, presence, *Visus.*
Visita, bisiting, *Visitatio.*
Visitar, to bisite, *Visere, inuisere.*
Vistuario, a wardrop, or bestrie, *Vestiarium.*
Vitualla, bittailes, *Victus.*
Vituperable, to be despised, *Vituperabilis.*
Vituperar, to dispraise, *Vituperare.*
Vituperio, despraise, reproch, *Vituperium.*
Viscocho, bisket bread, *Bis coctus panis.*
Vizconde, a bicount, *Vicecomes.*

V O

Vocable, a word, *Vocabulum.*
Vocabulario, a dictionarie, *Dictionarium.*
Vocal, a bowell, *Vocalis.*
Vocativo, the bocatiue case, *Vocatiuus casus.*
Voga, rowing, *Remorum impulsio.*
Volumen, a bolumne, *Volumen.*
Voluntad, will, *Voluntas.*
Voluntario, boluntarie, *Voluntarius, spontaneus.*
Voluntarioso, willing, *Voluntarius.*
Voluntariosamente, boluntarily, *Volenter.*
Vomitar, to bomite, *Vomere.*
Vomito, bomiting, *Vomitus.*
Vos, vosotros, yee, *Vos.*
Votar, to bowe, to giue the boice, *Vouere.*
Voto, a bowe, a boice, *Votum.*
Vozinglero, a lewde talker, *Verbosus.*

V u

Vulgar, common, *Vulgaris.*
Vulgarmente, commonly, *Vulgo.*
Vulgo, the common people, *Vulgus.*
Vuestro, yours, *Vester.*

X A

Xabon, soape, *Sapo, smegma.*
Xabonero, a soaper, *Saponarius.*
Xagua, a kinde of herbe in the Indies, *Herba quædam Indica.*
Xaharrar, to plaster a wall, *Malshare, trusillare.*
Xaques, a checke at chesse, a budget in a saddle, *Pera.*
Xaqueca, the megrim, *Grauedo capitis.*
Xaquima, a halter, *Capistrum, restis.*
Xara, a bramble, a shaft, *Sagitta.*
Xaramago, wilde rape, *Syluestris raphanus.*
Xarave, syrope, *Potio, syrupus.*
Xarcias, the cords in a ship, *Armamenta, Funes nautici.*

Zeme,

X E
Xeme, a span, *Spithama.*
Xerga, serge, *Sagum.*
Xenable, mustarde, *Sinapis.*
Xerguerito, a goldfinche, *Carduelis.*
Xergon, a strawe bed, *Culcitra, stramentaria.*

X I
Xibia, a cuttle fish, *Sepia.*
Xibion, cuttle bone, *Sepium.*
Ximia, an ape, *Simia.*
Xira, cheere, *Epulum.*
Xiringa, a string, *vide* Siringa.

X V
Xugo, iuice, *Succus.*
Xugoso, full of iuice, *Succidus.*

Z A
Zagano, a drone, *Fucus.*
Zagal, a shepheard, *Pastor.*
Zaguan, a patch, *Porticus, cryptoporticus.*
Zamarilla, a shepheardes cloake, *Penula pastoris.*
Zambra, a kinde of boate, *Cymbæ genus.*
Zangano, a dore bee, *Cephen.*
Zanges, zagues, water bottle, *Lagena, vtriculus.*
Zarco, grey eied, *Glaucus.*
Zargatona, fellwort, *Psyllium.*
Zarzahan, a kinde of cloth which the moores make, *Pannus puniceus.*
Zarzagavillo, a cold winde, *Ventus rigidus.*

Z E
Zebra, a kinde of mule, *Mula.*
Zebretana, a tiller bowe, *Balistæ genus.*
Zelo, zeale, *Zelus.*
Zero, a cypher in Arithmeticke, *Cyphra.*

Z I
Zimborio, a chapple, *Capella.*
Zizaña, cockle, *Lolium.*

Z O
Zodiaco, the zodiacke, *Zodiacus.*
Zohori, one that seeth wel, one that findeth springs by the earth, *Aquæ siue metalli inuentor.*
Zorra, a foxe, *Vulpes.*
Zorzal, a thrush, *Turdus.*

Z V
Zuane, a swan, *Cygnus.*
Zuiza, bull baiting, also a shew or muster of soldiors, *Bubetia, lustratio.*
Zufre, brimstome, *Sulfur.*
Zumbas, busting, humming, *Susurri.*
Zumbar, to hum, to buzze, *Susurrare.*
Zumbido, humming, buzzing, *Susurrus.*
Zurrador, a currier, *Coriarius.*
Zurzir, to patch, *Sarcire.*
Zurra, darbuena zurra, to strike, *Cædere, serire, percutere.*

FINIS.

www.ingramcontent.com/pod-product-compliance
Lightning Source LLC
Chambersburg PA
CBHW020812230426
43666CB00007B/970